The Eisenhowers Reluctant Dynasty

Steve Neal

From a farm during the French and Indian Wars to the White House during one of the most turbulent eras of American history, this is the first comprehensive study of one of America's celebrated families. Concentrating on the last three generations of Eisenhowers—from Ike and Mamie to David and Julie—it is filled with fascinating detail and a wealth of anecdotes.

The Eisenhowers, in contrast to such families as the Roosevelts, Tafts, and Kennedys, have built a tradition of public service without running for office themselves. In addition to Ike's unique role in the shaping of our country we learn more about the contributions of his admired wife, Mamie, his brother Milton (to whom he referred as "the brightest member of the family"), and his son, John, an esteemed writer on military subjects.

(*continued on back flap*)

The Eisenhowers
Reluctant Dynasty

Steve Neal

Doubleday & Company, Inc., Garden City, New York
1978

The illustrations used on the endpapers were provided courtesy of The Dwight D. Eisenhower Library, the Kansas City *Star*, Penn State Photo, Wide World Photos, and George Cserna.

The author would like especially to thank Milton Eisenhower and John Eisenhower for permission to use various family letters quoted in this volume.

Library of Congress Catalog Card Number 77-80904
ISBN: 0-385-12447-3

PRINTED IN THE UNITED STATES OF AMERICA
FIRST EDITION

For Susan,
whose book this is also

Contents

Preface

Following the publication of my profiles of John and Mamie Eisenhower in the Philadelphia *Inquirer*, several newspaper colleagues suggested that I undertake a biography of the Eisenhower family. Though there were scores of books about Dwight D. Eisenhower, I soon found that there had not been a comprehensive study of the family.

When I approached John S. D. Eisenhower in January of 1976 he gave me his full cooperation. John opened his files to me and encouraged other members of the family to cooperate, and there were no restrictions imposed. I was free to make my own judgments and interpretations. Through the courtesy of Dr. Milton S. Eisenhower, his correspondence with President Eisenhower was made available to a writer for the first time.

The Eisenhower Library in Abilene, Kansas, is the most important center for primary-source material and its staff helped locate family records and correspondence for this project. I am particularly indebted to director John E. Wickman, associate director Don Wilson, and archivist Susan Jackson. My good friend Becki Berg provided me with relevant documents from the collections of the Library of Congress. Joe Gradel of the *Inquirer* library was enormously helpful.

Milton and John Eisenhower talked at length with me about their careers and of their relationship with President Eisenhower. These interview sessions were always pleasant and informative.

Barbara Eisenhower was unfailingly open and cooperative, and an interview with Mamie Eisenhower offered valuable insights into that most private of recent first ladies. I am grateful to numerous friends and associates of the Eisenhowers for answering questions about the family.

Useful background on the eighteenth-century Eisenhowers of Pennsylvania was provided by David Boldt who has edited a history of colonial Philadelphia.

On many occasions I received useful suggestions from Gerard McCauley, my agent. Finally, I am most appreciative to Lisa Drew of Doubleday whose advice, encouragement, and effective editing made this book possible.

Chapter One

THE NEW COUNTRY

The *Europa* was making its final voyage of the year from Rotterdam to the New World, and when a November storm seemed in the offing as it entered Delaware Bay, a decision was made to discharge the passengers—mostly German immigrants—just inside Cape Henlopen at what is today Lewes, Delaware. From there they would complete the trip to Philadelphia aboard three smaller sailing vessels, called shallops, that were used to carry passengers and freight, mostly grain, along the coastline of the Delaware Bay. The *Europa*'s captain presumably had no interest in battling his way up the bay against a squall and was eager to reach his Virginia destination and then be underway back toward Rotterdam before the big winter storms came sweeping across the North Atlantic.

And so it was that Nicholas Eisenhower, fifty, and his three sons first set foot on North American soil in November of 1741 on the site of what had been more than one hundred years earlier the first European settlement in the Delaware Bay. A Captain Pieter Hayes had established a whaling station on Lewes Creek in 1631 at the request of the Dutch West India Company. That first settlement had been destroyed by Indians during its first winter, but after that false start, settlement had steadily spread through the region, at first under the auspices of the Dutch and

Swedish, whose officials had maintained an uneasy truce, and since 1681, by the English, and in particular by William Penn.

As the Eisenhowers proceeded north toward Philadelphia up the coast of present-day Delaware, they could see many signs of settlement, including the log cabins of the Swedish settlers, with their distinctive herringbone patterns, and occasional small towns. The market place in New Castle, Delaware, where Penn himself had first landed in 1682, had been in continuous use for 109 years on the occasion of the Eisenhowers' sailing by, and many brick and wooden homes now lined its streets. Forest had been cleared from the flat, fertile lands of Delaware and signs of the recently completed grain harvest were presumably still on view. (A century later, a small community a short distance up the Appequinimink Creek from the bay would change its name from Cantwell's Bridge to Odessa, in the mistaken belief that it would become a grain shipping port similar in importance to the Russian port on the Black Sea.)

The increasing evidence of settlement, however, had not changed appreciably the scene of stirring pastoral beauty that Penn had reported: "The soil is good, air serene and sweet from the cedar, pine and sassafras, with wild myrtle of great fragrance. Fish in abundance, especially shad and (rock) fish. Oysters are monstrous for bigness. In the woods are diverse fruits . . . and flowers that for color, largeness and beauty excel."

Philadelphia was a major port. On a typical day as many as a hundred merchant ships were in port—loading, unloading, or waiting to do so. And there would be a like number of shallops, barges, and other smaller craft that shuttled between Philadelphia and the smaller ports up and down the bay. The city was the second-largest English-speaking city in the world, after only London, and was the major port of entry in this period, and the arrival of German immigrants from the *Europa* was a matter of administrative routine. Two Philadelphia physicians went out to the shallops carrying the passengers from the *Europa* and examined them. While passage across the Atlantic was notoriously difficult, and conditions squalid at best, the passengers of the *Europa* seemed to have come through in at least normal health. "We have carefully examined the state of health of the passengers on board the three shallops, brought from the Capes from the *Europa*," the doctors reported, "and found no disease on board that is infectious." What disease, if any, they might have found on board that was not infectious, they did not disclose in their report.

The Eisenhower men then apparently reported promptly to the courthouse on High Street, a three-story brick building with an ornate cupola that had been built in 1709 and which rose, according to one account, "almost majestically above the city's teeming produce markets." There, they took the oaths of allegiance to the Commonwealth of Pennsylvania and the British Crown. What the Eisenhowers and the other passengers from the *Europa* may have thought of this busy and reportedly rather foul-smelling metropolis, in which literally every tenth house was a bar or tavern, has not been recorded for posterity. The Eisenhowers would not, in any event, be staying in the city long. They were here for other purposes.

They were here in fact to participate quite directly in Penn's "Holy Experiment." Penn, who had received title to the lands along the Delaware Bay (Delaware, New Jersey, and Pennsylvania Bay) from King Charles II in settlement of a large debt that the Crown owed his admiral father, was himself a religious refugee, who had twice been jailed in England for preaching the Quaker faith.

After William Penn had lined up his Quaker countrymen to become the craftsmen, merchants, and speculators in his new colony, there remained the problem of getting farmers to till the soil and grow the food. To solve this problem, he had gone to the Rhineland in Germany to give what were, in effect, sales talks to the German farmers, even handing out plans for building a house in the New World (plans which, incidentally, turned out to be impractical). But what Penn was basically offering these Protestant German farmers was an escape from the ravaging bands of soldiers, vindictive religious persecution, and ever-spreading plagues of pestilence that characterized life in the Rhineland at the time. The result was a flood of emigration from Germany to Pennsylvania, of which the Eisenhowers were to become a part.

The literal translation of their family name was "iron hewer." Metalworkers in the Odenwald who bore the name Eisenhauer were known to have lived there at the time of Charlemagne. As early as 1446, they owned land near Breitenbrunn. With the occupation passing from father to son, the vocational trade also became the family name. According to family legend, the Eisenhowers numbered among them some medieval German warriors. By the sixteenth century, the family was committed to pacifism and a new religious sect, having been influenced by the teachings of reformer Menno Simons, the father of the Mennonite movement. Challenging the authority of church and state, Simons urged his followers to reject materialism and militarism. Among his early converts were the Eisenhowers, then living in the Rhine province of Bavaria. During the Thirty Years War which ravaged Germany from 1618 to 1648, the Mennonites were persecuted by the armies as they destroyed farms and obliterated towns and villages.

The Eisenhowers fled first to Switzerland seeking religious freedom and then to Pennsylvania. Like so many other of their Pennsylvania Dutch brethren, they settled in Lancaster County after traveling west from Philadelphia via Conestoga wagon along the old Lancaster Turnpike. In the case of the Eisenhowers, they lived in the community of Bethel Township which later became part of Dauphin County. According to colonial records, Nicholas filed application in January of 1753 for 120 acres of wooded land.

It was Eisenhower's misfortune to acquire his new farm as the French and Indian War was about to explode on the Pennsylvania border. Encouraged by the French, the Delaware and Shawnee tribes made frequent raids on pioneer households. British General Edward Braddock's defeat near the Ohio River in 1755 was to have the effect of leaving colonial settlements undefended. Indians were terrorizing isolated farms, slaying the inhabitants and taking scalps, burning buildings and crops, and killing livestock. Much of the white population sought sanctuary in the more densely populated region of southeastern Pennsylvania.

On August 12, 1756, the Pennsylvania *Gazette* reported that Indians had attacked the Eisenhower farm: "By a letter from Fort Henry in Berks County dated August 7th, there is advice that the Indians are hovering about that neighborhood, some of them have been seen almost every day and that they had burnt the house of Nicholas Eisenhower." Shortly afterward, five neighboring farmers were slain and five children kidnapped by Indians. Apparently undaunted, Eisenhower rebuilt his log cabin and continued farming on the homestead.

Records do not indicate when Nicholas or his wife, Anna Margaretha, died. It is known that he was still living as late as December 19, 1759, when he witnessed the will of one of his sons. Earlier that year he deeded the farm to Peter, the eldest Eisenhower son.

Peter was one of the first owners of commercial property in Fredericksburg, having purchased sixty-four front feet on Market Street in 1761 with the stipulation that he would build a substantial building within eighteen months. Sometimes identified as "Peter Ironcutter," he was a prominent local merchant. In June of 1779, he sold the Nicholas Eisenhower farm for 2,200 pounds. By this time he was sixty-three and most of his children were grown and well established. One of his sons, Frederick, had been killed in action during the American Revolution.

With the Revolution came a renewal of Indian raids on the Pennsylvania frontier. Britain's Parliament had approved the use of Indian warfare against the colonialists and on July 3, 1778, some three hundred Americans were massacred near the northeastern Pennsylvania settlement of Wyoming. Many of the settlers, their homes and farms destroyed, fled to the southeast. The Continental Army effectively retaliated by capturing Fort Niagara, which had been the source of British supplies to the Indians, and in the same campaign wiped out some forty Indian villages.

This last great Indian offensive may have been a factor in Peter's decision to sell his father's farm. During this period two friends were killed by Indians. One David Emrick, who had sold land to Peter, was taken prisoner along with his family. When Emrick became tired, the Indians reportedly killed him and impaled his baby on the sharp end of a sapling and waved it in the air.

Whatever his reasons, Peter moved thirty miles to the west and paid 3,300 pounds for 170 acres at the foot of the Blue Mountain near the Harris Ferry (now Harrisburg) and the Susquehanna. It was to be his home for the rest of his days. For its time, the farm was a considerable operation with several houses, barns, stables, and outbuildings. When Peter died, at eighty-six, in 1802, he left seventeen children, the youngest of whom was the second Frederick, destined to become the great-grandfather of Dwight D. Eisenhower. In his will, Peter directed that his oldest son, John, should assume control of the farm and that "any overplus" be used for "raising and clothing and schooling" of the four youngest children. In a supplement to the document, written in 1801, Peter said of his wife that nothing, "not even the value of a spoon could be disturbed or taken from her as long as she remains my widow."

As his inheritance, Frederick received $266 in three installments. In 1817, he married Barbara Miller, five years his senior and a member of a Mennonite sect known as the River Brethren because they held river baptisms. The farm methods of the Pennsylvania Dutch were conservative but highly successful. Dr. Benjamin Rush of Philadelphia said the German farms could be identified "by the fertility of their fields, the luxuriance of their meadows, and a general appearance of plenty and neatness in everything that belongs to them."

Although most of his family were farmers and he himself had farmed, Frederick became a weaver. With Barbara he moved to Millersburg and built a three-story frame house with a large workshop area on the first floor and living quarters on the upper two stories. Among other things, Frederick wove linen tablecloths, pillowcases, coverlets, and bedspreads. One of his hand-woven coverlets is on display at the Eisenhower center in Abilene.

Frederick was reputed to have been a strict disciplinarian and on one occasion gave his son John a severe beating for harmlessly embellishing a story. The father is said to have later regretted the harsh punishment.

Of the nineteenth-century Eisenhowers, the most formidable personality was Frederick's son Jacob, who rose to a position of influence and prestige as the minister and leader of the Lykens Valley River Brethren. From boyhood, Jacob had been scholarly and bookish. His 1847 marriage to Rebecca Matter, a member of an old and established River Brethren family, brought Jacob a considerable dowry. In 1854, Jacob and Rebecca purchased a one-hundred-acre tract of land in Elizabethville, north of Harrisburg.

According to records at the Dauphin County courthouse, the Eisenhowers paid $3,698.46¾.

Their expansive nine-room, two-story, red brick house became the social center of Elizabethville. A large meeting room on the first floor had been designed for use as a church meetinghouse and it was also used for spelling bees between area schools, prayer meetings, and other gatherings. Anyone seeking overnight shelter could find a bed in the attic cobbler shop which the Eisenhowers kept available for unexpected guests. A large Pennsylvania Dutch barn was the architectural centerpiece of the farm which included a fruit orchard, a vineyard, some one hundred beehives, large sloping fields for grain and vegetables, and a spring in the back yard that provided water for the assorted family enterprises.

Jacob's sermons attracted River Brethren from beyond Dauphin County for he was a renowned orator who still delivered sermons in German, the first language of most of the members of the Elizabethville community.

For Jacob, the Civil War posed a moral dilemma. Though he had long opposed slavery, he was an outspoken pacifist. Some members of the Eisenhower family enlisted in the Union Army. As a minister, Jacob would not endorse the war, but he did make known his admiration for Abraham Lincoln and named one of his fourteen children (six lived to maturity) after the President.

In the early 1870s, the Eisenhowers and fellow members of the Brethren began discussing a possible move to the West. Most of them lived comfortably on bountiful farms, but they talked with enthusiasm about even greater opportunities in Kansas. The spirit of the frontier beckoned and younger members of the congregation were interested in building a new land much as their ancestors had done generations earlier in Pennsylvania.

Jacob's aging father, Frederick, was skeptical about undertaking a long journey to a strange country, yet when the River Brethren departed for Kansas in March of 1878 the eighty-four-year-old patriarch of the Eisenhower family was among them.

Jacob financed the family's journey by selling the Elizabethville property for $8,500 and the sale gave him enough capital to help his children in later years. The Pennsylvania River Brethren left Harrisburg with more than fifteen carloads of freight. They settled at Abilene, Kansas, which had been one of the most celebrated frontier towns as the northern terminus of the Chisholm Trail and the western terminus of the Kansas-Pacific Railroad. It was the prototypical cattle town and with the longhorns came cowboys, gamblers, gunfighters, and prostitutes. An illustrious town marshal, "Wild Bill" Hickok, brought order to Abilene in the early 1870s. When the railroad expanded westward, most of the lawless elements went elsewhere.

A history of Kansas, published in the 1880s, described the Brethren as "one of the most complete and perfectly organized" groups "that ever entered a new country."

Dickinson County was prime farmland with streams of pure water, soil that was rich and deep, timberland, orchards and groves, and, importantly, little wasteland. Jacob bought a 160-acre tract south of the Smoky Hill River and went about constructing a Kansas version of his Pennsylvania farm—a large house with the first-floor meeting room for the Brethren, a huge barn, and windmill. His entire farm was "improved land" with a meadow, pasture, orchard, and large fields of corn and wheat.

Jacob wanted his son David to help manage the farm, but the younger Eisenhower was bored with the mundane day-to-day responsibilities of farming and wanted to study engineering. With Jacob's financial assistance David entered Lane University, a small institution of higher education operated by the River Brethren at Lecompton, Kansas. Though Lane did not have an engineering department it offered a range of liberal arts and vocational courses, and David studied mechanics, mathematics, Greek, rhetoric, and penmanship.

One of David's classmates was Ida Stover, an attractive and popular young woman from Virginia. Higher education for women had been considered improper in Virginia and the strong-willed and energetic Ida was also defying River Brethren tradition in her determination to receive a college education. There was intense competition among the male students of Lane for dates with Ida. David, shy, quiet, and reflective, was thoroughly captivated and made her his chief interest. By the end of his sophomore year he abandoned plans for an engineering career and turned his full attention to Ida. During spring term of 1885, David and Ida were engaged.

Married in the college chapel on September 23, 1885, David and Ida would not return to Lane University. Instead they returned to Abilene where they hoped to begin a family and make their home in Dickinson County.

Chapter Two

AN AMERICAN FAMILY

David's marriage began with great hopes and aspirations. His father had given him two thousand dollars and 160 acres of choice farmland. If David wanted to follow in the tradition of his agrarian ancestors he was well prepared to do so.

Eager to strike out on his own, he mortgaged the farm and spent Jacob's cash gift to begin his own business, a general store, in the village of Hope, which was twenty-eight miles south of Abilene. Because of his meager background in business, David brought in a young businessman named Milton Good as his partner. Having worked in an Abilene clothing store, Good possessed considerable experience and is said to have been personable and outgoing, a "natural" salesman.

Above their store, the Eisenhowers and the Goods lived in adjoining apartments, where they frequently entertained other young couples at dinner parties. Some of the townspeople noted that the Eisenhowers seemed to be living "too high," yet the business was prospering and its partners and their wives were popular members of the community.

In the fall of 1888 the happiness ended quite abruptly. The business failed and David was financially ruined. In the process he lost everything—his store, the farm, and his reputation. Efforts were made to place the blame elsewhere. It was alleged, for example, that Milton Good and his wife had mysteriously vanished overnight with all of the store's cash. However, no charges were ever pressed or substantiated against Good.

David fled from the scene of his humiliation for he was fully aware that his inattention to detail, lack of experience, and poor judgment had been factors in his undoing, yet he lacked the strength to face that reality in Kansas. Seeking refuge from his defeat, David found a ten-dollar-a-week job in the roundhouse of the Cotton Belt Railroad at Denison, Texas, four hundred miles from Abilene. Ida, pregnant with a second child, stayed in Kansas. Their first son, Arthur, was born in 1886, and the second, Edgar, was born in January of 1889.

To pay off David's creditors, the Eisenhowers retained a lawyer to liquidate the general store's inventory. While the bills did get paid, Ida became suspicious of the lawyer's methods and bought some lawbooks to learn bankruptcy law. Years later, Edgar Eisenhower said that his mother was concerned because the lawyer provided neither an accounting of the sale nor a letter of explanation. In the end, Ida did not take the lawyer to court. Not long after giving birth to Edgar, she took her two infant sons and traveled to Denison, where the family was reunited.

It was a difficult period. Plagued with self-doubts after his business debacle, David was earning barely enough to pay family living expenses.

A third son, David Dwight, was born October 14, 1890, in the tiny house by the railroad tracks. Though Ida named her son for his father she called him by his middle name to avoid confusion. Another reason that Ida preferred "Dwight" was her aversion to nicknames with their easy informality. She did not want her third son to be known as "Junior" or "Dave" and it did not please her that her older children would be called "Ed" and "Art." Adhering to his mother's wish the son reversed the names and he would apply to West Point as Dwight David Eisenhower. When he became an international figure as "Ike," Ida still referred to her son as Dwight. Once, in a letter to Mamie Eisenhower, Ida would ask who "this Ike" was whom she had written about.

The Eisenhowers did not remain in Texas for long. Friends and relatives urged them to return to Dickinson County. Jacob was anxious for them to come home because his wife, Rebecca, had died, and the local bank, in which he had invested much of his once considerable holdings, had failed. David's brother-in-law, Chris Musser, had been appointed foreman of the Belle Springs Creamery in Abilene, a business which was organized and operated by the River Brethren and was housed in a large, new building on the eastern edge of town. When Musser sent a letter to Denison that offered his brother-in-law a position as plant engineer, David quickly accepted.

If the reunion with the Kansas Eisenhowers was a happy occasion, it did not signal a change in David's fortunes. His salary was "less than fifty dollars a month," not much more than he had earned in Texas. As one of the poorest families in town, the Eisenhowers lived in a small house near the railroad tracks that might well have been described as a shack. On the other side of the railroad tracks lived the more affluent and socially prominent families of Abilene.

"I have found out in later years we were very poor," said Ike in a post-World War II visit to Abilene. "But the glory of America is that we didn't know it then. All we knew was that our parents could say to us that opportunity was all about us. All we had to do was to reach out and take it." Of all the Eisenhowers none seemed to enjoy the companionship of millionaires and captains of industry more than Ike, whose memories of an impoverished boyhood were never forgotten.

In 1898, David's brother Abraham Lincoln Eisenhower, Abilene's veterinarian, sold his practice and moved to California, and he sold his home to David and Ida. It was a modest, two-story white frame house on South Fourth Street with a three-acre tract, which provided a family garden, and Ida carefully planned how the garden would be used, for the family raised its own produce.

Religion was a dominant influence in the Eisenhower home with the family participating in a weekly Bible meeting in the living room and the sons attending Sunday school at the River Brethren church. At the weekly family sessions the Eisenhower sons took turns reading biblical passages and they were able to recite many verses by rote. Years later Milton recalled that his parents quoted freely from the Bible and were embarrassed on the rare occasions that one of them had to look up a scriptural reference. As a schoolgirl Ida had once memorized 1,365 biblical verses in six months.

In later years David and Ida left the River Brethren and searched for another sect. One of the groups they joined, the "Bible Students," sometimes held prayer meetings at their house and Ida played the piano as the group sang hymns. Ida would eventually become a member of the Jehovah's Witnesses and David's religious quest led him to mysticism. The most unusual expression of David's beliefs was an enormous wall chart that he drew of the Egyptian pyramids. It was ten feet high and six feet wide, and, according to David, the chart contained prophecies for the future as well as confirmation of biblical events. Captivated by the bizarre drawing, the sons spent hours studying David's creation.

Such unorthodox if not eccentric views were not forced upon the children. Encouraged to reach their own conclusions, the sons later joined more conventional Protestant denominations, yet they ardently defended the convictions of their parents. By setting standards and values of high principles the parents had given their sons a quiet strength.

Though the family increased in size, its income was much the same. Roy was born in 1892; Paul, born in 1894, died in infancy; Earl was born in 1898, and Milton in 1899. That David and Ida were able to feed such a growing family was largely because of the fertile soil of their three acres that included a vegetable garden, strawberry patch, and fruit trees; they also had cows, chickens, and a smokehouse.

Well liked by fellow employees at the creamery, David had the reputation of "standing up for his men" if management harassed someone under his supervision. When young men came to work it was David who patiently assisted them until they were broken in. At the same time, he worked to improve his own capabilities, taking a correspondence-school course to gain certification as a refrigeration engineer so that he would not be left behind when the creamery began manufacturing ice and ice cream.

Politics was rarely discussed at the family dinner table although it was known that David and Ida were Republicans. During the 1896 presidential campaign the three oldest sons—Arthur, Edgar, and Dwight—demonstrated an interest in the contest between Republican William McKinley and Democrat William Jennings Bryan, the "Boy Orator of the Platte." There were monumental issues between the candidates and the sudden rise of Populist sentiment must have alarmed the conservative folk of Abilene. What made the campaign so appealing to the Eisenhower boys was the proliferation of bright celluloid campaign buttons. For the first time, campaign buttons were being mass produced in colorful red, white, and blue designs. Most of the Eisenhower classmates sported bright new McKinley buttons.

For the brothers the highlight of the year was McKinley's visit to Abilene. In a torchlight parade the Eisenhower boys carried torches for their candidate. "There was a certain amount of disrespectful laughter," Ike would recall, "but we got through the parade in our fashion, with no singed hair and without undoing McKinley."

Of far greater interest to the youngsters than political campaigns were the illustrious stories of the "Wild West." As elderly townspeople recounted tales of Wild Bill Hickok, the brothers listened with fascination. In their play, the Eisenhowers emulated the gunfighters of the Old West—Billy the Kid, Wyatt Earp, Jesse James. When they learned to read, the boys eagerly consumed the latest in pulp literature about their heroes, and Ike in later years would become a devoted aficionado of Zane Grey.

As youngsters they were taught to follow the code of the Old West. "It was," said Ike years later, "meet anyone face to face with whom you disagree. You could not sneak up on him from behind . . . without suffering the penalty to an enraged citizenry. If you met him face to face and took the same risks as he did, you could get away with almost anything, as long as the bullet was in front."

Always prepared for a good fist fight, Dwight and Edgar became known as "tough guys." Arthur, the eldest brother, was less athletic and not a fighter. Indeed, Edgar admitted that he thought of Arthur as "somewhat of a sissy." Most of the Eisenhower fistic battles were at the expense of young men from Abilene's more fashionable North Side. The Eisenhower sons often wore threadbare clothes which made them different from other students. In Ike's fifth-grade class picture he was the only student wearing overalls—the others wore Sunday-dress clothes. Edgar sometimes wore his mother's old button shoes. When other children taunted the brothers a fight often ensued.

When Edgar and Dwight took their red coaster wagon loaded with vegetables to the North Side to sell their produce the class antagonism became even greater. According to Edgar the upper-class housewives treated them contemptuously. "They made us feel like beggars," he said years later. For his part, Ike said he suffered no such abuse.

Stories of the fighting abilities of the Eisenhower brothers soon became part of local folklore. Edgar was "Big Ike" and Dwight was "Little Ike," and they took pride in their roughneck images. Edgar's reputation was made when he knocked out a taller and bigger youngster named Davis from the North Side. To the students watching him, Edgar must have seemed like a street-corner version of "Gentleman Jim" Corbett bringing down the illustrious John L. Sullivan. Though never the brawler that his older brother was, Ike was nonetheless a formidable adversary. In his most storied fight, no doubt embellished with each retelling, he fought for "more than an hour" against a stronger, more powerful youngster from the North Side named Wesley Merrifield. "It seemed like a week," Ike said half a century later. Some classmates urged Merrifield and Dwight to fight and they formed a circle around the two boys. Arthur Eisenhower recalled that Merrifield used his superior strength and speed to repeatedly strike Dwight's head. According to Arthur, "Dwight's face became a swollen and bleeding mass of flesh. His eyes and lips became all wounds." Most observers thought Dwight would soon collapse. Though staggering from the heavy punches and still bleeding, Dwight refused to concede and began to fight back. Many of Dwight's punches were wide but others reached Merrifield's head and soon he, too, became bruised. Merrifield, who had punched at will in the early going, lost much of his power. Like George Foreman struggling against the "rope-a-dope" of Muhammad Ali, Merrifield became weary and frustrated. It was a stalemate with both Dwight and Merrifield struggling to remain on their feet. Finally, they conceded that it was indeed a draw.

Unquestionably the most painful ordeal of Dwight's youth was his confrontation with blood poisoning. When he lacerated his knee the cut caused him little concern because his leg had been scratched many times. But two days later Dwight's leg was discolored, swollen, and becoming increasingly painful. The family doctor immediately recognized the blood poisoning and said that the leg would have to be amputated for Dwight to survive.

For the youngster whose most glittering accomplishments had been on the athletic field the prospect of facing life as a cripple may well have seemed a death sentence. Dwight told his parents and the doctor that he would rather die than permit amputation. When the others left Dwight's room Edgar remained and promised that he would do what he could to stop the operation. Dwight's condition worsened as he screamed, went into delirium and then into a coma. The doctor insisted that only amputation would save Dwight and warned the family that they would be responsible for the boy's death. Despite the doctor's grim predictions the black swelling subsided and Dwight recovered. To the deeply religious Eisenhowers it was nothing less than a miracle. Within three weeks Dwight was able to walk again.

In 1904, Dwight entered the freshman class at the town high school which was located on the first floor of Abilene's City Hall. One floor below the school was the town jail and an Eisenhower classmate said school was once disrupted when a prisoner used dynamite in an escape attempt. The red brick building was also the headquarters for the fire department and Dwight served with other male students as a "volunteer" fireman. "When the firemen rang the bell, the boys, Dwight among them, responded immediately by skipping classes to help man the old two-wheeled hose cart. . . . If Dwight didn't get to the hose cart he was among those who sprinted to the store to buy treats for the girls."

As a student Dwight was able to maintain respectable grades in spite of the demands of athletics and his part-time employment at the creamery. The school yearbook of 1909 said, "Dwight is our best historian and mathematician. His interest in History is one of his outstanding traits as a scholar." According to the class prophecy Dwight was destined to become a Yale history professor and Edgar would one day become President of the United States.

"I remember that whenever the teachers called on Dwight he could always recite," said his classmate Winifred Williams. "I never heard him say, 'I don't know.' "

History was always Dwight's favorite subject and was to become a lifelong passion. His high school history courses were less stimulating than what he learned from his own reading. A local newspaper editor, Joe Howe, permitted Dwight to borrow volumes from his extensive personal library. Dwight's choices were inevitably history and biography with the *Life of Hannibal* emerging as his favorite. Though afforded the same borrowing privileges from Howe's library, other students were said to have been intimidated by the ponderous chronicle of the Punic Wars that Dwight read with such enjoyment.

On a social level Dwight seems to have been shy and somewhat insecure. In the school's caste system the North Side elite would not accept South Side roughnecks into the most prestigious social fraternity, the Bums of Lawsy Lou. One of Dwight's classmates, Lelia Grace Picking, said the fraternity's membership was restricted to students "who had their way through school provided and were financially able, so they did not have to spend so much time in chores and working." Dwight's exclusion from their social gatherings meant that he was unable to have a true relationship with the attractive Gladys Harding whom he wistfully admired from a distance.

Whatever social credentials they lacked, Dwight and Edgar were the school's leaders on the athletic field. Such was their influence that on one occasion they would inform a startled but delighted freshman that he was going to be the starting pitcher on the school's baseball team. Of the two brothers Edgar was the superior athlete, "the greatest football player in the class" according to the school yearbook. Although Edgar was two years older than Dwight they were high school classmates. In grade school Edgar had been an indifferent student and barely managed to pass the eighth grade. Ordered by his father to repeat the eighth grade, Edgar refused, which prompted David to withdraw him from school. For two years Edgar worked at the creamery and his physical development during that period proved an asset when he returned to school in 1904.

At the time, high school athletics were loosely organized and received no funding from the school. Dwight organized a community fund-raising campaign to purchase modern athletic equipment for the baseball and football teams, and he also secured official school recognition for the Athletic Association. In the 1909 yearbook he wrote, "Early in the fall of 1908, the High School boys organized an Athletic Association for the year. After electing Dwight Eisenhower president, Harry Makings vice-president, and Herbert Sommers secretary and treasurer, we proceeded to do business. Deciding not to play any baseball that fall, we started on football at once."

In the spring of 1909, Edgar and Dwight graduated together. Though Dwight talked vaguely about going to Kansas University in the fall he questioned whether he had the ambition. By contrast Edgar knew that he wanted to study law at the University of Michigan. Still bitter about the lawyer who handled his bankruptcy, David was very much against Edgar's career choice and offered to help pay his son's expenses if only he would pursue a more respectable trade. As an alternative David proposed that Edgar study medicine at the University of Kansas. Edgar and Dwight had already made an arrangement in which one of them would attend college every other year while the other took a job and paid for educational expenses. Under the plan it would take eight years for the brothers to graduate. As the oldest it was decided that Edgar should attend college during the first year of the program.

Over the next year Dwight sent his brother two hundred dollars that he earned as the night foreman in the creamery. In 1909, he began dating a girl named Ruby Norman and their relationship became close without serious commitment. Staying behind in Abilene left Dwight with a sense of restlessness. He wanted to escape the small town and discover new worlds, but his ambitions were still unfocused.

Those goals became more sharply defined the following summer when he renewed his friendship with Everett E. "Swede" Hazlett, Jr., a high school classmate who had just received a congressional appointment to the United States Naval Academy. It was actually Hazlett's second appointment. A year earlier he had failed the entrance examination and the intervening months had been spent preparing for another try, which came through the patronage of a Kansas congressman. "I had seen just enough of Annapolis to be tremendously enthusiastic about it and to know that there was nothing I wanted quite as much as to be a naval officer," said Hazlett years later.

Impressed by Hazlett's enthusiasm, Dwight listened attentively to the stories of Annapolis. Hazlett was a member of a North Side family and in high school was occasionally challenged by South Side boys. "I felt protective," Ike later recalled and he told friends, "to lay off." Dwight became Hazlett's closest friend. "I liked him most for his sterling qualities," said Hazlett. "He was calm, frank, laconic and sensible, and not in the least affected by being the school hero."

In the summer of 1910, the two friends spent many evenings together at the creamery where they played poker in the engine room. For refreshments they took ice cream from the company's freezer and at other times took eggs and chickens which they cooked on a shovel in the boiler room. So close was the friendship that Hazlett proposed that Dwight apply for the Naval Academy. Hazlett pointed out that it was an opportunity for free education, a career as a naval officer, and a chance to play college football against big-time competition.

It took little argument, for Dwight realized the difficulty in financing a college education. Furthermore, he was anxious to study military history from professional soldiers. Dwight was troubled that this decision might disappoint his strongly pacifist parents, but he also knew that they had always been independent and would want him to make his own judgment.

He wrote both Kansas senators, requesting an appointment to either of the service academies. After learning that one of the senatorial appointments had been filled, Dwight concentrated on Senator Joseph L. Bristow, whose home was in neighboring Salina.

On August 20, 1910, Dwight wrote Bristow:

> I would very much like to enter either the school at Annapolis, or the one at West Point. In order to do this, I must

> have an appointment to one of these places and so I am writing you in order to secure the same.
>
> I have graduated from high school and will be nineteen years of age this fall.
>
> If you find it possible to appoint me to one of these schools, your kindness will certainly be appreciated by me.
>
> Trusting to hear from you, concerning this matter, at your earliest convenience, I am respectfully yours,
>
> Dwight Eisenhower.

Abilene's most prominent citizens were approached by Dwight and asked to write letters to Senator Bristow. Among those recommending him were newspaper publisher Charles M. Harger, merchant J. B. Case, and local postmaster Phil Heath. By the time Dwight was finished soliciting endorsements, Bristow received more than twenty letters promoting the appointment. With so many recommendations Dwight expected a quick response, yet for several weeks there was no word from Washington. On September 3, 1910, he wrote a second letter to Bristow:

> Sometime ago, I wrote you applying for an appointment to West Point or Annapolis. As yet, I have heard nothing definite from you about the matter but I noticed in the daily papers that you would soon give a competitive examination for these appointments.
>
> Now, if you find it impossible to give me an appointment outright to one of those places, would I have the right to enter this competitive examination?

This time Bristow responded quickly and advised Dwight that examinations were to be held the following month in Topeka. Hazlett began tutoring lessons, sharing with Ike the methods he had learned at preparatory school. "Ike's God-given brain sped him along and soon he was way ahead of his self-appointed teacher," said Hazlett.

Uncertain how he would fare, Dwight took a train to the state capital where he took the test with a field of applicants, many of whom had been studying for months. As it turned out, Swede's confidence in Ike was amply justified. Among the candidates willing to attend "either" service academy Dwight had placed first with an over-all percentage of 87½. He was second among West Point applicants and first among Annapolis applicants. When the young man who won the West Point competition was unable to accept the appointment, Senator Bristow named Ike in his place.

For Hazlett it was a tremendous disappointment. "This was a cruel blow," he said years later, "and Ike didn't like it any better than I did. All his hopes had been aimed at Annapolis and he felt that, through me, he knew a good deal about it." Swede suggested that Ike write Senator Bristow, stressing that he "greatly preferred the Navy" and "beg for a reconsideration." Dwight said he would not "look any gift horse in the mouth." He did, however, consider Hazlett's suggestion until Swede discovered a rule specifying that midshipmen had to enter the Naval Academy prior to their twentieth birthday. When the next class entered Annapolis Dwight would be nearly twenty-one. This could be countered easily enough, said Hazlett. A birth certificate was not required for admission, and Ike could "knock off a couple of years." Such a strategy was firmly rejected by Ike.

On October 25, he wrote Senator Bristow: "I wish to thank you sincerely for the favor you have shown me in appointing me to West Point."

That same fall Ike returned to Abilene High School for "graduate work" where he took several science courses ostensibly to prepare for college. A more compelling reason seems to have been Dwight's interest in playing another season of football. For the first time he would not be playing in Edgar's shadow. Since graduation Ike had gained weight and speed and in 1910 he had matured noticeably. Playing tackle Ike gave performances that were at times spectacular. Opposing coaches were dazzled when, as a defender, he would break through the line to drop their quarterbacks from behind. This fifth high school football season struck Ike as a fine tune-up for what he hoped would be a football career at West Point.

In January of 1911, Dwight reported to Jefferson Barracks in St. Louis where he would take the West Point entrance examination. Overwhelmed by the sights and sounds of St. Louis, the first big city that he had ever seen, Ike left the barracks one night to explore the metropolis. He had gone with a fellow applicant and within a few hours they were lost. When they knocked on a door to seek directions the two young men were held at gun point by a suspicious bartender. By the time they found their way back it was well past curfew. Afraid that authorities might disqualify them from the examination the two applicants scaled a wall and quietly made their way back to the sleeping quarters.

The next day Dwight was recovered sufficiently to pass his examination with high marks. At last his future seemed secure.

As Dwight left Abilene for West Point in June, Ida and David wept softly.

Chapter Three

AMONG BROTHERS

Ike was the third brother to leave Abilene. It was not easy for him to cut lifelong ties. Before undertaking his journey to the East, Dwight traveled north for two sentimental reunions. In Chicago, he visited Ruby Norman, then a music student at the Chicago Conservatory. He spent several days with his girlfriend. And they were to correspond regularly for the next two years. In Ann Arbor, he stayed with Edgar. Ike was so impressed with the University of Michigan and Edgar's collegiate life style that he wondered if his decision to go to West Point was the right one.

Edgar did not enjoy the same spectacular success in athletics at the university as he had done at Abilene High School. He lost some twenty pounds as a result of illness and was never able to regain the power which had made him a fearsome running back. He did not even play football at Michigan but did manage to participate in track and baseball. Edgar bluntly termed his performance in college athletics as "rotten." Dwight had reason to believe that he might succeed where Edgar had failed. He wanted nothing more than to become a star on the Army football team. Everything else was secondary.

He arrived at West Point on June 14, 1911, along with 264 other incoming cadets. It was a hot, sweltering day and the discomfort was intensified by the hazing by upperclassmen. Ike was assigned to the "beast barracks." He later described the discipline and harassment as "strenuous" and for others, "unendurable." His roommate, who was also from Kansas, wept repeatedly in discussing these matters with Ike. The unfortunate cadet withdrew from the Academy early in the term. Ike was older than most of the upperclassmen barking commands at him and laughed privately about his predicament. His background in athletics and as a member of a large family made him less vulnerable to the strain and tension which overcame some of his classmates.

Ike and his second roommate, Paul Hodgson, from Wichita, both became stars on the Cullum Hall (plebe) football team that fall. They were viewed as potential varsity lettermen and suddenly found themselves addressed with respect by some upperclassmen. Ike was a halfback, a much more glamorous position than he had played back in Abilene. He was a strong, quick running back, who was difficult to bring down. He was also a fine blocker and aggressive defensive player. After the football season ended, Ike enhanced his athletic reputation by participating in boxing, track, and baseball.

There was little distinguished about Ike's academic record in his first year at West Point. He was one-hundred-twelfth in mathematics, eighty-second in drill regulations, thirty-ninth in history, thirtieth in military engineering—and fifty-seventh out of a class of two hundred-twelve in over-all scholastic standing.

The one bright spot on Dwight's grade sheet was English, where he stood tenth in the class. Hodgson later recalled that Dwight would agonize over English themes for several days. It was said he could write polished essays in less than thirty minutes. Hodgson said Ike's paper would invariably receive a much higher grade than his own. The lucid, unpretentious Eisenhower prose, which won high marks at West Point, was to be an invaluable asset in his military and civilian careers.

Ike was promoted as one of the brightest prospects of Army's 1912 football team. Sportswriters described him as the "huge Kansan" and a "plunging halfback." Several went so far as to predict he was destined for All-America recognition. His photograph was widely published in eastern newspapers. The build-up for Dwight was unusual because he was listed as a reserve behind senior

Geoffrey Keyes, Army's most versatile ball carrier. But Keyes was injured shortly before the first game.

In the season opener, against Stevens Institute, Ike helped lead the Cadets to a 27–0 victory. A week later, he was credited with sparking Army to a 19–0 triumph over Rutgers University. The New York *Times* described Ike as "one of the most promising backs in Eastern football" on the basis of his performance against the Scarlet Knights. Swede Hazlett recalled "the consternation at Annapolis when the sports pages brought news of a great new Army halfback who could do everything and who was running wild against all opponents." Hazlett clipped a three-column photograph from a New York newspaper of Dwight punting and tacked it on his wall.

Ike found himself playing a secondary role when Keyes returned for the Yale game. Keyes ran well and Ike remained on the sidelines. That afternoon must have been particularly frustrating for Dwight because Army lost, 6–0. Keyes starred again in the next game as Army defeated Colgate 18–7. But Dwight saw considerable action. The West Point yearbook, *The Howitzer,* noted that "Eisenhower in the fourth quarter could not be stopped."

On November 9, Army was to play the Carlisle Indian School from central Pennsylvania. Carlisle was coached by Glenn S. "Pop" Warner and featured the most extraordinary athlete of the day, James Francis Thorpe. In 1911, Thorpe had been named a halfback on Walter Camp's All-America team. In the summer of 1912, he had achieved the unique athletic feat of winning both the decathlon and the pentathlon at the Olympic Games. He was regarded as the world's greatest athlete, a tribute King Gustav V had paid him at Stockholm. So Army was up against no mere mortal but a legend. It was a challenge that Ike and his teammates welcomed, an opportunity to compete against America's first superstar.

Thorpe was too much for Army. A West Point sportswriter said that Thorpe's "wonderful and spectacular runs" were the most remarkable ever witnessed at the Academy. Ike played much of the game on defense. His assignment and that of another Army back was to double team Thorpe. Years later, Ike was to boast about a perfect "high-low" tackle he and his teammate made which momentarily stunned Thorpe. But Thorpe broke free for a first down run on the very next play.

It was a long afternoon for Ike. Thorpe ran for two touchdowns, passed for another, kicked three field goals and three extra points. Thorpe returned an Army kick ninety yards for a touchdown which was nullified by a penalty. On the next play, Thorpe ran ninety-five yards for a touchdown.

Ike was the only Army player singled out for his performance in newspaper accounts of the Carlisle victory. But his knee was injured. Marty Maher, the team trainer, obtained a special brace for Ike. He was pronounced fit to play in the next game, against Tufts College.

The Tufts game was to have given Ike a final workout before the all-important Navy game. Army won, 15–6. But Ike twisted his knee while breaking through the Tufts line and was carried from the field. He was hopeful it was only a minor injury and that he would be back in uniform for the Navy game, but Dr. Charles Keller, the Academy's chief surgeon, solemnly advised him that he would not be able to play again that year. Indeed, Keller said Ike's athletic career might be over.

Ike shattered the knee several days after his release from the hospital. At a riding drill, in the Riding Hall, Dwight was ordered to participate in all movements of the drill. The drillmaster disputed the advice of Dr. Keller that Ike should be excused from mounting and dismounting. Ike's roommate, P.A., argued that he did not have to risk injuring himself further. "I've got to do it," Ike told Hodgson. "He as good as called me a liar."

The knee buckled and his cartilage and tendons ripped when Ike completed the drill.

Returning to the hospital, Dwight underwent surgery and treatment for nearly four days. The process was "so painful that I scarcely slept," Ike said.

Dr. Keller told him, "You'll never play football again. You may not even graduate."

It was a terrible setback for Dwight, who had come so close to his ambition of success as a big-time college football player. "The end of my career as an active football player had a profound effect on me," Ike later said. He described himself as "almost despondent" and on several occasions considered resigning from the Academy. "Life seemed to have little meaning," he said.

However, Ike was to demonstrate his adaptability by involving himself in football in other ways. He became a varsity cheerleader and coach of the junior varsity football team.

The adjustment was a painful one. In an undated letter to Ruby Norman, Ike wrote: "Seems like I'm never cheerful any more. The fellows that used to call me 'Sunny Jim' call me 'Gloomy Face' now. The chief cause is this game pin of mine—I sure hate to be so helpless and worthless. . . . Anyway I'm getting to be such a confirmed grouch you'd hardly know me."

Ike was, by his own admission, far from a model cadet. He viewed the spit-and-polish regimentation of West Point somewhat irreverently. And this attitude resulted in numerous demerits. His behavior was more daring than defiant. If he did not take the rules seriously, neither did he take himself seriously.

When some imperious upperclassman ordered Dwight to his room for "special instruction" in "full-dress coat," he decided to obey the order literally. He reported to the room half nude. The upperclassman was outraged. But Dwight wryly noted, "Nothing was said about trousers, sir." The incident earned him demerits and established his reputation as the class maverick.

Most of his transgressions were minor—showing up late for formation, late for meals, brass buttons poorly polished, room in disorder, dirty washbasin, and failing to execute "right into line" properly. For these and similar demerits, Ike was to rank ninety-fifth in conduct in a graduating class of one hundred sixty-four. Dwight attributed his facility for collecting demerits to "a lack of motivation in almost everything other than athletics." He looked contemptuously on classmates who were too cautious to risk getting demerits. In at least one instance, he violated the code by smoking in the hall and blowing smoke into the room of a well-behaved cadet. The cadet was petrified about the possible consequences. Ike flashed his wide grin. He was having a good time, as in the old days in Abilene.

Ike received a month's furlough in the summer of 1913 and returned home to visit his family. It was an unannounced visit and the family was as surprised as it was delighted. There had been some changes. David, the father, had left the Belle Springs Creamery to become superintendent of the local gas plant. The new job did not substantially increase the family income, but he had become disenchanted at the creamery and, after more than twenty years there, wanted to make a move.

The family circle seemed smaller. Edgar was still at Michigan. Arthur, who had been the first to leave, in 1905, was a messenger boy for the Commerce Trust Company of Kansas City, Missouri. One of Arthur's roommates at a boardinghouse had been Harry S. Truman, a bookkeeper for the Union National Bank who also worked as an usher at the Grand Theater. Truman was to continue to speak warmly of Arthur long after his break with Ike, recalling that Arthur did not know how to turn on a gas jet when he first came to the boardinghouse. Arthur did not stay in close touch with other family members. "He was the black sheep," one family member says.

Another brother, Roy, had embarked on a professional career. He was working in a drugstore in nearby Ellsworth. Roy, the least athletic of the Eisenhower brothers, had worked part-time in an Abilene drugstore during his high school years. Shortly after leaving high school, he took a special course in pharmacy. He was then accredited by the state of Kansas as a druggist. From all accounts, he was highly successful at his profession. Within a few years he would own his own store at Junction City, Kansas. Dwight visited Roy frequently during his 1913 furlough.

The younger brothers, Earl and Milton, were perhaps most excited by Ike's visit. To them he was more than an older brother, he was the town hero, the local boy who had made his mark in the East.

Ike was not modest about this new role. He wore his West Point uniform when he walked in downtown Abilene. The townspeople seemed as proud of him as his own family. For the first time he was able to get a date with the striking Gladys Harding. She even invited him to her family's fashionable North Side home.

But Ike still found time to play poker and reminisce with old high school teammates. In spite of his football injury, he still appeared to be strong and rugged. His friends urged him to fight

Dirk Tyler, a black porter and professional boxer. Dwight's friends said that Tyler had become the town bully. When Ike met Tyler, he was verbally challenged by the massive fighter. They agreed to a match in the basement of a local department store. A large crowd gathered to see the West Point football letterman and the Kansas City heavyweight. Ike, who wore an elastic stocking to protect his knee, later said that the sight of Tyler in the ring was intimidating. Indeed, Ike became concerned with self-protection.

Tyler rushed at Ike, throwing and missing with his right hand. Ike's counterpunch stunned Tyler. Within seconds, Ike had landed with a flurry of punches and Tyler was defenseless. He knocked Tyler cold with a final right uppercut. Ike said his impressive performance was less than it seemed. Tyler, for all his brawn, had no finesse. "He telegraphed his punches from a mile away," Ike said.

Once again, Ike had added luster to the family's already formidable athletic reputation. A fine light heavyweight was lost when Ike returned to West Point.

Ike was an Army cheerleader on November 1, 1913, when an unknown western team, Notre Dame, came to West Point. The Cadets were undefeated and rated by sportswriters as the best team in the country. In the first period, Army moved against Notre Dame at will. But Irish quarterback Gus Dorais suddenly began using a new play—the forward pass. Throwing to end Knute Rockne, Dorais led Notre Dame to a 35–13 victory. The Fighting Irish suddenly became recognized as a national football power and the style of the game took on a new look.

"Everything has gone wrong," Dwight wrote the following week, "including the football team, which got beaten most gloriously by Notre Dame last Saturday. The only bright spot is, just now, that trouble with Mexico seems imminent. We may stir up a little excitement yet. Let's hope so—at least."

Ike may have been eager for action against Pancho Villa, yet his most cherished ambition was to serve in the Philippines. In anticipation of such an assignment, he bought tropical uniforms with his uniform allowance.

But football continued to be his great interest at West Point. He designed black and gold cheesecloth capes which spelled out

"Army" when designated cadets stood in the grandstands. Ike described his enthusiasm about Army's 22–9 victory over Navy in a November 1913 letter to Ruby Norman:

> Back from N.Y. and we surely turned the trick—22–9. Oh you beautiful doll! Some game, some game! Just a small crowd saw us do it, you know. Just 45,000 people. Sure was sad! Three touchdowns and a field goal for a total of 22 points. You should have seen us after the game. Oh! Oh! Oh! Believe me, girl, I *enjoyed* myself. Course I couldn't raise a riot for I was in uniform—but I went down to Murray's in a crowd of four—and we danced and ate—and oh say—the joy of the thing is too much—I feel my reason toppling.

He took a measure of pride in his performance as coach of the Cullum Hall (junior varsity) football team. Officially, Dwight was assistant to an officer. "But he knew little of the game," Dwight recalled. The varsity coach made it known that Ike was to be given wide authority. A number of Dwight's players later won their "A." In 1914, Cullum Hall compiled a three and one record, including the season finale, a dramatic triumph over traditional rival New York Military Academy.

Ike's academic record contained few hints of future prominence. He finished sixty-first in a class of one hundred sixty-four. With one hundred demerits in his final year at West Point, Dwight placed one-hundred-twenty-fifth in conduct. He was not embarrassed by his rating in conduct and discipline. Years later, he would criticize another general by saying, "He's always been afraid to break a regulation."

There were sharp differences of opinion about Ike's potential as an officer. One instructor said he was "born to command." Another instructor recalled, "We saw in Eisenhower a not uncommon type, a man who would thoroughly enjoy his army life giving both to duty and recreation their fair values (but) we did not see in him a man who would throw himself into his job so completely that nothing else would matter."

Swede Hazlett, visiting Ike during his own graduation leave, said, "It was no surprise to find that he was just about the most outstanding man in his class, generally liked and admired. Had he not indulged in so many extracurricular activities he could easily have led his class scholastically. Everyone was his friend—but with no loss of dignity or respect."

The Howitzer, West Point's yearbook, described Dwight as a "Mexican athlete—good at throwing the bull." In a yearbook profile, written by roommate P. A. Hodgson, Dwight was satirized:

> This is Señor Dwight David Eisenhower, gentlemen, the terrible Swedish-Jew, as big as life and twice as natural. He claims to have the best authority for the statement that he is the handsomest man in the Corps and is ready to back up his claim at any time. At any rate you'll have to give it to him that he's well developed abdominally—and more graceful in pushing it around than Charles Calvert Benedict. In common with most fat men, he is an enthusiastic and sonorous devotee of the King of Indoor Sports and roars homage to the shrine of Morpheus on every possible occasion. However, the memory of man runneth back to the time when the little Dwight was but a slender lad of some 'steen years, full of joy and energy and craving for life and movement and change. 'Twas then that the romantic appeal of West Point's glamor grabbed him by the scruff of the neck and dragged him to his doom. Three weeks of "Beast" gave him his fill of life and movement and as all the change was locked up at the Cadet Store out of reach, poor Dwight merely consents to exist until graduation shall set him free.
>
> At one time he threatened to get interested in life and won his "A" by being the most promising back in Eastern football—but the Tufts game broke his knee and the promise. Now Ike must content himself with tea, tiddledywinks, and talk, at all of which he excels. Said prodigy will now lead us in a long, loud yell for—Dare Devil Dwight, the Dauntless Don.

The class of 1915 was to become known as "the class the stars fell on." Ike perceptively wrote this about Omar Bradley in *The Howitzer*: "If he keeps up the clip he's started, some of us some day will be bragging, 'Sure, General Bradley was a classmate of mine.'"

As graduation approached, Ike was again haunted by his football injury. The head of the medical department, upon reviewing Dwight's records, informed Cadet Eisenhower that while he could graduate, he might not get an army commission. If this happened, Ike retorted, he probably would go to Argentina and live among the gauchos. Several days later, Ike turned down a commission in the Coast Artillery. "It was a sedentary, immobile sort of life," he later explained. Dwight began looking into a trip to the Argentine. Finally, he received his commission when he promised not to serve in the cavalry.

Secretary of War Lindley M. Garrison spoke about duty and sacrifice in his West Point commencement address. Ike's thoughts about the speech are not recorded. But his return to Abilene that summer was long remembered. Dwight was warmly received by old friends and neighbors. Little Ike had not let them down.

In the meantime, Edgar, Big Ike, was practicing law in the mill town of Tacoma, Washington. He had graduated, with a law degree, from the University of Michigan in 1914. His favorite subject had been constitutional law, which he had studied under Henry M. Bates, the dean of the law school. Edgar later cited the influence of John Marshall on his own interpretation of the Constitution.

Like Dwight, Edgar "considered quitting school several times." But his fear of returning to Abilene as a manual laborer, "a plain, everyday street cleaner," compelled him to remain at Ann Arbor. He refined his study methods to a point where he graduated in the top half of his class. Edgar became interested in the Pacific Northwest through his classmate Charles Johnson, from Tacoma. As students, Eisenhower and Johnson defended another student at a trial. "Our client was a Hindu student who had left his lodgings without paying rent," Edgar recalled. "The lad had complained he was cold all of the time." The student lawyers won their case.

"On my way West after graduation I stopped off at Abilene to see the family," Edgar said. "I rather dreaded telling Mother that

I was going way out to the Pacific Northwest. One by one, our family was gradually breaking up."

Edgar arrived in Tacoma during the early autumn of 1914. He prepared for the state bar examination in the law offices of Bates, Peer and Petersen in the National Realty Building. Upon passing the bar, Edgar was admitted into the firm. He was a pioneer lawyer in the self-proclaimed "Lumber Capital of America." In his first trial, he startled the presiding judge by charging that "the whole case was a frame-up" and questioning the integrity of the opposing lawyer. "Only an inexperienced kid would have made such a blunder," Edgar later confided. "But the funny part of it is, the lawyer in question was later disbarred for being dishonest."

Chapter Four

IKE AND MAMIE

As a newly commissioned second lieutenant, Ike was assigned to the 19th Infantry at Fort Sam Houston in San Antonio, Texas. It was a less exotic tour than the Philippine assignment he had coveted. But Ike discovered that "many of the members of the West Point Class of 1915 went to the least desirable places." Actually, Dwight seemed close to realizing the ambition he had confided to Ruby Norman of becoming involved in President Wilson's counterrevolutionary intervention in Mexico.

Ike's reputation as a football coach and erstwhile Army halfback was a considerable asset. No sooner had he arrived in San Antonio than a local military academy offered him $150 to coach their football team. Dwight politely declined, explaining that such a responsibility would conflict with his official duties. Shortly afterward, Ike was summoned by Major General Frederick Funston. "It would please me and it would be good for the Army if you accept this offer," Funston said.

So Ike began coaching the Peacock Military Academy. He demonstrated the same commitment and enthusiasm which had proven so successful in his earlier coaching. His team compiled a winning record against larger schools. The War Department took notice. Ike was becoming known as an able and innovative young coach.

Something happened in early October of 1915 which diverted Dwight's attention from football and all other activities. He met Mamie Geneva Doud, an attractive, slender, dark-haired girl, whose family maintained a winter home in San Antonio. "Ike and I first met at Fort Sam Houston one Sunday afternoon," Mamie recalled long afterward, "when my parents and I stopped off at the fort to say hello to a friend, Mrs. Hunter Harris, wife of a major."

While the Douds visited with Mrs. Harris, Ike walked past. Mrs. Harris asked him to "meet some friends." At first, Dwight said he was on duty and unable to pause. "He's the woman hater of the post," Mrs. Harris told Mamie. Ike changed his mind and came across the street to meet the Douds.

"He looked me over carefully and, to the surprise of everyone, invited me to go with him on his inspection rounds," Mamie said. She remembered Ike as "just about the handsomest male I had ever seen." Moreover, she was intrigued by the "woman-hater" description.

For his part, Dwight seems to have been immediately taken with "a vivacious and attractive girl, smaller than average, saucy in the look about her face and in her whole attitude." As they walked through the fort, Ike said, "Now, Miss Doud, this is an army post, and the men in the barracks are not expecting ladies. I suggest that you keep your eyes to the front."

Mamie, lighthearted and independent, "immediately looked to the left and right—to his obvious discomfiture."

Ike was eager to spend another evening with her. But much to his disappointment, he found that Mamie was the belle of the post. The next afternoon Dwight managed to annoy the Doud family maid by calling between fifteen and twenty times asking for Mamie. When she returned, from a family fishing trip, Ike called again. He invited her to go dancing that night. She was busy, she explained. Dwight asked about the following night. She was engaged. Then he asked about taking her to the Majestic Theater on Saturday. She said she had already accepted dates for the next three "big nights" at the Majestic. Finally, Ike said, "How about four weeks from now?"

Mamie accepted. "I had a few other beaux, and I wasn't about to give them up immediately," she said. "But Ike was never easily discouraged. He simply outpersisted the competition."

Ike was invited by Mamie to a cookie and grape juice party several days after their phone conversation. At this affair, Dwight is said to have made a positive impression on Mamie's parents. The Douds were a close-knit family and Ike was quick to sense the importance of building a friendly relationship with Mamie's sisters and parents. Although they came from a more prosperous background, Dwight viewed the differences in social status as unimportant.

The Doud family had come to the New World from Guilford, England, in 1639. In England, they had been members of the landed gentry with great manor houses and their own coat of arms. They settled in Connecticut and helped found the town of Guilford. Mamie's grandfather, Royal Houghton Doud, established a wholesale grocery firm in upstate New York and later made a fortune as founder of a Chicago meat-packing enterprise. With the daring of a gambler, Doud invested his considerable finances in the Alaskan gold rush, not as a prospector but as a supplier. Like so many others, he lost his fortune.

John Sheldon Doud, Mamie's father, had been more of a pragmatist. He had attended the University of Chicago and Northwestern University. At the age of twenty-eight, he organized his own meat-packing firm, John S. Doud Company, in Boone, Iowa. Within eight years, he had made enough money to retire and move his family to Colorado. They first settled in Pueblo, then moved to Colorado Springs, and finally Denver, where a great Victorian house was built for them on Lafayette Street.

Mamie's mother, Elvira Mathilde Carlson, was the daughter of Swedish immigrants. The father, Carl Carlson, had come from Dagos Socken, Sweden, in 1868. His wife, Johanna Marie, followed the next year. They moved to Boone, Iowa, where Carl became manager of a flour mill. He later bought the mill and became a leading citizen of the community. He was spokesman for the large Scandinavian population and active in Republican Party affairs.

John and Elvira had four daughters—Eleanor, Mamie, Eda Mae, and Mabel Frances, who was known as "Mike." Eleanor, a year older than Mamie, had died of a heart ailment at the age of seventeen. In Denver, Mamie attended Miss Walcott's School, a girls' finishing school. There were still traces of the Old West in Denver. Mamie years later remembered seeing such colorful characters as William F. "Buffalo Bill" Cody and Molly Brown of Leadville.

"Mother is basically a Westerner in outlook and upbringing," John Eisenhower has said. "From the West she derived many of her salient characteristics: friendliness, coupled with a passion for her own privacy, a strong will, and a rather black-and-white outlook that makes her intensely loyal to people and institutions that she considers on her side."

One of the techniques Ike employed in his courtship was getting the Douds interested in his football team. They began attending the Saturday afternoon games, and by the end of the season, it was apparent that Dwight ranked first among Mamie's suitors.

He did not have a great deal of money to spend on her. When he took Mamie out for dinner, it was for ordinary Mexican food—tamales, chili, or enchiladas. They often attended vaudeville shows at the Orpheum, a local theater. For her nineteenth birthday, on November 14, Ike bought her a silver jewel case.

Mamie's acceptance of the expensive jewelry box convinced her parents that she was indeed serious about Dwight. They advised her of the inevitable hardships she might experience as a military wife. John Doud bluntly noted that Ike could become a casualty of the Great War. If anything, this observation made Mamie more determined to marry Dwight.

"He proposed, and I accepted—right after Christmas," she recalled. Ike ordered an engagement ring, a duplicate of his own West Point class ring, from Bailey, Banks and Biddle in Philadelphia. It arrived some weeks later and he presented it to her on Valentine's Day.

When Dwight sought permission from her father, he was somewhat defensive about his modest income. He told Doud that future promotions and pay raises were probable. Doud, who had reared Mamie in luxurious surroundings, was encouraging. He said that Mamie would be on her own. Ike was advised not to expect sudden advancement in income. An enduring marriage, Doud said, is not necessarily linked to social and economic status.

Doud did, however, intervene when Dwight proudly announced that he had been approved for transfer to the aviation section of the Army. Ike was elated about the move. "I liked the idea of flight training," he said. It was an opportunity for genuine excitement to be an aviation pioneer, and at the same time, earn 50 percent more pay. Dwight saw it as a means of breaking out of the football-coach stereotype in which the War Department had cast him. The Douds listened in silence as Ike broke the news. Finally, John Doud explained that he could not permit the marriage if Dwight was so "irresponsible" as to become a flyer. Mamie agreed with the ultimatum.

Ike solved the dilemma by refusing the transfer. It was a decision he had no cause to regret. As an aviator, his military career would have been considerably different. Mamie's influence on Dwight's growth and advancement is said to have been profound. "She takes full credit for smoothing the edges off the rough-and-ready Kansan and for teaching him some of the polish that later put him in good stead," John Eisenhower has noted. "It would have been Colonel Dwight David Eisenhower, if it weren't for Mamie," asserts Kevin McCann, a longtime aide to Eisenhower. "He had lived in a fairly narrow environment in Abilene. When he was at West Point, it was practically a monastic institution. Mamie came out of a much more sophisticated environment. In their early years together, Mamie was a broadening influence on Eisenhower." So for that matter were the elder Douds who treated him as a son.

Mamie's fears for Ike did not prevent him from applying for General John J. Pershing's "Punitive Expedition" against Mexican guerrilla Pancho Villa. Partisans of Villa, such as American journalist John Reed, had portrayed him as a Robin Hood with "Napoleonic" military genius. Wilson ordered Pershing to capture Villa, whom he blamed for the slaying of nineteen Americans at Chihuahua. Dwight's application to participate in the mission was passed over. There would be no battle stars earned in revolutionary Mexico.

Ike and Mamie were married at noon on July 1, 1916, in the

music room of her family's Denver house. She wore a white lace gown and Dwight wore his tropical dress white uniform. He did not sit down, Mamie recalled years later, in order to keep the crease in his trousers. After the ceremony, Ike cut the wedding cake with his sword. Later, he attempted to preserve Mamie's wedding bouquet by pouring melted candle wax over the flowers. But this effort, Mamie said, "french-fried the flowers into a shriveled brown mass."

There was additional reason for celebration that afternoon. Dwight received a promotion to first lieutenant and his monthly pay increased to $151.67.

For their honeymoon, the Eisenhowers went to the Colorado mountain resort of Eldorado Springs. Then, from Denver, they took a Union Pacific train to Abilene to meet Ike's family. David, who had written Mamie a warm letter before the wedding, met them at the station at four in the morning. Ida Eisenhower prepared them a fried chicken dinner instead of breakfast. Dwight's parents and brothers took an immediate liking to Mamie. And she was similarly impressed with them. If there had been doubts about the often uneasy relationship between families and married children, the stopover in Abilene did much to dispel them. It was a brief visit because only eight hours later they took the train south to San Antonio.

For a young woman who had grown up in an elegant home, accustomed to being waited on by servants who addressed her respectfully as "Miss Mamie," the apartment at Fort Sam Houston must have seemed about as livable as a tool shed. The bedroom was empty. Ike's uniforms filled the only closet. She described the living-room furniture as "horrible." Mamie's walnut bedroom suite from Denver and an oriental rug which they had received as a wedding gift soon gave the Eisenhower home a more distinctive look. Mamie was given charge of the family finances and supervised the purchase of everything from furniture to Dwight's clothes. Ike, who disliked shopping, willingly turned over such duties to his wife.

As was often the case with young women in her social circle, Mamie did not like to work in the kitchen. Dwight often said that when she married, her only culinary knowledge consisted of making fudge and mayonnaise. Because of this, the Eisenhowers ate their meals at the officers' mess. The food in the mess, which cost them sixty dollars each month, was often served cold and without seasoning. Mamie surprised Ike by purchasing a wooden icebox so that they could prepare meals at home. She did some cooking. But Dwight quickly became the regular cook. His specialities were pot roast, chicken, steak, and vegetable soup. They sometimes entertained other couples on the post at informal buffet suppers. Mamie would play the piano, which she rented for five dollars a month, and the group would sing popular songs of the period.

In spite of his winning record the previous fall, Ike was relieved of his coaching job at Peacock Military Academy. A former football star at the University of Texas was hired to replace him. As luck would have it, Dwight was asked to take over the football program at St. Louis College, a large Catholic school. The additional income was a major factor, no doubt, in Ike's acceptance of the job, for the school's football team had been on a losing streak that had begun five years earlier. His rebuilding program at the Catholic school must have been the major sports story in San Antonio that year. Eisenhower's team was tied in the first game, then went undefeated until the city championship game which they lost. A trademark of all his teams was a strong passing offense. "I always tried to open up the game," he later wrote.

San Antonio was not the safest community. When Ike headed a military police patrol, he narrowly missed being shot on a dark street. On another occasion, he was fired at from close range by a drunken soldier. He gave Mamie one of his revolvers and taught her how to use it. But one evening when a prowler attempted to break in through the bedroom window, she called neighbors instead of using the revolver. As it turned out, the prowler escaped into the night—and Mamie's revolver was so well hidden, tucked in a bedroll behind the piano, that its value as a deterrent was at best questionable.

By the spring of 1917, Ike seemed confident that the United States would join the Great War in Europe. He made no secret of his desire to go overseas. Any future opportunities for high military command seemed to hinge on his getting combat experience on the Western Front. President Wilson had been officially neutral since the outbreak of hostilities in 1914. He had won reelection in 1916 with the slogan "He kept us out of war." Wilson knew the slogan was fraudulent. "I can't keep the country out of war," he told a member of his cabinet. "Any little German lieutenant can put us into the war at any time by some calculated outrage."

The United States was not dragged into the war by treaty commitments. Nor was it directly threatened. Britain's efforts to starve Germany by blockade had some economic impact in the United States. But Germany's efforts to starve Britain with submarine warfare caused a much greater emotional backlash in the United States. Wilson took a position of moral superiority throughout this period, condemning British "navalism" and German "militarism." Germany tipped the balance against itself by launching unrestricted warfare with submarines and U-boats. The sinking of three American ships in March and the disclosure of the Zimmermann note, a proposal by the German foreign minister that Mexico attack the United States, aroused prowar sentiments in the United States.

Wilson's deliberations were analyzed later by Winston Churchill, who wrote: "The action of the United States with its repercussions on the history of the world depended, during the awful period of Armageddon, upon the working of this man's mind and spirit to the exclusion of almost every other factor." Wilson, Churchill said, "played a part in the fate of nations incomparably more direct and personal than any other man."

On April 2, 1917, Wilson went before a joint session of Congress to obtain a declaration of war against Germany. Only through intervention, Wilson said, could Germany be punished for challenging America. "It is a fearful thing to lead this great peaceful people into war," he said. "Civilization itself seems to be hanging in the balance. But the right is more precious than the peace, and we shall fight for the things we have always carried nearest our hearts—for Democracy. The world must be made safe for Democracy."

Ike had been assigned to help organize and train a new regiment, the 57th Infantry, the day before Wilson's speech. He had decidedly mixed feelings about this task. It separated him from friends and associates in the 19th Infantry—and from Mamie. He was transferred to Leon Springs, some thirty miles from San Antonio. Mamie was unhappy about the separation, a condition of military life to which she never became fully accustomed.

"It used to anger me when people would say, 'You're an army wife, you must be used to Ike being away.' I never got used to him being gone," Mamie said nearly sixty years later. "He was my husband. He was my whole life."

Mamie must have missed Ike a great deal because she took a considerable risk in visiting him. Her father had given them a four-year-old Pullman roadster as a gift. Mamie had never driven the automobile and had no particular desire to learn. Ike left the car behind when he was transferred. There was no transportation for Dwight to visit her at San Antonio. So, with remarkable determination, Mamie decided to attempt to drive the Pullman to see Ike. Painfully aware of her lack of driving skill, she began her journey soon after dawn in an effort to avoid any traffic. It was, by all accounts, an uneasy trip as she trembled and maneuvered her way to the camp. She had telephoned Dwight to advise him that she would be coming. It was fortunate that she had made the call. As she drove through the camp gate, where Ike was waiting, Mamie cried, "Ike! Get on, get on quickly—I don't know how to stop this thing!"

Dwight ran to the side of the Pullman and jumped on the running board, opened the door, and stopped the car. He spent the rest of the day giving her driving lessons. On future visits, he suggested that she arrange for a more experienced driver to accompany her.

In the meantime, Ike worked with seemingly tireless energy in preparing the men of the 57th for battle. He was promoted to captain on May 15. The men whom he trained, so eager to go overseas, were destined to spend the war on garrison duty in Houston.

He was ordered to Fort Oglethorpe in Georgia, as an instructor in their Officers' Training Camp, in mid-September. It was with some bitterness that Ike received these orders. He wanted to be on the real battlefields in Europe, and Mamie was expecting their first child any day. A son, Doud Dwight, was born on September

23. Mamie soon called him "Icky." Her parents came to San Antonio to be with her. John Doud made Mamie's burden somewhat lighter by giving her a one-hundred-dollar monthly allowance.

Dwight was next ordered to serve as an instructor at the Army Service School at Fort Leavenworth, Kansas, in early December. This enabled him to stop in San Antonio for a visit, however brief, with Mamie and his new son. Ike was becoming increasingly restless as an instructor. The newspapers were publicizing the achievements of some of the brightest young officers—Brigadier General Douglas MacArthur, commander of the Rainbow Division, and Captain George Patton, aide to General Pershing and himself field commander of a tank unit. Ike lusted for such opportunities. For weeks, he had written the War Department with requests to go overseas. His applications had been rejected. At Leavenworth, he received a reprimand from the War Department for appearing to second-guess his superiors. The post commandant also reprimanded Dwight. This was more than Ike could tolerate. He snapped back that all he was asking was a chance to go to battle. The commandant took no further action.

For all his resentment at being left in training camps, Dwight seems to have exerted his best efforts at working with the young soldiers. A letter written by another soldier, shortly after his arrival at Leavenworth, says: "Our new Captain, Eisenhower by name, is, I believe, one of the most efficient and best Army officers in the country." Ike's official record indicates that his superiors took a similar view. Again and again, his ability to train others and his leadership qualities are praised.

In February, Ike reported to Camp Meade, Maryland, where tank units were being trained for combat. This at long last seemed to be Dwight's chance for overseas duty. It "put new spirit into me," he said. His dream became reality—or so it seemed—in mid-March when word came that he would be leaving for Europe in command of the 301st Tank Battalion. His jubilation was soon tempered by the news that overseas duty had been precluded by another assignment. On March 24, he was ordered to take a less glamorous command, at the Tank Training Center, Camp Colt, Gettysburg, Pennsylvania. "My mood was black," Ike remembered years later.

The Camp Colt command hardly compared with the trenches in France, nor did it compare favorably with other training centers. Although it was a tank school, there were no tanks. Indeed, it had been all but abandoned by the Army. Dwight was left to improvise and use his already renowned "organizational ability."

One benefit derived from this dubious command was that Mamie and their infant son could be with him. As Mamie was packing and readying for the move to Gettysburg, an older friend advised her to pack lightly. Military families were always on the move, the friend said. In order not to exhaust herself by moving heavy furniture, Mamie was urged to sell her furnishings. She decided to do just that on the premise that the cash could be used to purchase secondhand furniture in Pennsylvania. Mamie sold her walnut bedroom set, living-room furniture, lamps, dishes, glassware, and rugs for ninety dollars. Later, she would readily admit to having been "hoodwinked by an older woman."

"How could I have been so gullible?" she said years later. "I know I was young, but not that young. Surely I could have applied simple arithmetic and figured out that ninety dollars would never replace another apartment. What I exchanged for nine ten-dollar bills cost originally over nine hundred dollars. It's a wonder Ike didn't wring my neck."

Mamie and Icky traveled four days by train in their April journey from San Antonio to Gettysburg. Mamie credited a kind-hearted porter with making the trip smoother. The porter kept her supplied with warmed feeding bottles of milk for Icky, and with cans of hot water for bathing the child. She found the last stretch of her journey, a five-hour local train from Washington to Gettysburg, the most difficult. With no porter to assist her, she quickly became tired. Her spirits were much improved when Ike met her at Gettysburg's railroad station. For the first time, they were going to live together, with their son, as a family.

They lived in a large, old, white-pillared brick colonial house which overlooked the campus of Gettysburg College. It had formerly been occupied by the men of Sigma Alpha Epsilon fraternity and was thus perfectly suited for entertaining. As the commander's wife, Mamie was required to host dinners for generals and other officers, visiting congressmen, and other important figures who came to inspect the camp. The Eisenhower residence became a popular center for bridge, which Mamie played during the afternoon with other army wives, and poker, Dwight's favorite game. If living in such a large house had its advantages, it also had considerable drawbacks. Mamie said the old SAE house was "so poorly heated that I thought I was going to freeze to death."

Ike transformed the camp into the Army's showcase Tank Training Center. He was rewarded for his performance with promotions—to major in June, and to lieutenant colonel on October 14, his twenty-eighth birthday. Some ten thousand men were under his command. They learned the new mobile warfare, with its new tactics and operations, in lectures and on maneuvers. During the summer, Dwight received three small French Renault tanks which enabled him to simulate battlefield situations.

With his appreciation of military history, Ike chose Big Round Top, a strategic location during the Battle of Gettysburg, for firing maneuvers. Before the arrival of the tanks, he arranged for flatbed trucks to be delivered on which machine guns and cannons were mounted. "The firing might have been greater than during the great battle," he wryly noted. Dwight was thoroughly captivated by the most historic of American battlefields. He took Mamie on long drives, recounting in detail the fateful events of July 1863. According to Mamie, he "knew every rock on that battlefield."

His responsibilities at Camp Colt sometimes brought him into conflict with politicians and local businessmen. When Ike forced an officer to resign for cheating fellow soldiers in a card game, he was confronted by the officer's father and their congressman. Despite much pressure, Dwight would not compromise. He demonstrated the same rigid commitment to principle when a Gettysburg hotel, in defiance of his orders, served liquor to uniformed soldiers. Military guards were stationed at the hotel, and it was declared off limits to the regiment. The local congressman protested at the urging of the hotel operator, but Ike, with the blessing of the War Department, prevailed.

"Eisenhower was a strict disciplinarian," said Claude J. Harris, who was his administrative assistant at Camp Colt, "but most human, considerate." Harris said Dwight "was always available to confer with his officers on either military or personal problems." Ike was said to be somewhat reticent during this period. "He shied at publicity," Harris said, "preferring to remain in the background."

That Dwight was held in high regard by his men was evidenced by a September 21, 1943, resolution by Camp Colt alumni, recommending him as a presidential candidate. While they professed to have "no knowledge or concern as to the political affiliations or beliefs" of Eisenhower, they urged his election on the basis of his "leadership qualities."

His considerable achievements at Camp Colt still fell short of what he hoped to accomplish overseas. Ike continued to ask the War Department to assign him to such duty. Finally, his wish was granted. He was scheduled to sail to France in November, where he would command his own unit. But the Armistice was signed and the Allies victorious on November 11—one week before he was to leave for Europe. Fate had again blocked Dwight's aspirations for fame and glory in Europe.

Mamie and Icky had left Gettysburg for the Doud home in Denver when word came in early November that her younger sister, Eda Mae ("Buster"), was gravely ill. By the time she reached Chicago, Mamie received a telegram that Eda Mae was dead. She arrived in Colorado just in time for her sister's funeral. Eda Mae was buried beside Eleanor; both of the Doud sisters had died at the age of seventeen. Mamie had a heart murmur from childhood that apparently resulted from rheumatic fever. After the tension and grief of her younger sister's death, she was ill for more than a week. But she soon recovered.

For the next five months, she remained in Denver with Icky and her family while Ike worked with the Tank Corps at Fort Dix, New Jersey, and Fort Benning, Georgia.

Ike was giving retirement from the Army at least some consideration. Among his options was a high-paying job offer from an Indiana businessman who had been a soldier at Camp Colt.

"As for my professional career, the prospects were none too bright," Dwight later wrote. He was certain that his future in the Army was restricted to "meaningless" paperwork. "If not depressed, I was mad, disappointed," he said, "and resented the fact that the war had passed me by."

Ike was flattered when Colonel Ira Welborn, director of the Tank Corps and his superior, recommended him for the Distinguished Service Medal early in 1919. But in sending father David Eisenhower a copy of the recommendation, he was not optimistic about his chances.

Dear Dad,

Just sending you above—as thought you'd be interested. There is no chance of my getting one of the medals—but it shows Colonel Welborn's opinion of me.

Devotedly,

Son

Two years later, Welborn, feeling that Ike had been slighted, resubmitted the recommendation. In 1922, he tried again and succeeded.

The award read: "While Commanding Officer of the Tank Corps Training Center, he displayed unusual zeal, foresight, and marked administrative ability in the organization, training, and preparation for overseas service of technical troops of the Tank Corps."

Welborn wrote Ike that "It may seem like a posthumous award —it has been so long coming—but that will soon be outgrown."

Dwight's wartime rank was reduced to captain in the summer of 1920. But he was promoted to major in December. If there were no battle stars from the Great War, Ike could boast more administrative experience than most young officers. Because others received more public recognition, Dwight was underestimating his own stature and potential.

Chapter Five

THE YOUNGER BROTHER

He was always conscious of the need to excel. As the youngest of the seven Eisenhower brothers, Milton had to make his own identity. By the time he was thirty, he would be recognized as the family prodigy and one of the most prominent young officials in the federal government.

His childhood may have been more difficult because both parents had wanted a girl when he was born on September 15, 1899. "My father was sorry he never had a girl," Earl Eisenhower said years later. "He used to sit on our front porch and make friends with every little girl that came by. I know he was miserable because Milton wasn't a little girl."

Much to his discomfort, Milton wore shoulder-length curls until he was five years old. In a 1902 family portrait, his long hair contrasts sharply with that of the other brothers. At the age of four, he had scarlet fever. It was a terrifying ordeal for the family. For six weeks he was quarantined in his room. The family doctor said Milton might not survive. Although he lived, his body was so ravaged by the disease that his eyes were permanently weakened and his body left frail and spindly.

Painfully insecure during much of his childhood, Milton was moved easily to tears by the teasing of his brothers. He had a fear of dark places which his brothers frequently tested by pushing him into the attic and the hayloft of the family barn. Milton so dreaded the laughter of others that he never enjoyed being the target of humor.

As a youngster, he was "anxious to make good in athletics." He wanted to earn the respect of his brothers in the same manner they had won local prestige. But Milton was too weak and uncoordinated to make his mark in sports. "I practiced baseball for many hours," he said. "But I was so butter-fingered that I could only make the third team in high school." In football, he was acutely aware of his physical limitations. He became the water boy. Only in track was Milton able to compete. He practiced by running "several miles a day" and won a position as a sprinter on the high school team.

If he was unable to find athletic glory, Milton nonetheless made a name for himself at Abilene High School as a scholar. Milton received twenty-six "ones"—equivalent to "A's"—out of thirty-one courses. He credited his impressive achievements to a study method learned from Anna Hopkins, a teacher who lived for a year in the Eisenhower home. Her method made such a difference that his Latin instructor accused him of using a "pony" on an examination. Milton credited another teacher, Miss Ruth Hunt, with helping him develop a readable literary style. His earlier writings were somewhat ponderous and dispassionate, he said. But Miss Hunt inspired him to approach writing with creativity and imagination. He soon found an outlet for his writings. One of his teachers, Ruth Harger, was the daughter of the publisher of the Abilene *Daily Reflector*. Milton told her that he was giving some thought to lying about his age and joining the Army. She strongly disapproved and secured him a job on her father's newspaper.

Charles Moreau Harger was to have a profound influence on Milton. Harger, a graduate of Harvard University, was a figure of power, prestige, and prominence. He was a prolific writer and frequent contributor to such national magazines as *The Saturday Evening Post* and *Harper's*. As the chairman of the Kansas Board of Regents, he controlled the growth of state colleges and universities. The tall, slender Harger was aloof and distant from most residents of Abilene. "People thought he was snobbish," Milton said. "But he was a complete intellectual who never stopped thinking. It would irritate people when they would pass him on the street and he wouldn't speak. He was always preoccupied with his thinking. When he ran for Congress, this trait worked against him. Even though he was superbly qualified, he was badly defeated."

In any event, Harger took an almost paternalistic interest in Milton. "The greatest thing that ever happened to me was my association with him," Milton would say more than sixty years later. "He became almost a second father to me." From the start of their relationship, he worked to broaden Milton's literary horizons. "I had read the Rover Boys, Horatio Alger, Robert Louis Stevenson, and Mark Twain," Milton said. "But Mr. Harger had a large library and began selecting books for me." Within a short period of time he was reading volumes on the ethics of journalism, economics, and Gibbon's *Decline and Fall of the Roman Empire*.

Milton's political views were more pronounced than other members of the Eisenhower family. He was an admirer of President Woodrow Wilson, which was no small commitment in the conservative town. "It was almost looked down on to be a Democrat," Milton said. "My enthusiasm for Wilson began when I learned that he came from the same part of Virginia that my mother did," he said. "I became interested in Colonel Edward House [Wilson's adviser and confidant] when my parents told me that he came from Texas—and Ike was from Texas."

Milton was one of Wilson's most vocal supporters in Abilene during the campaign of 1912. If, at thirteen, he seemed precocious to Republican elders, they at least listened. Unlike so many school children, his views were distinctly his own. Milton followed the presidential campaign by reading three newspapers. And when Wilson was elected, he was jubilant. His Wilsonian idealism was somewhat tempered by Harger's thoughtful criticism of Administration policies. But Wilson remained his "idol" for a number of years. Indeed, Milton hoped to pattern his own career after Wilson by "going into government or education."

"It was quite an unusual thing for a young lad to have those ambitions in Abilene," Milton said later.

As his political philosophy matured, he became more skeptical about Wilson. "He was a man of very great faults," Milton said. "He was stubborn—and unwilling to compromise. He had a messianic complex and was convinced of his own infallibility. In foreign policy, he was probably the most imperialistic President we have had in modern times."

One of Milton's earliest and most notable journalistic accomplishments was an interview with William Jennings Bryan. Most newspapers of the day were persecuting Bryan for his pacifist arguments; he had resigned as Secretary of State to protest Wilson's increasing hard line against Germany. The New York *World* accused Bryan of "treachery." The New York *Times* said he had a "befuddled mind." The Cleveland *Plain Dealer* condemned him for "treason." Bryan carried his message to the American public as the leading speaker on the Chautauqua circuit. Milton, barely out of high school, was intimidated by Bryan's reputation. He had heard a story that Bryan refused to answer any questions from a reporter in Kansas City, whom he accused of misquoting.

"When Bryan got on the train for Denver, he put on his pajamas and got into a lower berth," Milton said. "Then suddenly, from the upper berth, came this reporter. He threatened to yell if Bryan didn't talk—and the great man would have been caught in an embarrassing situation."

Milton located Bryan in the barbershop of the Union Pacific Hotel. Somewhat nervously, he waited for him in the hotel lobby. When Bryan appeared, Milton asked for an advance copy of his speech so that he could meet an early deadline.

Bryan explained that he never used a text. But he said, "Sit down and I'll tell you what I'm going to say." He then dictated a newspaper story, with quotes and background, and gave Milton a recent photograph of himself to accompany the article. As he was preparing to leave, Milton asked Bryan about Wilson. What followed was a remarkable critique of the Wilson foreign policy which outlined how America became entwined in the Great War. "I would never have succeeded as a career reporter," Milton later admitted, for he "did not write about our personal conversation." Although Bryan made no such stipulation, Milton treated their talk as confidential.

Harger was so impressed with Milton's story about Bryan that he gave him a 50 percent raise—from eight dollars a week to twelve. Milton told him that Bryan was the real author of the article. Harger smiled and said, "If you can get the real authority to do much of the work for you, you deserve whatever pay you get!"

Milton was nicknamed "Scoop" after "Scoop, the Cub Reporter," a popular comic strip of the day. "I was a complete neophyte," Milton said. "Not long after I started, I picked up some interesting gossip on the street. Kansas had been a consistently dry state and the news concerned some suspicious-looking kegs. In my lead, I wrote: 'Last night, a truck was seen backing up to the local creamery. And some suspicious-looking kegs were taken into the creamery.' When I turned the story in, I was quite happy with it. But Mr. Harger brought it over to me. He had crossed out 'local creamery' and written 'into the home of David J. Eisenhower.'" Milton said he never again was tempted to use gossip or hearsay information in an article.

He frequently received assistance from townspeople in his reporting. "When I covered the dedication of a new Catholic church, the local priest helped me. All the dignitaries from Kansas were there—political and religious leaders—as was a cardinal from Chicago. I wrote the material about the crowds and the color. And the priest developed the religious material for me." Harger congratulated Milton on the church article. "That's good reporting," he said. "If you insist on accuracy, you have to go to the authorities to get it."

Harger urged Milton to attend college if he still planned a career in education or public service. So, in the summer of 1918, Milton enrolled at Kansas State College. It was a "largely wasted term," he said, because he was drafted into the Student Army Training Corps. Like other freshman men, he spent more time at military drill than he did in the classroom. The SATC retarded any opportunity for intellectual development. "It was 85 percent military training and 15 percent education," he said.

He returned to Abilene that fall as "temporary editor" of the newspaper. Harger had gone East to be with an ailing family member and had asked Milton to take over the daily operations of the *Reflector*.

The war in Europe remained the biggest news of the day. Abilene, like most other American towns, was polarized and divided about the war. "Nearly everyone in town was down on pacifists and all things German," Milton said. "Since my parents fell into both categories, they were especially suspect. Mother was so outspoken that she was in danger of being arrested. It was only the intervention of an influential friend, J. B. Case, one of the original builders of the Union Pacific Railroad, that kept her out of jail. He really went to bat for Mother." Other American pacifists were less fortunate. Socialist leader Eugene Victor Debs was indicted, convicted, and sentenced to ten years in prison under the Espionage Act for denouncing the war.

Milton played up the war in his news columns with banner headlines, a major departure from Harger's more conservative style. "For the first time in the war, the Americans and the Allied troops were making real progress against the Germans," Milton said. "So I put streamer headlines on the front page." Harger, upon hearing of the altered format, was indignant. The *Reflector's* headlines were traditionally one or two columns. He telephoned his copublisher and asked, "Should I come out to straighten things up?"

"Stay where you are," the partner said. "Our circulation has increased by one hundred and twenty-eight."

Milton earned enough money during this period to enroll at Kansas State University in 1919. He was an industrial journalism major. It was a pragmatic choice for he made no secret of his ambition to someday succeed Harger as publisher of the Abilene *Daily Reflector*. Milton continued to work for Harger during his vacations. Because he was financing his own education, it took him six years to graduate. In 1922, he left school to work as director of information for a group of public utilities at Abilene. At Kansas State, Milton earned a comfortable income as a correspondent for the Kansas City *Star* and the Topeka *Daily Capital*. He also was a frequent contributor to such agricultural journals as the *Kansas Farmer* and the *Iowa Farmer*. "I would find a good photograph and write a feature about it," Milton said years later.

His most important responsibility was serving as editor of the *Kansas State Collegian*. Milton received the appointment as a freshman. Although the position traditionally went to an upperclassman, he had more experience than any other applicant. He also received strong support from members of his social fraternity, Sigma Alpha Epsilon. "Some fraternity brothers told me that they were absolutely certain I could get the job," Milton later recalled. "And, they added, it paid fifty dollars a month." By Milton's description, the newspaper was "practically an adjunct of the School of Journalism." He would assign and edit stories under the supervision of the faculty. As editor, he struck up a friendship with college president William M. Jardine. "I'd bring in stories or questions to him that I had doubts about," Milton said.

He found a sympathetic listener in Jardine. Indeed, he was no less influential in Milton's development than Charles Harger. Jardine, a tall, balding, agricultural scientist, brought Milton into his family circle, where he was a frequent dinner guest. Milton became acquainted there with L. R. Eakin, a Manhattan banker and merchant, who was Jardine's close friend. Milton later met Eakin's daughter, Helen Elsie, a high school student. When she entered Kansas State, Milton began dating her.

"My first date with her was when I was a senior and she was a freshman," he said. "We went to dances together, played golf before breakfast occasionally, and discovered we had the same interests."

In the meantime, Milton was winning honors and awards in several fields. He was chancellor of the local creative writing club and won a gold medal in the college's short-story contest. He also was tapped for membership in Phi Kappa Phi, the scholastic honorary for scientific schools. He gained additional recognition as the best college orator at Kansas State. In 1921, he won the gold medal at the Missouri Valley speech contest. A newspaper report in the Columbia *Missourian* said, "Mr. Eisenhower was especially to be commended for his delivery. His voice was deep and clear, his gestures unforced. With a sufficient amount of ardor, he presented his argument convincingly."

In his senior year, Milton was appointed a teaching assistant in the Speech and English departments. He also worked as a proofreader for *The Industrialist*, the college's official newspaper. All of these activities kept him in touch with president Jardine. They also enabled him to accumulate considerable savings. "I began as a freshman with forty dollars," Milton said. "I worked my way through school—and graduated with seventeen hundred dollars in the bank."

Asked by L. R. Eakin what he would most like to do, Milton said his greatest ambition was to attend Harvard Law School but that he could not afford it. Eakin offered to pay Milton's expenses without any reimbursement. Though Milton was deeply moved by Eakin's generosity, he did not take him up on his offer. So Milton remained at Kansas State.

Upon graduation, Milton was appointed an instructor in the journalism school. It was a low-paying job, but he accepted it as an opportunity to launch a teaching career. He was so well-known to college administrators that his future at Kansas State seemed bright indeed. Milton took some graduate courses which, he hoped, were the beginning of his doctoral program.

His lectures and studies were interrupted by an appendicitis attack and surgery. He received a note from president Jardine:

> Dear Milton,
>
> What in the world has gone wrong with you? I was just twenty-six years of age when I had my appendix cut out and I have been glad ever since. No doubt the next thing I hear of you doing is accepting a college presidency somewhere.

Shortly afterward, Milton received another job offer. Some months before, a Republican National Committee field representative had been on the campus to help Milton organize a college Republican club. Having outgrown his earlier enthusiasm for Wilson, Milton became an avid Republican. Milton made a positive impression on the RNC man. He recruited one hundred members and was elected club president. The RNC man casually suggested that Milton ought to apply for a diplomatic post in the State Department. Milton filled out an application, took a written test, and "forgot about the matter." Just as he was settling into his teaching routine, a telegram came from Secretary of State Charles Evans Hughes. Milton was offered a consular post in Edinburgh, Scotland.

He was faced with a dilemma. For years he had contemplated the relative merits of a career in education or government. Now, it seemed, he had to make his decision. Milton was restless and uneasy when he approached Jardine to discuss his alternatives. "Well," said Jardine in an even tone, "that's the sort of thing you have to figure out for yourself. But you're fired. There's no place at this institution for you the next two years. If you want to come back then, I'll see what I can do for you."

The president's swift action stunned Milton. He had expected Jardine to urge him to remain at Kansas State. "I'm not sure that rules about giving a faculty member a year's notice were in existence then," Milton said, "but I wasn't conscious of them."

When Jardine smiled, Milton laughed about his "firing." He wired his acceptance to the State Department, and asked a local travel agency to secure train tickets to New York and reservations on the S.S. *United States,* which was soon scheduled to sail for England.

Thus began Milton's half century of government service. He was ill-prepared for the world of international affairs. "My naïvete was monumental," Milton was to remember some years later. But he learned quickly. Among his duties were handling applications from thousands of prospective emigrants, writing reports about Scottish industry, and arbitrating local disputes involving American citizens. He also did studies for the U. S. Commerce Department. Since the days of ancient Greece, consuls have played an important role in developing international trade.

Much of the work was drudgery. "We are the Cinderellas of the diplomatic service," another consul once lamented. But for Milton and such ambitious members of his generation as Charles E. Bohlen, the consular service was to be an apprenticeship for distinguished careers in government and international diplomacy.

Milton found time to take some graduate courses at the University of Edinburgh. He lived at Ramsay Lodge, a university dormitory. At first, Milton was subjected to some heckling from Scottish students. He suffered for several days and then retaliated by making fun of their speech. There was apparently no bitterness, as Milton became a frequent drinking companion. He often engaged in debates with students over world affairs, a role which found him defending American foreign policy.

In 1926, Milton was invited to return to the United States. President Coolidge had named Jardine as his Secretary of Agriculture, and Jardine wanted Milton to become his assistant. Milton, though flattered, declined the offer. "I couldn't accept a political appointment," he said. "I was still rather security conscious. I was in the Foreign Service, saving fifty dollars a month, and I was essentially engaged to Helen through correspondence. I wasn't about to run any risks by taking a position with uncertain security."

Secretary Jardine induced the Civil Service Commission to send Milton a competitive test. "Fortunately, I finished first," Milton said. "This seemed to be for me the real entrance into the federal service that I had dreamed of in my high school days."

Milton looked forward to his arrival in Washington, where Helen had just graduated from George Washington University. But his transfer stalled when Secretary of State Frank Kellogg objected. President Coolidge's intervention at Jardine's urging moved Kellogg to approve Milton's release. Milton was in Washington in time for a brief reunion with Helen; the Eakins were preparing to leave on a world tour, which meant that there would be another long separation between Milton and Helen.

Because of his civil-service classification, Milton became "the first career assistant to a Cabinet member." He was twenty-five when he moved into his own office at the Department of Agriculture. Though he was younger than his colleagues, he was already considered an expert in agriculture. Secretary Jardine gave him weighty responsibilities. Milton prepared Jardine's congressional testimony and speeches, answered much of the Secretary's correspondence, and signed Jardine's signature to the letters.

Jardine was not the easiest person to write speeches for. He was a man of limited oratorical gifts. "He could butcher the King's English more than any other public figure who ever lived," Milton said, "but he always made sense." Milton frequently accompanied Jardine on his trips. On one such occasion, they were in Butte, Montana, where Secretary Jardine was to address the National

Wool Growers. Much to Milton's surprise, he found himself seated at the head table.

"I was greatly embarrassed when the toastmaster asked me to say a few words," Milton would recall many years later. "Even though I was a pretty skillful public speaker, I became flustered. So I blurted out, 'I don't make speeches. I only write them.'"

Secretary Jardine rose with a twinkle and said, "Anything good I say is mine. Any mistakes are Milton's."

Jardine found Milton invaluable. They had gotten on well since their first meeting at Kansas State and their relationship became even more intimate. During a visit to Kansas, Secretary Jardine traveled to Abilene to have dinner with the Eisenhower family. "Mother had a woman from the church serve so that she could serve as hostess," Milton said. "Jardine always liked to have a cocktail before dinner. I had to find some liquor. So I went to Mr. Harger, who gave me a bottle of mixed martinis. I put it in the refrigerator to get it chilled. Mother came in and said, 'What does it taste like?' I gave her a teaspoon, she made a funny look and said, 'Don't tell Sister Tolliver.'"

The Jardine visit to the Eisenhower home was of great social significance in Kansas. To have a member of the President's cabinet as a dinner guest was the envy of every North Side household. Milton's sudden prominence in the nation's capital had not gone unnoticed in Abilene. The local newspapers had reported that he had been to White House teas and state dinners. By the standards of his home town, Milton was a genuine celebrity.

From the moment Milton joined the Department of Agriculture, he was involved in one of the great issues of the day—the McNary-Haugen farm-relief bill. The measure was an outgrowth of the postwar agrarian depression. While the rest of the country prospered, agriculture fell on hard times. Prices on farm products dropped by some 35 percent. The crisis deepened when farmers glutted the market. Many farm mortgages were foreclosed. Recovery was so slow that progressive leaders and farm organizations called for extraordinary measures. In 1924, the farmers endorsed the McNary-Haugen bill, legislation which called for a federal farm board to purchase surplus commodities and sell them abroad at the world price—or keep them off the market until prices rose.

Senator Charles L. McNary of Oregon, a plain-spoken Republican liberal, and Secretary of Agriculture Henry C. Wallace were leading advocates of the farm-relief plan. President Coolidge and Secretary of Commerce Herbert Hoover were its principal opponents. As president of Kansas State, Jardine had attacked the McNary-Haugen bill. When Wallace died in 1924, Coolidge replaced him with Jardine, recommended by Hoover because he was "opposed to all paternalistic legislation."

McNary-Haugen, defeated by congressional vote in 1924 and 1926, became a symbol of agrarian discontent. Milton, who understood the temper of the times better than Coolidge or Jardine, described McNary-Haugen as "an ingenious measure." He was hopeful that Coolidge would be willing to accept at least a modified version of the bill.

When the bill finally passed in 1927, Coolidge threatened a veto. Milton, working with Jardine, prepared a conciliatory statement for Coolidge to consider for a veto message. Coolidge rejected it and instead sent an uncharacteristically strident veto message. The President sternly warned against using the "coercive powers of government" for "price fixing." While Coolidge acknowledged that there was an agricultural crisis, he offered no solution.

A year later, McNary-Haugen again passed in both houses of Congress. The farm situation had shown no improvement, but Coolidge remained in opposition. Milton attempted to revise the Administration's policy on farm parity. He proposed tax credits for farm land, lower freight rates for agricultural products, higher tariffs on foreign farm products, and farmer-controlled cooperatives to supervise production and distribution of farm products. Milton and Secretary Jardine presented their amendments to Coolidge at the White House, who briefly examined the document before dismissing them.

Unhappily enough, Coolidge ignored Milton's advice. His second veto message was even more uncompromising than the first. Coolidge said McNary-Haugen was "bureaucracy gone mad" and would subject farmers to the "autocratic domination" of government.

Milton was bitterly disappointed. "I thought the President should have worked with McNary and other congressional leaders," he said, "but he just let it die." It was not, however, a resignation issue. Milton preferred to work for reforms from within the system rather than his most likely alternative—on an isolated college campus.

His advancement had been nothing less than remarkable. At twenty-six, he was adviser and confidant to a Cabinet member. Two years later, he would be appointed director of information for the Agriculture Department, the youngest person ever to hold the position. He was a more confident, more self-assured young man than the boy orator from Kansas State. Arthur S. Flemming, who came to Washington in 1927 as a graduate student at American University, met Milton that fall. "He was a very articulate person," Flemming was to recall years later. "He had a very fine understanding of the issues of the day—and was very much involved in them. I was most impressed that a young man would already be working at such a high level."

Milton and Helen were married on October 12, 1927. Dwight, in dress uniform, was best man. Helen cut the wedding cake with his sword. Whatever Milton's frustrations about Coolidge policies, he and Helen clearly enjoyed Washington social life. They became well acquainted with the Coolidges at White House receptions and dinners.

Secretary Jardine fell out of favor with Coolidge late in 1927. Coolidge took himself out of the 1928 presidential race with his "I do not choose to run" statement. Almost immediately, Jardine began lining up farm-belt support for his close friend Herbert Hoover. Milton, in opening the Secretary's mail, discovered a handwritten presidential reprimand:

> Jardine—
>
> Remember you are working for me.
>
> Calvin Coolidge.

Milton quickly sensed that Coolidge was hoping for a popular movement to draft him on the 1928 ticket. At any rate, Jardine's star quickly faded at the Coolidge White House. No longer was he invited to social functions or private conferences. But with

Hoover on the ascendancy, Jardine's future seemed more promising. Milton, with the security of civil service, watched the Machiavellian maneuvering with wonder and amusement.

In looking back on his service in the Coolidge administration, Milton described the quiet President as "a narrow and stubborn man who was woefully uninformed in some very important areas. Coolidge was such a firm believer in the free enterprise system," Milton said, "that he wanted no governmental interference whatsoever. Had a workable plan been adopted, the Depression might have been much less devastating than it was."

Milton's efforts at such reform were thwarted. But he had tried, and his efforts were duly noted.

Chapter Six

SOLDIER ASCENDANT

Ike returned to Camp Meade in the spring of 1919, entering the Infantry Tank School, where he would remain for three years. The Tank Corps was much better equipped than it had been at Camp Colt. There was an abundance of tanks—German, British, French, and American models. Dwight was given command of several heavy-tank battalions.

One of the benefits of Camp Meade was Ike's friendship with Colonel George S. Patton, Jr. Patton was the most illustrious of the World War I Tank Corps officers. According to legend, he had ridden into battle sitting astride one of his tanks and waving a sword. He wore pearl-handled revolvers and had used them to kill one of Pancho Villa's top lieutenants in the Mexican border war. His flamboyant style was the antithesis of Ike's firm but low-key leadership. But they became fast friends; they shared a mutual interest in military history and tactics and had lengthy discussions about their reading. Another common bond was Patton's zest for athletics. He had been a football star at Army and an Olympic shooting champion. Mamie and Beatrice Patton were friendly, but their relationship does not seem to have been close.

Ike and Patton both agreed that troops supported by a tank company were infinitely superior to those without tank support. They were pioneers in tank warfare and sought to convince others of its importance. For starters, they wrote articles for military journals. Dwight called for a new, medium-sized tank. "The tank is in its infancy," he wrote, "and the great strides already made in its mechanical development only point to the greater ones still to come. The clumsy, awkward, snail-like pace of the old tanks must be forgotten, and in their place we must picture this speedy, reliable and efficient engine of destruction." Ike recommended, in his *Infantry Journal* article, that a tank company be included in the infantry division. Patton, writing for *Cavalry Journal*, argued along similar lines.

Their superiors were not amused. Dwight was ordered to report to the chief of infantry. "I was told that my ideas were not only wrong," he later recalled, "but dangerous and that henceforth I would keep them to myself. Particularly, I was not to publish anything incompatible with solid infantry doctrine. If I did, I would be hauled before a court-martial."

Such threats effectively silenced their campaign, but they also drew Ike and Patton "even closer." They continued to experiment with tank maneuvers. During one such operation they narrowly escaped when a cable snapped, slashing down trees and bushes. On another, the engine was knocked off a heavy tank, while they were riding inside.

Patton made an important contribution to Dwight's career in the autumn of 1919. He introduced him to General Fox Conner, then chief of staff of the American Expeditionary Force in Washington and one of the most influential strategists of World War I. Conner was considered a brilliant student of military doctrine and history. Patton had briefed Conner about Ike's tank background and their theories. Following dinner at Patton's quarters, Conner engaged Dwight in a long and detailed conversation. Later, Ike was to cite this meeting as a major turning point in his career.

At Camp Meade, Dwight spent three years as the football coach. He was ordered to take the job by General Samuel D. Rockenbach. As in earlier seasons, Dwight produced a winning record.

It was some months before Mamie and Icky could join him in Maryland. At first, there were no living quarters for families. But some wartime barracks were converted into duplex apartments.

Ike discovered some broken-down furniture at the camp dump which he repaired for their own use; he also sent for the furnishings from their Camp Colt home which had been left behind in Gettysburg. He prepared a dressing table for Mamie out of wooden orange crates. They slept on army cots. Mamie would never purchase furniture on credit. She insisted that everything be paid for promptly, which meant that they were slow in accumulating furniture. Still bitter about her sale at Fort Sam Houston, Mamie searched secondhand stores and auctions for bargains.

Dwight and Mamie enjoyed family life at Camp Meade; they shamelessly pampered and displayed Icky. Dwight took him to parades and football games, even to tank drills. In the summer of 1920, the Eisenhowers visited the Douds in Colorado. By the time they returned, Patton had been transferred to Fort Myer. Ike spent more and more time with his three-year-old son. He bought him a Christmas tree and, as a gift, a bright red "kiddie car."

The holiday festiveness was dampened several days before Christmas. Icky came down with what appeared to be a bad cold. A nurse and the post doctor said there was no cause for alarm. Indeed, they said he would be fully recovered in a day or two. The fever did not subside. Icky's face became flushed and contorted. The fever increased. In a second examination, the post doctor gave a startling diagnosis—scarlet fever. Ike, who had witnessed Milton's struggle for life against this dreaded disease, was shaken. Mamie, suffering from a high fever, was confined to the apartment. Her mother and sister cut short their holiday visit in Iowa to come to Maryland and comfort her.

Dwight kept a vigil for Icky at the post hospital, where specialists from the Johns Hopkins Medical School were brought in to treat the boy. So contagious was the disease and so uncertain the cure that Dwight was seldom allowed inside Icky's room. He kept watch through a porch window and waved at his son.

Icky died on January 2, 1921. Dwight and Mamie were devastated. "We were completely crushed," he later said. "This was the greatest disappointment and disaster in my life, the one I have never been able to forget completely."

Mamie said, "For a long time, it was as if a shining light had gone out in Ike's life. Throughout all the years that followed, the memory of those bleak days was a deep inner pain that never seemed to diminish much." Dwight would send flowers to Mamie on Icky's birthday the following year and for the rest of his life.

There were more disappointments, though none so profound. Ike applied to the Infantry School at Leavenworth, hoping to do well enough there to qualify for the Command and General Staff School. Once again, he was turned down by superiors. Each time he had attempted to prove himself as a future commander there had been setbacks and even reprimands. That he did not return to civilian life during this period does not mean that he was not tempted to do so.

His military future, however, still held promise. His army file for the Camp Meade years indicates that he was well regarded. One entry states, "Major Eisenhower is preeminently qualified for the detail he seeks. He has force, character and energy as well as knowledge." Such reports and the long discussion two years earlier kept Dwight high on General Fox Conner's list of bright young officers. When Conner was put in command of the 20th Infantry Brigade at Camp Gaillard in the Panama Canal Zone, he asked Ike to become his executive officer.

Dwight readily accepted. But his request for transfer was vetoed by both his commanding officer and the War Department. That summer Conner's close friend, General John J. Pershing, became chief of staff. At Conner's request, he had Dwight assigned to Panama.

He and Mamie sailed for Panama, on the army transport *Cambrai*, on January 7, 1922. Some of their fellow passengers became seasick. It was a turbulent voyage as a heavy storm rocked and jolted the ship. Ike and Mamie found the trip uncomfortable, but they took a measure of pride in not having missed a meal because of the weather or illness.

Mamie was appalled by their house in the Panama jungle. She called it "a double-decked shanty, only twice as disreputable." It had been abandoned for a decade and had fallen into disrepair in the humid climate. The house had been constructed by the French during their aborted effort to excavate the Canal. It was built of flimsy planking and had a sheet-iron roof, which leaked during frequent thundershowers. They were frequently disturbed by bats, a problem which Ike confronted with his dress military sword.

If living conditions were primitive at Camp Gaillard, it was well worth the price. Dwight and Conner's official relationship soon formed the basis for a close friendship. "I never saw two men more congenial than Ike Eisenhower and my husband," Mrs. Conner said years later. "They spent hours discussing wars, past and future."

Conner told Dwight that a second world war, much greater in scope than the just-ended war, was inevitable. He said the Treaty of Versailles would fail because Germany was too powerful to be restrained. The League of Nations might have been an effective deterrent, Conner said, but America's failure to join it made war all the more likely. When that war came, Conner wanted Ike to be ready for a high command.

Dwight said his three years with Conner were "sort of a graduate school in military affairs and the humanities, leavened by the comments and discourses of a man who was experienced in his knowledge of men and their conduct." Conner rekindled Dwight's interest in military history. He chose books for him to read, including works of philosophy, historical fiction, and military history; he introduced him to Plato, Tacitus, Nietzsche, and Clausewitz. His questioning was so precise that Ike read Clausewitz's *On War* no less than three times. He traced the battles and campaigns on old maps and charts, discussing the key strategic decisions with Conner.

They also spent much time discussing World War I. Conner was much impressed with Dwight's ability to comprehend the lessons of the recent war. He paid Dwight the ultimate compliment in comparing him to wartime protégé Major George C. Marshall. "Eisenhower, you handled that just the way Marshall would have done," Conner would say in praise.

Mamie was less than fascinated by Panama. She did not like the climate, the seemingly endless battle to keep animals out of her house, and the isolated jungle location of Camp Gaillard. The marriage became strained. "I never knew exactly how Ike felt," Marian Conner recalled, "as he knew Mamie was wearing down a path to my front porch." Mrs. Conner gave her some advice on how to revive her life with Dwight. "You mean I should vamp him?" Mamie asked. "That's just what I mean," Mrs. Conner said. "Vamp him!"

Mamie began wearing her hair in a more fashionable short cut and with bangs, which made her look older and more mature. She left for Denver in the summer of 1922 to have a second child. John Sheldon Doud Eisenhower was born on August 3. Ike received a leave and was present for his son's birth.

When they returned to Panama, the Eisenhowers were spiritually renewed more than at any time since Icky's death. Mamie became more active in camp affairs. She became chairman of a fund-raising committee seeking to build a post maternity hospital. Mamie was troubled that there was no children's hospital for the camp's enlisted men. Mrs. Conner gave her strong support and the backing of her husband. She also secured two American film stars, Lila Lee and Thomas Meighan, who were then working on a motion picture in Panama, to appear at a benefit program. Mamie organized bridge tournaments, picnics, and white-elephant sales to raise more money. Through her leadership, the hospital became a reality.

Dwight and Mamie were visited in 1923 by Swede Hazlett. It had been nearly eight years since the boyhood friends had seen each other, but they had frequently corresponded. Hazlett said Ike's World War I letters included some "griping because I was overseas while he was kept at home."

Hazlett, by then commander of his own submarine, spent three weeks in the Canal Zone while his vessel was undergoing repairs. Dwight was surprised to see Hazlett and favorably impressed by his naval command. For his part, Swede was pleased to find Ike so involved in his work. Ike, he said, "had been largely responsible for drawing up war plans for the defense of the area. He explained them to me with the enthusiasm of a genius. He had also fitted up the second-story screened porch of his quarters as a rough study, and here, with drawing boards and texts, he put in his spare time refighting the campaigns of the old masters. This was particularly unusual at a torrid, isolated post, where most officers spent their off hours trying to keep cool and amused."

Actually, most of Hazlett's visit seems to have been spent doing just that. "Ike got me astride a horse again," he recalled later, "and we rode the bosque trails." They played poker in the evening. "This latter was bad news for me," Hazlett commented, "for Ike and his army friends set a much higher standard for the five-card game than did the Navy."

Hazlett took Dwight for a dive in Panama Bay when the submarine was repaired. "He enjoyed it thoroughly," Hazlett said years later. "I never had a passenger who was more avid for information. Whenever I was otherwise engaged he wandered through the ship, chatting informally with the crew, and they responded readily. I really believe that by the time he left the ship he knew almost as much about submarines as I did."

On Hazlett's last night in Panama, Ike and Mamie attended a farewell party with Swede at the Union Club. They would not see him again until 1935.

Dwight continued to learn from General Conner. His efforts to retain Conner's high confidence did not endear him to some junior officers. Ike was said to have been irritable and intolerant as Conner's chief of staff. There is no doubt that he was strongly dedicated to Conner and his bluntness may have been a reflection of that commitment.

By the fall of 1924, Dwight was hoping for a transfer. The years with General Conner had been invaluable. But Panama was not a pleasant climate for his family, and his official function no longer presented a challenge. When the transfer came, Ike was unhappy. The War Department ordered him back to Camp Meade to coach still another football team. He saw himself going "back into the rut I had started to dig for myself a decade earlier." He was resentful of the football-coach stereotype.

Ike was the backfield coach for what was built up as an All-Army team. The head coach was his former West Point teammate Vernon Prichard. Their mission was made exceedingly difficult by the War Department. Unlike the other services, the army coaches could not recruit nationally. They were limited to soldiers at Camp Meade. As a result, they lost nearly every game. Small colleges trounced them. So did the Marines in what had been promoted as the "Big Game."

Near the end of the season, Ike was again named commander

of a tank battalion. He made still another effort to gain admission to the Infantry School; the chief of infantry turned him down. Dwight's arguments were in vain. He was instructed to go to Fort Benning and take over a light tank battalion.

Shortly afterward, Ike received a telegram from General Conner that stated: "No matter what orders you receive from the War Department, make no protest, accept them without question."

Conner had left the Canal Zone and was serving as Deputy Chief of Staff. He knew of Dwight's frustrations within the infantry. So, with characteristic subtlety, Conner outmaneuvered the chief of infantry. He arranged for Ike's transfer to a recruiting station near Denver. The telegram had been sent to soften this apparent blow. For an officer of Dwight's experience, such an assignment might have seemed an invitation to early retirement. But the wily general had, in making Ike a lowly recruiter, transferred him from the infantry to the adjutant general's office. Conner then persuaded the adjutant general to place Dwight in the Command and General Staff School.

Dwight's bitterness at the recruiting station orders, only slightly mollified by Conner's letter, turned to ecstasy upon news of his nomination to Leavenworth. He was to describe the training, years later, as "a watershed in my life."

After his initial jubilation, there was some uncertainty. The appointment meant that he had bypassed Infantry School. Most of the 274 other officers would have the advantage of that preparatory schooling. An insensitive infantry officer told Ike that he would probably fail. Dwight wrote General Conner for advice on how to best prepare for the intense competition.

Conner's reply was reassuring. "You may not know it," he wrote, "but because of your three years' work in Panama, you are far better trained and ready for Leavenworth than anybody I know. You will feel no sense of inferiority."

Ike began his studies in August of 1925. As Conner had predicted, he showed a remarkable capacity to absorb knowledge and solve complicated military problems. Dwight approved of the innovative methods of instruction. There were no written examinations, no learning by rote. The major technique was called "war gaming," deciding how a student would lead his command in hypothetical situations. General Conner had spent three years developing Ike's aptitude for military theory and strategy. Dwight was so self-confident at Leavenworth that he declined to participate in a study group which he considered a waste of time.

His closest friend in the class was Major Leonard T. Gerow, whom he had served with in the 19th Infantry at Fort Sam Houston. Perhaps because Gerow had graduated first from Infantry School, Ike thought studying with him would be worthwhile. Dwight converted his third-floor study at Otis Hall into "a model command post." They drew maps and plotted tactical moves. Their room was closed to other classmates. The teamwork was profitable to both men. They excelled in "war games" competition and graduated first and second in their class. Ike finished two-tenths of a percent higher than Gerow.

Another old friend, Colonel George Patton, was an instructor at the Command School. In congratulating Dwight on his top ranking, Patton said, "Major, some day I'll be working for you."

A celebration was held at the Muehlbach Hotel in Kansas City. Arthur Eisenhower, then vice president of the Commerce Trust Company, arranged for some bootleg liquor. Ike and Mamie, Gerow and his wife, and some friends attended. Although Dwight was an off-key singer, he put aside his inhibitions and belted out such songs as "Abdul the Bulbul Ameer" and "Casey Jones."

The glittering performance at Leavenworth did not assure him of immediate rewards. He was transferred back to the infantry with orders to report to Fort Benning and command a battalion.

Some War Department bureaucrats still considered him little more than a football coach. He was contacted about taking an ROTC job on a college campus where he would be paid an additional $3,500 to coach the football team. Ike refused. A more enticing offer came from the Command School. He was sounded out about a teaching position. The War Department, however, said that Fort Benning had priority on Dwight's services. At Benning, Ike was disgusted when he was given another coaching assignment. He turned down the head coaching job. But he became backfield and offensive coach. It was, much to his relief, Dwight's last autumn on the sidelines.

He was summoned to Washington in December by General

John J. Pershing, the steely-eyed hero of World War I. Pershing, on the recommendation of General Conner, had assigned Dwight to the Battle Monuments Commission. Ike had some reservations about the position; it was indoor work and promised to be dull. But Mamie helped persuade him to accept the assignment. She had much confidence in General Conner's suggestions.

Dwight took the assignment and soon found himself writing a guidebook to the American battlefields in Europe. His job was to synthesize thousands of pages of maps, statistics, official reports, and other material into a readable narrative. He quickly sensed that his efforts might produce something more significant than a descriptive text. It was an opportunity to write military history for a general readership. Moreover, it was to give him a thorough education in the terrain of strategically important France.

His studies with General Conner and at the Command School had given him more than adequate preparation for the guidebook job. The greatest difficulty facing him seemed to be a six-month deadline. He received much help from Milton, whom he saw each night. When the book was published, Dwight gratefully acknowledged Milton's contribution "to anything which may be considered creditable, appearing herein as a result of my efforts."

The *Encyclopaedia Britannica* was to describe Ike's guidebook as "an excellent reference work on World War I."

General Pershing, who had proposed the guidebook, was pleased with Dwight's work. In a letter to the chief of the infantry, Pershing commended Dwight's "splendid service" and "superior ability." He also wrote, "What he has done was accomplished only by the exercise of unusual intelligence and constant devotion to duty."

Ike was selected as a student for the Army War College that spring. It was a most coveted assignment for any officer with aspirations for a general's star. Still, Xenophon Price, General Pershing's chief military aide, told Dwight he would be making a mistake leaving the Battle Monuments Commission. "Every officer attached to the Commission is going to be known as a man of special merit," Price said.

But Ike was more interested in the school. "For once," he retorted, "the Department has given me a choice. And for once I'm going to say yes to something I'm anxious to do."

He graduated on June 30, 1928, finishing first in his class for the second time. His record at the Army War College was to figure heavily in future promotions; it also made his services more in demand. Dwight was offered an assignment on the War Department General Staff or a return to the Battle Monuments Commission. The guidebook was to be revised and the job included traveling to France for firsthand study of the battlefields. Mamie convinced him that the foreign assignment was the better opportunity.

They settled in Paris in July, moving into a hotel. Later, with the help of some American friends, they found an apartment on the Rue d'Auteuil, on the right bank of the Seine. In the fall, John attended the McJanet School for American children, which was only a block away. The Battle Monuments Commission office was close enough so that Ike walked home for lunch. Mamie studied French, hoping to learn enough so that she could communicate with her cook and with tradesmen. But she was unable to master French grammar and came to rely on a pocket dictionary. Dwight had studied French at West Point and had taken a refresher course in Washington. But he, too, had difficulty with the language. Because of the large American military community in Paris, the Eisenhowers did not feel isolated. Their home was the scene of so many festive evenings that a friend, Captain George A. Horkan, nicknamed it the "Club Eisenhower" and called the Mirabeau Bridge the "Pont Mamie." It was a much different environment than the famed Left Bank salon of Gertrude Stein, where artists and writers gathered. Ike described himself as "an unsophisticated Kansan" and his idea of French culture was visiting a war museum.

Dwight spent months visiting the major battlefields of the Western Front—Cantigny, Château-Thierry, Saint-Mihiel, the Meuse-Argonne. He took detailed notes on logistics, transportation, strategy, and terrain. Ike often joined highway workers for lunch; he would offer them fruit or wine and, through his chauffeur, engage in friendly conversation. Occasionally, Mamie and John would accompany him. A half century later, John would vividly remember the ruins of Verdun where he came across a human skull. As a six-year-old, he was captivated by his father's stories about the battles; later, he became an avid collector of war souvenirs. If the hobby was educational, it also presented some hazards. John started to kick a hand grenade, not realizing that the pineapple-shaped object was an explosive, but he was quickly grabbed by the chauffeur. John was careful not to offend his father. "I was scared to death of him," he would recall years later.

There were several family vacations. Ike took Mamie to Belgium, Switzerland, Germany, and southern France. At the end of John's school year, the family went to San Remo on the Italian Riviera. It was Dwight's first exposure to nations he would have so much to do with in later years. The holiday junket was less than enjoyable. John was stricken with whooping cough, and by the time he recovered, the vacation had ended.

The Eisenhowers returned to Washington in November of 1929. Dwight was assigned as a staff officer in the office of the Assistant Secretary of War. The Wall Street stock market was collapsing as Ike settled into his new job. The country was falling into the greatest domestic crisis since the Civil War. And Ike would be in the nation's capital watching two administrations attempt to cope with the disaster. His considerable experiences, he hoped, would lead to his own rendezvous with destiny.

Chapter Seven

WASHINGTON APPRENTICESHIPS

In the 1920s, Ike and Milton were both eager, hard-working, and ambitious young men. Milton was already a figure of some prominence in Washington, one of the bright stars of the Coolidge administration, a man who had many friends on Capitol Hill and among the growing Washington press corps. Dwight, hoping to enhance his own standing in the nation's capital, looked to his younger brother for companionship and advice. It was Milton who had provided much of the editorial assistance for the battlefield guide. He also told Ike much about how Washington worked, explaining the subtleties and nuances of the federal government. Milton took Dwight to parties and dinners where he could mix with government officials and journalists. Years later, a reporter would remember Milton approaching him at one such affair, saying, "Please don't go until you've met my brother; he's a major in the Army and I know he's going places." Ike got along well in such company. He was known best as "Milton's brother." But he left a positive impression as an officer who liked people, understood the civilian viewpoint, and was willing to listen to the opinions of others.

One of the journalists Dwight met through Milton was Harry C. Butcher, the personable editor of *The Fertilizer Review*, the house organ of the National Fertilizer Association. Like the Eisenhowers, Butcher was a Midwesterner. He was a native of Iowa and it was noteworthy that, like Milton, he had paid for his college education by writing for farm magazines. Milton was responsible for Butcher's opportunity to join the Columbia Broadcasting System. When Milton first came to Washington, he lived with Sam Pickard, the head of the Agriculture Department's radio information service. Pickard soon left the department to become an executive at CBS. Butcher, who had visited Milton frequently at Pickard's home, struck Pickard as a good choice to head the CBS Washington office. Butcher took the job with enthusiasm.

Butcher's introduction to Dwight came in 1927 at Pickard's house. Ike, then coaching football at Fort Benning, had brought his team north to play at Fort Myer. His team won, and after the game he celebrated with Milton and some friends. "Ike was very easy to talk to," Butcher would recall a half century later. "He was just one of the boys. That evening he showed us one of his favorite stunts. He would stand erect against the wall and fall stiffly to the floor, quickly catching his hands before his nose hit the floor."

Ike endeared himself to the other men by bringing some bootleg gin to the informal affair. Later, Butcher said, Dwight would make bathtub gin for his friends. "Ike had more access to alcohol through the commissary," he said. "We thought he made good gin."

Butcher and his wife, Ruth, would become close friends of Ike and Mamie's, with whom they often played bridge. Dwight and Butcher took up golf and played at the District of Columbia Soldiers Home. On one hole, they were required to hit over a fifty-foot stone wall. "Ike hit a wood [golf club] and the ball came screaming back at us," Butcher said. "We ducked just in time." Dwight seemed to have a penchant for narrowly escaping injury. Butcher once showed him a fountain pen gas bomb designed as a deterrent against mugging. "Ike took it out on the back porch," Butcher said. "He wanted to find out how it worked. He gave it a push and the gas came burning into our eyes."

Ike and Mamie lived at the Wyoming Apartments, a massive six-story building located just behind Connecticut Avenue; Milton's home at 24th Street and Massachusetts Avenue was within walking distance. Dwight spent many evenings sharing his thoughts with Milton. "We were not only intimate," Milton said, "but we found that we liked to talk over our problems together." Ike later observed, "Our thought processes dovetailed very closely."

For Dwight, his Washington assignment meant working for General of the Armies John J. Pershing. The tall, sober Pershing was the father of the modern American Army. Under his direction, the American Expeditionary Force had broken the stalemate along the Western Front. He was universally regarded as the architect of victory in the Great War. He had retired on September 13, 1924. But as chairman of the American Battle Monuments Commission, he continued to devote himself to the memory of his men.

Pershing, Ike thought, was cold and aloof. As a young man, Pershing was said to have been full of wit, spirit, and humor. But in 1915 a fire at San Francisco's Presidio had claimed the lives of his wife and three of his four children. The tragedy was said to have changed Pershing into a stiff, taciturn man. "I never got to know him well," Dwight said, describing him as "rather reserved" and "remote." Ike was somewhat amused by the efforts of an enterprising editor of the *Army-Navy Journal* to launch a Pershing presidential campaign in 1928. Pershing had been prominently mentioned as a candidate in 1920 but had renounced a political career. The would-be kingmaker was unable to convince Pershing to change his mind. Although Dwight visited with the editor, he did not become involved in the dubious campaign.

Working for Pershing was often frustrating. When the general asked Dwight to draft speeches, he invariably rejected them. Dwight's efforts at drafting letters for him were better received; however, Pershing would carefully edit and in some cases rewrite the letters. Pershing exhibited high regard for Ike's knowledge of military history and his ability to write simply and logically. Pershing, who was then working on his memoirs, asked Dwight to read the manuscript.

Ike dutifully spent several days reading the book. He thought the diary format was confusing and told Pershing so.

"General," Dwight said, "everything in that war, as far as the

Army is concerned, pointed up to the two great battles, Saint-Mihiel and the Argonne. Now, I don't believe you should tell the story in those two chapters in the form of a diary. It takes the reader's attention away from the development of the battles and it just follows your own actions, your own decisions, and your own travels.

"There's no reason to ignore your diary," Ike went on. "You can intersperse comments which will show where you were, what you were doing, and what you were thinking. This kind of treatment would give authenticity to the story you are telling."

Pershing listened attentively. "Write me something," he said.

Ike spent many hours of off-duty time on this project. To be the literary aide and collaborator of America's greatest soldier seemed a singular honor. Dwight rewrote the two chapters on the battles. Pershing indicated that he was pleased. But he added, "Before I use them, I want to send for Colonel Marshall."

Several days later, Marshall came to Pershing's office. Ike had never met Marshall before. However, through General Conner, he had become familiar with Marshall's work. Marshall conferred with Pershing most of the afternoon. Ike was not invited to participate in the discussion.

Marshall stopped by Dwight's office after the session. He told Ike that he had vetoed the two chapters. "I think they're interesting," Marshall said. "But General Pershing likes consistency. It would be a very hard thing for him to accept this abrupt change for these two subjects and then go right back into his diary."

Ike politely disagreed with Marshall. But Pershing had already decided. Dwight would later criticize the book, published in 1931 as *My Experiences in the World War*. Pershing received the Pulitzer Prize for history, an honor which Ike would never attain.

There were more difficulties working for Pershing. Dwight found that the general "had one deplorable habit"—he always arrived more than an hour late for social engagements. Ike, who often served as a temporary aide, was embarrassed more than once trying to explain Pershing's absence to an anguished host.

Dwight and Mamie entertained frequently and sometimes had high-ranking War Department policymakers at their parties. They were, in turn, frequently invited to the homes of Ike's superiors. Secretary of War Patrick J. Hurley, the brash, flamboyant Oklahoma millionaire, invited the Eisenhowers for dinner. Mamie is said to have charmed Hurley. Years earlier, when she met Secretary of War Newton Baker, she had committed a rare faux pas. Baker asked, "What does your husband do best, Mrs. Eisenhower?" She answered: "He plays an awfully good game of poker."

Mamie decided that the Wyoming Apartments were not the proper setting to return the Secretary's hospitality. They invited the Hurleys to dinner at the Willard Hotel, where Ike and Mamie received a special rate as members of the Saturday Night Dinner Dance Club. It was uncommon for a junior military officer to host a Cabinet officer. But Mamie said, "They had been wonderfully kind to us, so we couldn't see why we shouldn't return their hospitality." Mamie ordered an elegant floral arrangement for their table. "The party flowers cost almost as much as it took to feed us for a week," she said. "Added to the dinner check, they really upset our budget." The Eisenhowers compensated for this extravagance by dining on meat loaf and stew for some days afterward.

Ike had caught Hurley's attention while working in the office of the Assistant Secretary of War. He had drafted a plan for industrial mobilization which suggested how American industry could best respond to another war. Dwight reviewed the reports of Bernard Baruch's War Industries Board of 1917–18. He met with Baruch and such captains of industry as Walter S. Gifford of American Telephone and Telegraph and Daniel Willard of the Baltimore and Ohio Railroad. Baruch exercised a real influence over Ike, persuading him that wage and price controls should be adopted in the event of war. Dwight found opposition to Baruch's policies in the War Department, but he incorporated them in his report.

When a federal commission held hearings on war profiteering, Ike briefed industrial moguls in advance. He later wrote an article for *Infantry Journal* about the hearings and described the witnesses against the munitions makers as "a retired admiral of the Navy, two ministers of the Gospel, a leader of the Socialist Party, an oculist, editors of magazines of so-called 'pacifist' leanings, and officials of various peace organizations." He added, "A listener gained the distinct impression that the members of this group, with possibly one or two exceptions, were earnestly and unselfishly laboring for promotion of an idea which they implicitly believed." Dwight concluded the article with a summary of his plan for industrial mobilization.

During this period, Ike helped organize the Army Industrial College, and lectured on his comprehensive industrial mobilization plan. He was contributing, in a modest way, to the growth of the military-industrial complex.

Milton, still a high official in the Department of Agriculture, confided to his brother that he was less than enchanted with Arthur M. Hyde, the new Secretary of Agriculture. When Hoover was elected President, most political observers felt that Jardine would remain at Agriculture. Hoover had been responsible for Jardine's appointment by Coolidge, and Jardine had been among Hoover's earliest supporters for the presidency—at the cost of his relationship with Coolidge.

Hoover broke the news to Jardine several weeks before the Inauguration, explaining that he wanted to appoint Hyde as Agriculture Secretary. Hoover soothed Jardine and said that the real agricultural czar would be the chairman of the new Federal Farm Board. Jardine was offered that post, but with wounded pride he left government. He would return in 1930 as ambassador to Egypt.

There were some people in the farm belt who were pleased by Jardine's departure, feeling that he had been too much of an Administration pawn. Though Hyde was not a McNary-Haugenite, he was a political moderate. He had once supported the presidential candidacy of Illinois progressive Frank Lowden. And he had been a candidate for statewide office on the "Bull Moose" Progressive ticket in 1912. Eight years later, as a Republican, Hyde was elected governor of Missouri. His administration had increased support for the state's public schools and built 7,640 miles of highways.

Hyde's chief qualification for the Cabinet appointment seems to have been that his administration published brochures of technical information for farmers. Although he owned three farms, Hyde did not operate them. He was a small-town lawyer and Ford automobile dealer. "He isn't a dirt farmer nor yet a scientific agriculturist," wrote one columnist. "He is a politician who knows more about farmers than farming."

From the start, there was friction between Milton and Hyde. When they went to the White House to study President Hoover's farm message, Hyde readily approved it. Milton, reflecting the sentiments of farm leaders, made some thoughtful criticism. Hyde disagreed with Milton but conveyed his dissent to a presidential aide. Hoover was not persuaded. His farm message was delivered without Milton's suggestion. Hoover called for the creation of a Federal Farm Board "to promote the effective merchandising of agricultural commodities in interstate and foreign commerce, and to place agriculture on a basis of economic equality with other industries."

Some congressmen reiterated arguments which Milton had raised. Clarence Cannon of Missouri said the Hoover proposal "fails by every major test. It does not make the tariff effective. It does not control the surplus. And it contains no provision against overproduction."

The bill passed. But with the decline of farm prices deepened by the stock market crash, the Federal Farm Board failed to provide adequate support. It had established national cooperatives in grain, wool, cotton, beans, livestock, and pecans. In ordinary times the board might have succeeded, but it lost $345 million in three years.

If Milton's independence did not impress Hyde, it earned the respect of presidential assistant George Akerson. In 1929, Akerson told Milton that he was recommending him to President Hoover for a position on the White House staff. Milton did not get the job because the budget only permitted two full-time assistants to the President. Later, Hoover secured appropriations for two additional staff members.

The rift between Milton and Secretary Hyde continued. When a Republican senator charged that Milton was manipulating the department's press service to benefit the Democrats, Secretary Hyde questioned Milton. It was something of a point of pride with Milton that he was a civil servant first and Republican second. He pointed out that his work was as nonpartisan and objective as possible. Much to Milton's disgust, Secretary Hyde defended him by telling the senator that Milton was a Republican partisan. Milton objected to such classification. Secretary Hyde brought the issue to the White House—and President Hoover ruled in Milton's favor: Career officials should preserve their nonpartisanship. The tall, angular Hyde still would not concede on this point. He ordered Milton to make an ad hominem attack on Democratic Senator Pat Harrison of Mississippi who had been critical of the Agriculture Department. Milton instead wrote a statement defending the department and ignoring Harrison. He would resign if Secretary Hyde demanded that he become the department's political hit man. Hyde told Milton they would have a "showdown" meeting with President Hoover. Milton quickly notified his friend Akerson about Hyde's intentions. When Hoover received them in the Oval Office, he listened to both men. Milton stood Hyde's attack without flinching. At the end of the meeting, Hoover gave Secretary Hyde a firm but gentle reprimand.

Milton's writing skill and journalism background had helped propel him upward at the Agriculture Department. He organized the "National Farm and Home Hour," a national radio program, and, in 1929, began editing the *Yearbook of U.S. Agriculture*. In 1930, he was coauthor of *The U. S. Department of Agriculture, Its Structure and Functions*, which was long recognized as the standard work on the department. If Secretary Hyde disapproved of Milton's nonpartisanship, he seems to have recognized the quality of his work. Milton was indispensable to farm editors and writers as well as the radio networks.

His staff included several bright young editors, among them John R. Fleming, who would later serve as foreign editor of *U.S. News & World Report*. Fleming, a Democrat, had done editorial work in Massachusetts and Ohio before joining Milton's staff in May of 1930. He stayed with Milton and Helen in his early days in Washington. Fleming recalled years later that Milton made certain that none of his staff wrote political speeches for Secretary Hyde. "As civil servants, we couldn't be expected to do political work," Fleming said.

"Milton always did his homework," Fleming said. "At budget

meetings, I was struck by how well he knew information about all areas of the department budget. The budget people always listened when he spoke."

In the meantime, Ike was still working as an aide to the Assistant Secretary of War. But more and more of his work consisted of writing reports, letters, and statements for the Chief of Staff, General Douglas MacArthur. Dwight was dazzled by MacArthur, who was already something of a military legend. MacArthur was the son of General Arthur MacArthur, once the Army's senior ranking officer. But the younger MacArthur's own accomplishments qualified him as a military aristocrat. He had graduated first in his class at West Point (1903). He had served as an aide to his father and to President Theodore Roosevelt. In World War I, he had earned the Distinguished Service Medal, Distinguished Service Cross, seven Silver Stars, and numerous other decorations for his combat leadership in the Aisne-Marne, Saint-Mihiel, and Meuse-Argonne offensives. At the end of the war, MacArthur was appointed superintendent of West Point, where he raised academic standards. During the 1920s he rose from brigadier general to four-star general. President Hoover appointed him chief of staff in 1930. At fifty, MacArthur was the youngest officer ever appointed to the position. He cut a dashing figure. "If Caesar didn't look like MacArthur, he should have," said one admirer. His command of English and his oratorical powers were remarkable. There were already some reports of MacArthur's flaws. He was described as aloof, egotistical, pretentious, and arrogant. But his defenders insisted he was modest, charming, and unselfish. Dwight, for his part, was grateful to serve as a subordinate to MacArthur.

There were, to be sure, some differences with MacArthur. Dwight was uneasy with MacArthur's attitude about partisan politics. While Ike had strong political opinions, he kept them to himself when he was on duty. MacArthur was straightforward in expressing his right-wing political views in any situation.

Dwight did not approve of MacArthur's handling of the bonus army in the summer of 1932. The marchers included thousands of war veterans who had come to Washington from all parts of the country; they wanted to collect the "adjusted compensation certificates" which Congress in 1925 had voted to pay them in

1945. Many of them had lost their jobs in the Depression, so they felt justified in asking for an early payment for their wartime service. Congressman Wright Patman of Texas introduced a bill authorizing immediate payment.

Between fifteen and twenty thousand veterans were in Washington by June. President Hoover voiced his opposition to the Patman legislation. One prominent Republican, Columbia University president Nicholas Murray Butler, said: "It is absolutely essential that the organized raids on the Treasury in the name of the war veterans should, despite the cowardice of Congress, be resisted and repelled." Ike apparently shared this view. He later said the bonus marchers "seemed to feel that they should be regarded as a special class entitled to special privileges."

The bonus march was organized in Portland, Oregon, by Walter W. Waters, a former army sergeant and unemployed cannery superintendent. As commander of the "Bonus Expeditionary Force," Waters became the spokesman for the movement. His men voted that there would be "no panhandling, no drinking, no radicalism" and no "indulgence in talk attacking the government or engaging in any actions unbecoming a gentleman and a soldier."

In Washington, Superintendent of Police Pelham D. Glassford was sympathetic to the veterans. Glassford had been the youngest brigadier general in World War I, and he had dealt with other hunger marches during the Depression. Glassford wanted the veterans to return to their homes, but he took pains to see that they were provided for during their stay in Washington. He located food and housing for the former soldiers. The police were ordered to provide first aid for them. Glassford sent the Marine band to play songs for the veterans, obtained baseball equipment for them, and convinced local businessmen to donate groceries and other supplies. Glassford made daily visits on his blue motorcycle, maintaining a dialogue with the bonus marchers.

The bonus marchers lobbied on Capitol Hill. On June 14, the House of Representatives passed the Bonus bill; however, three days later, the Senate killed the measure. Most of the veterans retreated to their Washington encampments. There was no violence and only a scattering of boos. Will Rogers commented that they held "the record for being the best behaved" of any "hungry men assembled anywhere in the world."

Meanwhile, the Hoover administration was becoming more and more embarrassed by the presence of the veterans. Hoover and MacArthur charged that many of the bonus marchers were dangerous radicals. But, in fact, they were what they purported to be —veterans who had fallen on hard times. Communists had made efforts to infiltrate the bonus army, but they were unsuccessful. The bonus army purged radicals from its ranks. Hoover refused to meet the veterans. The Army reinforced its troops in the Washington metropolitan area. Hoover conferred with Secretary of War Hurley and MacArthur over possible evacuation of the veterans. At the War Department there were numerous proposals about how to accomplish that goal. Brigadier General George Moseley suggested arresting the bonus marchers and detaining them in concentration camps on "one of the sparsely inhabited islands of the Hawaiian group not suitable for growing sugar" where "they could stew in their own filth." MacArthur promised bonus-march leaders that the veterans would be allowed to leave the capital area in orderly fashion.

Hurley confided that the bonus marchers had been so law-abiding that force would be required to drive them away. The District commissioners ordered Glassford to forcibly evacuate veterans from abandoned buildings on Pennsylvania Avenue which had been slated for demolition. A brief scuffle ensued when police attempted to carry out the order. Glassford assured district commissioners that the situation was under control and asked for more time so that tensions would ease. The commissioners, without Glassford's knowledge, appealed to the White House for federal troops. Hoover immediately granted their request.

MacArthur personally led the troops which included cavalry with drawn sabers, six tanks, and machine guns. Ike argued against MacArthur's appearance on the scene. He said it was "highly inappropriate" for the Chief of Staff to become involved in a local dispute. "General MacArthur disagreed," Dwight recalled, "saying that it was a question of federal authority in the District of Columbia, and because of his belief that there was 'incipient revolution in the air' as he called it." MacArthur not only ignored

Dwight's dissent, he ordered him into uniform to participate in the assault. In Dwight's War Department post, he was required to wear civilian clothes. John Eisenhower recalls that his father came home "and started pulling into his boots, expressing displeasure about the difficulties of getting a uniform out just over a short period of time. In those days, pulling on boots was a real pain. Took a lot of talcum powder."

The Chief of Staff wore his formal parade attire with seven strips of ribbons and decorations. Dwight's photograph, standing behind MacArthur, appeared in *Time* magazine the following week. His displeasure with MacArthur is not evident in the picture. But Dwight did not approve of his chief's heavy-handed tactics. MacArthur swiftly evacuated the Pennsylvania Avenue buildings with bayonets and tear gas; the downtown buildings had been the only area affected by the presidential order. Secretary Hurley and President Hoover did not want the troops to cross the 11th Street Bridge to evacuate the largest veterans' encampment at Anacostia Flats.

Hurley twice sent messages to MacArthur with instructions not to move into Anacostia. Ike watched MacArthur ignore the orders. The troops kept marching. When they charged into the encampment, blue tear-gas bombs were thrown into tents. Shacks were set aflame. Soldiers poured gasoline on the packing crates, chicken coops, fruit crates, and canvas tents. The flames were soon two hundred feet high. A seven-year-old boy was bayoneted in the leg when he attempted to rescue his rabbit from a tent. The infant child of another veteran would die from the tear gas. Major George Patton, leading the cavalry into the camp, discovered that one of the men he routed had saved his life on the Western Front.

Ike took little pleasure in seeing American soldiers routing American citizens. "The whole scene was pitiful," he later observed. He was saddened to see Anacostia Flats burning and the veterans helplessly fleeing. By the time the Army was through, the bonus marchers' camp had been reduced to ashes and rubble. As MacArthur was leaving the scene, Ike warned him not to go back to the War Department. With his keen sense of public relations, Dwight knew that the bonus march assault had been a disaster, not to mention a defiance of presidential orders. He cautioned MacArthur that reporters would be waiting for him at the War Department. "I suggested it would be the better part of wisdom, if not of valor, to avoid meeting them," Ike said. It was Eisenhower's contention that the troop movement "had not been a military idea really, but a political order." Thus, Dwight argued, President Hoover and Secretary Hurley should accept responsibility.

MacArthur, who had rejected Ike's earlier advice, paid no more attention to this suggestion. He told a group of correspondents: "That mob down there was a bad-looking mob. It was animated by the essence of revolution. The gentleness, the consideration with which they had been treated had been mistaken for weakness, and they had come to the conclusion beyond the shadow of a doubt, that they were about to take over in some arbitrary way either the direct control of the government or else to control it by indirect methods. It is my opinion that had the President not acted today, had he permitted this thing to go on for twenty-four hours more, he would have been faced with a grave situation which would have caused a real battle. Had he let it go on another week, I believe the very institutions of government would have been very severely threatened. . . . There were, in my opinion, few veteran soldiers in the group that we cleared out today; few indeed. I am not speaking by figures because I don't know how many there were. But if there were one man in ten in that group who is a veteran, it would surprise me."

This diatribe was to taint MacArthur's image. In Hyde Park, Governor Franklin D. Roosevelt, then in the midst of his presidential campaign, told an adviser that MacArthur, on the basis of this performance, was "one of the two most dangerous men in America." While President Hoover gave public support to MacArthur, he privately condemned his actions. Ike later said, "I think this meeting led to the prevailing impression that General MacArthur himself had undertaken and directed the move against the veterans and that he was acting as something more than the agent of civilian authorities."

Dwight was appointed to MacArthur's staff in February of 1933. His office was next to MacArthur's, separated only by a slatted door. When MacArthur wanted him, he raised his voice. It has been suggested by one of his biographers that Ike was chosen to help repair MacArthur's reputation. Clearly, Dwight was more sensitive to public opinion than the imperious Chief of Staff. Ike had none of the trappings of power. MacArthur had the only chauffeured limousine in the War Department. When Dwight was asked to make one of his frequent trips to Capitol Hill as the department's lobbyist, he was not offered use of the limousine; he was not even provided with cab fare. Ike had to fill out a special form to receive two streetcar tokens; he took a trolley car on official business.

Roosevelt had soundly defeated Hoover in the 1932 election, and on Saturday, March 4, 1933, he was inaugurated. For the country, the new President inspired hope and confidence. In his inaugural address Roosevelt said:

> We do not distrust the future of essential democracy. The people of the United States have not failed. In their need they have registered a mandate that they want direct vigorous action. They have asked for discipline and direction under leadership. They have made me the present instrument of their wishes. In the spirit of the gift, I take it.

There was a sense of movement and excitement in Washington. Boldness and innovation had replaced the tired, discredited mentality of the Hoover administration. Roosevelt had promised a New Deal. He brought with him a brilliant collection of advisers and policymakers: Rexford G. Tugwell, Adolf Berle, Raymond Moley, Harry Hopkins, Felix Frankfurter, William O. Douglas. They were indeed the best and the brightest of a new generation. They carried with them a new vision and sense of purpose that government could solve any crisis. Washington replaced Wall Street as the economic center of the country. MacArthur and Ike watched the events with some skepticism. Dwight grumbled when the Army was asked to help supervise the mobilization of the Civilian Conservation Corps. The project enlisted some 300,000 men for conservation work in the nation's forests. "Dad was very disturbed about the Army being saddled with the CCC problem," John Eisenhower recalls. "He felt that the Army was trapped enough already without having to take on this extra chore of the CCC." One night Ike told his family, "Well, maybe we can use the reservists to help us out a little bit in the CCC chore." As it turned out, the Officers' Reserve Corps handled most of the burden.

In the Agriculture Department, Milton was now working for a new secretary, Henry Agard Wallace. "Secretary Wallace was one of the best Cabinet members I ever knew," Milton would say more than forty years later. "A new style and vigorous action became apparent the moment he was sworn in."

Wallace, shy and mild-mannered, was a social reformer and ideologue. Although he was, at forty-five, one of the youngest members of the Cabinet, his experience was vast. Wallace's father, Henry C. Wallace, had been Secretary in the Harding and Coolidge administrations. His grandfather, the first Henry Wallace, could have been Secretary in the McKinley administration. But he preferred his role as farm leader and editor of *Wallace's Farmer*, the family's newspaper. Young Henry had worked on the editorial staff of *Wallace's Farmer* since his graduation from Iowa State College in 1910. He became an associate editor and when his father joined the Harding cabinet, took over the paper. Wallace was, at the same time, deeply interested in scientific research. As a youngster, he became a protégé of black scientist George Washington Carver. Under Carver's tutelage, Wallace began experimenting with crossbreeding at the age of eight. Years later, his scientific experiments would produce a high-yield strain of corn which earned him an international reputation as a plant geneticist. Wallace was also a pioneer in the field of agricultural economics. In 1915, he had devised the first corn-hog ratio chart which determined whether a farmer would profit more by selling his corn or by feeding it to hogs. Wallace also developed a system of forecasting corn yields on the basis of rainfall and temperature records. He forecast the coming farm depression in a 1920 brochure on agriculture prices. During the 1920s, he rose to a position of prominence in the agrarian movement. His father, he felt, had been betrayed in the Cabinet. Their bête noire had been then-Secretary of Commerce Herbert Hoover. The elder Wallace's efforts to obtain better farm prices had been thwarted by

Hoover. When Wallace died in 1924, he was a defeated, saddened man. The son continued his father's fight for the McNary-Haugen bill. The Wallaces had been Republican stalwarts. But in 1928 Henry A. Wallace left the party of his father and grandfather to support Democrat Al Smith against Hoover; Smith had endorsed the McNary-Haugen bill. In 1932, Wallace vigorously supported Roosevelt. Many of his editorials were quoted by Roosevelt in farm belt campaign speeches. His appointment as Secretary of Agriculture was well received both in the department and in farm states.

There was much similarity between Wallace and Milton. Both were born and reared in the Middle West and began their adult careers by writing for farm journals. They supported the principles of the McNary-Haugen bill, advocated land-use planning, and improvement of farm productivity. They were men of ideas, determined that there must be a change in farm policy. If there were similarities, there were also notable differences. Milton was dapper and well groomed; Wallace wore baggy suits, with a loose-fitting necktie. Milton was an old hand on the Washington cocktail circuit; Wallace was awkward and ill at ease at such gatherings. But in the department and at Cabinet meetings, Wallace was confident, impressive, and firmly in control.

"I never knew a man who possessed greater intellectual honesty than Henry Wallace," Milton said years later. "He was completely dedicated. He knew how to delegate authority. He trusted people to whom he delegated authority, and he was an ideal administrator."

In his first meeting with Agriculture Department officials, Wallace praised their educational and research work. He also told them that he was launching a New Deal in agriculture and, in the process, would transform the department into an action agency. The Agricultural Adjustment Act was soon devised by Wallace and farm economists to raise the prices of major American farm crops. It paid farmers for leaving part of their acreage unplanted, which was expected to help eliminate the surplus. The AAA also aimed to raise farm prices through the new subsidy principle; funds for which were to be raised by taxing processors of farm products.

Roosevelt and Wallace chose George Peek as AAA administrator, the most prominent figure in the agrarian uprising of the 1920s and the architect of McNary-Haugenism. Peek had worked closely with the first Secretary Wallace and had advised Roosevelt on farm problems in the 1932 campaign. He was a prickly old curmudgeon and regarded himself as the real head of the department. Peek did not disguise his contempt for Milton, whom he considered a member of the "Jardine-Hoover clique." Peek would not speak to Milton when he saw him at the department or on the golf course. He suggested that Wallace fire Milton.

Wallace ignored Peek's advice. "It irked Peek when Wallace, in driving need of help, found Eisenhower so competent and conscientious as to merit promotion almost immediately to a sort of deputy undersecretariat," wrote Russell Lord, an aide to Wallace.

Secretary Wallace told Peek and others that "Milton Eisenhower is the best young executive in the department." He cut Peek short with "Nothing doing" when the AAA head repeated the suggestion. Peek urged appointment of a Democrat as information director.

"Wallace became an intimate friend after this episode," Milton said years later.

As editor of *Wallace's Farmer*, Wallace had been in an excellent position to judge Milton's work as information director. He approved of what he had seen. Numerous people had urged Wallace to retain Milton. Charles Burton Robbins, an Iowa insurance executive and Wallace family friend, had been Assistant Secretary of War in the Hoover administration. Early in 1933, he wrote Wallace: "There is a young man in the office whom I wish particularly to commend to your attention. His name is Milton Eisenhower, who is head of the Bureau of Public Information, and is, of course, a civil-service employee. His brother, Dwight, is Major in the Regular Army and was in my office during my period of service as Assistant Secretary of War. I think the Eisenhower boys are topnotchers in every respect, and Dwight is considered one of the finest of the younger officers in the Army.

"I am not asking you for anything in the way of particular promotion or anything of that sort for him," Robbins added. "But if you are looking for a good man to do a good job I think you will find that Eisenhower will fill the bill."

Milton considered leaving the department during the Peek dispute. He had earlier been offered the editorship of a national magazine and a ten-thousand-dollar salary. Wallace's loyalty to him was amply repaid. "Although Milton was a Republican, he felt things were in pretty bad shape," a former aide later recalled. "By 1932, he thought it was necessary to have a new administration. His sympathies were with the new administration. He was delighted with the appointment of Wallace."

George Peek did not limit his criticism to Milton. He spoke of Wallace's "elastic mind" and questioned the department's commitment to the farm movement. His differences with Wallace became so great that President Roosevelt removed him from the department, making him a special adviser on foreign trade. Within a short time, Peek broke with Roosevelt. In 1936, he campaigned actively for Republican Alf Landon. So Wallace's decision to back Milton was vindicated by events.

Wallace complained to Milton about his inability to get his viewpoint across to Roosevelt. The President, it seemed, would tell stories and anecdotes throughout their meeting. With his sense of insecurity, Wallace felt rejected. Indeed, Wallace lost his temper with the President.

Milton, at Wallace's invitation, accompanied the Secretary to his next session with President Roosevelt. It was at this point that Milton began his first truly close association with an American President. Though Milton had worked for Roosevelt's two Republican predecessors, he had performed such tasks through presidential assistants. So this meeting was a key moment in Milton's career. He had no difficulty in communicating with Roosevelt. He was a more patient listener than Wallace. If there was a right way and a wrong way of dealing with Roosevelt, Milton seemed to grasp the right way. Wallace was so impressed by Milton's easy rapport with Roosevelt that he later sent Milton alone to the Oval Office. "The Secretary got his messages through to the White House much more effectively through a third person," Milton said later. "And I was delighted to be the intermediary." Roosevelt frequently served Milton lunch at their meetings. Milton also would accompany Rexford G. Tugwell, Undersecretary of Agriculture, to White House sessions. Tugwell, who had been an economics professor at Columbia University, was one of the charter members of the "Brain Trust." As such, his views had done much to shape the early New Deal. "Milton Eisenhower was very cooperative," Tugwell said, "and very active." Tugwell's ideas about agriculture excited Roosevelt and Wallace. Milton helped translate some of them into legislation.

Among the agricultural innovations were the Soil Conservation Service, the Rural Electrification Administration, and the Resettlement Administration, which Tugwell headed. The resettlement agency sought to move farmers from submarginal land to a better location. Three "greenbelt" towns were built near bucolic countrysides.

Milton shared Wallace's disappointment when the Supreme Court struck down the Agricultural Adjustment Act. To Milton, it seemed that the recovery efforts of the New Deal were being thwarted by the aging conservatives on the high court. He had doubts about the checks and balances system, in which he had always maintained a blind faith. Moreover, Milton feared—correctly, it turned out—that the rejection of the AAA would spell fiscal disaster. The farmers had themselves funded the program through the processing tax. "Wallace and I both knew that when the act was discarded, the Treasury would have to pay," Milton said. "And we felt that this would set loose a cycle which no one could stop. The Treasury has paid as much as $7 billion in one year to finance farm programs."

He did not agree with some New Deal policies. However much Milton admired Roosevelt and Wallace, he felt frustrated when he disagreed with them. At one point, he offered Wallace his resignation. There would be no loud protest, he explained. He would leave quietly, in the old-boy tradition.

Wallace asked Milton to explain his grievances. Milton described his differences with Wallace on international trade. Wallace listened and smiled, and told Milton that dissent was welcomed and that he liked to hear divergent viewpoints. Wallace talked Milton into remaining.

If Milton was a conservative within the New Deal, he was still the liberal of the family. He and Helen now lived in a remodeled regency house in a Falls Church, Virginia, neighborhood which had been developed by L. R. Eakin. Harry Butcher and John Fleming were frequent visitors; so were Dwight and Mamie. Milton and Ike often debated political issues. Milton was the idealist, Ike the pragmatist. Milton's knowledge of political theory and his own experiences in government gave him a built-in advantage, but Dwight's ability to recite facts and statistics often compensated. Milton said that Ike's rebuttals would sometimes leave him "embarrassed."

Four of the Eisenhower brothers gathered for a reunion at Milton's house in the winter of 1934. Edgar was in Washington to represent lumber interests while the National Recovery Act's lumber code was being prepared. Earl, working as an electrical engineer in southwestern Pennsylvania, drove through a blizzard to see his brothers. A lively discussion ensued. Edgar denounced the New Deal's social programs as unconstitutional. Ike joined Edgar in attacking Roosevelt and creeping socialism.

Milton found himself defending the New Deal against his two older brothers. Earl also spoke out for Roosevelt. The four men spent most of the night in a lively and, at least to them, entertaining discussion. When it ended, no minds had been changed.

Ike was envious of his brothers. This reunion may have reinforced doubts about his own career. Arthur's success in banking had been almost a Horatio Alger rise. Edgar, though full of bluster, had reason to take pride in his work. His corporate law practice was among the largest in the Pacific Northwest. Dwight had seen Milton grow from a wunderkind into a presidential confidant. By contrast, Ike had not won promotion in a decade. He told his son, John, that his class would not reach the grade of colonel until 1950—when, at sixty, he would be near retirement age.

In a sense, Ike considered himself a failure. His old friend Swede Hazlett, who had just been promoted to commander, arrived in Washington in 1935 for a tour of duty at the Navy Department. "I saw him frequently," Hazlett said. "He was still the same old Ike." However, Dwight confided his disappointment. "He was still a major with no immediate prospects," Hazlett said.

He noted that Ike would "gripe about the Army promotion system, and how much better the Navy system was." Hazlett "consoled him with the thought that in case of war the Army would expand so much more rapidly that it would eventually pull way ahead in promotion of the Navy."

Dwight was not convinced. He nearly resigned from the Army shortly afterward. A national newspaper group offered him a position as their military editor. For a variety of reasons, the job appealed to Ike. His salary, as MacArthur's aide, was $3,000. The newspaper job would pay him more than five times what he was making. Furthermore, it would keep him close to his army friends. He could write honest and informed assessments about the American military. His work on the Battle Monuments Guide had made his reputation, in military circles, as a writer. If war came, Ike would have a chance to make his mark as a war correspondent. Richard Harding Davis, Stephen Crane, and John Reed went on to literary prominence after doing just that. Ike was tempted to accept; it was a logical decision.

But if war was coming, Dwight did not want to be an outsider. He talked about the newspaper job with Milton. If Ike resigned his commission, Milton knew that his brother would continue to live in the nation's capital. Their family circle would continue unbroken. But after weighing all his options, Dwight decided to remain with MacArthur. Milton supported his brother's decision.

"We seldom disagreed," Milton later said. "When we did it was a rare exception. During this period, we were together three nights a week. I can't help but think our association had a profound influence on me. Since it was an intimate relationship, it was also a beautiful human relationship."

Their jobs drew them physically apart in 1935, but they kept in close contact through correspondence. MacArthur, who had written a letter praising Ike's skill at handling complex problems, was stepping down as Chief of Staff. His new assignment was chief military adviser to the Philippine Government. MacArthur asked Dwight to help devise a defense program for the islands. Then, Ike said, MacArthur "lowered the boom on me." He asked Dwight to come along to the Philippines as his chief assistant. Ike explained that he preferred troop duty and that his family did not want to transfer to the islands. MacArthur made the request an order, arguing that Dwight had worked with him for a long time and that bringing in a new person would make his job more difficult. "I was in no position to argue with the Chief of Staff," Ike said.

MacArthur would not give Dwight a specific terminal date for the Philippine tour, and the vagueness troubled Dwight. But MacArthur did allow Dwight to choose an army associate to go along with them. Ike picked Major James B. Ord, a West Point classmate. Ord had worked with Dwight on the Philippine defense plan, spoke fluent Spanish, and was known for "his quickness of mind and ability as a staff officer."

Ike departed for the Philippines in September 1935. Mamie and John stayed in Washington for another year. John, who had just been elected class president at the John Quincy Adams Junior High School, wanted to graduate with his class.

"My mother was not terribly keen on going to the tropics again," John recalled years later. "I think she'd had rather a bad time of it down in Panama. The combination of circumstances led to Mother's and my staying in Washington for another year."

In Dwight's absence, Milton assumed the role of family patriarch. Mamie and John were often dinner guests at Milton's home. Mamie's parents visited them several times. The Wyoming Apartments was also the setting for Mamie's bridge club.

Milton was getting closer and closer to the center of action in the New Deal. Roosevelt, always searching for bright young talent, seemed particularly taken with him. Secretary Wallace made him the department's trouble shooter. The assertive Secretary of the Interior Harold Ickes attempted to transfer the Forest Service into his department. Milton successfully lobbied at the White House to keep the agency under Wallace's jurisdiction. Wallace charged Milton, among others, with drawing up a master plan to reorganize the entire department. The New Deal's innovations had transformed Agriculture from a relatively small institution into the largest executive department, but this rapid growth was not achieved without inefficiencies.

Secretary Wallace summoned Milton on a spring morning in 1937. He asked him to join him for a walk to the Washington

Monument, followed by luncheon in the department's dining room.

"Milton," Secretary Wallace said, "are you aware of the conflicts in the action programs of the department?" Under the New Deal's land-use programs, some farmers were urged to reduce their wheat and cotton acreage, while others were urged to increase it. The Agricultural Adjustment Administration, Soil Conservation Service, Farm Security Administration, and Tennessee Valley Authority were dispensing contradictory regulations. Newspapers and politicians had criticized the farm bureaucracy's massive waste. Milton had been concerned about it.

Wallace then dropped a surprise. "I want you to set up an agency with the mission of overcoming these conflicts. I've thought about this a great deal. I've discussed it with Paul Appleby and Rex Tugwell and they agree on what has to be done. You'll get our full support," Wallace said. "I don't expect you to perform miracles. This will be an extremely difficult task and you will surely make mistakes." Nevertheless, Wallace expected "steady progress" to assure Roosevelt and Congress that the department was reforming itself.

Milton's title was Coordinator of the Office of Land-Use Planning. He was "placed in a position second in responsibility to the Secretary's." Indeed, Milton was rapidly becoming Wallace's Harry Hopkins. He found the prospect somewhat awesome, but he accepted without hesitation. Milton also retained his post as information director. He delegated much of those duties to subordinates.

"My job," Milton recalled forty years later, "was to remove the conflicts between all these new programs." His first move was to call a meeting of all agency heads, where he explained his goals and listed some of the conflicts he hoped to resolve. The meeting was a disaster. "I got no cooperation whatsoever," he said. "Each of the agency heads said that what they were doing was absolutely essential."

Shortly afterward, Milton began a program of local and regional coordination. Through this process, he hoped to circumvent the parochial interests of the bureaucrats. Each of the department's baronies had local farm advisory committees. Milton sought to persuade them to determine "the maximum economic potential of their farm lands, consistent with a conservation objective." Achieving this, he would then work to adapt national regulations to eliminate conflicts at the local level. Milton managed to sign an agreement with forty-eight land-grant colleges and universities on methods of cooperation. Milton's efforts at restoring order had been modestly successful, but he found that the real problem could be eliminated only by creating one central system. He recommended merging the action agencies into twelve common regional headquarters. Numerous state offices would be abolished, but the disorganization would be greatly reduced.

"Milton, this is political dynamite," Wallace said. "You'd better get the approval of President Roosevelt because that's where the political heat will be the hottest." Wallace suggested that Milton launch the reorganization in the north central states. "That's my country," Wallace said. "And if you make Milwaukee the regional headquarters, you'll have to move an office out of Des Moines, my home town. But perhaps if we demonstrate the importance of putting selfish interest aside for a nobler cause, it will set a good example."

Milton took maps and charts to a luncheon meeting with President Roosevelt, showing how the reorganization would simplify the politics of agriculture. "The political criticism will be substantial," Roosevelt cautioned. "You can bet that some of the loudest critics will be the very same senators and congressmen who have been attacking the programs you have been trying to correct." Roosevelt approved the plan. "Go ahead, Milton," he said. "I'll stand behind you."

Phase one of reorganization was a smashing success. The north central states were cooperative. The new headquarters in Milwaukee was far more efficient than the far-flung state offices had been. Milton's phase two focused on the southeastern states. As part of the reorganization, the regional office of the Soil Conservation Service was to be transferred from Spartanburg, South Carolina, to Atlanta. Senator James F. Byrnes of South Carolina opposed the move. Byrnes was an ally Roosevelt could not afford to alienate. He had been Roosevelt's link to the powerful southern committee chairmen in the Senate and had helped secure passage of many

New Deal measures in spite of his own conservatism. So when Byrnes delivered a petition with 200,000 signatures, Roosevelt personally received him.

Milton was soon called to the White House. Roosevelt was less jovial than he had been in their past meetings. "Milton," he said, "that coordinating program of yours is causing me a lot of trouble. I'm sorry but I'm going to have to ask you not to move the Soil Conservation office out of Jimmy's state. I need Jimmy Byrnes."

The order bothered Milton. All his efforts, the long months of planning, the pledge of presidential support had been thrown aside. "You understand, Mr. President, if we give in here that this really means the end of the program in all parts of the country. If we surrender here, then the next move will bring even greater pressure."

Roosevelt assured Milton that he understood, explaining that he still favored efficiency and reorganization. However, he told Milton that each presidential decision had to be made in a larger context. "I have to look at the totality," Roosevelt said.

Milton returned to the Agriculture Department to break the news to Secretary Wallace. Their program had been a political casualty, but Milton had been a team player in this policy dispute. Roosevelt would not forget it.

Chapter Eight

THE COMING STORM

As Ike was leaving for the Philippines, General Fox Conner's prediction of another world war seemed more probable than ever. The Japanese had conquered Manchuria and established a satellite government. Japan was now preparing to invade northern China. In Europe, the Fascist powers were planning a policy of aggression and warfare against their democratic neighbors. Italy's Mussolini, with his bombast and penchant for elegant uniforms, seemed comical at times, but Germany's Hitler was clearly a dangerous threat to Western civilization. He had slain political rivals and thrown millions of his countrymen into concentration camps. The horrors of Nazism, with its anti-intellectualism and barbarism, were becoming more and more evident.

The American people were skeptical about the events in Europe. According to public-opinion polls, they did not think the United States should intervene in another European war. Some thought that war-mongering internationalists were a greater threat to the peace than Hitler. In 1934, Senator Gerald P. Nye of North Dakota conducted a Senate investigation into the munitions industry. His committee concluded that American entry into World War I was due to the machinations of the munition makers, not to "make the world safe for democracy." Nye made a series of speeches attacking the "merchants of death." He said that Europe should pay for their own wars. "If the Morgans and other bankers must get into another war, let them do it by enlisting in the Foreign Legion."

Isolationism had become a powerful political force. Indeed, it was a movement so broad that its adherents ranged from reactionaries like Colonel Robert R. McCormick of the Chicago *Tribune* to Socialist Norman Thomas. President Roosevelt recognized the threat posed by the Fascist dictators, but much as it troubled him, he had to deal with an isolationist Congress and nation. His ability to act was limited. He described his policy as "watchfully waiting."

Dwight's knowledge of history convinced him that the isolationists were wrong. No great power could ignore events in the rest of the world. His assignment in the Philippines would further his education for high command. At the same time, it would teach him about working with political leaders.

By congressional act, the Philippines had been transformed into a commonwealth in 1935. A decade later, the government would be completely independent. President Manuel L. Quezon had turned to MacArthur for a defense program that would thwart Japanese aggression. Ike and Major Ord devised a plan for a National Defense Act at an annual cost of 50 million pesos, or $25 million. MacArthur vetoed the plan as too expensive for the young government. He suggested a 50 percent reduction. Dwight and Ord presented an alternative plan which greatly reduced military pay, training time, and armaments. Ike "thought such a makeshift force would be rejected out of hand as worthless for defense."

Their proposal was rejected, but for a different reason. President Quezon told MacArthur he needed a plan that could be supported on a budget of 16 million pesos. Ike and Ord made radical cutbacks. They eliminated an artillery corps, the navy, and the air force. They shrank the army from twenty thousand to eight thousand men. MacArthur accepted the final proposal. As it turned out, Quezon had some difficulty getting funding for even this skeleton force from his national assembly. But with imperial Japan on the move, it was passed.

Dwight liked his work in the Philippines. One of his first projects was to organize a military academy modeled after West Point and to establish a reserve system. He also helped prepare the strategy and tactics for defense of the islands. Because of the paltry military budget Ike said, "We had to content ourselves with an attempt to produce a military adequate to deal with domestic revolt."

He found that it was necessary to organize a small "air force" if only to get to the training stations in the mountains and far-flung islands. Ike designed the air strips and bought several planes. The U. S. Army Air Corps loaned two flight instructors. Ike himself took flying lessons and was issued a pilot's license. He noted, "My reflexes were slower than those of the younger men. Training me must have been a trial of patience."

Dwight's flying nearly cost him his life on two occasions. His instructor, Captain William Lee, was flying him from a remote mountain town to Manila in the fall of 1936. As they were taking off, the plane narrowly missed crashing into a mountain ridge. The other incident occurred on one of his earliest solo flights. A sandbag, which had been strapped in the light plane for balance, snapped loose and fell against the control stick. Ike struggled to pull back the controls and guided the plane to a rough landing. His friend Major Ord was less fortunate. He was killed when a Philippine air cadet crashed a plane into the mountains. Ike later wrote, "Without my friend, all the zest was gone."

President Quezon was impressed with Ike. He liked him for his wit and candor, and his attention to detail. Ike was given an office in the presidential palace at Malacanan. When Quezon discovered Dwight's skill at bridge, he frequently invited him to spend weekends aboard the presidential yacht, the *Casiana*. Quezon also invited Ike to his office for long discussions, where they talked of the defense plans, taxes, education, government corruption, and many other topics. Ike became more of a presidential confidant than MacArthur, partly because of the general's unusual working schedule. "He never reached his desk until eleven," Ike said. "After a late lunch hour, he went home again. This made it difficult for Quezon to get in touch with the general when he wanted him."

Unhappily, Dwight's relationship with MacArthur hit a low

point. In a letter written not long before their departure for the Philippines, MacArthur had praised Ike:

"I have been impressed by the cheerful and efficient devotion of your best efforts to confining, difficult, and often strenuous duties, in spite of the fact that your own personal desires involved a return to troop command and other physically active phases of Army life, for which your characteristics so well qualify you." MacArthur said these qualities were "convincing proof of the reputation you have established as an outstanding soldier . . . this reputation coincides exactly with my own judgment."

Ike had sharp differences with MacArthur. He thought MacArthur's desire to be named field marshal of the Philippine Army was "rather fantastic." Dwight told him that being a four-star American general was honor enough. "Why in the hell do you want a banana country giving you a field marshalship?" he asked. When President Quezon agreed to bestow the title, Ike urged MacArthur to turn it down. He told the general it was "pompous and rather ridiculous to be the field marshal of a virtually nonexisting army."

MacArthur received the lofty commission in an elaborate ceremony at the presidential palace. It was MacArthur's passion for such military pomp and ceremony which led to their break. MacArthur told Ike that "the morale of the whole population would be enhanced if the people could see something of their emerging army in the capital city, Manila." The general's assistants were asked to bring in military units from throughout the islands to a central campsite near the city. "We told the general that it was impossible to do the thing within our budget," Ike later recalled. But MacArthur, undeterred, ordered them to continue organizing the parade.

President Quezon, surprised to learn of the planned troop movements, asked Dwight what was happening. "I was astonished," Ike said. He had been under the impression that MacArthur had cleared the project with Quezon. An angered Quezon called MacArthur and canceled the parade. According to Dwight, the president "was horrified to think that we were ready for a costly national parade in the capital."

MacArthur was "exceedingly unhappy" with his staff. He

sternly criticized Ike and Major Ord for going ahead with preparations for the parade, claiming that he had only wanted them to quietly investigate the possibility. "General MacArthur denied he had given us an order, which was certainly news to us," Dwight said. Sharp words were exchanged. "All you're saying is that I am a liar," Ike said, "and I am not a liar, and so I'd like to go back to the United States right away." MacArthur smiled and said: "Ike, it's just fun to see that damn Dutch temper." The general said the episode had been merely "a misunderstanding."

For Ike, however, it was no small matter. "This misunderstanding caused considerable resentment," he said. "And never again were we on the same warm and cordial terms." In later years MacArthur would become resentful and jealous of Dwight's prominence. He would then denounce his erstwhile subordinate as "the apotheosis of mediocrity." Dwight wryly noted that he "studied dramatics under MacArthur."

There were some high moments. Dwight received his long-awaited promotion to lieutenant colonel in July 1936, and his family had rejoined him. He and Mamie lived in an opulent, air-conditioned suite in the Manila Hotel with a view of Manila Bay. The centerpiece of the apartment was a huge crystal chandelier. Mamie furnished their apartment with bamboo chairs and settees, porcelain lamps, and a rosewood bench. Their income went much further in Manila than in Washington as Dwight received his regular army income and $500 a month from the Philippine Government. They did not socialize with the MacArthurs, but they mixed often with American businessmen.

The tropical climate was an ordeal for Mamie, who spent most of her time inside the apartment. Her health, always fragile, was severely tested. On one occasion she suffered a stomach hemorrhage during a drive to the mountain town of Baguio where John attended school. She fell into a coma. Ike rushed to the hospital as soon as he was notified. He remained there until her recovery became certain. Because the climate was more comfortable in the mountains, she stayed there for several months afterward.

Ike, too, had health problems. He lost weight. He suffered periodic attacks of bursitis and a painful intestinal ailment. A bland diet seemed to correct the latter affliction. However, twenty years later, surgery would be required after another attack.

In July of 1938, Ike and his family sailed to the United States. They visited Denver and Abilene, spending time with the Douds and the Eisenhowers. Dwight also used this trip to lobby for increased aid for the Philippines. The War Department ignored him, so Dwight called on General Malin Craig, the Chief of Staff. He persuaded Craig that the defense of the Philippines was indeed vital to American interests. Craig immediately sent word that Dwight was to be accommodated. The Army provided some World War I Enfield rifles and some Lewis and Browning machine guns. Since the War Department appropriations had been relatively low, the Army was unable to provide airplanes or mortars. Ike purchased arms and supplies from American manufacturers. He also bought several more airplanes for the Philippine Air Corps.

Ike found more discussion of a coming European war. Germany reclaimed the Rhineland and Italy marched into Ethiopia. Hitler and Mussolini had entered the Spanish Civil War. In December of 1937, the Japanese had sunk an American navy gunboat in China. Though the Japanese government apologized, their aggression against China went on. Their bombing of Shanghai and the sacking of Nanking rallied world opinion behind the Chinese. The isolationists had won a victory of sorts when President Roosevelt had signed the Neutrality Act of 1937.

Roosevelt had not abandoned his commitment to human rights, however. In a speech in Chicago, on October 5, 1937, he said: "War is a contagion, whether it be declared or undeclared. It can engulf states and people remote from the original scene. . . . It seems unfortunately true that the epidemic of world lawlessness is spreading. When an epidemic of physical disease starts to spread, the community approves and joins in a quarantine of the patients in order to protect the health of the community against the spread of the disease." He warned that if the Fascist powers continued their assault against other nations, "Let no one imagine that America will escape, that America may expect mercy, that this Western Hemisphere will not be attacked."

The speech was a signal that American policy was shifting. So was public opinion. A February 1938 Gallup poll indicated that 69 percent of the population favored helping England and France if the Fascist powers challenged them. Ike was shocked by the reports of Nazi persecution of the Jews. At the Army-Navy Club in Manila he was surprised to find some people speaking out in Hitler's defense. Ike was sympathetic to the plight of European Jews. His attitude was apparently well known to the Jewish community in Manila and elsewhere for he was invited to help devise a plan for an orderly emigration of European Jews. "Through several friends, I was asked to take a job seeking in China, Southeast Asia, Indonesia, and every country where they might be acceptable, a haven for Jewish refugees," Dwight later recalled. His annual salary would be $60,000, plus expenses.

The politics of rescue intrigued Dwight, who described the offer as "appealing." Yet with war clouds on the horizon, he declined the offer. The Roosevelt administration would attempt, without success, to find a place for the refugees in Latin America and Africa. The American State Department shamefully succeeded in restricting immigration quotas and sending thousands of Jews to certain death. Nothing would so horrify Ike during World War II as the firsthand inspection of the Nazi death camps.

Dwight was certain that General Conner's prophecy would soon become reality. He became even more certain on a warm September night in Manila while visiting a friend, Colonel Howard Smith. The two officers listened to an old shortwave radio, using earphones to hear a broadcast from London. British Prime Minister Neville Chamberlain, who months earlier had promised world peace as he signed the Munich Pact, was declaring war against Germany. The Nazis had invaded Poland.

"You can imagine what a bitter blow it is to me that all my long struggle to win peace has failed," Chamberlain said. He went on, "It is the evil things that we shall be fighting against—brute force, bad faith, injustice, oppression, and persecution—and against them I am certain that the right will prevail."

In a letter to Milton, Ike wrote his reaction to the speech. "After months and months of feverish efforts to appease . . . the final result will be that Germany will have to be dismembered."

The following day, Ike asked MacArthur for his release. "General," he said, "in my opinion the United States cannot remain out of this war for long. I want to go home as soon as possible. I want to participate in the preparatory work that I'm sure is going to be intense."

MacArthur urged him to remain in the Philippines where his work was meaningful and important. Ike said that the War Department had given him noncombat responsibilities in World War I. And he did not want it to happen again. MacArthur said he would not stand in Dwight's way.

President Quezon argued that Ike should stay; he offered him a blank contract for his services. "You fill in any figure you want, any figure you think is reasonable," Quezon said. Dwight tactfully refused. "No amount of money can make me change my mind," he said. "I want to be there if what I fear is going to come about actually happens."

Later, Quezon presented Eisenhower with a $100,000 annuity policy to "show his appreciation of all Ike has done for the Philippine nation." Dwight was touched by this gesture, but would not accept it. The persistent Quezon said it would assure security for Mamie. Dwight said that was his responsibility.

At a farewell luncheon in the Malacanan Palace, Dwight was awarded the Distinguished Service Cross. "Whenever I asked Ike for an opinion I got an answer," Quezon said. "It may not have been what I wanted to hear, it may have displeased me, but it was always a straightforward and honest answer."

Mamie pinned the award on his white uniform. The citation said: "Through his outstanding achievements in the service of the Philippine Government he has increased the brilliance of his already enviable reputation, and has earned the gratitude and esteem of the Filipino people."

On December 13, 1939, the Eisenhowers sailed from Manila. General MacArthur and his wife were on hand to exchange farewells. By Christmas, Dwight and his family were in Hawaii; they celebrated the New Year in San Francisco.

Ike reported to Fort Ord, where he became executive officer of the 15th Infantry. There he encountered George C. Marshall for the second time. Marshall was by then Chief of Staff. "Have you learned to tie your own shoes again since coming back, Eisenhower?" Marshall asked. He was referring to the servants and houseboys who performed such duties in the Philippines.

"Yes, sir," Dwight said, flashing his grin. "I am capable of that chore, anyhow."

At Fort Ord, Dwight made the argument that the Nazis could probably conquer the Low Countries—Holland and Belgium—by using modern weapons. France, too, he said, was vulnerable. From personal experience, Ike noted that Japan was likely to seize isolated colonies in the Pacific—and increase pressure on the Americans. He questioned whether the American armed forces were ready. Dwight sometimes grew testy when his remarks were taken lightly. He was soon nicknamed "Alarmist Ike."

In March, Ike was transferred to Fort Lewis, Washington, with the 15th Infantry. He richly enjoyed the assignment. Most of the troops had just returned from China; they were seasoned and experienced soldiers. As luck would have it, Dwight was not given adequate weapons, equipment, or staff officers for his regiment. There were other problems, too. Enlisted men complained about irregularities in their charge accounts at the Post Exchange. Ike personally investigated the charges and rectified the situation.

The manpower and weapons shortages did not prevent Ike from conducting intensive combat training. The rugged terrain of western Washington provided an ideal setting for war maneuvers. Dwight later recalled such obstacles as "stumps, slashings, fallen logs, tangled brush, hummocks, and hills." He commanded his own battalion in the maneuvers. "I sweated and accumulated a grime of cake dust," he said. "At night, we froze."

His troops liked him. When Ike was inspecting the kitchen, he reportedly sliced a raw onion and grabbed a handful of raw hamburger. As he continued through the kitchen, he ate the red hamburger and the onion. "By God, that must be a tough guy!" said one of the cooks. "Raw meat!"

Ike still anxiously hoped for a field command. He was elated to receive a letter from old friend George Patton. The letter indicated that Patton was due to head one of the new armored divisions. He wanted Dwight as his regimental commander.

This seemed to be the assignment Ike had long been waiting for. With boyish enthusiasm, he wrote to Colonel Mark Clark, a friend who was then serving on the General Headquarters Staff. Dwight told Clark he hoped the Chief of Infantry would leave him alone. The Patton opportunity was not one to be missed.

Events continued to confirm what Dwight had been saying all along. Another world war was inevitable. Germany seized both Denmark and Norway in the spring of 1940. The neutral Low Countries also were conquered by Hitler's armies. In news reports, Ike watched with keen interest the evacuation from Dunkirk of some 338,000 soldiers and civilians. The Royal Air Force and some 850 British vessels had made the mass exodus possible.

With ruthless efficiency, the German war machine drove through France. On June 25, France fell. Hitler controlled Western Europe. Against the advice of his general staff, Hitler decided to invade England. The RAF and the Luftwaffe fought the Battle of Britain. German air raids on London and rural areas took a heavy toll. Walter Lippmann wrote: "Our duty is to begin acting at once on the basic assumption that the Allies may lose the summer, and that before the snow flies again we may stand alone and isolated, the last great democracy on earth." A national poll said that only 30 percent of all Americans thought Hitler could be defeated. Britain's new Prime Minister, Winston Churchill, bravely vowed to "defend our Island whatever the cost may be." Roosevelt sent Churchill fifty destroyers to help the Allied cause. In the meantime, a treaty between Germany, Italy, and Japan united the Axis powers in their quest for a new world order.

In September of 1940, Congress passed the Selective Service Act. The personal lobbying efforts of General Marshall and Secretary of War Henry L. Stimson had made the difference. Isolationist forces had fought the legislation with vigor. Roosevelt had publicly endorsed a selective service bill. The draft went into effect on October 16.

Dwight faced a difficult choice in the middle of November. He received a telegram from his onetime Command School classmate, Leonard Gerow, a brigadier general and chief of the War Plans Division in the War Department:

> I need you in War Plans Division do you seriously object to being detailed on the War Dept General Staff and assigned here please reply immediately.

Dwight was genuinely torn. Such an assignment would put him on the threshold of high command, but it also would remove him from combat duty. He wrote Gerow: "Your telegram, arriving this morning, sent me into a tailspin." In his anxiety, Ike suffered an attack of shingles.

In a long letter to Gerow, Dwight said his desire for field command outweighed his ambition for the War Plans Division. However, he said Gerow should decide his fate. Ike also noted that General Charles F. Thompson, commander of the Third Division, wanted him as chief of staff. Gerow withdrew his request in deference to Thompson.

Dwight became chief of staff of the Third Division on November 30, 1940. Fort Lewis was division headquarters, so Ike remained in the Pacific Northwest. He was not comfortable with this position. In a letter to Gerow, he lamented: "In trying to explain to you a situation that has been tossed in my teeth more than once (my lack of extended troop duty in recent years), all I accomplished was to pass up something I wanted to do, in favor of something I ought to do, and then . . . find myself not even doing the latter."

There were some benefits to living in the Pacific Northwest. Edgar Eisenhower lived less than fifteen miles from Fort Lewis. The two brothers were able to spend much time together. They golfed, discussed politics, drank cocktails, and reminisced about Abilene. It was, Mamie said, "a regular picnic," when Edgar came.

Edgar took an almost paternal interest in John Eisenhower. John had stayed briefly with Edgar and his daughter Janice while attending Stadium High School in Tacoma. Edgar had become estranged from his own son, Jack, but he took an instant liking to John. Although the youngster resisted most of Edgar's reactionary political ideas, he treated his uncle with respect. Moreover, John was an outstanding student at the local high school. Edgar wanted to pass his prosperous law practice over to another family member. He offered John a proposition.

"If you'll study law," Edgar said, "I'll pay your way through any college for four years, and then through four years of law school. I'll take you into the law firm as soon as you graduate. You'll make a lot of money."

John was flattered, but he had no difficulty in turning Edgar down. "I can argue with you, Ed, and love it," John said. "But I could never work for you." Years later, John said, "I've made a lot of mistakes. But that was not one of them. It would never have worked out."

John had another career in mind. He told his parents that he wanted to apply for a West Point appointment. Ike warned him of the pitfalls of a military career. He pointed to his own lack of promotion, the low pay scale, and the frustrations of dealing with the War Department bureaucracy. Dwight offered to finance John's education "even if it extends over eight to ten years." The arguments were not persuasive. John was determined to follow his father into the Army. He had watched Dwight turn down several lucrative job offers to remain an officer.

Ike asked Milton to help organize a letter-writing campaign for a Kansas appointment to West Point. "The tragedy of the whole thing," Ike wrote, "is that six years ago there were at least half a dozen people on the Hill that would have been delighted to give me such an appointment. In fact, I obtained such appointments for other boys, merely on a personal request. All those men, except possibly Mr. Powers of New Jersey, have disappeared from the rolls of Congress. In any event, politicians have such short memories that any direct request of mine would now be simply tossed into the wastebasket."

Milton enlisted the help of Charles M. Harger, the Abilene newspaper publisher. Harger recommended John's appointment to the local congressman. But after some discussion the congressman told Harger that he had already promised the appointment to a Manhattan boy. "It seems clear that there is nothing further to do in the case of Congressman Rees," Ike wrote.

Harger and Milton both recommended John to Senator Arthur Capper. "I think that nothing will have more effect in the end," Dwight wrote Milton, "than your close contacts with the Senator's secretary." Senator Capper invited John to take a competitive examination for the appointment. John went to Washington for the test and enrolled at Millard's Academy, a West Point preparatory school. He stayed with Milton and Helen at their Falls Church house.

Thirty-six young men took the examination for Capper's appointment. John scored a 92 in the civil service test and finished first. Indeed, it was the highest score a Kansas applicant had ever received. "Last night he received word from Senator Capper notifying him that the Senator would appoint him to West Point," Milton wrote Harger on November 14. "The Eisenhower family will be eternally grateful to you and the others who supported John."

Ike was proud of John's performance. The appointment had been earned instead of a patronage gift. John wanted to return to Fort Lewis to celebrate with his parents.

"At this moment I cannot make an intelligent reply to your proposal that you come home after Christmas," Dwight wrote on November 20, "because I don't even know that I am to be here! There is now being discussed the possibility of my coming to Washington. I think the chances are about 50–50, but the matter should be settled, one way or another, within a few days."

Dwight did not like the rainy Pacific Northwest climate. He also learned that Mamie hoped for a transfer to Washington. "Today we're having a typical winter day in the Northwest," Dwight said in November, "rainy and dark! But we've been fairly fortunate so far—and have our nice days to break the long stretches of rain and fog."

He was still a staff officer at Fort Lewis, which was a disappointment. Ike continued to correspond with friends about his wish to be with troops. "I know that General Marshall is not concerned with the assignment of such small fry as myself," he wrote in one of these letters. But, in fact, Marshall and the War Department were very much aware of him.

Ike was promoted to chief of staff for the Ninth Army Corps in early March. He was suddenly responsible for all posts, forts, camps, stations, and other military installations in the northwestern United States.

A few days later, on March 11, a longtime ambition was realized. He was promoted to full colonel. It was his most cherished moment in uniform. Weeks earlier, he had doubted whether the promotion would ever come. Now, with the "chicken wings" on his shoulders, Ike was jubilant. His enthusiasm soured when some well-meaning colleagues predicted he would soon be a general.

"Damn it," he told John. "As soon as you get a promotion they start talking about another one. Why can't they let a guy be happy with what he has? They take all the joy out of it."

Ike began an intensive training program for his division. No sooner had this started than he was transferred to Third Army Headquarters, at Fort Sam Houston, in San Antonio. Lieutenant General Walter Krueger had asked Marshall for a chief of staff for the Third Army. Dwight had been recommended by his old friend General Mark Clark, whom Marshall had asked to screen officers.

The Third Army was preparing for the Louisiana maneuvers, the biggest peacetime war maneuvers in the nation's history. As chief of staff, Ike was charged with devising strategy and tactics for some 240,000 men against the Second Army, whose troop strength was 180,000. "Old Louisiana hands warned us that ahead lay mud, malaria, and mosquitoes," Dwight later recalled.

"We're having some difficulty getting used to Texas heat," Ike wrote in July. "But it's not so severe as I remembered it. They tell me that when I go to the Louisiana maneuvers I'll find out what disagreeable weather is. But I figure I can take it."

Mamie was sentimental about her return to the scene of their courtship and their first home together. They arrived in San Antonio on the twenty-fifth anniversary of their marriage. Their spacious colonel's house was much different from the cramped apartment they had occupied in 1916. The town, too, had changed a great deal. Dwight surprised Mamie that morning with a platinum watch with diamonds, for her anniversary gift.

A few days later, Mamie received a less pleasant surprise. "Our furniture arrived yesterday," Ike wrote John on July 16, "and we were disappointed in the results of shipping by van. A good many pieces of dishes and furniture were broken, and I have to go out this afternoon to try to settle the matter with the shipper. I hope we don't have to move again for a long time."

Mamie also was troubled by the problems of running a five-bedroom house without servants. Her burden eased considerably when she acquired the services of Private Michael McKeogh, who had been a bellhop at the Plaza Hotel in New York for seven years. She was then able to run the household and entertain.

In August, Ike went to Louisiana for the maneuvers. The preliminary maneuvers were held in August. The "war" began in mid-September. It was a military spectacular. More than one thousand planes were used. Several tank divisions fought each other. Paratroopers were dropped for combat exercises. The maneuvers were costly and some civilians were skeptical of their value. One senator told General Marshall the exercise was too expensive, particularly because the troops had made so many errors. "My God, Senator," Marshall retorted, "that's the reason I do it. I want the mistakes down in Louisiana, not over in Europe, and the only way to do this thing is to try it out, and if it doesn't work, find out what we need to make it work."

The maneuvers were covered widely in the nation's newspapers. The Third Army, following Dwight's master plan, won the early engagements. Bad-weather conditions threatened to turn the tide. But the Third Army columns continued to close the ring and nearly captured the commander of the Second Army. Marshall was mightily impressed by Ike's performance; so was the cluster of newspapermen covering the maneuvers. Robert S. Allen and Drew Pearson wrote in their syndicated column that "Colonel Eisenhower" had "conceived and directed the strategy that routed the Second Army." Dwight, they wrote, "has a steel-trap mind plus unusual physical vigor [and] to him the military profession is a science and he began watching and studying the German Army five years ago."

He was still relatively unknown, far from a household word. One wire-service photograph taken during the maneuvers showed Ike conferring with General Krueger and British Major A. V. Golding, who were correctly identified. According to the caption, the third man was "Lt. Col. D. D. Ersenbeing." "At least," Dwight said later, "they got the initials right."

Marshall stressed the importance of the Louisiana maneuvers in a speech before the American Legion Convention. "The present maneuvers," he said, "are the closest peacetime approximation to actual fighting conditions that has ever been undertaken in this country. But what is of the greatest importance, the mistakes and failures will not imperil the nation or cost the lives of men."

Years later, Marshall would describe the Louisiana mock war as the best training his World War II generals would receive. "All of them learned a great deal," he said. In addition to Ike, Omar Bradley, George Patton, and Courtney Hodges had starred in the maneuvers. Patton, who commanded a tank division for the losing Second Army, had demonstrated his flair and fighting ability in defeat.

Ike seemed to enjoy the challenge of the maneuvers. But he was still hoping for a field command. In a note to Gerow, he wrote: "Handling an Army staff that has had very little chance to whip itself together has its tough points—in spite of which I am having a good time. But I would like a command of my own." He expressed some embarrassment over the Allen and Pearson "Washington Merry-Go-Round" column. As a staff officer, he said that Krueger, not he, should have received the credit.

As the maneuvers ended, Ike received a telegram advising him that he was being nominated by the President for brigadier general. He received his first star in a formal ceremony at Fort Sam Houston. "That was my proudest moment," Mamie Eisenhower was to recall years later.

Ike tried to view his promotion with some perspective. "One thing is certain," he wrote a friend. "When they get down to my place on the list, they are passing out stars with considerable abandon."

Chapter Nine

GENERAL IKE

The United States was running out of time. By a single vote, Congress had passed an extension of the Selective Service Act. In another close vote, Congress had revised the Neutrality Act. President Roosevelt was preparing to wage an undeclared war against Germany on the Atlantic Ocean. "Everything is to be done to force an incident," Roosevelt advised Prime Minister Churchill in a secret cable. His incident came when a German submarine attacked the American destroyer *Greer* near Iceland. Roosevelt described the attack as "piracy legally and morally." He responded by warning that Nazi ships would now enter the North Atlantic "at their peril." It was, in effect, a declaration of war.

Another crisis now loomed in the Pacific. Prince Fuminaro Konoye, the moderate Prime Minister of Japan, had proposed a summit conference with Roosevelt to avert disaster. But on October 17, the Konoye government was replaced by General Hideki Tojo. The new Japanese Prime Minister was a militarist, imperialist, and ardently pro-German. Joseph C. Grew, the American ambassador to Japan, warned that Tojo's leadership increased the possibility of war. Japanese envoys arrived in Washington to negotiate with Secretary of State Cordell Hull, but the talks did little to ease the tension. The Japanese Foreign Office imposed a three-week deadline on the talks which left little time for diplomatic maneuvering. Roosevelt and the American service chiefs suggested a six-month truce with Japan. Germany, they agreed, was the greater threat, "the most dangerous enemy."

There was little reason for optimism. Imperial headquarters in Japan had never expected a peaceable solution. Secretary of the Navy Frank Knox predicted a confrontation. Some observers thought diplomatic progress was being made; the mere fact that talks were going on gave them hope. "It seemed that the Japanese bluff had been called and war at least, temporarily, averted," Ike said. An editorial in his San Antonio newspaper proclaimed that Japan did not wish to fight. Other commentators agreed.

Ike had been studying and evaluating the recent Louisiana maneuvers. The weaknesses and inefficiencies which were exposed during the exercises troubled him. He was in the process of suggesting corrective measures on Sunday morning, December 7. That afternoon he went to bed, tired and exhausted, leaving orders not to be disturbed. In two weeks, he was scheduled for a Christmas leave. Ike and Mamie would spend two weeks in the East and be reunited with John at West Point.

The news of Japan's raid on Pearl Harbor changed those plans. An aide awakened Dwight to tell him the Japanese had wiped out the United States fleet. Ike put on his uniform and returned to his office.

The next day, President Roosevelt declared war on the Axis powers with his ringing "Day of Infamy" address. "Our two nations are now full comrades-in-arms," he wrote Churchill.

For five days, Ike helped dispatch Third Army units to the West Coast in anticipation of possible Japanese attacks. Patrols were sent to the southern border and along the Gulf of Mexico. Dwight was at the center of the maelstrom, charged with sending instructions to one hundred other stations. On Friday, December 12, he received a call from the War Department. "Is that you, Ike?" Colonel Walter Bedell Smith asked. "Yes," Dwight said. "The Chief says for you to hop a plane and get up here right away," Smith said. "Tell your boss that formal orders will come through later."

Ike was disappointed. He did not know what the new assignment would bring. His first reaction was that the War Department was putting him on the shelf again. "The message was a hard blow," he said. Service with combat troops seemed unlikely.

He called Mamie and asked her to pack a suitcase, and sent Milton a telegram asking him to meet him at Union Station. Sadly he canceled plans for the Christmas vacation. Dwight arrived in Washington on Sunday, one week after Pearl Harbor. Milton met him at the great concourse. "I see you got my wire," Dwight said. Milton said that Dwight could stay with his family at Falls Church. Dwight accepted the offer.

"I'll have to check in at the War Department first," Ike said. Milton drove his brother to the old Munitions Building, which then served as General Marshall's headquarters.

Dwight's previous meetings with Marshall had been brief encounters. Marshall had become Chief of Staff as the war began in Europe. He had traveled across the country, advising officers to prepare for wartime mobilization. Marshall was well aware of the Army's limitations and deficiencies. More than anyone else, he was responsible for reinstating the draft. His task was rebuilding America's armed forces.

Marshall was a graduate of Virginia Military Institute. He did not engage in the camaraderie of West Point alumni; his outward personality seemed cool, detached, reserved. He was reputed to have a fiery temper, though it was seldom seen by others. His bearing and air of command impressed soldiers and political leaders. Marshall did not tolerate failings in others and kept a personal list of officers who had displeased him. Ike had enormous respect for Marshall, whom General Fox Conner had described years earlier as a "genius" in military command. Marshall had been impressed by Dwight in their earlier meetings. Indeed, Marshall tried to lure Ike from the Battle Monuments Commission to join his own staff at Fort Benning, but circumstances prohibited such a transfer. Marshall, however, did not forget Dwight. The strong recommendations of Conner and Pershing were important in Ike's selection for high command, but Marshall wanted to observe the Kansan firsthand.

For twenty minutes, Marshall described the situation in the Pacific. Suddenly he asked, "What should be our general line of action?"

Ike was taken aback. He hesitated momentarily. "Give me a few hours," he said.

"All right," Marshall said, dismissing him.

Dwight sensed that Marshall was testing him. His response might well determine his place on Marshall's list. Leaving Marshall's office, he went to find a desk in the War Plans Division. Studying a map of the Pacific, Ike pondered all options. He selected Australia as the base for the defense of the Philippines. Despite the difficulties, Dwight felt that the Philippines must be defended. He would recommend to Marshall doing "whatever was remotely possible."

He returned to Marshall with a proposal. "General," Ike said, "it will be a long time before major reinforcements can go to the Philippines, longer than the garrison can hold out with any driblet assistance, if the enemy commits major forces to their reduction. But we must do everything for them that is humanly possible. The people of China, of the Philippines, of the Dutch East Indies will be watching us. They may excuse failure but they will not excuse abandonment. Their trust and friendship are important to us. Our base must be Australia, and we must start at once to expand it and to secure our communications to it. In this last we dare not fail. We must take great risks and spend any amount of money required."

Marshall said, "I agree with you. Do your best to save them."

Ike was appointed head of the Philippines and Far Eastern Section of the War Plans Division. His old friend Gee Gerow was chief of War Plans. The assignment was still somewhat unsettling. On Saturday, Dwight wrote General Krueger:

> This is literally the first minute I have had to make even the briefest kind of report to you. I arrived here Sunday morning and have been working incessantly ever since with never more than a few brief hours for sleep.
>
> My immediate assignment is as an assistant to Gerow to lighten the burden of this office. The rapid, minute-to-minute activities of the Army seem to be centered through this place, because no one else is familiar with everything else that has been planned in the past. As quickly as this work can be cen-

tralized properly the pressure should ease up some, but there is no prospect of it becoming "normal."

Up to yesterday I was determinedly clinging to the hope that I could return to your headquarters at a reasonably early date. That hope went glimmering when I found out last night that my transfer has been made a permanent one. I was not consulted and naturally I have never been asked as to any personal preference. This is of course exactly as it should be, but it does not prevent my telling you how bitterly disappointed I am to have to leave you, particularly at this time. . . .

Ike's work schedule was busier than ever; he left Milton's home before eight in the morning and seldom returned until eleven at night. Dwight later recalled that he never saw Milton's home in the daylight during this period. Helen always had a hot meal ready for Ike when he returned. Milton, by then one of President Roosevelt's most prolific trouble shooters, resumed his earlier role as Dwight's confidant and alter ego. Dwight described his work load in a letter to Brigadier General LeRoy Lutes, who had been newly assigned to the War Department: "Just to give you an inkling as to the kind of madhouse you are getting into—it is now eight o'clock New Year's Eve. I have a couple hours' work ahead of me, and tomorrow will be no different from today. I have been here about three weeks and this noon I had my first luncheon outside of the office. Usually it is a hot-dog sandwich and a glass of milk. I have had one evening meal in the whole period."

The Japanese had quickly established their dominance of the Far East. In the days following Pearl Harbor, they conquered Thailand, Singapore, Guam, Hong Kong, Borneo's rich oil fields, and the Philippines. General MacArthur withdrew his soldiers to the Bataan Peninsula. The Japanese drove General Joseph Stilwell out of Burma.

Not surprisingly, Ike took the news hard. He had felt a strong commitment to the Philippines, morally and personally. He sought to build up forces in the Far East.

"I've been insisting the Far East is critical—and no other side shows should be undertaken until air and ground there are in satisfactory state," he wrote on January 1. Ike sent former Secretary of War Patrick J. Hurley to the Philippines with ten million dollars in cash to hire ships to break the Japanese blockade of the Philippines. Hurley's mission was a failure. Ship owners did not want to risk their vessels against the Japanese. Dwight later persuaded the British to make the ocean liner *Queen Mary* available for transporting fifteen thousand soldiers to Australia. The *Queen Mary* was so fast that it did not require escorting vessels, and Dwight was confident that a submarine couldn't overtake it. However, he was startled to receive an intercepted cable. An Italian spy had notified his government of the *Queen Mary*'s destination. Ike kept the message to himself. He did not want Marshall and others to share his agony and anxiety over the ship's fate. When news came that the *Queen Mary* had docked in Australia, Dwight went to Marshall.

"General," he said, "I want to tell you something. I sent a division to Australia via the South Atlantic and then we got word that she had been sighted and the Italians knew where she was going. Of course, they passed that on to the Germans. I have lived a long life in these past days until I could tell you. It's all right now. She is there. I didn't want to show you that message until now. There was nothing you could do about it, so I just didn't want to show it to you and let it bother you."

Marshall paused and said, "Eisenhower, I received that intercept at the same time you did. I was merely hoping that you might not see it and so I said nothing to you until I knew the outcome."

Once again Ike had scored points with the Chief of Staff. In his first meeting with Dwight, Marshall said: "Eisenhower, the department is filled with able men who analyze their problems well but feel compelled always to bring them to me for final solution. I must have assistants who will solve their own problems and tell me later what they have done." From then on, Dwight was determined to "report to the General only situations of obvious necessity or when he personally sent for me."

Ike did not care for the War Department's infighting and what he perceived as petty rivalries. "Tempers are short! There are lots of amateur strategists on the job—and prima donnas everywhere. I'd give anything to be back in the field," he wrote then.

Marshall soon made it known that Dwight should not plan on a field command. "I want you to know that in this war the commanders are going to be promoted and not the staff officers," Marshall said. "You are a good case. General Joyce wanted you for a division commander and the Army commander said you should have corps command. But, Eisenhower, you're not going to get any promotion. You are going to stay right here on this job and you'll probably never move. While this may seem a sacrifice to you, that's the way it must be."

Ike, whose hopes for combat duty in World War I had been rebuffed by the War Department, could not contain his bitterness. His temper flashed. "General," he said, "I don't give a damn about your promotion. I was brought here to do a duty. I am doing that duty to the best of my ability and I am just trying to do my part in winning the war." He stormed out of Marshall's office and, at the door, turned to see Marshall smile.

The setbacks in the Pacific made Dwight's position in the War Department all the more frustrating. "There is a lot of big talk and desk hammering around this place," he wrote, "but far too few doers. They announce results in advance—in a flashy way and make big impressions, but the results do not materialize and then the workers get the grief."

He noted the Japanese triumphs on his yellow pad. "The news from Wavell is all bad," he wrote on January 30. "Troops in Malaya giving up and going back to Singapore. . . . What a mess. We are going to regret every damn boat we sent to Iceland." The next day, he wrote, "Events move too fast. . . . Day by day the case looks worse. . . ."

Ike worked hard to influence the War Department to aid MacArthur in the Far East. But he was converted to the department's Europe-first strategy. His efforts to assist in the Far East did not undercut departmental policy. The Pacific theater was a holding operation against the Japanese.

"Tom Handy [Col. Thomas Handy, a WPD colleague] and I stick to our idea that we must win in Europe," Ike wrote on January 27. "Joe McNarney not only agrees—but was the first one to state that the French coast could be successfully attacked. It's going to be one h— of a job, but, so what? We can't win by sitting on our fannies giving our stuff in driblets all over the world—with no theater getting enough. Already we're probably too late in Burma—and we'll have to hurry like hell in Ceylon."

Major General McNarney, a West Point classmate, had been in London as chief of staff of a special army observer group. He returned to the War Department as Deputy Chief of Staff. His blunt talk about Europe weighed heavily with Ike.

"The struggle to secure the adoption by all concerned of a common concept of strategical objectives is wearing me down," Dwight wrote. "Everybody is too much engaged with small things of his own—or with some vague idea of larger political activity to realize what we are doing—rather, not doing. We've got to go to Europe and fight—and we've got to quit wasting resources all over the world—and still worse—wasting time. If we're to keep Russia in, save the Middle East, India, and Burma, we've got to begin slugging with air at West Europe; to be followed by a land attack as soon as possible."

Ike was appointed head of the War Planning Division in February. As Gerow, departing for a troop assignment, turned over his office, he told Dwight: "Well, I got Pearl Harbor on the book, lost the P.I., Singapore, Sumatra, and all the N.E.I. north of the barrier. Let's see what you can do."

As chief of WPD, Ike had to be a spokesman for the direction of the war effort. During February he began making recommendations for the over-all strategy against the Axis powers. His February 28 secret memorandum for Marshall differentiated between operations "whose current accomplishment in the several theaters over the world is necessary to the ultimate defeat of the Axis powers, as opposed to those which are merely desirable because of their effect in facilitating such defeat."

Dwight put top priority on holding the United Kingdom "which involves relative security of the North Atlantic sea lanes"; keeping Russia in the war "as an active enemy of Germany"; and maintaining position in the India-Middle East region to "prevent physical junction of the two principal enemies" and "keep China in the war." He added, "It is extremely doubtful that any single one of these mandatory missions could be long accomplished if we should fail completely in either or both of the other two."

He gave a lower priority, "desirable," to the security of Alaska, maintaining bases west and southwest of Hawaii, the security of Burma, South America south of Natal, Australia, and bases on the West African coast. "This distinction between the necessary and the desirable must be rigidly observed because of limitations on shipping, equipment, and trained troops," he said.

In the same memorandum, Ike gave an early indication of American plans for a cross-Channel invasion. "The United Kingdom is not only our principal partner in this war," he wrote, "it offers the only point from which effective land and air operations against Germany may be attempted." Dwight called for "immediate and definite action" to keep Russia in the war. "Russia's problem is to sustain herself during the coming summer, and she must not be permitted to reach such a precarious position that she will accept a negotiated peace, no matter how unfavorable to herself, in preference to a continuation of the fight."

Marshall was learning more about Ike's intelligence, his ability to deal with long-range problems, and his capacity to assume responsibility. On each count, Dwight impressed him.

Ike handled the pressure gracefully. His opinions were sometimes overruled, yet his influence continued to grow. On March 10, he wrote: "Gradually some of the people with whom I have to deal are coming to agree with me that there are just three 'musts' for the Allies this year—hold open the line to England and support her as necessary; keep Russia in the war as an active participant; hold the India-Middle East buttress between Japs and Germans. All this assumes the safety from major attack of North America, Hawaii, and Caribbean area.

"We lost 8 cargo ships yesterday. That we must stop, because any effort we make depends upon sea communications."

Ike's father, David Eisenhower, died that same day, at seventy-nine. Because of his responsibilities, Dwight was unable to return to Abilene for the funeral. Indeed, the next day Dwight met with President Roosevelt to show him a draft of a presidential message to Chiang Kai-shek. "I was instructed by the President not to hand Dr. Soong an exact copy of the message," Dwight wrote in his diary. "I am merely to contact Dr. Soong tomorrow and inform him of the general nature of the radiogram." (Soong was Chiang's brother-in-law and special envoy to Roosevelt.)

As Ike sat at his desk that night, he wrote that his father's death had been a great blow. "I have felt terribly," he wrote. "I should like so much to be with my Mother these few days. But we're at war! And war is not soft—it has no time to indulge even the deepest and most sacred emotions. I loved my Dad. I think my Mother the finest person I've ever known. She has been the inspiration for Dad's life, and a true helpmate in every sense of the word. I'm quitting work now—7:30 P.M. I haven't the heart to go on tonight."

Dwight continued his eulogy to his father the following day:

> My father was buried today. I've shut off all business and visitors for thirty minutes—to have that much time, by myself, to think of him. He had a full life. He left six boys and, most fortunately for him, Mother survives him. He was not quite 79 years old, but for the past year he has been extremely old physically. Hardened arteries, kidney trouble, etc. He was a just man, well liked, well educated, a thinker. He was undemonstrative, quiet, modest, and of exemplary habits—he never used alcohol or tobacco. He was an uncomplaining person in the face of adversity, and such plaudits as were accorded him did not inflate his ego.
>
> His finest monument is his reputation in Abilene and Dickinson County, Kansas. His word has been his bond and accepted as such; his sterling honesty, his insistence upon the immediate payment of all debts, his pride in his independence earned for him a reputation that has profited all of us boys. Because of it, all central Kansas helped me to secure an appointment to West Point in 1911, and thirty years later, it did the same for my son, John. I'm proud he was my father! My only regret is that it was always so difficult to let him know the great depth of my affection for him. David J. Eisenhower 1863–1942.

The death of his father made Ike more conscious of family responsibility. Later that month he took a weekend vacation with

Mamie to visit John at West Point. This had been the first break in Dwight's intensive work schedule since coming to Washington. "We thoroughly enjoyed our visit at the Academy," Dwight wrote John on March 29. "I wish we could come up to spend Sunday about once a month, but it is impossible." Almost as an afterthought, Ike told his son about a promotion. "I was appointed a Major General day before yesterday, so apparently the Chief of Staff did not mean what he said about making me serve in the War Department in the grade of Brigadier."

On March 30, Ike wrote his brother Edgar about the prospects of a lengthy war. "You are no more anxious than I am to get this war over with," he wrote. "The difficulty is that there are so many things that we didn't do in the past twenty years that their accomplishment now is a matter of weeks and months. It cannot be done in a minute. There is no use going back over past history either to regret or to condemn; although I was one of those that for the past two years have preached preparedness and tried to point out the deadly peril into which the United States was drifting. I don't see any point now in telling anyone else that he was wrong. We have got a fearful job to perform and everybody has got to unify to do it. No other consideration can now be compared to that of defeating the powers that are trying to dominate us. If they should win we would really learn something about slavery, forced labor, and loss of individual freedom."

In the meantime, Marshall asked Ike to turn his attention to the European command structure. Marshall and presidential confidant Harry Hopkins went to London in early April to consult with Churchill about a cross-Channel invasion. Three plans were discussed: Bolero, the concentration of American forces in Britain for the European invasion; Sledgehammer, an emergency landing on Europe in 1942; and Round-up, the proposed cross-Channel attack in 1943.

Shortly after Marshall's return, Ike wrote: "Bolero is supposed to have the approval of the Pres. and Prime Minister. But the struggle to get everyone behind it, and to keep the highest authority from wrecking it by making additional commitments of air-ship-troops everywhere is never ending. . . . The actual fact is that not 1 man in 20 in the govt. (including the W. and N.

Depts) realizes what a grisly, dirty, tough business we are in! They think we can buy victory!"

Marshall asked Dwight to make a study of the organization and the command structure needed in England. He also asked Dwight to consider the type of officer to head the operation.

On May 11, Ike described at length to Marshall the qualifications of the commanding general:

> As a first condition, he must enjoy the fullest confidence of the Chief of Staff in order that he may efficiently, and in accordance with the basic ideas of the Chief of Staff, conduct all the preparatory work essential to the successful initiation of Bolero. All planning in England for the U. S. Ground Forces, Air Forces, and the S.O.S. must be cleared through him; otherwise his position will be intolerable. . . . Next, he should be an officer who will, in any one of several possible roles, fit perfectly into the final organization—no matter what that may be. It is impossible at this time to predict with certainty that Bolero is going to develop along the lines now visualized. Unforeseen events may finally compel a defensive role in that theater, with the main effort of the U. S. Army executed elsewhere. . . .
>
> If Bolero develops as planned, there will come a time when United States Forces' activity and interest in that region will be so great as to make it, for an indefinite period, the critical point in all our war effort. When this comes about, it is easily possible that the President may direct the Chief of Staff, himself, to proceed to London and take over command. The officer previously serving as Commander should be one who could fit it (and would be acceptable to the new Commander) as a Deputy or as a Chief of Staff. This will insure continuity in planning and execution, and in understanding.

Ike did not nominate anyone for the job. His assistant, Colonel Albert C. Wedemeyer, proposed Marshall, with Dwight as Chief of Staff. Of all potential candidates, only Dwight seemed to fit the qualifications set by himself. Marshall had already settled on him. He sent Dwight to London in late May, to inspect U.S. headquarters and recommend any changes that were necessary. "I sent Eisenhower and some others over so the British could have a look at them," Marshall later admitted. "And then I asked Churchill what he thought of them. He was extravagant in his estimate of them, so then I went ahead with my decision on Eisenhower."

On his return, Ike recommended Deputy Chief of Staff McNarney for the London post, citing "his complete familiarity with the British organization and methods of planning, together with his characteristic of patience, which he possesses to noticeable degree at no sacrifice of energy and force."

"Patience is highly necessary," Ike wrote, "because of the complications in British procedure." Dwight also recommended a promotion, to lieutenant general, for the European commander. "There will soon be at least 4 Major Generals in the command, and the promotion is logical for that reason."

He brought Marshall a directive for the commander on June 8. Ike suggested that Marshall carefully study the report before sending it to London. "I certainly do want to read it," Marshall said. "You may be the man who executes it. If that's the case, when can you leave?"

For the first time, Marshall had told Dwight that he was destined for a truly major role in the war. Ike recorded his reaction in his diary: "The C/S told me this a.m. that it's possible I may go to England in command. It's a big job—if the U.S.-U.K. stay squarely behind Bolero and go after it tooth and nail, it will be the biggest American job of the war. Of course command now does not necessarily mean command in the operation—but the job before the battle begins will still be the biggest outside of that of the C/S himself."

Three days later, Ike wrote: "The C/S says I'm the guy. He also approves Clark for Corps C.G. in England and gives us the II Corps. Now we really go to work. Hope to leave here by plane on 22nd."

Ike hoped to begin immediate preparations for the cross-Channel invasion. But the British Cabinet had vetoed such a plan on the day of his appointment. Churchill met with Roosevelt at Hyde Park to urge an operation in French North Africa. The British and American general staffs preferred an attack on Western

Europe. They were unanimously against a second front in North Africa. Churchill, however, benefited by the news of the German conquest of Tobruk in Libya. That British defeat revived Churchill's pet project. Roosevelt was plainly sympathetic.

The responsibilities of Dwight's command were thus uncertain as he prepared to depart for London. Ike wrote a friend, General Spencer Ball Akin, on June 19, about his new assignment: "In a day or so I'll be leaving Washington. This has been a tough, intensive grind—but now I'm getting a swell command and, of course, am highly delighted that I got away with this job sufficiently well to have the Chief accord such recognition to me. Incidentally, the Chief is a great soldier. He is quick, tough, tireless, decisive and a real leader. He accepts responsibility automatically and never goes back on a subordinate. We're particularly fortunate in having him for a Chief of Staff. It has been a pleasure to work directly under him."

Ike spent his last weekend in Washington with his family. John had received a special leave from West Point. The fall of Tobruk made Dwight seem tense and pensive, John recalled years later. Ike's European command brought his son a certain prominence at West Point. "From that point on," John said, "I was treated a little differently, even by my classmates."

Ike assumed his command, in London, on June 24. As the leader of American forces, he quickly became a symbol to the British. He received the warmest of welcomes from the British and reciprocated by disciplining American officers who flaunted their Anglophobia.

He was assigned a suite at the luxurious Claridge's, London's most elite hotel. "I feel as though I were living in sin," he said. Within a few days, he moved to more modest quarters in the Dorchester Hotel, sharing a suite with Harry Butcher, who had left his job as head of the CBS Washington office to become Dwight's naval aide. "What he wanted," Butcher said, "was an old friend around to whom he could talk eye to eye, without having to worry about subservience."

The American and British press focused their attention on the new commander. Though Ike had never before conducted a press conference, he soon demonstrated a winning rapport with reporters. They were impressed by his candor, his willingness to share background information, and his friendliness. Ike told subordinates to treat reporters as members of the Allied team. "When we talk of public relations, I have a feeling that I will gain a reputation as an expert in this field," Butcher said. "I'll be getting the credit for Ike's good sense, for he is the keenest in dealing with the press I've ever seen, and I have met a lot of them, many of whom are phonies." Butcher noted that Ike "thinks the less he's in the papers, the better," yet with photographers "no one but a Sunday-school teacher with a class of nice girls could have been as obliging as Ike."

Dwight modified censorship rules to permit names of his subordinates to be used in news dispatches. According to Butcher, this was done "partly to avoid having stories repeatedly carrying his own name."

Still, the cult of personality which would result in his election to the presidency a decade later was already beginning. *Collier's* and *Life* were among the first American publications to publish major features about him. Edward R. Murrow, in a July broadcast for CBS, portrayed Ike as a representative of the "great American middle class." Murrow added, "I don't know whether Eisenhower is a good general or not."

Ike was troubled by the uncertainties of his mission. His goal, supported by Marshall, was the cross-Channel invasion. The British resisted. On July 11, Dwight wrote Marshall: "The British Staff and Prime Minister have decided that Sledgehammer can not repeat not be successfully executed this year under the proposition that the invading force must be able to remain permanently on the continent."

Churchill and the British continued to press for a North African invasion followed by an attack through the "soft underbelly" of Axis-occupied Europe. If Churchill had his way, Ike might well be relegated to a secondary role. There were even rumors that he was only an interim theater commander. "It is a rather lonely life I lead," Dwight wrote Milton on July 24. "Every move I make is under someone's observation and, as a result, a sense of strain develops that is entirely aside from the job itself."

Not long afterward, Ike disclosed the same uncertainty to General Brehon Somervell. "It is so easy to lose contact with the War Department and with the developing situation as it affects the U.S.," he wrote, "that frequently I am overcome by a 'lost' feeling and have a desperate desire to jump on a fast plane and come over for a twenty-four-hour visit."

Marshall, Harry Hopkins, and Admiral Ernest J. King came to London in late July in a final effort to persuade the British to the cross-Channel invasion. Churchill and the British chiefs did not waver. Marshall and Ike were bitterly disappointed. Dwight told Butcher that the Allies "must prepare for the possibility of a Russian collapse."

Marshall threatened to shift to a Pacific-first strategy if the British did not go along with him. The British chiefs were at first worried by Marshall's ultimatum. However, Churchill was confident that Roosevelt would never abandon Europe. With the British adamantly opposed to Sledgehammer, the Americans were forced to consider alternatives. Roosevelt wanted Americans to meet Nazi Germany in combat as soon as possible. Ike was convinced the British had made a disastrous mistake. He predicted July 22, the date of the rejection of Sledgehammer, might be remembered as "the blackest day in history."

Ike's disappointment was brief. On July 25, Marshall and the British chiefs designated him as supreme commander for Torch, the invasion of French North Africa. Roosevelt had resolved the Anglo-American dispute by deciding on the North African operation. Oran and Algiers on the Mediterranean and Casablanca on the Atlantic coast of Morocco were chosen as three strategic harbors to be seized by amphibious operations.

Control of North Africa and the Mediterranean was of the utmost importance to the Allies, who sought to preserve the short sea routes to India and Australia. Hitler and Mussolini wanted to take the Suez Canal, which would make their domain world-wide. In 1942, German Field Marshal Erwin Rommel's advance through Egypt and Libya had forced the British into retreat. Rommel's use of tanks, artillery, and infantry had already earned him a reputation for military genius. Churchill himself paid tribute to the abilities of "The Desert Fox" in a House of Commons address. By the fall of 1942, the tide had reversed. On October 23,

British General Bernard L. Montgomery struck Rommel's forces at El Alamein. The battle continued for more than a week, ending in a decisive victory for Montgomery. It was recognized as a signal triumph for the Allies and a hopeful omen for Torch, then in its final planning stages.

Ike described the planning period for Torch as "the most trying of my life." The British and American strategists had quarreled for weeks over the scope of the operation. The British wanted to concentrate on Mediterranean landings for the quickest possible drive to Tunisia. The Americans argued for a landing on the Atlantic coast of French Morocco, stressing that Fascist Spain could close its pincers at the Strait of Gibraltar and thus contain the Allies within the Mediterranean. The Americans prevailed only after Roosevelt and Churchill reached agreement on Casablanca. Ike, striving to weld a unified Allied command structure, had been neutral during the controversy. He was the conciliator, to whom a close-knit organization and coalition solidarity were all important.

Torch was further complicated by the political situation in French North Africa. The government of Vichy France, headed by Marshal Henri Pétain, had signed a peace treaty with Germany, although it was officially neutral. The United States had recognized the Vichy regime. Roosevelt and Churchill disliked and distrusted General Charles de Gaulle, leader of the Free French. The British, however, had fought Vichy French soldiers in North Africa and the Middle East earlier in the war. Because of these hostilities, Torch was purported to be an exclusively American operation. It was not known if the Vichy French would resist American landings. Like Franco's Spain, they were viewed with uncertainty and doubt.

Ike's political adviser on North Africa was Robert Murphy, a maverick American diplomat with more than a decade of service in France. Since 1940, he had been American consul general in Algiers and Roosevelt's personal envoy to French Africa. Under an assumed name, Murphy traveled to London to brief Ike in September. "The General seemed to sense that this first campaign would present him with problems running the entire geopolitical gamut," Murphy said. "As it certainly did. And in those days, Eisenhower, in accordance with military tradition, still preferred to regard himself as a soldier who paid attention to politics only when military operations were affected. . . . Eisenhower listened with a kind of horrified intentness to my description of the possible complications."

Butcher wrote in his diary at the time: "Ike feels we are sailing a dangerous political sea, and this particular sea is one in which military skill and ability can do little in charting a safe course."

If at all possible, Ike was to secure support of the French high command. The French maintained a standing army of 120,000 men in North Africa to supervise their colonies. Because of persistent leaks from De Gaulle's Free French headquarters and of Pétain's collaboration with the Nazis, Ike could not take either French group into his confidence about Torch. Yet he was charged with the difficult task of getting the French to permit the Americans to make their landings in North Africa without resistance and, if possible, getting them to resist German or Italian movement into Tunisia. Allied headquarters learned that German and Japanese intelligence had alerted Vichy to the possibility of Torch.

The Allies considered it vital to win over a prominent French spokesman to whom the French colonial forces would rally. Murphy thought he had the perfect candidate in Henri Giraud, an aging French general who had been a popular hero of World War I and whose reputation had most recently been enhanced by his daring escape from a Nazi fortress. Giraud had previous experience in North Africa and was well thought of by Arabs. Moreover, he was still on friendly terms with both De Gaulle and Pétain.

Giraud was smuggled from southern France by submarine for a secret meeting with Ike on Gibraltar. The meeting was frustrating for both men. Giraud had been led to believe that he would be named Allied commander and demanded the ranking role in the occupation of French soil. He also asked further that the Allied forces instead be sent to southern France to battle the Germans there. Ike tactfully explained that such arrangements were not possible. He fashioned a compromise: Giraud would be recognized as leader of the effort against Axis aggression in North

Africa and commander in chief of all French forces in the region and governor of French North Africa.

"In my anxiety to keep Giraud with us, even though it is too late for him to assist us in the role in which we especially desired him, I conceded every point he made except only that I must remain directly responsible to the Combined Chiefs of Staff for operations of the Allied force until different arrangements could be made with the consent of the two governments," Ike wrote in his report to Marshall.

The Allied landings met bitter French resistance at Oran and Casablanca. There was little resistance at Algiers. After Torch had already begun, Giraud broadcast by radio an appeal to his countrymen in North Africa to join him in uniting with the Allies. He then departed for Algiers.

Unhappily, Giraud proved to be a paper tiger. His message carried no weight.

As luck would have it, Admiral Jean François Darlan, commander in chief of Vichy France's armed forces, minister of defense, and the heir apparent to Pétain, happened to be in Algiers at the time. Darlan had real authority, including control of the powerful French fleet. He was, in many ways, the most controversial and hated of all Vichy leaders. His diatribes against Britain and De Gaulle and his collaboration with the Nazis had worked to give him the image of a Fascist. Murphy had a long-standing relationship with Darlan and thought his cooperation in North Africa might be achieved through careful diplomacy. Murphy had most recently been in communication with Darlan's son. The son, a young French officer stationed in Algiers, had been stricken with polio. Darlan had made a sudden visit from Vichy to be with him.

Murphy had earlier received secret messages from Darlan which indicated the Vichy admiral was indeed willing to participate in French-American military operations. However, American Admiral William D. Leahy, who had been U.S. ambassador to Vichy and knew Darlan well, had cautioned Murphy that Darlan was "ambitious and dangerous."

Darlan's reaction to Murphy's overture was not encouraging. He accused the Americans of a "massive blunder," arguing that had they only waited the French would have joined them in combined operations in France and North Africa. Darlan had been given orders by Pétain to cooperate with the Germans whom Vichy had authorized to make use of bases in Tunisia. Murphy was unable to persuade Darlan to do otherwise, and Germany established its position in Tunisia.

Ike dispatched his deputy, General Mark Clark, to put additional pressure on Darlan. By threatening to imprison him, Clark secured a cease-fire order from Darlan which ended the fighting at Casablanca and Oran. Darlan also told the French not to fight the Germans. The Nazis took over southern France the next day, and Darlan repeated the cease-fire order, this time with orders to resist the Germans. In return for Darlan's aid, Ike granted him authority in French North Africa and agreed to retain Vichy officials and continuation of Vichy policies, which included persecution of Jews, concentration camps, and laws suppressing civil liberties.

The Darlan "deal" became a major political controversy. Public opinion was sharply divided in Britain and the United States. Ike was criticized and condemned in the liberal press for collaborating with the arch collaborator. Roosevelt himself was troubled by the damage the Darlan alliance would do to the image of the Anglo-American partnership. Ike grumbled, "I regret that I must use so much of my own time to keep explaining these matters."

Ike said "military expediency" dictated the Darlan "deal." Churchill had told him: "If I could meet Darlan, much as I hate him, I would cheerfully crawl on my hands and knees for a mile if by doing so I could get him to bring that fleet of his into the circle of Allied forces." To this end, Darlan proved no more effective than Giraud. The French fleet did not join the Allies but sank itself at Toulon as Germans prepared to board some of the 177 vessels. De Gaulle called it "the most pitiful and sterile suicide imaginable."

Darlan was unable to bring French officials in Tunisia over to the Allied side in time to prevent the German takeover. His cease-fire order in North Africa had come when the Allies had already established their position and authority. General Marshall, defending Ike, said Darlan's cease-fire had saved 16,200 American casualties. During the invasion the Americans had suffered 1,800 casualties. American planners had estimated 18,000 casualties. So, theoretically, Ike had saved lives by his move.

The controversy went on. In Europe, the resistance movements expressed shock and disbelief that Americans would collaborate with "quislings." British commentators were no less harsh. Their message was that Ike, a hayseed from Kansas, had been taken in by the wily Fascist opportunist. On this point, Dwight was deeply sensitive. "The only thing that made me a little peeved about the matter was that anyone should think I was so incredibly stupid as to fail to realize I was doing an unpopular thing, particularly with those who were concerned with things other than winning the war—which is my whole doctrine and reason for existence," he wrote in a letter to his brother Edgar.

Ike attempted to calm his family about the criticism and was philosophical about the unfavorable publicity. In a letter to John he wrote: "From what I hear of what has been appearing in the newspapers, you are learning that it is easy enough for a man to be a newspaper hero one day and a bum the next. The answer is that just as one must not let his head get swelled too much by a bit of acclaim, he must not be too upset and irritated when the pack turns on him."

He became defensive about the beating he received in the public prints. Speaking to his British political adviser, Harold Macmillan, he said: "I can't understand why these long-haired, starry-eyed guys keep gunning for me. I'm no reactionary. Christ on the mountain! I'm as idealistic as hell."

In the wake of criticism, Ike felt compelled to send a cable to his superiors explaining the decision. "There may be a feeling at home that we have been sold a bill of goods," he admitted with typical understatement. He emphasized that the agreement pertained only to North Africa and by no means committed the United States to Darlan's claim to the helm of French government. "Roosevelt was deeply impressed by it," said Robert Sherwood, the playwright then serving as an aide to FDR. "As he read it with the same superb distribution of emphasis that he used in his public speeches, he sounded as if he were making an eloquent plea for Eisenhower before the bar of history."

When the storm of criticism intensified, Roosevelt was urged by Marshall and Secretary of War Henry L. Stimson to make a public defense of Ike. The alternative was a loss of credibility from which the three-star general might never recover. To reject the Darlan deal would mean relieving Ike from command.

Secretary of the Treasury Henry Morgenthau attacked the deal. In London, Foreign Secretary Anthony Eden was bitterly critical of Ike. Darlan "can make rings, diplomatically, round Eisenhower," Eden said. Edward R. Murrow ripped the deal in a commentary, saying, "Are we fighting Nazis or sleeping with them?"

Against this background, Roosevelt could hardly remain silent. Privately he was supporting Dwight, yet the temptation to repudiate the Darlan pact must have been strong. Hopkins, Samuel Rosenman, and Robert Sherwood told Roosevelt to go public with his stand. A statement was drafted by Elmer Davis, Archibald MacLeish, and Milton Eisenhower, the three top officials from the Office of War Information. Roosevelt made heavy revisions, which irritated Milton but made the language sharper.

Roosevelt said:

> I have accepted General Eisenhower's political arrangements made for the time being in Northern and Western Africa.
>
> I thoroughly understand and approve the feeling in the United States and Great Britain and among all the other United Nations [Allies] that in view of the history of the past two years no permanent arrangement should be made with Admiral Darlan. People in the United Nations likewise would never understand the recognition of a reconstituting of the Vichy Government in France or in any French territory.
>
> We are opposed to Frenchmen who support Hitler and the Axis. No one in our Army has the authority to discuss the future Government of France and the French Empire. . . .
>
> The present temporary arrangement in North and West Africa is only a temporary expedient, justified solely by the stress of battle.
>
> The present temporary arrangement has accomplished two military objectives. The first was to save American and British lives, and French lives on the other hand.

The second was the vital factor of time. The temporary arrangement has made it possible to avoid a "mopping-up" period in Algiers and Morocco which might have taken a month or two to consummate.

Roosevelt's public approval gave Ike a much-needed vote of confidence. He wrote Marshall on November 17, "I am pleased that you and the President saw the thing in realistic terms and realize that we are making the best of a rather bad bargain."

The political controversy and the atrocities of the Vichy Fascists persisted. On November 18, Dwight told his chief of staff, Walter Bedell Smith: "Since this operation started, three-quarters of my time, both night and day, has been necessarily occupied in difficult political maneuver." Later that day, he wired Smith: "My whole interest now is Tunisia. When I can make the Allies a present of that place the Agent [Churchill] can kick me in the pants and put in a politician here who is as big a crook as the chief local skunk."

Milton Eisenhower came to Algiers on December 11 in his capacity as associate director of the Office of War Information. President Roosevelt had sent Milton to North Africa to make reports on the Darlan arrangement, the work of OWI in broadcasting propaganda there, and the problem of French refugees who had fled the Nazis. Milton showed Ike a summary of the negative news reports and commentaries about the Darlan deal. Dwight was hurt and upset.

Milton took it upon himself to try to repair his brother's reputation. He startled Robert Murphy with a blistering lecture about Darlan. Murphy had expected Milton to put pressure on the Allies to release the thousands of political prisoners held by Vichy police. "I was preparing to explain this complicated situation," Murphy said, ". . . but my visitor soon made it clear that he had come to Algiers mainly because he was concerned about his brother's reputation." Milton said that some commentators were denouncing Ike as a Fascist. According to Murphy, he said, "that unless drastic action were taken immediately, the General's career might be irreparably damaged."

"Heads must roll, Murphy!" Milton said. "Heads must roll!"

Milton wanted some of the more prominent Vichy officials removed from power. Murphy said such "drastic action" could not happen overnight.

Ike told Milton, "If I could just get command of a battalion and get into a bullet battle, it would all be so simple." By this time, Dwight was having as much difficulty on the military front as he was with the political situation. The Allies had been unable to move into Tunisia before the Germans reinforced it. On Christmas Eve, Ike conceded that the race for Tunisia had been lost in the rain and the mud. "I think the best way to describe our operations to date," he said, "is that they have violated every recognized principle of war, are in conflict with all operational and logistic methods laid down in textbooks, and will be condemned in their entirety by all Leavenworth and War College classes for the next twenty-five years."

Butcher wrote of Ike's frustration: "If he ever gets Tunisia, he'll be a changed man; now he's like a caged tiger, snarling and clawing to get things done."

North Africa became less complicated for Dwight when Darlan was assassinated on December 24. Mark Clark said Darlan's death "was like the lancing of a troublesome boil." Dwight sent a handwritten letter to Madame Darlan expressing his sympathy: "I feel that we have lost a most valuable ally and a competent supporter." He told Butcher that Darlan's death did end the problem but no doubt would create more.

Giraud, a popular choice, was appointed to succeed Darlan. Roosevelt, Churchill, and De Gaulle at last seemed at peace. Marshall told Dwight to concentrate on the battle for Tunisia and "delegate international diplomatic problems to your subordinates."

Murphy's willingness to collaborate with the most venal elements of the Vichy regime soon brought Dwight into another controversy. "Now that poor Darlan has been killed we've got this Giraud, and no one can attack his record," Ike told British political adviser Harold Macmillan. "We have made Giraud the boss. Of course we're going to make changes. We are going to get a new governor for Algeria. It's a guy called Pie-row-ton. They tell me he's a fine guy."

Much to his horror, Macmillan subsequently discovered that "Pie-row-ton" was Marcel Peyrouton, who had served as the cruel and brutal minister of the interior at Vichy, heading the secret police and supervising the arrests and executions of those who fought the Nazis. Peyrouton had also been responsible for a code of anti-Semitic laws and had signed De Gaulle's death warrant.

When the appointment was announced, Ike again found himself in the eye of a hurricane. Writing in his diary, he noted: "Peyrouton's appt to succeed the worthless Chatel has been received with howls of anguish at home. Who do they want? He is an experienced administrator and God knows it's hard to find many of them among the French in Africa."

Peyrouton arrived in Algiers while Roosevelt and Churchill held their January summit conference in Casablanca. Dwight, suffering from a chronic cold and under the strain of the Tunisia military setback and Vichyite political controversies, was ill at ease. "Ike seems jittery," Roosevelt confided to Harry Hopkins.

Butcher wrote in his diary: "Eisenhower's neck is in a noose and he knows it." Earlier that month Ike had been shaken when he learned of a message Roosevelt had sent Churchill: "I agree that Eisenhower has had to spend too much time on political affairs but Marshall has sent him very explicit instructions on this point," Roosevelt wrote. "I don't know whether Eisenhower can hold Giraud in line with another Frenchman running the civil affairs but I shall soon find out."

Ike was unsure of his position at Casablanca. There were reports that he was a marked man, that because of his political blunders and the stalled military advance, he would be replaced by a more proven commander such as Sir Harold Alexander. What happened at Casablanca was revealing of Ike's personal style. He spoke to Roosevelt and Churchill with candor and modesty, acquitting himself remarkably well. Because of his years in the Philippines, he was ignorant of European politics, he admitted. The State Department had approved Peyrouton's appointment, but Ike took responsibility. He told Roosevelt that generals might make mistakes and be fired yet governments could not. He was ready to accept the consequences.

Roosevelt and Churchill were pleased with the way Ike had

made his case. Indeed, they agreed that he should be given the supreme command and a fourth star. The forces under Alexander in Tunisia were to come under Dwight's command. Alexander was to become Ike's commander of ground forces. The British won another delay for the cross-Channel attack at the conference. Roosevelt agreed to commit Allied troops to an invasion of Sicily in 1943, following the Tunisian campaign.

Churchill praised Ike in announcing this appointment to Parliament. "I have great confidence in General Eisenhower," the Prime Minister said. "I regard him as one of the finest men I have ever met."

The British high command thought Ike would be further removed from the military aspects of the war, becoming a chairman of the board. General Alan Brooke said Dwight's appointment "could not help flattering and pleasing the Americans insofar as we were placing our senior and experienced commander to function under their commander who had no war experience." As Alan Brooke saw it, Ike would be pushed "into the stratosphere and rarefied atmosphere of a Supreme Commander, where he would be free to devote his time to the political and inter-allied problems, whilst we inserted under him one of our own commanders to deal with the military situations and to restore the necessary drive and coordination which had been so seriously lacking."

Ike made it known that he would be no figurehead, letting others take responsibility for the key decisions. He rejected the British tradition of command by committee, saying that he would hold authority "under the principle of unified command." Through his forceful stand, he saw the British recognize him as Supreme Allied Commander. In a letter to John, Ike said the speculation about a British general for the supreme command had been justified. "Such a development could easily have come about," he said, "and I assure you I would have been very proud to serve under Alexander or any other of the seniors in this region. They are extraordinarily able men. However, you must not worry what happens to me in this war, particularly with regard to rank and assignment. Personal fortunes mean nothing—the job is to win the war. I am still a Lieutenant Colonel of the regular Army, and I think a pretty good one."

In February, the Allies suffered an embarrassing setback. Rommel staged a fierce attack through the Kasserine Pass with Panzers and infantry, supported by the Luftwaffe. Faulty intelligence had contributed to the success of the German thrust. Sources had predicted an attack from the north, but Rommel's thrust came from the south. The Allied air-support system was poorly coordinated and the inexperience of American infantry and armored units was painfully evident. There were more than five thousand American casualties.

Rommel moved northward, expecting a supporting attack by Arnim's Fifth Panzer Army to help deliver the knockout blow. When the reinforcements did not materialize, Rommel retreated. Ike, sensing Rommel's withdrawal, called for an immediate counterattack. His commanders, still reeling from the earlier attack, were hesitant. Their inaction permitted Rommel to escape. Ike subsequently removed General Lloyd Fredendall as commander of the II Corps. Fredendall had lost Dwight's confidence, and his steadiness as a combat commander was questionable at best.

The debacle at Kasserine Pass was not easily forgotten. Ike wrote Gerow: "I wish that every Division Commander could go up there right now and see the consequences, the appalling consequences, of failure to achieve in advance some measure of battlefield discipline, to teach his men the essentials of scouting, patrolling and security. . . . We have the greatest material in the world but our men must learn what a serious business this is, they must know that their own lives depend upon the thoroughness with which they learn the lessons taught, and officers that fail to devote themselves completely and exclusively to the task must be ruthlessly weeded out. Considerations of friendship, family, kindliness, and nice personality have nothing whatsoever to do with the problem. . . . For God's sake, don't keep anybody around that you say to yourself, 'He may get by'—he won't."

In the command shakeup, Ike called Patton from Morocco to replace Fredendall. At Patton's request, Omar Bradley was appointed his deputy. Ike regarded Patton as the dynamic, aggressive leader he needed to capitalize on the American defeat. "Morale in the II Corps was shaken and the troops had to be picked up quickly," Ike later recalled. "For such a job Patton had no superior in the Army."

Dwight lectured Patton about his battlefield flamboyance. "Your personal courage is something you do not have to prove to me," he said, "and I want you as Corps Commander—not as a casualty." Patton's major duty, Ike said, was to rehabilitate his forces. "You must not retain for one instant any man in a responsible position where you have become doubtful of his ability to do his job. We cannot afford to throw away soldiers and equipment and, what is even more important, effectiveness in defeating our enemies, because we are reluctant to damage the feelings of old friends. This matter frequently calls for more courage than any other thing you will have to do, but I expect you to be perfectly cold-blooded about it."

Patton succeeded in rebuilding the American units, yet Alexander persisted in having doubts about their effectiveness. Alexander enraged Patton and irritated Ike by using the Americans in a secondary and supporting capacity. When Alexander cut the Americans out of the plans for the final drive on Tunis, Ike intervened. The Americans were to have their own sector, he said. Alexander reminded Dwight of the disaster at Kasserine Pass. Dwight's rejoinder was that the British had been given much American equipment which might have prevented that defeat. Alexander unleashed Patton.

The joint Anglo-American offensive moved forward against stubborn Axis resistance. On May 7, the Allies captured Tunis. Six days later, some 275,000 German and Italian prisoners were taken, including the leading commanders. The victory in North Africa meant Ike had passed the test as military and political events closed in on him.

Churchill cabled Ike his congratulations "on the brilliant result of the North African campaign by the Army under your supreme direction."

As the fighting ceased, Ike had little time to celebrate the conquest of Africa. The invasion of Sicily and Italy, described by Churchill as Europe's "soft underbelly," was on the horizon.

Chapter Ten

PRODIGY'S PROGRESS

President Roosevelt summoned Ike to the Oval Office for a meeting in early June of 1942. Winston Churchill and General Mark Clark were there to discuss plans for the first Allied offensive. When the conference ended, Roosevelt detained Ike.

"You know what I've been doing all morning?" Roosevelt asked. Ike said he didn't know. "Well," Roosevelt said, "I've been trying to decide among four competing bureaus where to put your baby brother. He's giving me an awful lot of trouble. I have to decide which will be lucky enough to get him."

Service in three administrations had given Milton more experience in shaping national policy than most of Roosevelt's trouble shooters. As a civil-service career man, he had a strong sense of independence and growing confidence in himself. In 1939, he had been offered a deanship at Penn State. The college administrative post interested him, but he was reluctant to leave the Roosevelt administration where his rapport with the President and his immediate superior, Secretary Henry A. Wallace, had given him power and influence. Milton wrote Ike, then in the Philippines: "Finally, I am not certain that I would be entirely happy in work that lacked the rigorous demands on many fronts that I encounter here."

Milton remained at Agriculture, but within a year he was having second thoughts about his decision. Wallace in 1940 became Roosevelt's Vice President. If Milton was pleased with Wallace's nomination and election to the nation's second highest office, he was also disappointed that Wallace was leaving the department where so much had been accomplished under his leadership. The appointment of Indiana hog farmer Claude R. Wickard as Wallace's successor offended Milton. "Wickard was a practical farmer," Milton said years later, "yet he had no capacity for running a great department. He was by no means the intellectual that Wallace and Tugwell were. And he would not delegate authority as Wallace had done so skillfully. He didn't trust anyone."

Wickard, a thick-set man of medium height, looked and talked like a small-town farmer. After a term in the Indiana legislature, he came to Washington in the 1930s as assistant director of the corn and hog section of the AAA. He later became director of his section and, in the winter of 1940, became Undersecretary. His promotion to Secretary came in August, following the Democratic Convention. Milton resigned as information director to devote his full efforts to his duties as land-use coordinator. His difficulties with Wickard began almost from the moment the new Secretary took office. An aide to Wickard shocked Milton by asking him the purpose of the land-use coordinating agency. Milton coolly explained the four-year history of the agency. Wickard further irritated Milton by placing additional responsibility on him. Milton became associate director of the Agriculture Extension Service.

Milton was becoming disenchanted with the department. His small staff could not handle the land-use coordinating office load and still manage the extension service. Wickard did not seem to grasp Milton's function nor listen to his advice. Milton found Wickard "inept, insensitive, and ignorant." He was scarcely able to contain his scorn.

"No offer could have induced me to leave the department," Milton later recalled. "I liked my work, was proud to have been in the department, and was devoted to its purposes. But I started losing interest."

Roosevelt kept Milton in government by giving him special assignments, some of them unrelated to agriculture. Shortly after Pearl Harbor, he asked Milton to draft plans for an Office of War

Information. Roosevelt did not want the type of propaganda network which George Creel had used during World War I to create national hysteria. He asked Milton to design a system which would provide an adequate flow of information to keep Americans and the Allies informed about the war. At the same time, the report was to recommend means of counteracting Axis propaganda. Milton proposed an Office of War Information with foreign and domestic divisions. It was an important report and Roosevelt seemed receptive to its presentation.

Milton returned to the Agriculture Department, where his office was studying a conservation plan for the seven states of the Tennessee Valley Authority. The TVA program overlapped and conflicted with four Agriculture Department agencies. Milton went to Tennessee in an attempt to resolve the differences. When he arrived in Tennessee, he received a call from the White House instructing him to report to the President.

The next morning, Milton met Roosevelt. The President, uncharacteristically, did not engage in small talk or banter. His eyes were bloodshot. He appeared pale and haggard. "Milton," he said, "your war job, starting immediately, is to set up a War Relocation Authority to move the Japanese-Americans off the Pacific Coast. I have signed an executive order which will give you full authority to do what is essential. The Attorney General will give you the necessary legal assistance and the Secreatary of War will help you with the physical arrangements." Roosevelt added, "The greatest possible speed is imperative." Milton asked and received permission to transfer his staff from the coordinating office to the War Relocation Authority. Roosevelt abruptly terminated the meeting.

A spirit of vengeance, retribution, and war hysteria had taken hold of much of the country after Pearl Harbor. Americans were not prepared for the humiliating defeat in the Pacific and vented their frustration by punishing Japanese-Americans. In California, Governor Culbert Olson and Attorney General Earl Warren fired Japanese-Americans from civil-service jobs and revoked their licenses to practice law and medicine. In New York, Mayor Fiorello La Guardia warned them not to ride on the city's subways or buses, or walk the streets.

Columnist Westbrook Pegler wrote that "the Japanese in California should be under armed guard . . . and to hell with habeas corpus until the danger is over." The volcanic Pegler's suggestion had little impact. But Walter Lippmann, the nation's most respected journalist, joined the campaign to intern Japanese-Americans in concentration camps. Lippmann said a Japanese attack on the western United States was probable. "It is a fact that the Japanese have been reconnoitering the Pacific Coast for a considerable period of time, testing and feeling out the American defenses," he wrote. Lippmann noted a certain reluctance by the Administration to enact "a policy of mass evacuation and mass internment," yet "the Pacific Coast is officially a combat zone: some part of it at any moment may be a battlefield. Nobody's constitutional rights include the right to reside and do business on a battlefield." Attorney General Francis Biddle was later to describe the Lippmann columns as a decisive factor in adopting the repressive policy.

Secretary of the Navy Frank Knox said fifth-column work had been responsible for Pearl Harbor and urged the camps to prevent future sabotage. General John DeWitt, head of the Western Defense Command, said, "The Japanese race is an enemy race and while many of them have become 'Americanized' the racial strains are undiluted." In a report to Washington, he wrote: "The very fact that no sabotage has taken place is a disturbing and confirming indication that such action will be taken." He called for concentration camps for all Japanese-Americans.

Secretary of War Henry L. Stimson also took a hard line. "Their racial characteristics are such that we cannot understand or even trust the citizen Japanese," Stimson said.

Opponents to Japanese-American internment had seen evidence to the contrary. Curtis B. Munson, a special representative of the State Department, had made a comprehensive investigation into the Japanese-Americans. Munson reported a strong admiration and attachment to the United States. Indeed, he wrote, "There is no Japanese problem on the Coast. There will be no armed uprising of Japanese. There will undoubtedly be some sabotage financed by Japan and executed largely by imported agents." Munson said, "For the most part the local Japanese are loyal to the United States or, at worst, hope that by remaining quiet they can avoid concentration camps or irresponsible mobs. We do not believe that they would be at the least any more disloyal than any other racial group in the United States with whom we went to war."

Munson said that Knox's undocumented charges of "fifth column activities" prior to Pearl Harbor had needlessly fanned racial prejudices. He suggested a statement of encouragement to Japanese-Americans from the "President or Vice President, or at least [someone] almost as high." The document was to remain classified until after the war, and Munson's recommendations were overruled.

The Japanese-Americans had already endured years of discrimination in their adopted country. The 1924 Immigration Act banned further immigrants from Japan and denied citizenship to some 47,000 Japanese then living in the United States. These aliens, known as the Issei, could not own land, vote, or intermarry with whites. Their children, the Nisei, were American citizens by birth. They attended public schools and many of them helped their parents in small businesses such as farms or commercial fishing boats. Ninety percent of the nation's 127,000 Japanese-Americans lived on the Pacific Coast.

In the weeks after Pearl Harbor, they suffered hateful abuse. California Attorney General Earl Warren ordered banks to impound their funds. Merchants, including grocery stores, prohibited them from shopping. "Japs Shaved—not responsible for accidents," said a sign in a California barbershop. Vigilante mobs in Los Angeles and San Francisco broke windows in Japanese shops. Fishing boats were vandalized and fishing nets ripped apart.

Warren, at the time a candidate for governor of California, contributed further to the anti-Japanese hysteria by publicly charging that Japanese farmers had carefully and with malice "infiltrated themselves into every strategic spot in our coastal and valley counties." There were 5,135 Japanese-operated farms in California, covering 226,094 acres and with an estimated value of $65 million. In addition, the Japanese owned nearly half of the truck crops and some 1,000 produce stores with a value of more than $60 million. Among the white population, there was some economic motivation for the internment of all Japanese. The Native Sons and

Daughters of the Golden West, an organization whose members included prominent politicians, newspaper publishers, and businessmen, had spent more than thirty years trying to get rid of the Japanese. Warren's manipulation of the Japanese issue was not unlike the race baiting of other successful California politicians.

Warren told federal officials not to be deceived by the apparent loyalty of the Japanese-Americans, that this was a clear sign of how skillful their sabotage was. "It looks very much to me as though it is a studied effort not to have any until the zero hour comes," he said. A few days later, Warren asserted, "There is more potential danger among the group of Japanese who were born in this country than from the alien Japanese." There was much irony in Warren's leadership in the fight for removal and segregation of the Japanese for in later life he was to become a crusader for racial equality, deeply committed to freedom and social justice.

West Coast congressmen pressed for internment with near unanimity. A congressional committee held hearings in California, putting further pressure on Roosevelt. One of the President's closest friends, U.S. District Judge Jerome Frank, had written in December, "If ever any Americans go to a concentration camp, American democracy will go with them." A Japanese-American witness appearing before the committee asked, "Has the Gestapo come to America? Have we not risen in righteous anger at Hitler's mistreatment of the Jews? Then, is it not incongruous that citizen Americans of Japanese descent should be similarly mistreated and persecuted?" The congressmen concluded that Japanese-Americans represented a dangerous threat.

Attorney General Francis Biddle, a Philadelphia patrician with impeccable liberal credentials, was abhorred by the lynch-mob fervor. He wrote Roosevelt: "A great many West Coast people distrust the Japanese [and] various special interests would welcome their removal from good farm land and the elimination of their competition."

Biddle had publicly defended Japanese-Americans the day after Pearl Harbor. "There are in the United States many persons of Japanese extraction whose loyalty to the country, even in the present emergency, is unquestioned," he said. "It would therefore be a serious mistake to take any action against these people."

Biddle's support of civil liberties was privately ridiculed by Roosevelt. When Biddle made another plea for fairness, Roosevelt said civil liberties might apply to 99 percent but to deal firmly with the rest. Secretary of War Henry L. Stimson, whose racial views were almost a caricature of a Rudyard Kipling rajah, had won the battle for Roosevelt's mind. Stimson, not Biddle, received presidential authority to act on the evacuation. Although other cabinet members—Interior Secretary Harold Ickes and Treasury Secretary Henry Morgenthau—were also in opposition to internment, they were not consulted on the formation of the policy. Biddle made no more public utterances to try to reverse the developing policy. He advised Roosevelt that the Justice Department found no evidence of a future Japanese attack on the American mainland. Moreover, the FBI said there had been no sabotage. Biddle was for the rest of his life haunted by his failure to stand up to Stimson and Roosevelt. "If Stimson had insisted, had stood firm, as he apparently suspected that this wholesale evacuation was needless, the President would have followed his advice," he later recalled. "And if . . . I had urged the Secretary to resist the pressure of his subordinates, the result might have been different. But I was new to the Cabinet, and disinclined to insist on my view to an elder statesman whose wisdom and integrity I greatly respected."

Roosevelt signed the now infamous Executive Order 9066 on February 19, 1942, waiving the civil liberties of Japanese-Americans and approving their wholesale evacuation into concentration camps. There were only murmurs of protest. On Capitol Hill, only Senator Robert A. Taft denounced this abrogation of individual freedom. The liberal journals were strangely muted. Even the American Civil Liberties Union, which would later describe these events as "the worst single wholesale violation of civil rights of American citizens in our history," gave tacit support to the internment order. Socialist leader Norman Thomas, a cofounder of the ACLU, was critical of his liberal brethren. "What is perhaps as ominous as the evacuation of the Japanese," Thomas said, "is the general acceptance of this procedure by those who are proud to call themselves liberals."

Milton was appointed director of the War Relocation Authority on March 10. He was, years later, to remember this assignment as "the meanest, toughest, most unpleasant of my career." Yet if his conscience was troubled by the most shameful episode, he chose conformity rather than conviction. Until the fateful meeting with Roosevelt, Milton had known little about the Administration's plan for concentration camps. "The problem of the Japanese-Americans on the West Coast seemed remote and insignificant," he said.

Milton met with Assistant Secretary of War John J. McCloy and Biddle for further briefing. McCloy, an early advocate of the Japanese detention, promised full military assistance. Biddle gave Milton the services of Assistant Attorney General Tom Clark as WRA legal counsel. "The choice of Clark under the circumstances was not a fortunate one," Biddle wrote in his memoirs. Clark became a concentration camp stalwart. Milton's Agriculture Department staff responded to their WRA transfer "with enthusiasm," Milton said.

On March 25, Milton met with General DeWitt and agreed to terminate a "voluntary" evacuation program, suggesting mandatory detention for all males. DeWitt, whose racist excesses were boundless, argued that women and children should also be evacuated. Milton also met with representatives of the Japanese-American Citizens League. Their poise and dignity impressed him greatly. "I feel most deeply that when the war is over . . . we as Americans are going to regret the avoidable injustices that may have been done," he wrote in an April 1 letter to Secretary Wickard.

At a conference in Salt Lake City with the governors of ten western states, Milton suggested that Japanese-Americans could find work in the private sector in the intermountain states. He had planned to suggest a prevailing wage and health-benefit package. The governors heatedly shouted him down. Arizona Governor Sidney P. Osborn said his state would not "propose to be made a dumping ground for enemy aliens." Idaho's Chase Clark said, "Japs live like rats, breed like rats, and act like rats. We don't want them." The governors were hostile to anything less than concentration camps. Milton did not have the political strength to force a more moderate policy. Only Roosevelt could have reversed it and he had already sanctioned their demands. Milton, shaken by the meeting, which in 1977 he still described as his most traumatic experience, went along. "I spent little time pondering the moral implications of the President's decision," he later recalled.

In April and May, most of the evacuation was carried out. Two Issei committed suicide in San Francisco to avoid the humiliation and indignity of the concentration camps. Thousands of Japanese families lost their heirlooms, furniture, china, and other valued possessions. Swindlers and commercial predators descended in mobs upon Japanese homes, warning the soon-to-be evacuated families to sell their goods for a pittance or face confiscation of their property. Some families destroyed cherished objects rather than submit to the junk dealers and vultures. Businesses and farms were bought for bargain prices. The Federal Reserve Bank of San Francisco recommended liquidation to evacuees. The bank later reported that Japanese-American losses were some $400 million. Less than 10 percent would be recovered in court settlements over the next three decades. Not since the Indian wars had the American Government destroyed the economic structure of an entire people. The accumulated savings of a lifetime had vanished suddenly and almost overnight for most families. Soldiers shouted, "Out, Japs!" as truck convoys came for the evacuees.

Milton had originally proposed "small CCC sort of camps" where the Japanese-Americans could participate in work projects for the war effort and receive prevailing civilian wages. The Army and War Department persuaded him that it was impractical to establish fifty to seventy-five small camps. Larger camps, housing from five to six thousand, were easier to keep under armed guard. The Japanese were first stationed at fifteen "assembly centers," which included the Rose Bowl at Pasadena, racetracks in Santa Anita and Tanforan, the Livestock Pavilion in Portland, Oregon, and a brewery in Yakima, Washington. Families were housed in horse stalls, grandstands, and cheaply constructed shacks. The guards startled the internees. "This evacuation did not seem too unfair until we got right to the camp and were met by soldiers with guns and bayonets," recalled one Nisei. "Then I almost started screaming." There was no privacy in the camps, which came as a culture shock to the modest Japanese. The latrines included rows of built-in toilets without partitions or doors; constipation became widespread. Women were forced to bathe in outdoor shower stalls within view of the armed guards. Several families were herded together to sleep in one communal room or stall. Mud mixed with raw sewage after spring rainfall.

During April and May, Milton settled on sites for the ten concentration camps. They were on desolate desert flatlands east of the Sierra Nevada mountains, on the Gila desert in Arizona, and at Tule Lake, in an isolated corner of northern California's Siskiyou County. Milton told a congressional budget committee that camp construction "is so very cheap that, frankly, if it stands up for the duration we are going to be lucky." He said some camps might expect extreme weather conditions "as high as 130 degrees in summertime."

Milton referred to the camps as "evacuation centers," never admitting they were concentration camps. Yet Roosevelt himself termed them "concentration camps" and the Japanese considered themselves prisoners behind the barbed wire and guard towers. The camps denied them any more privacy than the "assembly centers" had permitted. Families shared single rooms with strangers. The mess-hall meals were devoid of milk, meat, fresh fruit, or vegetables, and more reminiscent of a prison diet than military-prepared food. Their dishes were often unwashed, for there was almost no hot water. All Japanese phonograph records and reading materials were confiscated with the exceptions of Bibles, hymn books, and dictionaries. The camp newsletters, published by the internees, could publish only brief announcements or propaganda favorable to the WRA. Those who questioned such procedures were thrown into solitary confinement.

"This whole policy of resort to concentration camps is headed . . . toward the destruction of constitutional rights . . . and toward the establishment of racial discrimination as a principle of American government," the *Christian Century* wrote. "It is moving in the same direction Germany moved." Milton did not welcome such criticism, and he referred mail critical of the policy to the War Department.

He wrote the White House on May 15: "As you know, quite a little mail is being received by the President from liberal groups and kindhearted people protesting the evacuation. Much of it questions the military necessity of the program. . . . Since this Authority cannot appropriately speak on military questions, we have been forwarding it to the Assistant Secretary of War John McCloy. May I suggest that such mail be sent directly to Mr. McCloy?"

Interior Secretary Ickes did not think Milton had done an adequate job and attacked his record at a June 5 meeting of the Cabinet. Vice President Wallace wrote in his diary: "Ickes criticized Milton Eisenhower for doing a bad job in relocating the Japs on the Indian reservations. When it was suggested, however, that Eisenhower be returned to Agriculture and the whole matter be put into the hands of Interior, he backed rapidly away from the problem. The Attorney General and various others spoke most highly of Eisenhower's capacity." Ickes, not one to give up easily, wrote Roosevelt a confidential note ten days later: "I have it from several sources that Eisenhauer [*sic*] is sick of the job."

Milton was, in fact, weary of the dismal experience. He had not told Roosevelt many of the sad details of the racist repression, nor had he gone public with his views of the camps. On June 16, Roosevelt relieved Milton of the WRA post with the provision that he find a suitable successor. Milton was told that another wartime assignment awaited him, the associate directorship of the Office of War Information. By coincidence, Milton had been invited to a party at the home of Dillon Myer, with whom he had worked at the Agriculture Department. As the evening went on, he asked Myer about becoming WRA director. "The past three months had been the toughest of my career," Milton said years later, "and I had lost a year's sleep." Myer recalled that Milton "was practically ill" and told him: "I can't sleep and do this job. I had to get out of it." Myer agreed to take the job if Roosevelt wanted him. Roosevelt quickly made the appointment official.

In his concluding report Milton wrote Roosevelt: "The future of the program [WRA] will doubtless be governed largely by the temper of American public opinion. Already public attitudes have exerted a strong influence in shaping the program and charting its direction. In a democracy this is unquestionably sound and proper. Yet in leaving the War Relocation Authority after a few extremely crowded weeks, I cannot help expressing the hope that the American people will grow toward a broader appreciation of the essential Americanism of a great majority of the evacuees and of the difficult sacrifice they are making."

Milton suggested that Roosevelt "issue a strong public statement in behalf of the loyal American citizens who are now bewildered and wonder what is in store for them." He also urged, "at the appropriate time . . . a more liberal wage policy."

"If public opinion had permitted," he wrote, "it might have been preferable in many ways to pay WPA wages to members of the work corps and to provide their families with subsistence in addition. This would have been more in keeping with the spirit of the Geneva Convention. I sincerely hope that changing public attitudes will later on permit a change in this severe wage policy."

Roosevelt, who showed little sensitivity to the plight of the Japanese-Americans, was not responsive to Milton's recommendations. Indeed, nearly a year later he would forward a complaint about the WRA by Ickes to Milton for comment, forgetting that a new director had been appointed. By this time, Milton was ready to speak out about the injustices of the camps.

His letter to the President was candid:

> My friends in the War Relocation Authority, like Secretary Ickes, are deeply distressed over the effects of the entire evacuation and relocation program upon the Japanese-Americans, particularly upon the young citizen group. Persons in this group find themselves living in an atmosphere for which their public school and democratic teachings have not prepared them. It is hard for them to escape a conviction that their plight is due more to racial discrimination, economic motivations, and wartime prejudices than to any real necessity from the military point of view for evacuation from the West Coast.
>
> Life in a relocation center cannot possibly be pleasant. The

> evacuees are surrounded by barbed wire fences under the eye of armed military police. They have suffered heavily in property losses; they have lost their businesses and their means of support. The State Legislatures, Members of the Congress, and local groups, by their actions and statements bring home to them almost constantly that as a people they are not welcome anywhere. States in which they are now located have enacted restrictive legislation forbidding permanent resettlement, for example. The American Legion, many local groups, and city councils have approved discriminatory resolutions, going so far in some instances as to advocate confiscation of their property.
>
> Furthermore, in the opinion of the evacuees the Government may not be excused for not having attempted to distinguish between the loyal and the disloyal in carrying out the evacuation. Under such circumstances it would be amazing if extreme bitterness did not develop.

Milton said the WRA could either "build permanent relocation centers" or "strike out vigorously in helping the loyal become reabsorbed in normal American communities during the war period." He preferred the second alternative and indicated that Myer was striving to do just that. For all his good intentions, Myer was unable to bring about large-scale releases. In 1944, the Supreme Court upheld the internment as Justice Hugo Black wrote that military considerations rather than racial prejudice were behind the camps. "To cast this case into outlines of racial prejudice, without reference to the real military dangers which were present, merely confuses the issue," wrote Black. Justice Owen J. Roberts, dissenting, wrote that the policy was "nothing but a cleverly disguised trap to accomplish the real purpose of military authority, which was to lock him [Korematzu] up in a concentration camp."

The role which Milton had played in the tragedy was not easily forgotten. He said the "only pleasant memory" of the period was the presentation of a gift to him by Mike Masaokoa on behalf of the Japanese-American Advisory Committee. Milton said Masaokoa expressed gratitude for trying to carry out the evacuation in their interest. "I believe to this day that most of the evacuation could have been avoided had not false and flaming statements been dinned into the people of the West Coast by irresponsible commentators and politicians," Milton wrote in his memoirs, published in 1974. "I have brooded about this whole episode on and off for the past three decades, for it is illustrative of how an entire society can somehow plunge off course."

Yale historian John Morton Blum has written: "Eisenhower and his successor, Dillon Myer, both decent men, had hoped to pursue a principled policy, but it developed predictably that a principled internment, like a principled evacuation, was no more possible than a principled genocide."

Other historians have been more critical. Eugene V. Rostow wrote in the *Yale Law Journal* shortly after the war:

> The course of action which we undertook was in no way required or justified by circumstances of war. It was calculated to produce both individual injustice and deep-seated social maladjustments of a cumulative and sinister kind. . . . We believe that the German people bear a common political responsibility for outrages secretly committed by the Gestapo and the SS. What are we to think of our own part in a program which violates every democratic social value, yet has been approved by the Congress, the President and the Supreme Court?

Milton was for years publicly silent about his WRA period and until the recent declassification of WRA papers and the publication of his memoirs there was little documentary evidence that he had disagreed with the policy. Some observers have made the argument that Milton was a "war criminal." Historian Roger Daniels, in his study *Concentration Camps USA*, concluded: "By the stern standards of the Nuremberg Tribunal then, Eisenhower, who acquiesced in an atrocity and who helped to execute it, was as guilty as Gullion, the Provost Marshal General, Bendetsen, DeWitt, McCloy, Stimson, Roosevelt, and all the other prime architects of policy."

Above all, Milton had been the team player. Like most

members of government, he did not consider resigning under protest. Had he been more vociferous in his criticism, the horrors of the internment policy would have shocked many Americans. But loyalty to the President, especially in wartime, was of greater urgency to Milton than democratic ideals. His conscience would painfully remind him of his silence during that fateful spring.

Milton's next assignment, as associate director of OWI, was more to his liking. The Bureau of the Budget had requested him, and the Agriculture Department wanted him back, but Roosevelt thought OWI was the most critical area for Milton's organizational talents. The director was Elmer Davis, then fifty-two, a native of Indiana and Rhodes scholar who had become one of the pioneers of radio commentary. Davis had given up a fifty-three-thousand-dollar salary with CBS to request active service in the Navy. Roosevelt persuaded him to take the OWI directorship and Davis agreed if the President also named an associate director "skilled in governmental organization and information matters." The New York *Herald Tribune* said Milton had been chosen because he was "an expert in cutting snarled red tape and had a specialist's knowledge of which heads are useful and which should be lopped off."

Some months earlier Milton had outlined the proposal for OWI: a merger of the Office of Facts and Figures, the Office of Government Reports, the information service of the Office of Emergency Management, and a part of Colonel William J. "Wild Bill" Donovan's Office of Coordinator of Information.

The executive order which authorized OWI said its function was "to coordinate the dissemination of war information by all federal agencies and to formulate and carry out, by means of the press, radio and motion pictures, programs designed to facilitate an understanding in the United States and abroad of the progress of the war effort and of the policies, activities, and aims of the government."

Davis had an early confrontation with Admiral Ernest King for withholding news about an American defeat in the South Pacific on the basis that it would have given the Japanese an opportunity to inflict far greater damage. Davis sharply disagreed. From then on, Milton served as his liaison with the War and Navy departments.

Milton met daily with Davis. They both sat down with agency chiefs who comprised the Board of War Information. Members of the group included Archibald MacLeish, former Librarian of Congress and head of the OFF; playwright Robert Sherwood, Roosevelt's most gifted speech writer and head of OWI's overseas branch; and *Look* publisher Gardner Cowles, Jr., head of OWI's domestic branch, Davis; and Milton. This panel, which shaped OWI policy, had diverse opinions about how far it could go. MacLeish, an outspoken liberal and internationalist, wanted OWI to define the ideals America was fighting for. Milton, always cautious, disagreed. "We know," he wrote Davis, "that in the end the people as a whole will decide . . . and we may also be certain that we will not be completely satisfied with the decision. For that decision will be a compromise between widely divergent economic and political views.

"We must maintain our policy of objectivity," he said. "OWI . . . should continue to be thought of primarily as an information agency." Milton advised MacLeish: "Our job is to promote an understanding of policy, not to make policy." MacLeish still did not accept the concept of a mere news agency, or "issuing mechanism."

In any case, Davis backed Milton. Davis left his associate most of OWI's administrative duties. Milton's task in eliminating the overlapping functions of the parent agencies was reminiscent of his Land Use Co-Ordinating Office. When the Board of War Information adopted a policy, Milton was charged with implementing it. The *American Political Science Review* noted in February of 1943: "The product in large measure of the work of its associate director, M. S. Eisenhower, the OWI brings to the public opinion problems facing the United States a degree of unified control and direction hitherto unattained."

Through his position Milton was able to help protect Dwight's reputation. His December 1942 flight to North Africa did involve work on a propaganda program for the Mediterranean theater and a presidential study on refugee relief in North Africa, but some observers felt he viewed Dwight's career as the paramount issue.

"I was of course concerned about the criticism being leveled at General Eisenhower," Milton wrote years later. On Milton's return, he spoke with Roosevelt, Vice President Wallace, and Chief of Staff George Marshall about Robert Murphy, Dwight's political adviser.

"He feels that Murphy has given his brother, General Eisenhower, poor advice," Wallace wrote in his wartime diary. "Milton feels very strongly that his brother should not be called on to do both military and political work but he also feels that his brother ought to have sound political advice. Milton thinks that Murphy is bad either because of lack of ability or shorthandedness."

Milton's protests about Murphy did not force the recall of the reactionary, pro-Vichy, State Department official, yet his defense of Ike and his presence in North Africa may have helped his elder brother persevere through his first political crisis. The assassination of Darlan was, however, a greater factor in Dwight's survival. When the sinister Peyrouton was named governor of Algeria in January, Milton again complained to Wallace about the Murphy influence. *The New Republic* editorially called for Murphy's removal. However, the White House and State Department supported their embattled diplomat. As Dwight's position became more secure, Milton was less outspoken about the quality of his advisers.

Some of the newsmen in OWI questioned Milton's commitment to disseminate anything more controversial than facts and figures. Palmer Hoyt, a onetime Western novelist and publisher of the Portland *Oregonian*, succeeded Cowles as OWI's domestic chief in 1943. "Milton just wasn't a guy of great decisive qualities," Hoyt said later.

Hoyt had authorized an investigation of gas rationing and pricing. His reporters uncovered price fixing and other irregularities. Oil-company officials, Hoyt said, tried to block the release of the report, as did Interior Secretary Ickes. "I didn't get any help from Milton," Hoyt said. "He just wouldn't stick his neck out. I finally told Ickes that we goddamned well were going to release it."

If Milton was hesitant to get involved in such infighting, he chafed when overseas OWI broadcasters attacked the political settlement in Italy which followed Mussolini's resignation. OWI commentators described King Victor Emmanuel and the new premier, Marshal Pietro Badoglio, as "Fascists." Although both men were, in fact, Fascists, Roosevelt angrily spoke out against OWI at a news conference. Milton said the OWI men had been guilty of "insubordination, almost treason." Sherwood defended them for reporting the truth. Davis and Milton did not. Roosevelt was dubious about OWI for the duration of his presidency. On a personal level, Milton continued to hold Roosevelt's friendship and perform special assignments for the White House. He was Roosevelt's personal agent in setting up the Quebec Conference with Churchill, where limited recognition was given to the Free French headed by De Gaulle. After setting the agenda with British, American, and Canadian diplomats, Milton arranged to make the return flight to Washington on a British two-engine plane. A fire broke out while the plane was in flight and Milton prepared to parachute before it was brought under control. The plane returned to Canada for repairs and Milton secured another flight.

Kansas State College approached Milton about succeeding F. D. Farrell as president. Davis gave Milton permission to talk with the college regents. After a brief visit to Kansas, Milton returned to Washington and received a formal offer by mail.

Milton wrote Dwight on April 12 that he was leaning toward acceptance, confiding that he might "feel that I was running away from a necessary and pretty arduous war post."

Dwight responded on April 20: "I regard the position described in your letter as one of public trust and offering opportunities for public service to challenge the talents of any man. I think the only question to be decided is whether or not your present position can be adequately filled by another individual without diminishing the coordination with other important governmental agencies. From your personal viewpoint, this should appear to be a real opportunity and it, therefore, becomes merely a question of the greatest service you can render the country at this time. Assuming that your leaving your present position would not precipitate any organizational crisis, my own inclination would be to accept the job in the belief that over a period of years it would allow you to be a real factor toward influencing a healthy development of young America."

Later that week, Dwight wrote Charles Moreau Harger, one of those responsible for Milton's nomination: "I felt he should accept the presidency. It is an outstanding position of service and one in which he can be of substantial assistance to prosecution of the war."

Milton found Dwight's comments reassuring, although he later said one motivating factor was that he thought the presidency would be easier than his Washington career. Indeed, he anticipated opportunities to write articles for national magazines and engage in scholarly research. He was also tiring of the occupational hazards of OWI. Roosevelt had not, he said, helped rebuild the "prestige and strength of OWI."

He accepted the Kansas State offer in mid-May and took office on July 1. "I was eager to be, for the first time in my life, the top man in an organization," he recalled years later. Milton's one condition was that the regents allow him to continue his government service as an unpaid consultant. But he never saw Roosevelt again, for the college presidency would prove to be more demanding and time-consuming than he had ever expected.

Chapter Eleven

THE SUPREME COMMAND

The American high command had wanted to begin preparations for the cross-Channel invasion following the triumph in North Africa. But at Casablanca the British had successfully argued for the thrust into Europe's "soft underbelly," invasions of Sicily and then Italy. Ike was to remain as Supreme Commander. The July 10 invasion of Sicily was the greatest amphibious assault in history, some 250,000 soldiers landed along a front of one hundred miles. Ike had been urged to postpone the invasion by some of his subordinates. As would later be the case at Normandy, the operation was threatened by stormy weather. The sea became rough and choppy, throwing ships off course. High winds were upsetting flight patterns. Ike was against postponement because it might force a delay of up to three weeks. When General Marshall asked him about the uncertain weather conditions, Dwight answered decisively: "The operation will proceed as scheduled in spite of an unfortunate westerly wind that may interfere somewhat with the landing of U.S. troops."

There were some difficulties in the landings, yet the weather worked to Allied advantage. The Italians had not expected an attack under such conditions and were caught by surprise. They offered feeble resistance as the Allies took seven beaches in southeastern Sicily. Ike's gamble had worked. His concept of beach landings was effectively demonstrated and would become standard Allied strategy.

The rest of the campaign was harder as the 350,000 Germans and Italians mobilized and fought back. Bad weather hampered Allied airborne landings and resulted in some mistaken antiaircraft fire by the Allies. For more than a month, the fighting continued. Patton again exhibited his innovative and aggressive leadership as his Seventh Army pushed northward to Palermo, then turned eastward and beat Montgomery's British Eighth Army to capture Messina, which closed the campaign. Some 135,000 Axis troops were taken prisoner and 32,000 were killed or wounded. Another 100,000 retreated into Italy. The Allies suffered 25,000 casualties. Although the campaign had taken longer than Ike expected, his victory was of enormous strategic and psychological importance. The Mediterranean was now an Allied sea route. Mussolini was deposed and arrested by the Fascist Grand Council after Patton's stunning victory at Palermo. The new government, headed by Marshal Pietro Badoglio, promised allegiance to the Axis, but secretly began peace negotiations with the Allies. The Germans, who had infiltrated into the highest levels of Italian Government, sent reinforcements to northern Italy. Field Marshal Albert Kesselring, the German commander in southern Italy, anticipated an Allied invasion and occupied most of the region.

Ike wrote Marshall after Sicily was in Allied hands: "Your personal approval is the highest award I could seek. . . . We are all extremely proud of the smooth functioning during the Sicilian campaign of the Allied team, among all services. The aggressiveness, determination, skill and cooperative spirit of all naval, air and ground units were exemplary."

He elaborated on the Sicilian campaign in an August 18 letter to John: "The Sicilian campaign is finished. Naturally, it is always a disappointment when a single one of your enemy escapes but, in this particular case, the most strenuous efforts of air, ground and sea could not prevent the German getting some of his troops back across the Straits of Messina. However, he was a thoroughly beaten enemy and was glad to save what he could."

For Ike, the greatest crisis of the Sicilian invasion and one of the most thorny problems he faced during the war, was the Patton slapping incident. Patton was among Ike's oldest friends and was rapidly becoming a military legend. His indomitable spirit and his gift for inspiring American troops moved Ike to observe that Patton's army was "a fighting force that is not excelled in effectiveness by any other of equal size in the world." Yet if Patton's self-confidence and impulsiveness were assets on the battlefield, the same hubris away from the combat zone nearly destroyed his career. When Patton was visiting some military hospitals on August 10, he was deeply moved by the agony and suffering of wounded soldiers. He slapped and verbally abused two soldiers afflicted with battle neurosis, describing one of the men as a "yellow son of a bitch." The soldier wept and Patton ordered him out of the hospital. "I won't have these brave men here who have been shot seeing a yellow bastard sitting here crying," Patton said. Ike received a report of the incident one week later from his surgeon general.

Ike told the surgeon general, "I guess I'll have to give General Patton a jacking up." He ordered an investigation, but he was hesitant to make the matter public. "If this thing ever gets out," Ike said, "they'll be howling for Patton's scalp, and that will be the end of Georgie's service in this war. I simply cannot let that happen. Patton is indispensable to the war effort—one of the guarantors of our victory." A cover-up was thought to be the safest method of keeping the preeminent Allied field commander in uniform. Ike told Butcher that he "might have to send Patton home in disgrace."

He wrote Patton a stern letter of reprimand:

> I am attaching a report which is shocking in its allegations against your personal conduct. I hope you can assure me that none of them is true, but the detailed circumstances communicated to me lead to the belief that some ground for the charges must exist. I am well aware of the necessity for hardness and toughness on the battlefield. I clearly understand that firm and drastic measures are at times necessary in order to secure desired objectives. But this does not excuse

> brutality, abuse of the sick, nor exhibitions of uncontrollable temper in front of subordinates. . . .
>
> It is acutely distressing to me to have such charges as those made against you at the very moment when an American Army under your leadership has attained a success of which I am extremely proud. . . . If there is a very considerable element of truth in the allegations accompanying this letter, I must so seriously question your good judgment and your self-discipline as to raise serious doubt in my mind as to your future usefulness.
>
> No letter that I have been called upon to write in my military career has caused me the mental anguish of this one, not only because of my long and deep personal friendship for you but because of my admiration for your military qualities; but I assure you that conduct such as described in the accompanying report will not be tolerated in this theater no matter who the offender may be.

Patton apologized to the soldiers he had struck and wrote Ike a letter of apology. Ike had promised to keep the reprimand secret. However, some war correspondents learned of the incident and were able to document the charges. Their first proposal was to sit on the story only if Patton were removed from command. Dwight met with the three enterprising reporters: Quentin Reynolds of *Collier's*, Demaree Bess of *The Saturday Evening Post*, and Merrill "Red" Mueller of NBC. Ike, who had earlier taken the same correspondents into his confidence, was popular with the press corps. His briefings had given reporters more "inside" information than they were accustomed to getting from a commander of his standing. So when Ike pleaded on Patton's behalf, the war correspondents were sympathetic. A gentleman's agreement was reached with the reporters and the story was not filed.

Columnist Drew Pearson broke the story on November 21 during his national radio program. Pearson, sensing he had one of the biggest exclusives of the war, predicted that Patton would never again hold a position of responsibility. The commentator implicated Ike in the cover-up, charging that he had not so much as given Patton a reprimand.

Ike was further embarrassed when his own chief of staff, "Beetle" Smith, told reporters that Patton had never been reprimanded. A great storm of protest followed. Congressmen threatened to veto Patton's promotion to major general. The war correspondents vented their frustration and remorse at having participated in the cover-up. Ike received hundreds of letters from parents and American citizens which questioned his handling of the affair. Marshall himself asked for an explanation.

In his response, Ike explained the incident and his reprimand. "It is true that General Patton was guilty of reprehensible conduct with respect to two enlisted men," he advised Marshall. "After exhaustive investigation, including a personal visit to Sicily, I decided that the corrective action as described above was adequate and suitable in the circumstances. I still believe that this decision is sound. As a final word it has been reported many times to me that in every recent public appearance of Patton before any crowd composed of his own soldiers, he is greeted by thunderous applause."

Patton had reason to be concerned about the pressures from Washington. Ike wired him: "It is my judgment that this storm will blow over because our reporters here have generally sent forward very accurate stories including an account of my action with respect to you and of your corrective measures. I must stress again to you the necessity for acting deliberately at all times and avoiding the giving way to impulse." Patton expressed his regret at causing Ike further trouble.

In the meantime, the Italian campaign was meeting heavy resistance. Montgomery and the Eighth Army had landed in Calabria, on the toe of southern Italy on September 3 with almost no resistance. On the same day, a secret armistice between Italy and the Allies was signed, to go into effect on September 8. Ike was to announce the surrender as the Allies went ashore at Salerno. Badoglio sent a message to Ike seeking a delay. "Badoglio has gummed up the works," Ike confided to Omar Bradley at lunch.

He did not intend to let Badoglio renounce the carefully negotiated treaty. He notified the aging Fascist: "I intend to broadcast the existence of the armistice at the hour originally planned. If you or any part of your armed forces fail to cooperate as previously agreed I will publish to the world full record of this affair. . . . I do not accept your message of this morning postponing the armistice. Your accredited representative has signed an agreement with me and the sole hope of Italy is bound up in your adherence to that agreement." Dwight did make one concession, calling a halt to an air drop on Rome, "on your earnest representation."

"Plans have been made on the assumption that you were acting in good faith," Ike concluded. "Failure now on your part to carry out the full obligations of the signed agreement will have most serious consequences for your country. No future action of yours could then restore any confidence whatever in your good faith and consequently the dissolution of your government and nation would ensue."

Ike did not hear from Badoglio, yet he went ahead with his broadcast from Algiers. In his familiar voice, he declared: "This is General Dwight D. Eisenhower, commander in chief of the Allied forces. The Italian Government has surrendered its armed forces unconditionally. As Allied commander in chief I have granted a military armistice, the terms of which have been approved by the governments of the United States, Great Britain, and the Union of Soviet Socialist Republics. . . . Hostilities between the armed forces of the United Nations and those of Italy terminate at once. All Italians who now act to help eject the German aggressor from Italian soil will have the assistance and support of the United Nations."

The Allied troops, only hours before their invasion, listened to Ike's message on the ships which would take them to the Italian mainland. The men were optimistic that their mission had been accomplished with the Italian surrender. Badoglio himself confirmed the terms in a broadcast over Radio Rome which he delivered ninety minutes after Dwight's announcement. The Italian Navy, obeying the armistice, sailed for Malta from Genoa, La Spezia, and Taranto. The fleet's flagship, *Roma,* was attacked and sunk by the Luftwaffe, but the rest of the fleet surrendered at Malta.

Those hoping for a peaceful conquest of Italy were bitterly disappointed. German forces were waiting when Lieutenant General

Mark Clark and the American Fifth Army landed at Salerno before dawn. They managed to control only four unconnected beachheads.

Ike reported to the Combined Chiefs of Staff that the invasion "will be a matter of touch and go for the next few days." He added, "If the enemy really appreciates correctly the size of our build-up, we are in for some very tough fighting."

The Germans launched massive counterattacks from the rocky hills above the beaches. On September 12, they nearly broke through the middle of the Allied beachhead. In the fierce battle, the Allies managed to hold their ground, supported by naval gunfire. Ike had also ordered tactical air support to check the German offensive. His strategy secured the beachhead and forced Kesselring into his northward retreat. Within two weeks, the Allies controlled Naples. At Salerno, Allied losses were more than fifteen thousand men—double the German casualties. The battle enabled Germany to consolidate its hold on northern Italy while staging a deliberate withdrawal from the south. The Germans disarmed Italian troops throughout Italy, in southern France, and the Balkans. They established a puppet government in northern Italy with Mussolini as chief of state. The mountainous terrain gave Germans a strategic advantage for the remainder of the campaign. Ike's decision to cancel the air drop on Rome was based on poor advice from General Maxwell D. Taylor of the 82nd Airborne Division and the frightened Badoglio. They had grossly overestimated German strength around the great city. Joseph Goebbels had written in his diary: "Naturally we shall not be able to hold Southern Italy. We must withdraw northward beyond Rome." Staying in Rome, Goebbels wrote, was "too dangerous." Kesselring agreed that Rome would be defenseless against an Allied air assault. Even after it was canceled, Italian soldiers there held the Germans at bay for two days.

After this lost opportunity, the Allies were to spend eight months in a bloody, seemingly fruitless struggle to capture Rome. Although the Allies had numerical superiority, the terrain occupied by the Germans was difficult to penetrate. War correspondent Ernie Pyle, who wrote vividly of the Italian campaign, said that American soldiers "lived like men of prehistoric times, and a club would have become them more than a machine gun." Miserable weather conditions placed additional burdens on them. All this might have been avoided had Ike held to his convictions in September.

He discussed his concept of an Allied command in a memorandum to Lord Mountbatten, who had just been named Supreme Allied Commander of the Southeast Asia theater. Mountbatten had asked him to write something "on the pitfalls to avoid and the line you consider one should take up" as a supreme commander. "Your senior commanders will probably be named for you by the Combined Chiefs of Staff and their duties may even be prescribed in some detail," Ike wrote. "Fundamentally this is an error since it tends to weaken an authority that has no legal basis, such as exists in a single national fleet, army or air force. Moreover, it can be wrecked at any moment not only by dissatisfaction on the part of either Government, but by internal bickering." He stressed that the commanders in chief must have "a great degree of independence," but that "all communications to the Combined Chiefs of Staff must pass through you and no one else must be allowed to send communications to that body."

Ike added: "To form your staff, start from the bottom up. Make sure that in every section . . . are officers of both nationalities and never permit any problem to be approached in your staff on the basis of national interest." He said that the British system of command should only apply in British Empire operations, but not in Anglo-American joint operations.

"The thing you must strive for is the utmost in mutual respect and confidence among the group of seniors making up the Allied command," he said. "All of us are human and we like to be favorably noticed by those above us and even by the public. An Allied commander in chief, among all others practicing the art of war, must more sternly than any other individual repress such notions. He must be self-effacing, quick to give credit, ready to meet the other fellow more than halfway, must seek and absorb advice, and must learn to decentralize. On the other hand, when the time comes that he himself feels he must make a decison, he must make it in clean-cut fashion and on his own responsibility and take full blame for anything that goes wrong." Several months earlier, Ike had rejected a suggestion to appoint an assistant for public relations. "I abhor the idea insofar as it implies that I should consciously seek publicity," Ike responded to General Charles Douglas Herron, who had made the proposal. "Perhaps my feeling on this matter has become crystallized into belligerence because of many years of service in Washington where I saw so many 'glory hoppers.' To me a press agent means phony or promoted stories which to the discerning speak for themselves."

Ike told Mountbatten that an Allied commander in chief was not a commander in the sense of personally leading a great fleet into battle, but "in no sense of the word, is he a figurehead or a nonentity. He is in a very definite sense the chairman of a board, a chairman that has very definite executive responsibilities. . . . He must execute those duties firmly, wisely and without any question as to his own authority and his own responsibility."

For all his self-effacing comments about publicity, Ike had become the best-known and most popular Allied commander. No other general received such consistently favorable coverage in the public press. He enjoyed the confidence of Roosevelt, Churchill, Stalin, and Allied military commanders. His popularity with soldiers was rated enormously high. He was the symbol of Allied victory in North Africa and Sicily and the general who forced the surrender of Italy. In the fall of 1943 he was even suggested as a presidential possibility. His friend George Allen had sent him a note along with a newspaper clipping about a New York City veterans' group which had endorsed him for the presidency. "How does it feel to be a presidential candidate?" Allen asked. Ike, flustered, wrote in pencil on Allen's note: "Baloney! Why can't a simple soldier be left alone to carry out his orders? And I furiously object to the word 'candidate'—I ain't and won't." In September, Walter Winchell disclosed in his radio broadcast that Ike was in line to become Roosevelt's vice-presidential running mate if Republicans nominated Douglas MacArthur for the presidency.

"So far, no one has had the temerity to mention to me, even by insinuation, the possibility that I might become interested in a political career," Ike wrote General George Van Horn Moseley. "When this war is won, I will be glad of the chance to take things easy. In any event, I can scarcely imagine anyone in the United States less qualified than I for any type of political work."

Arthur Eisenhower, Dwight's older brother and a prominent Kansas City banker, worried that speculation about a presidential race might tarnish Ike's military image. He wrote Dwight, reporting that more and more newspaper articles were promoting his candidacy. He urged Ike to assure President Roosevelt that he had no political ambitions. Arthur reported a luncheon conversation with Senator Harry S. Truman, his onetime boardinghouse roommate. "We commented briefly on this subject," Arthur said. "He agreed with me there was only one man today whose suggestion or intimation that you be the next President was worth a continental and that man is President Roosevelt. I hope all the rest will keep their mouths shut while you are carrying on the responsibilities of the commander in chief."

Ike replied that Arthur was overreacting. "It is true that I have seen, here and there, a few careless and ill-considered items in the newspapers; but this happens to any man whose name appears with some frequency in the public print. Certainly, I feel no necessity, as yet, for making any statement whatsoever because to do so would, I think, merely be making myself ridiculous."

He added, "For a soldier to turn away from his war duty for any reason is to be guilty of treachery to his country and disloyalty to his superiors. The President is my Commander in Chief. Nothing could sway me from my purpose of carrying out faithfully his orders in whatever post he may assign me."

At this time Ike was fully aware that Roosevelt controlled his destiny. He thought Marshall or British General Sir Alan Francis Brooke would be chosen to command Overlord, the invasion of Europe. His own name was most often mentioned as Marshall's successor as Chief of Staff. Ike said he would prefer remaining as commander of the Mediterranean theater instead of returning to Washington. Elliott Roosevelt, the President's son, later recalled Dwight's "nagging worry" that Marshall would become Supreme Commander in Europe "while he, Eisenhower, would be kicked upstairs into a desk job in the Pentagon." Secretary of the Navy Frank Knox, the blustery Chicago newspaper publisher and onetime Republican vice-presidential candidate, congratulated Ike on his imminent appointment as Chief of Staff. Knox said Marshall had already been designated as Europe's Supreme Commander. Mountbatten visited Dwight shortly afterward and confided that Brooke had been promised the command, but had stepped aside in Marshall's favor when it became clear that America would be the dominant partner in the operation. Ike made it known that he would like to be one of Marshall's field commanders in Europe. His overriding concern was to remain in an active military operation.

Marshall assumed he would get the European command and advised one of his assistants, Frank McCarthy, that they would probably be transferring to London. When General Pershing protested to Roosevelt that Marshall's transfer would be a grave error, Roosevelt told the World War I hero: "I want George to be the Pershing of the Second World War." Secretary of War Stimson said only Marshall possessed the authority and prestige to keep a doubtful Churchill behind Overlord. "To make it effective, he should be there very soon," said Stimson. Marshall's departure for Europe became the subject of controversy in Washington. Military and congressional leaders made the argument that Marshall was indispensable as Chief of Staff, the one man who understood the intricacies of global warfare and commanded the respect of all the services and Allied leaders. "Why break up a winning combination," asked Fleet Admiral Ernest J. King, Chief of Naval Operations and senior member of the Joint Chiefs of Staff, reflecting the view of the other Joint Chiefs.

Roosevelt met with Ike at Oran on the eve of the Cairo summit with Churchill and Chiang Kai-shek. Dwight took the President on a guided tour of the Tunisian battlefields and they talked of some of the ancient wars which had been fought in the region. As their conversation turned to more topical matters, Roosevelt said: "Ike, you and I know who was the Chief of Staff during the last years of the Civil War but practically no one else knows, although the names of the field generals . . . every schoolboy knows them. . . . That is one of the reasons why I want George to have the big command—he is entitled to establish his place in history." Roosevelt then told Ike what had long been rumored. He was scheduled to come back to Washington as Chief of Staff.

Later in the day, Admiral King gave Ike his seal of approval. "I hate to lose General Marshall as Chief of Staff," said King, "but my loss is consoled by the knowledge that I will have you to work with in his job." King also gave Ike some hope of remaining as a commander, predicting that Roosevelt would ultimately decide to keep Marshall in Washington.

Roosevelt was indeed beginning to have doubts about the wisdom of moving Marshall. At the Teheran Conference, Stalin asked Roosevelt who would command Overlord. Roosevelt said the issue had not been settled. Stalin retorted that he would not believe in the operation until the Allies chose a Supreme Commander. "Until that is done, Overlord cannot be considered as really in progress," said Stalin. The Soviet marshal asked Churchill point-blank if the British were truly committed to the cross-Channel invasion. Churchill vowed full British support and assured Stalin that the Supreme Command would be filled in a fortnight. Roosevelt, who always had difficulty in reaching decisions on filling key positions, could stall no longer.

By December 5, at the Cairo Conference, Roosevelt had come to the conclusion that Marshall's importance to the war effort in Washington precluded the glamour and place in history of commanding the great invasion. Roosevelt called Marshall to his villa and asked what his preference was. Although Marshall had looked forward to the Supreme Command and was the father of the cross-Channel invasion concept, he declined to give Roosevelt his opinion. Marshall said it was Roosevelt's decision, and personal feelings should not be a factor.

Roosevelt seemed greatly relieved. "I didn't feel I could sleep at ease if you were out of Washington," he told Marshall. Roosevelt then asked Churchill about Ike's appointment as Supreme Commander, and the Prime Minister approved it without hesitation. Churchill had told Ike earlier that he, Eisenhower, or Marshall were the only Americans he would accept as Supreme Commander. Marshall made no formal recommendation on the appointment, but for three years he had been grooming Ike for high command. He wrote the message to Stalin, signed by Roosevelt, announcing Dwight's appointment. Marshall sent Ike the handwritten note "as a memento" the next morning.

Ike's appointment became official on Sunday, December 5, yet he would not learn of his selection until Tuesday when he met Roosevelt in Tunis. "Well, Ike, you'd better start packing," Roosevelt said with a broad smile. Dwight's first reaction was that he was going to Washington as Marshall's successor. Roosevelt explained, "You are going to command Overlord."

Butcher wrote in his diary: "For the first time since we learned of the possibility of Ike's transfer, we now feel that we have a definite and concrete mission. This adds zest to living and interest in pursuing the objective. It has already made a remarkable difference in Ike. Now he is back to his old system of incessant planning and thinking out loud of qualifications of this or that man for certain jobs."

Roosevelt asked Ike if he would like to remain in the Mediterranean through the capture of Rome. Ike wisely chose to go to London. The Allies would not take the historic city for another seven months.

"Of all possible assignments this was the one that I least expected," Ike wrote Marshall, "since I had assumed that the decision was firm that you were to take that job on personally. However, immediately I learned of this from the President and upon receipt of your telegram from Cairo, I began figuring on the best way to organize the strictly American phases of this theater."

The appointment was made public on Christmas Eve, while Ike was in the process of putting together his Overlord staff. Churchill wanted Dwight's chief of staff, Beetle Smith, to remain in the Mediterranean as deputy to the British Allied commander. Dwight persuaded Churchill that Smith should move to London with him. The increased strain of his new job was in evidence when he accused Smith of insubordination for politely declining a dinner invitation. Ike threatened to let Churchill keep Smith in Italy, but he later apologized for this burst of temper. Smith, he often said, was his "ablest and finest officer." He never would have gone through with the threat to drop him. Marshall shared Ike's regard for Smith, but he expressed reservations about Eisenhower's choice of Patton as one of his commanders for Overlord. The Chief of Staff also was concerned that Dwight was gutting the command structure of the Mediterranean theater in favor of

Overlord. To a remarkable degree, Ike won the battle for key personnel—Smith, Patton, Bradley, Carl "Tooey" Spaatz, and British Air Marshal Arthur Tedder were all assigned to his command. Churchill kept Alexander in the Mediterranean, while assigning the vainglorious Montgomery as Dwight's British ground commander.

Marshall ordered Ike back to the United States for a visit and rest before taking command of Overlord. On December 29, he wrote: "You will be under terrific strain from now on. I am interested that you are fully prepared to bear the strain and I am not interested in the usual rejoinder that you can take it. It is of vast importance that you be fresh mentally and you certainly will not be if you go straight from one great problem to another. Now come on home and see your wife and trust somebody else for twenty minutes in England."

Ike did not think he had time to spare. He complained to Butcher that nothing could be accomplished in Washington, yet he must obey Marshall. Ike wrote Marshall on December 30: "With respect to my coming home you are mistaken in thinking that I fail to realize the desirability of a good rest. Moreover, I realize that there has been a very fine man operating in England. It happens that it is that particular man who has been urging me to arrive there as quickly as possible. The other feature of the affair is that I frankly feared that there would be no possibility of obtaining any rest through making a hurried trip to the United States. With several days consumed in travel each way and a conviction that I must get back here to turn over this theater to the new commanders at the earliest possible moment I feared I would simply be out of the frying pan and into the fire."

The long separation, inevitably, created strains between Ike and Mamie. Rumors had circulated about a wartime romance between Ike and his British driver, Kay Summersby. On numerous occasions, Mamie made references to Summersby in her letters to Ike.

Summersby was a fashion model and motion-picture actress before becoming Ike's driver in London and North Africa. She was beautiful, with high Garbo cheekbones, long, flowing hair, and a model's slender figure. "Kay was a diversion to Ike," Butcher recalled in a 1977 interview. "She was a breath of fresh air. She was witty and charming. As a driver during the blitz, she had been through a lot of danger. Ike appreciated that." Summersby narrowly escaped death in December of 1942 en route to joining Dwight in North Africa. Her ship, the *Strathallen,* was torpedoed by a German submarine and sank. She arrived in North Africa in a lifeboat. Her fiancé, American Colonel Richard R. Arnold, was later killed in Tunisia by a mine. In her book, *Past Forgetting: My Love Affair with Dwight D. Eisenhower,* published after her death, Summersby said their relationship became a serious one in North Africa. "Love had grown so naturally that it was a part of our lives, something precious that I had taken for granted without ever putting a name on it," she said.

Mamie had heard gossip about Ike and Kay from other military wives. Her correspondence was soon putting Dwight on the defensive. "Fear not about WAACs taking care of my house," Ike wrote her from Algiers on February 25, 1943. "I love you all the time—don't go bothering your pretty head about WAACs—etc., etc." Mamie expressed concern over a *Life* magazine article which mentioned that Summersby had gone to North Africa. "So *Life* says my old London driver came down!" he responded. "So she did—but the big reason she wanted to serve in this theater is that she is terribly in love with a young American colonel and is to be married to him come June—assuming both are alive. I doubt that *Life* told that. But I tell you only so that if anyone is banal and foolish enough to lift an eyebrow at an old duffer such as I am in connection with WAACs—Red Cross workers—nurses and drivers—you will know that I've no emotional involvements and will have none."

Summersby had, in fact, grown close to Ike. She was his secretary and confidante. She accompanied him to meetings with such world figures as Churchill, Roosevelt, and King George VI. Though she was still a British subject, and over the protest of Colonel Oveta Culp Hobby, head of the American Women's Army Corps, Ike arranged to have Summersby commissioned as a WAC lieutenant. Mamie was skeptical about what she was hearing. In one of her letters she asked Dwight about being "highly interested in Ireland." Kay Summersby was born Kathleen McCarthy-Morrogh in County Cork, Ireland.

Whatever his relationship with Summersby was, Ike's wartime letters to Mamie indicate that he still felt deeply about his wife. "Your love and our own son have been my greatest gift from life," he wrote. "I've never wanted any other wife—you're mine and for that reason I've been luckier than any other man." The publication in 1973 of *Plain Speaking* by Merle Miller, a series of interviews with the late Harry S. Truman, raised additional questions about Dwight and Summersby. Truman is purported to have said that Dwight was planning to divorce Mamie and marry Summersby, but that General Marshall vowed to "bust" him out of the Army if Eisenhower went through with his plans. Dr. Forrest C. Pogue, Marshall's official biographer and director of the Marshall Library, said he is doubtful that Dwight and Marshall ever exchanged such correspondence.

Summersby herself admitted in her book that she did not know of such a letter, but said she wanted to believe such correspondence had existed. Pogue said Marshall would have been shocked because of his friendship with Mamie. However, Pogue said it would have been out of character for Marshall to have given Dwight such a stinging reprimand. The historian has had unique access to Marshall's letters of reprimand and said none were as vitriolic as the document Truman described to Miller.

In any event, it was Marshall who brought Ike home for twelve days in January of 1944—for a reunion with Mamie. Dwight later told Summersby that he got into trouble with his wife for calling her "Kay" on several occasions. When Summersby made a visit to Washington that summer, Mamie treated her with cool disdain. She also asked one of Dwight's biographers, Kenneth Davis, not to mention Kay in his book.

Dwight and Mamie stayed together in January at Marshall's official residence at Fort Myer. They went to West Point in Marshall's private railroad car to have dinner with John, then in the midst of his final year at the Academy. Ike later flew to Kansas for a visit with his mother at Milton's presidential residence on the Kansas State campus. Mamie, who did not fly because of a heart murmur, remained in Washington. As Dwight departed for London, Mamie said she told him not to come back until the war had ended. "I can't bear to lose you again," she said. Ike later asked

Marshall for permission to move Mamie to London, which was denied by the Chief of Staff because it would show "favoritism" to a general when all other married American soldiers were lonely for their families.

On September 25, Ike wrote Mamie: "Of course, we've changed. How could two people go through what we have, each in his own way, and without seeing each other except once in more than two years, and still believe they could be exactly as they were. The rule of nature is constant change. But it seems to me the thing to do is to retain our sense of humor, and try to make an interesting game of getting acquainted again. After all there is no 'problem' separating us—it is merely distance, and that can some day be eliminated."

Mamie, always a formidable personality, was capable of putting Ike on the defensive by her correspondence. "It's true we've been apart for two and a half years and at a time under conditions that make separation painful and hard to bear," he wrote on November 12, 1944. "But you should not forget that I do miss you and do love you, and that the load of responsibility I carry would be intolerable unless I could have this belief that there is someone who wants me to come home—for good. Don't forget that I take a beating, every day. . . . I am not fussing at you. But please try to see me in something besides a despicable light—at least let me be certain of my welcome home when this mess is finished. I truly love you and I know that when you blow off steam you don't really think of me as such a black-hearted creature as your language implies."

Summersby's book describes a passionate but unconsummated romance. "His kisses absolutely unraveled me," she wrote, yet her book claimed Dwight was impotent. "Ike had a lot on his mind," said one former aide. "He was meeting Churchill, Montgomery, and other important leaders on an almost daily basis. Under those conditions . . . He had a lot on his mind."

John Eisenhower, who met Summersby in Europe and later served as her escort during her 1944 summer visit, said in a 1977 interview: "Nobody can bear witness that an incident did not happen. But the letters [his father's letters to Mamie] establish beyond any doubt in my mind that divorce never crossed my dad's mind." John recalled, "She was one of the crowd. She was very attractive. She was a bridge partner. Dad and everybody else was fond of her. I liked her too." John also confided that if he were to find written evidence that there had been an affair, he would not make the documents public. "If I found a real smoking gun letter," he said, "I'd probably destroy it. I haven't found any."

Ike's relationship with Summersby thus remains something of an enigma. They shared many experiences in the field, on the social circuit, and at quiet country retreats. It is clear that she was a comfort during some of the most tense moments of the war. He made no secret of his admiration for her, and she cared deeply for him. Churchill was said to have been alarmed by the Eisenhower-Summersby relationship, partly because Goebbels and the Nazis might exploit it for propaganda purposes, and also because as an Eiranean she was technically considered a security risk, prohibited from military secrets. As Ike's secretary, she was privy to the most classified Allied secrets and, in Butcher's absence, kept his diary. Another Churchillian fear was that Summersby might have a falling out with Ike and turn on him. Such concerns were groundless, for she was devoted to the Supreme Commander and the Allied cause.

Ike assumed the Supreme Command in London on January 13, 1944. He soon moved Supreme Headquarters, Allied Expeditionary Force (SHAEF) from his old offices at Grosvenor Square in downtown London to Bushby Park, a quiet village in the suburbs, where he and his staff could work closely together on planning the great invasion. There remained many skeptics, particularly among the British, about the cross-Channel strategy. Ike insisted that SHAEF quickly establish a spirit of optimism. Overlord would succeed, he told his associates, because it had to be a success. Ike was asked several months later by a reporter how a setback at Anzio in Italy would have changed the course of the war. "I was not there then," he replied, "but the Allies do not attack to be thrown back. I never considered failure because I do not ever let my mind think upon it that way."

While he was confident and assertive in dealing with the powerful, Dwight retained a sense of modesty. Roosevelt had earlier offered him the Congressional Medal of Honor, but he turned it down. "Ike said it was given for valor," Roosevelt later recalled, "and he hadn't done anything valorous." The President then awarded Dwight the Legion of Merit. Dwight wept at the ceremony and told Roosevelt he appreciated the medal more than any other. His rapport with soldiers was unique among commanders. His men called him "Ike," to his apparent delight. "When they called me Ike," he said, "I knew everything was going well." On a Christmas visit to the Isle of Capri, Ike was appalled to find great mansions reserved for himself and Spaatz. He was further outraged to find that the entire island had been designated an officers' recreation area. "Damn it," he said, "this is supposed to be a rest center for combat men, not a playground for the brass!" On Ike's orders, the island was made available to all Allied troops. It was more than a gesture, for he did not want his officers living like "big shots" while soldiers were dying in the mountains of Italy.

He spoke about his new command with humility. When John W. Burn, an Englishman, wrote expressing disappointment that Montgomery or Alexander had not been appointed Supreme Commander, he replied: "I well understand the feelings that prompted you to write your letter. . . . Moreover, I am the first to agree with you that any one of the generals you suggested, and possibly even any one of a number, would have been a better selection than that actually made for the accomplishment of my task. However, I hope you will agree that as long as this duty has been placed upon me by Great Britain and the United States, I have no recourse except to do my very best to perform it adequately."

Ike's organization at SHAEF was not unlike his Mediterranean headquarters, but it was much larger and more complex. More than ever, Dwight worked to achieve a unified command structure which would transcend Anglo-American differences. Smith was his closest associate and while they usually agreed, each was an eloquent advocate and could often influence the other's opinion. British Air Marshal Sir Trafford Leigh-Mallory was the Deputy Supreme Commander. Ike's immediate task was outlined in a directive from the Combined Chiefs of Staff: "You will enter the continent of Europe and, in conjunction with the other United Nations, undertake operations aimed at the heart of Germany and the destruction of her armed forces. The date for entering the

Continent is the month of May 1944. After adequate Channel ports have been secured, exploitation will be directed towards securing an arena that will facilitate both ground and air operations against the enemy."

He had not been satisfied with the early plans for the invasion at Normandy. The preceding September, long before his own name was linked with the invasion, Dwight's advice was sought by British Lieutenant General Sir Frederick Morgan of the European planning staff. His viewpoint was considered of some value on the basis of his success in the large-scale invasions of North Africa and Sicily. "The attack on a three-division front is fatally weak," Ike said then. "Were this my operation, I would insist on broadening it to a five-division front with two divisions in floating reserve."

Following his appointment, Ike conferred with Montgomery on the necessity of the more powerful assault. The field marshal, at Dwight's request, helped talk Churchill into supporting the larger scale thrust. Ike himself discussed the invasion at length in separate sessions with Roosevelt and Churchill. On January 23, he told the Combined Chiefs of Staff: "We are convinced that in all discussions full weight must be given to the fact that this operation marks the crisis of the European war. Every obstacle must be overcome, every inconvenience suffered and every risk run to ensure that our blow is decisive. We cannot afford to fail." He noted, "The present plan is limited to a three divisional assault. To ensure success we consider it essential to increase the assault force to five divisions. Nothing less will give us an adequate margin to ensure success." He said the larger operation would "be designed to obtain an adequate beachhead quickly and to retain the initiative."

Ike said he would prefer keeping the May 1 target date "to obtain the longest campaigning season." However, he would accept a one-month postponement rather "than risk failure with reduced forces on the earlier date." The British agreed to expand the attack, provided they were given another four weeks to produce more landing craft—and to give the Soviets time to launch their offensive on the Eastern Front which would divert some German troops from Western Europe.

Germany anticipated an Allied invasion. The Pas de Calais,

across the Channel at its shortest distance from England, was thought to be the most likely site for an amphibious assault. It was near the great port of Antwerp and would have put the Allies almost at Germany's front door. Their heaviest defense installations were built there and the Fifteenth Army was moved to the expected invasion site. Operation Fortitude, an Allied covert maneuver, helped further convince the Nazis that the major invasion was scheduled for the Pas de Calais. Omar Bradley later told Ike that Allied deception "was responsible for containing a minimum of twenty enemy divisions in the Pas de Calais during the first crucial months of the invasion." Hitler designated his most brilliant general, Field Marshal Erwin Rommel, as the defender of his "Atlantic Wall" from the North Sea coast south to the Spanish border. Rommel strengthened his defensive position with his characteristic efficiency. The beaches were mined and protected by underwater obstacles and barbed wire. Concrete fortifications were constructed with machine-gun installations.

German intelligence did not underestimate Ike. A Nazi officer, speaking at a Luftwaffe Adademy lecture on the invasion generals, said: "Eisenhower is an expert in operations of armored formations. He is noted for his great energy and hatred of routine office work. He leaves the initiative to his subordinates, whom he manages to inspire to supreme efforts through kind understanding and easy discipline. His strongest point is said to be an ability to adjust personalities to one another and smooth over opposite viewpoints. Eisenhower enjoys the greatest popularity with Roosevelt and Churchill."

Indeed, Churchill lauded Ike in a speech in the House of Commons on February 22, two weeks after the German report was delivered. Churchill said, "General Eisenhower, with whom we have worked for so long, so happily and so successfully, has been placed at the summit of the war direction." The Prime Minister said the Supreme Command had gone to the United States because of their "superiority of numbers" in the operation, yet he said Britain was still a full partner in the alliance. "Nothing like it has ever been seen before among allies," he said. "No doubt language is a great help, but there is more in it than that. In all previous alliances the staffs have worked with opposite numbers in each department and liaison officers, but in Africa General Eisenhower built up a uniform staff, in which every place was filled with whoever was thought to be the best man, and they all ordered each other about according to their rank, without the slightest regard to what country they belonged to. The same unity and brotherhood is being instituted here throughout the forces which are gathering in this country."

Ike was touched by the Churchillian tribute. "Despite the feelings of humility that must affect any honest man when he knows himself to be over-credited in any fashion," he wrote the Prime Minister, "I must confess to equal feelings of deepest gratification that you found it proper and appropriate to mention my name favorably before the House of Commons. I assure you that by the beginning of actual land operations in this theater the same perfection of team play in the higher Command and in the fighting units that characterized our operations in the Mediterranean will have been achieved here."

Churchill and Ike did, to be sure, have frequent clashes. At one point Dwight threatened to "go home" if he was not given command of Allied air operations. On March 22, he wrote, "If a satisfactory answer is not reached I am going to take drastic action and inform the Combined Chiefs of Staff that unless the matter is settled at once I will request relief from this Command." Ike finally secured command of airborne operations. He was less successful in his fight to preserve Anvil, the invasion of southern France which had been timed to coincide with the Normandy landings and drive the Nazis from France. Since the Mediterranean was now a secondary theater, Ike urged that vessels be sent from Italy for the more critical assault on southern France. Churchill vetoed any such action until after Rome had been taken. Only then could Anvil proceed as Ike wanted. Another concern was Roosevelt and Churchill's cavalier treatment of De Gaulle and the Free French. Dwight wanted the active support of French resistance groups. His own relations with De Gaulle were cordial and he had developed respect for the French general. Yet his commanders in chief, both of whom shared a hearty dislike for De Gaulle, kept the French leader out of the planning of Overlord and denied him the recognition Dwight was recommending.

In addition to the political and military pressures, there were personal strains during these anxious weeks. "Ike looks worn and tired," said an aide. "The strain is telling on him. He looks older now than at any time I have been with him." He burst into a rage upon learning that a newspaper reporter had acquired some of his letters to his aged mother and published them through a national syndicate. Ike considered legal action against the newspapers, but was advised that as a prominent figure he was unable to block such distribution of his personal writings. Anything he said was legitimate news. However, he did not like the notoriety. "When this war is over I am going to find the deepest hole there is in the United States, crawl in and pull it in after me," he wrote to an old friend. "As an alternative I am going to live on top of Pikes Peak or some other equally inaccessible place." He was becoming impatient with the volume of requests for autographs and favors from businessmen and others who had no connection with the Allied effort. "So long as you want my autograph only for young children or for people that are doing their full part in helping to win this war, I have no objection to sending a few signatures on to you," he wrote his brother Earl. "I merely don't like to be exploited by people who are doing nothing in this time of trial and struggle." Ike wrote Marshall: "I think, at times, I get a bit homesick, and the ordinary diversions of the theater and other public places are denied me." He asked for "an opportunity to become acquainted again with my son" by having John spend his June graduation leave in the European theater. Marshall readily agreed and John was to spend nearly three weeks with his father.

Patton again became the focus of controversy just as Congress was considering him and others for permanent promotion. "This I fear has killed them all," Marshall informed Ike. Patton's indiscretion came in a speech before a small Anglo-American women's group. He said, "It is the evident destiny of the British and Americans to rule the world." The remark was interpreted as an anti-Soviet diatribe in American newspapers.

"Apparently he is unable to use reasonably good sense in all those matters where senior commanders must appreciate the effect of their own actions upon public opinion and this raises doubts as to the wisdom of retaining him in high command despite his demonstrated capacity in battle leadership," Ike wrote. "I have grown so weary of the trouble he constantly causes you and the War Department, to say nothing of myself, that I am seriously contemplating the most drastic action." He wrote Patton: "I have warned you time and again against your impulsiveness in action and speech and have flatly instructed you to say nothing that could possibly be misinterpreted either by your own subordinates or by the public. . . . I am thoroughly weary of your failure to control your tongue and have begun to doubt your all-round judgment, so essential in high military position." Patton was summoned to SHAEF on May 1 for a meeting with Ike. To Marshall, Dwight wrote that he would probably have to send Patton back to the United States because "it appears hopeless to expect that he will ever completely overcome his lifelong habit of posing and of self-dramatization." Marshall replied that given Patton's experience against Rommel and in amphibious operations, perhaps he should be given another chance.

The unexpected boost Patton received from Marshall probably saved his command, for Ike did indeed change his mind about sending "Old Blood and Guts" home. He wrote Patton on May 3, saying: "I am once more taking the responsibility of retaining you in command in spite of damaging repercussions resulting from a personal indiscretion. I do this solely because of my faith in you as a battle leader and from no other motives. . . . No further action will be taken in this case and I expect you to plunge into the task of preparing your army with undiminished vigor at the same time that you exercise extreme care to see that while you are developing the morale and fighting spirit you will not be guilty of another indiscretion which can cause any further embarrassment to your superiors or to yourself."

Secretary of War Stimson approved of Ike's handling of the volatile Patton. "The judicial poise and good judgment, as well as the great courage which you have shown in making this decision, have filled me with even greater respect and admiration than I had for you before," wrote Stimson. In a secret message thanking Stimson for his vote of confidence, Ike confided: "Problems such as this one always present the difficulty that it is almost impossible, from this distance, to assess the effect upon public opinion in the United States. However, I am quite sure that from the viewpoint of Overlord the decision was a correct one."

Patton, who had bitterly criticized Ike to his aides when it appeared that his old friend might strip him of command, called the decision an "act of God." For Dwight, the arrangement had little to do with religious faith. "You owe us some victories," he said to Patton. "Pay off and the world will deem me a wise man."

In the months ahead, Patton would vindicate Ike's action with his dramatic pursuit of the Nazi armies. Yet he was not included in the invasion's D-Day operations and was to spend the intervening days as commander of a nonexistent army making maneuvers for Operation Fortitude. Because of their respect for Patton, the Germans were more easily convinced that Fortitude was the real invasion of Europe and Overlord was but a preliminary.

Ike drafted a message for his senior commanders in mid-May. By then, England was saturated with weapons, tanks, jeeps, ammunition, and some ten thousand airplanes. Every available space was utilized and some Britons joked that the weight of their arsenal might sink the island. "I feel strongly that as the day of our combined offensive approaches, it is necessary to make absolutely clear to our men the stark and elemental facts as to the character of our Nazi enemy, the absolute need for crushing him, if we are to survive," Ike wrote, "and, finally, to drive home the fact that we have defeated them before and can do it again. It is only necessary to steel ourselves to the task."

He was still concerned about the potential for Anglo-American hostilities if part of Overlord failed. "An Allied command cannot possibly be handled as would a completely homogeneous one," he wrote in his diary. "There always exists the danger that public reaction to a local tactical defeat will be that of blaming a Commander of another nationality." Yet the rivalries between commanders seemed less pronounced than had been the case in North Africa.

The Allies were ready for their historic assault by the first of June. Germany was struggling to hold Rome and on the Eastern Front the Nazis were reeling from the powerful thrusts of Stalin's armies. Plans for the invasion of Normandy were completed. The troops were well trained and anxious to cross the Channel. Only one factor remained which could delay them: the weather. Under normal weather conditions, Ike said the landings were "attended by hazards and difficulties greater than have ever before faced an invading army." The weather had been ideal during most of May, but on the day before the June 5 invasion rainstorms and heavy wind developed over the Atlantic. Ike was advised that forty-five-mile-per-hour winds would be hitting the Normandy beaches. He postponed the landings for twenty-four hours. The next day, Dwight met with top staff members and his meteorologists. The storm was still going on and their headquarters shaking from the gales of wind. However, the weather forecast indicated conditions would improve by the next morning. The sea would be calm and the skies partly cloudy. Some of the high command, including Leigh-Mallory and Tedder, urged postponement. Ike pondered his options for five minutes, knowing that rough weather could mean disaster yet also knowing it would be at least two weeks before the operation could be rescheduled and that some of the best weeks for campaigning had already been lost. He decided to take the risk. "Well, we'll go," he said, and D-Day had begun. Eisenhower's Chief of Staff W. B. Smith said it was Dwight's finest hour. "He responded with the instinct of a gambler," wrote military historian General S. L. A. Marshall, "lacking which, no battle commander may ever get off the pivot. His decision was not only morally of the highest order; it required a lightning appraisal of what could be accomplished in such a brief interval."

Ike visited troops who were being loaded into ships for the cross-Channel trip. That evening a war correspondent reported Dwight's eyes became moist as he met with paratroopers of the American 101st Division. "I would think that if a man didn't show a little bit of emotion, it would show that he was probably a little inhuman," Ike recalled years later in a television interview, "and goodness knows, those fellows meant a lot to me. But these are the decisions that have to be made when you're in a war." Soldiers of the 101st, their faces blackened for the air drop, seemed equally moved by the visit from their Supreme Commander. One paratrooper said, "Now, stop worrying. We'll take care of this for you, General."

That evening Ike wrote a note which was to be made public

only if the landing was a failure. Despite his long and successful efforts to build confidence in his command, he was prepared to accept full blame for any disaster. "Our landings in the Cherbourg-Havre area have failed to gain a satisfactory foothold and I have withdrawn the troops," he wrote. "My decision to attack at this time and place was based upon the best information available. The troops, the air, and the Navy did all that bravery and devotion to duty could do. If any blame or fault attaches to the attempt, it is mine alone." Ike later told Butcher that he had written similar notes before each of his previous large-scale amphibious operations, but had torn up the others. A defeat at Normandy would have been more his responsibility than any earlier setback for, more than anyone else, he had been the architect of the strategy and tactics of Overlord. "If it did fail," said Ike, "I was going into oblivion anyway. So I might as well take the full responsibility."

A similar message had been sent to Leigh-Mallory, who had predicted an 80 percent casualty rate. Ike told the British air marshal: "Those paratroopers are going to go as planned. You give me your objections, and I'll give you in writing my statement recognizing your recommendations to call off the air drops." As it turned out, air-drop losses were less than 4 percent, and the paratroopers were a decisive factor in the successful landing.

In the darkness, the Allied armada of 4,000 ships and 1,200 planes departed for Normandy. Once again the adverse weather conditions proved to be an Allied advantage. The Germans were so confident that the storm would delay the invasion that Rommel was celebrating a family birthday in Germany. Hitler was still convinced the assault would come at the Pas de Calais. Ike was pensive as he awaited word of the landings. "I have as yet no information concerning the actual landings nor of our progress through beach obstacles," he wired Marshall. "All preliminary reports are satisfactory. . . . The enthusiasm, toughness and obvious fitness of every single man were high and the light of battle was in their eyes."

The landings were a remarkable success. Only at Omaha Beach, where the Allies suffered 2,000 casualties had the forces been seriously challenged. "We were afraid the losses were bigger than they actually were," Dwight recalled years later. "Of all the attacks, that was the worst one." But Omaha and the other beaches were firmly controlled by the Allies at the end of the day. Some 132,000 Allied troops had come ashore and 23,000 had parachuted. Rommel's vaunted coastal wall had been penetrated.

In a rare tribute to the Anglo-American effort, Stalin said: "The history of war does not show any such undertaking so broad in conception, so grandiose in scale and so masterly in execution." Smith wrote: "I doubt that there has ever been a campaign in history where actual operations fitted so closely the initial plan of a commander, adopted so far in advance. Long before we set foot in Europe and tested the enemy's strength in battle, we had decided on the blueprint for his defeat." Churchill called it "the most difficult and complicated operation that has ever taken place."

Marshall, who visited Omaha Beach with Ike and the Joint Chiefs on June 12, told President Roosevelt: "Eisenhower and his staff are cool and confident, carrying out an affair of incredible magnitude and complication with superlative efficiency." By June 17, almost 600,000 men and 100,000 vehicles were in Normandy; and by the first week in July 1,000,000 soldiers and 500,000 tons of supplies were ashore. Ike's strategy and tactics had been a brilliant success. His gamble, too, was vindicated, for a terrible storm struck the French coast on June 19, which would have been the alternate D-Day. The invasion armada would have been caught in the worst weather in the Channel in twenty years. The American artificial port was destroyed in the storm and thus the British port became the Allied artificial harbor. On June 21, Ike wrote Marshall: "This is the third day that unloadings have practically ceased because of bad weather. Yesterday and today the weather has been so bad that sailings have had to stop from United Kingdom ports. . . . Bad weather on the coast has also permitted the enemy to bring up reinforcements and likewise interfered with our attacks."

Ike faced other problems besides the weather and the Germans. He was plainly disappointed in the performance of Field Marshal Montgomery, the acting Allied ground commander and commander of the British Twenty-first Army. Montgomery, as diminutive as he was arrogant, had served as a brigade major in the First

World War. In the early months of World War II, he had helped supervise the evacuation at Dunkirk. He became Britain's most celebrated commander in North Africa by turning back Rommel at the battle of El Alamein. Montgomery was a vanity case, who considered himself Ike's superior in both experience and ability. When they first met, in the winter of 1942, Montgomery reprimanded Ike, then an obscure American officer, for daring to smoke in his presence. Montgomery later boasted that he had "commanded in battle every unit and formation from a platoon to great armies" in contrast to Dwight, who "had never seen a shot fired in anger until he landed in North Africa." The field marshal also argued that Eisenhower was not a serious student of military history and lacked the knowledge to apply military science into battlefield practice. Always the loner, Montgomery criticized the Supreme Commander for relying too heavily on his staff. Ike came to question Montgomery's judgment at Normandy, for the British commander's operations fell far short of his preinvasion predictions. Ike, who favored an aggressive strategy, found Montgomery to be overly slow and cautious. He was concerned whether Montgomery would make any further progress when his forces became caught in a stalemate at Caen which lasted more than six weeks, although Montgomery had promised to deliver the area on D-Day. Montgomery retorted hotly that Dwight did not really understand the master plan for Normandy, for the British were drawing German fire to permit Bradley's First Army to advance.

Ike and the SHAEF high command had counted on Montgomery's success at Caen, which meant the opening of a direct route to Paris. In addition, the city was the capital and communications center of Normandy. The Americans had concentrated their efforts on the port of Cherbourg, located at the tip of the Cotentin peninsula. By the end of June, they had taken the port and captured 35,000 prisoners. The seizure of the port now made it possible for the Allies to send a much greater volume of supplies to Europe in a short period of time. Montgomery's forces had not yet entered Caen. Late in the month, he had promised a "blitz attack" and vowed to "continue battle on the eastern flank till one of us cracks and it will not be us." Ike hoped that his mercurial commander would repeat his North African triumph and was impressed by Montgomery's confident tone. "Please do not hesitate to make the maximum demands for any air assistance that can possibly be useful to you," he wrote the field marshal on June 25. "Whenever there is any legitimate opportunity we must blast the enemy with everything we have." Yet Montgomery called off his advance several days later because he anticipated a fierce German counterattack. He said the Nazi movement could be checked if his British and Canadian forces regrouped. The Supreme Commander thought Montgomery had fumbled an opportunity for a major breakthrough, but the massive German counterattack had been blocked. Rommel would not lead his Panzer divisions in a power thrust to drive the Allies into the sea.

Tedder and Smith were outspoken in their criticism of Montgomery. At SHAEF, the British strategists were no less disillusioned with him than Ike was. On July 7, Ike wrote Montgomery: "It appears to me that we must use all possible energy in a determined effort to prevent a stalemate or of facing the necessity of fighting a major defensive battle with the slight depth we now have in the beachhead. We have not yet attempted a major full-dress attack on the left flank supported by everything we could bring to bear." Montgomery was beginning to realize that Ike's criticism was shared by many others. Churchill himself thought Montgomery was overly cautious. In a letter to Dwight, Montgomery responded that a "very definite plan" was in preparation and it would "set my eastern flank alight."

Ike gave Montgomery the promised aerial support—more than 2,300 tons of bombs were dropped near Caen. Montgomery took the western half of Caen the next day, but called off his offensive before moving across the Orne River. Leigh-Mallory and Tedder were furious that Montgomery had not taken the air strips southeast of the city. Montgomery rationalized that it was a battle of position and expressed satisfaction with his performance. Ike called on Churchill "to persuade Monty to get on his bicycle and start moving." Montgomery then told Dwight his eastern flank would "burst into flames" and forecast a decisive triumph. Ike was delighted and told the hero of Alamein that his "brilliant stroke" would bring about a dramatic victory. Montgomery's attack was aided by more than 2,000 bombers as some 8,000 tons of bombs fell on Caen. He did take eastern Caen and said his mission had indeed been fulfilled. Ike was incensed at Montgomery's failure to deliver the promised breakthrough. Montgomery's advance had been only seven miles.

Ike wrote Montgomery, noting that the "tremendous air attack" had made him optimistic about the breakthrough. The Supreme Commander's disappointment was made clear. A month later, at the close of the Normandy campaign, Montgomery's erratic behavior once again cost the Allies a more spectacular victory. Germany was soundly defeated, having lost 10,000 soldiers with another 50,000 taken prisoner. Yet most of their Fifth and Seventh Panzer armies had escaped when Montgomery had not moved the interarmy group boundary to permit the Americans to close the Falaise-Argentan pocket. The German armies would regroup four months later for their most massive counterattack of the war. On September 1, Ike himself replaced Montgomery as Allied ground commander. Montgomery's bumbling and extreme caution had left no alternative. Montgomery was retained as commander of the Twenty-first Army group and his ego was massaged with a promotion to field marshal, Britain's highest military rank.

The Supreme Command was also to bring Ike into frequent collisions with Churchill. The Prime Minister was a figure of indomitable courage, whose energy and brilliant rhetoric helped Britain "rise to the level of events." He was also a man of excessive emotion and ego whose military judgment was often disastrous. Churchill once wrote that his interest in warfare began with a nursery passion for toy soldiers. During the First World War, he was the scapegoat for British setbacks at Gallipoli and the Dardanelles. The doomed assaults had been Churchill's idea and he was drummed out of his position as First Lord of the Admiralty. Following this humiliation, Churchill began active service on the Western Front and soon became commander of a battalion.

It took Churchill nearly a generation to recover his reputation and Britain's confidence. Had he died before the Second World War, he would have been remembered as a brilliant failure. During the 1930s, he urged his countrymen to prepare for an approaching war. From 1932 until the war, he led a one-man crusade to strengthen Britain's military establishment and resistance to

Hitler. When his foreboding prophecies were realized, Churchill was transformed from a quixotic dissenter to the symbol of a defiant nation. "My policy is to wage war," he said in his first broadcast as Prime Minister. "War without stint: war to the utmost." His capacity to inspire others was almost metaphysical. One British admiral said Churchill's faulty and dangerous strategy "cost thousands of lives" yet without him "we should have lost the war." Marshall and Ike had disagreed with Churchill's concentration on North Africa and Italy, and with his two-year postponement of the cross-Channel invasion. As Supreme Commander, Ike would not yield so easily. In July, Churchill called for the cancellation of the invasion of southern France, favoring a thrust from Italy into the Balkans. Ike insisted on going through with his own operation and said Churchill could appeal to Roosevelt. The President supported Ike, but the indefatigable Churchill made another proposition: shifting the landings from the Riviera to Brittany. Churchill advised his chiefs of staff that Dwight had already made the commitment to the west coast of France. He went to SHAEF to persuade Ike and for seven hours argued and pleaded with the Supreme Commander. At their next meeting, at 10 Downing Street, Churchill said if his strategic conception was rejected he might go to the King and "lay down the mantle of my high office." Churchill complained of American abuse and ill-treatment.

Ike stood his ground, but was troubled by Churchill's excited and impetuous remarks. "To say that I was disturbed by our conference," he wrote Churchill, "does not nearly express the depth of my distress over your interpretation of the recent decision affecting the Mediterranean theater. I do not, for one moment, believe that there is any desire on the part of any responsible person in the American war machine to disregard British views, or cold-bloodedly to leave Britain holding an empty bag in any of our joint undertakings. I look upon these questions as strictly military in character—and I am sorry that you seem to feel we use our great actual or potential strength as a bludgeon in conference. The fact is that the British view has prevailed in the discussions of the Combined Chiefs of Staff in many of our undertakings in which I have been engaged, and I do not see why we should be considered intemperate in our long and persistent support of Anvil." In closing, Ike appealed to Churchill's vanity: "I have leaned on you often, and have always looked to you with complete confidence when I felt the need of additional support."

Churchill replied, acknowledging the "kind" letter and offering congratulations "on brilliant operations in Anjou and Normandy." The Prime Minister had earlier told Ike, "Liberate Paris by Christmas and none of us can ask for more." The French capital was taken on August 25 as American and Free French forces made a triumphal entry, four months ahead of Churchill's goal. The invasion of southern France by Mediterranean Allied forces, which Ike would not compromise, meant the liberation of all France. The advances up the Rhône Valley had overpowered German resistance.

The decision to retain Patton had paid off handsomely. Patton's Third Army moved to France after D-Day and on August 1, they began surging through the Avranches gap. The Germans made a counterattack, but Patton whirled through the gap with astonishing speed. In three days, he had moved 100,000 soldiers and 15,000 tanks over one bridge and sent them plunging in three directions—westward into Brittany, southward toward the Loire River, and toward Le Mans in the east. His pursuit was successful, for the Germans were trapped and demoralized by his bold tactics. Hitler commented at the time: "Just look at that crazy cowboy general, driving down to the south and into Brittany along a single road and over a single bridge with an entire Army. He doesn't care about the risk, and acts as if he owned the world. It doesn't seem possible." Patton demonstrated what Ike had known all along, that he was without peer as a field commander.

For Germany, it was the beginning of the end. They had lost between 250,000 and 300,000 casualties in the Normandy campaign. Their situation was precarious and the Allies now debated how to sustain the momentum. Montgomery called for a narrow front with a "solid mass" of forty divisions under his command. The field marshal urged a single thrust over the northern edge of the Ardennes, into Germany, across the Rhine and culminating in Berlin. If Montgomery's proposal might have brought an early end to the war, it also contained severe risks. A German counterattack could inflict far greater damage on such a narrow front. Ike opted for the broad front, from Switzerland to the North Sea. He wanted "more than one string to our bow," making it all but impossible for Germany to block the Allied forward movement.

Montgomery told Ike it was unorthodox for him to be running ground operations. "The Supreme Commander must sit on a very lofty perch in order to be able to take a detached view of the whole intricate problem," said Montgomery. On September 5, Montgomery wrote Ike: "I consider we have now reached a stage where one really powerful and full-blooded thrust toward Berlin is likely to get there and thus end the German war." The Supreme Commander replied: "The bulk of the German Army that was in the West has now been destroyed. We must immediately exploit our success by promptly breaching the Siegfried Line, crossing the Rhine on a wide front and seizing the Saar and the Ruhr. This I intend to do with all possible speed. This will give us a stranglehold on two of Germany's main industrial areas and largely destroy her capacity to wage war, whatever course events may take. . . . Moreover, it will give us freedom of action to strike in any direction and will force the enemy to disperse, over a wide area, such forces as he may be able to assemble for the defense of the West." Montgomery would not abandon his conception and said the broad front "will prolong the war." Ike advised Marshall of Montgomery's single-thrust blueprint. "Examination of this scheme exposes it as a fantastic idea," he wrote. "The attack would be on such a narrow front that flanking threats would be particularly effective and no other troops in the whole region would be capable of going to its support. Actually I doubt that the idea was proposed in any conviction that it could be carried through to completion."

Ike did give Montgomery priority over the American forces for fuel and ammunition, since the British were heading into the Low Countries and the Allies needed possession of Antwerp, Europe's finest harbor. Brussels was taken on September 3 and Antwerp the next day, yet it would be more than two months before the seventy-mile channel to the great harbor would be cleared of German mines. Ike approved Montgomery's plan to seize the Pas de Calais before clearing the water approaches to Antwerp. The operation, named Market-Garden, was a daring effort to drop an "airborne carpet" along a marshy eighty-mile corridor and secure bridges over the Meuse, Waal, and lower Rhine rivers. The plan was to destroy V-weapon launching sites which were being used to strike England; trap German troops in western Holland; outflank the West Wall defenses; and get into position for an assault on the Ruhr. "I not only approved Market-Garden, I insisted upon it," Ike recalled years later. "What we needed was a bridgehead over the Rhine. If that could be accomplished I was quite willing to wait on all other operations. What this action proved was that the idea of 'one full-blooded thrust to Berlin' was silly."

The Allied armored and paratroop attack advanced sixty-five miles into the corridor, taking the bridges along the Meuse and Waal rivers. However, the attempt to gain a foothold on the lower Rhine and outflank the West Wall was rebuffed. Arnhem, the site of the all-important bridge, happened to be the mustering ground for a Panzer corps and headquarters for the German First Parachute Army. The Germans held the bridge and barred further Allied advances. Nearly twelve thousand Allied soldiers had been killed, wounded, or taken prisoner. Market-Garden was a devastating blow to the single-thrust concept and, at the same time, a tonic for Germany.

Because of the Market-Garden debacle and bad weather, the opening of Antwerp had been delayed for weeks. "I feel that Monty's strategy for once is at fault," said Brooke. "Ike nobly took all the blame on himself as he had approved Monty's suggestion to operate on Arnhem." The Allied campaign now seemed destined to continue for months. Montgomery, ever the gadfly, persisted in his requests to launch a single power thrust at Germany under his command. Ike wrote Montgomery a stern letter on the politics of the SHAEF command, on October 13:

> In order that we may continue to operate in the same close and friendly association that, to me at least, has characterized our work in the past, I will again state, as clearly as is possible, my conceptions of logical command arrangements for the future. If, having read these, you feel that you must still class them as "unsatisfactory," then indeed we have an issue that

must be settled soon in the interests of future efficiency. I am quite well aware of the powers and limitations of an Allied Command, and if you, as the senior Commander in this Theater of one of the great Allies, feel that my conceptions and directives are such as to endanger the success of operations, it is our duty to refer the matter to higher authority for any action they may choose to take, however drastic.

With one of your statements I am in emphatic agreement. That is that for any one major task on the battlefield there must be a single *battlefield* commander, a man who can devote his entire attention to that particular operation. This is the reason we have Armies and Army groups. When, however, we have a battlefront extending from Switzerland to the North Sea, I do not agree that one man can stay so close to the day by day movement of divisions and corps that he can keep a "battle grip" upon the overall situation and direct it intelligently. This is no longer a Normandy beachhead! Operations along such a wide front break themselves into more or less clearly defined areas of operation, one of which is usually the most important and best supported operation, the others secondary and supporting in character. The overall commander, in this case myself, has the function of adjusting the larger boundaries to tasks commensurate to the several groups operating in these several areas, assigning additional support by air or reinforcements by ground and airborne troops, when he has a general pool, and shifting the emphasis in maintenance arrangements.

Montgomery responded, "You will hear no more on the subject of command from me." He further wrote, "I have given you my views and you have given your answer. . . . I and all of us here will weigh in 100 per cent to do what you want and we will put it through without a doubt." The field marshal signed his letter, "Your very devoted and loyal subordinate." Ike notified Marshall: "We are having a sticky time in the North but Montgomery has at last seen the light and is concentrating toward his west, left, flank in order to clear up the Antwerp situation."

Throughout the fall, Hitler had been planning a full-dress counterattack to split the Allied front and rout its northern divisions. More than 700,000 new soldiers had been drafted from August to October, which enabled Hitler to create another twenty-five divisions. In spite of heavy Allied bombing, weapon production in Germany was higher than ever. The Allies were not expecting an offensive of major proportions. Hitler's appointment of elderly Field Marshal Gerd von Rundstedt as his Western commander seemed to confirm Allied intelligence reports that it was little more than a holding operation.

Ike was concentrating Allied strength for offensives in the north and south and in so doing permitted his defensive line to be stretched thin for some eighty miles across the Ardennes. The Allied command had no reservations about this fateful decision—they saw no possibility of a German attack across the heavily wooded Ardennes. In World War I, Marshal Foch had described the "almost impenetrable massif of the Ardennes" and the area had few good roads three decades later. Ike had commented several times on the weak American position in the area and said the Allies might be caught in "a nasty little Kasserine." Bradley and others said the Germans were not capable of moving through the forested terrain. Yet at dawn, on December 16, the Germans did attack the thinly held line, achieving complete surprise and quickly overpowering two American divisions. The Germans were not only familiar with the Ardennes, they had broken through its forests in 1870 and 1940 to crush French armies. Clouds and a heavy fog helped them launch this powerful thrust against the Americans. Hitler wanted his forces to break through to Antwerp, which would block Allied fuel supplies and split their armies. The Germans also hoped that the Battle of the Bulge would keep the Allies in check long enough for Nazi factories to rebuild the Luftwaffe, for a newly developed jet fighter had given them new hope of regaining air supremacy. Ike accepted blame for the Allied setback and transferred command of American troops north of the Bulge to Montgomery. Bradley ordered Patton, then advancing in the Saar, to make a ninety-degree shift and hit the German southern flank.

Ike did not panic in his hour of crisis. As the battle began, he was notified that President Roosevelt had nominated him for a fifth star. The vote of confidence could not have come at a better time. Ike viewed the German assault as a challenge and just as Fox Conner's strategy sessions had done years earlier, it brought out his best. On December 17, he wrote General Brehon Burke Somervell: "Yesterday morning the enemy launched a rather ambitious counterattack east of the Luxembourg area where we have been holding very thinly. In order to concentrate at vital points we have had divisions holding thirty-mile fronts. However, we have some armor that is now out of the line and resting. It is closing in on the threat from each flank. If things go well we should not only stop the thrust but should be able to profit from it."

Three days later, Ike reported to the Combined Chiefs of Staff that intelligence services "have become convinced that the full weight of the German reserves is being thrust into the attack within the area of the original penetration." Montgomery and Bradley, he wrote, were instructed to hold their flanks, gather all available reserves, and make thrusts against the Germans. Montgomery became even more imperious when he was given command of American forces in the north. Bradley said the field marshal "unfortunately could not resist the chance to tweak our Yankee noses." When it was reported that Montgomery might become Deputy Supreme Commander, with command of all ground forces, Bradley told Ike he would rather return to the United States. Montgomery did not get the promotion.

The Germans had shattered Allied optimism by both the surprise and ferocity of their attack. Only days before it had appeared that Germany was finished, yet with the Ardennes offensive the Nazis were threatening to win the war in the West. The Supreme Commander sent reinforcements to contain the Bulge and put his last remaining reserves, the 101st Airborne Division, at the vital road junction of Bastogne. The Germans had bypassed the town in their initial strike after encountering some resistance there. With the snow and ice closing secondary roads, Bastogne became essential to their plan. The Fifth Panzer Army turned back in a massive effort to overrun the Americans. Some 18,000 defenders held on as the Panzers encircled Bastogne. Fog and clouds had prevented Allied air support and the Germans were quick to take advantage. The weather cleared on December 23, and air attacks on the Panzers slowed their attack. Patton's Third Army smashed a hole through the German ring to reach Bastogne three days later, and the threat had ended. For another week, the fighting continued, but the Allies were on the offensive. Hitler's last desperate gamble had failed. Although the Allies had been delayed for some six weeks, the Germans had lost 120,000 men—double the Allied casualties. The American soldier had been given his severest test and prevailed. By January 18, the Bulge had been won and Ike was ready to implement his final assault against Hitler. As the battered Nazi armies retreated, Hitler prepared for his own death in the ruins of the Third Reich. Goebbels admitted in his magazine, *Das Reich*, "The 11th hour seems about to strike."

Ike had written Marshall on January 10, 1945, outlining the final campaign. "There has never been any question about our intentions of making the attack north of the Ruhr as strong as it possibly could be built up and placing it under command of one man. . . . Another point on which all have agreed is that the Ruhr itself cannot be attacked frontally and that in fact we should stay out of the area as long as we possibly can."

The British, economically depleted after years of war, still protested that Dwight's broad front was extending the war. They charged that Americans, with an abundance of manpower and resources, seemed in no particular hurry. Churchill, concerned about a potential Soviet presence in Central Europe, urged Ike to beat the Red Army to Berlin. "This has an important political bearing," Churchill wrote the Supreme Commander. Ike told Marshall, "Berlin itself is no longer a particularly important objective." Bradley told Ike that taking Berlin would cost 100,000 American casualties. Ike chose to concentrate on the Ruhr, where Germany's industrial might could be destroyed. Without the factories, Germany's war machine was broken.

The drive to the Rhine was launched in February. On March 7, a rainy afternoon, a task force of the U.S. Ninth Armored Division unexpectedly discovered a bridge across the Rhine, at Remagen, still spanning the river intact. By dusk, the First Army was on the east bank of the Rhine. Hitler had the officers who failed to demolish the bridge executed. He also dismissed Rundstedt, placing Field Marshal Albert Kesselring as Western commander in chief. Such moves were too late, for Ike had his foothold across the Rhine. At month's end, the Allies controlled the Rhineland.

An aide described the Supreme Commander as "immensely pleased" that the Rhine campaign had followed his long-standing conception with such precision. Even Field Marshal Brooke, who had vociferously opposed the plan, admitted that Dwight had been right.

On March 28, Ike wrote Stalin, "My immediate operations are designed to encircle and destroy the enemy forces defending the Ruhr, and to isolate that area from the rest of Germany. This will be accomplished by developing offensives around the north of the Ruhr and from Frankfurt through Kassel, until the ring is closed. The enemy enclosed in this ring will then be mopped up. . . . If we are to complete the destruction of the German armies without delay, I regard it as essential that we coordinate our action." Churchill still attempted to pressure Ike into moving into the Russian occupation zone and taking Berlin. Churchill viewed the Soviets as "a mortal danger to the free world" and would not easily back down. Ike wrote Marshall, recalling that Churchill had opposed the invasion of southern France, destroying the Rhineland defenses, and questioned his northern strategy. "Now they apparently want me to turn aside on operations," Dwight wrote, "in which would be involved many thousands of troops before the German forces are fully defeated. I submit that these things are studied daily and hourly by me and my advisers and that we are animated by one single thought which is the early winning of the war." To Montgomery, he wrote: "My plan is simple and aims at dividing and destroying the German forces and joining hands with the Red Army. . . . That place [Berlin] has become, so far as I am concerned, nothing but a geographical location, and I have never been interested in these. My purpose is to destroy the enemy's forces and his powers to resist."

Ike's forces closed the Ruhr pocket by April 1 in the greatest pincers movement ever brought off in Europe. Some 325,000 German soldiers were trapped inside, and on Hitler's orders they fought for nearly three weeks. When Field Marshal Walther Model's skillful resistance was finally divided by a north-south Allied thrust, Model committed suicide rather than follow Hitler's senseless orders.

After the Ruhr encirclement, Allied troops moved to the Elbe on April 11, where they awaited their meeting with the Russians. Hitler, who celebrated his fifty-sixth birthday on April 20, drank champagne with his cohorts while Russian bombs exploded outside the bunker. Ten days later, he committed suicide. Goebbels poisoned himself and his family the same day. Hitler's death meant the end of the European war. Patton's Third Army had made more advances into Czechoslovakia than the Russians, and Czech partisans urged Patton to take the city of Prague. The Russians reminded him that they had not taken Wismar in northern Germany at Eisenhower's request, which had kept them out of Denmark. Ike ordered Patton to halt because of the earlier precedent. Germany attempted to surrender to the Western Allies, but Ike would not receive the Nazi representatives until they surrendered to all of the Allies and had agreed to the surrender of forces in Norway and Denmark. He wrote the Combined Chiefs of Staff on May 7: "The mission of the Allied Force was fulfilled at 0241, local time, May 7th, 1945."

Ike was not present when the Nazi commanders signed the documents of surrender. Chief of Staff Smith presided over the rites of triumph. The Supreme Commander later received Marshal Jodl and said sharply that he would hold the German commander personally responsible for any violations of the surrender provisions. "Dad hated the Nazis so much that he didn't want anything to do with them," John Eisenhower recalled more than thirty years later. "He never forgot the horrors of the concentration camps." Ike had, in fact, become ill when he visited a camp near Gotha and saw a room of men killed by starvation. As the prisoners told him of the torture and bestiality, Ike may have remembered the job he had been offered while in the Philippines in which he would have worked to help evacuate Jewish refugees. Now, he could take satisfaction in having finally liberated them from the agony and tyranny of the Nazi era.

Marshall wrote Ike: "You have completed your mission with the greatest victory in the history of warfare. You have commanded with outstanding success the most powerful military force that has ever been assembled. You have met and successfully disposed of every conceivable difficulty incident to varied national interests and international political problems of unprecedented complications." The Chief of Staff, never given to fulsome praise, added: "You have been selfless in your actions, always sound and tolerant in your judgments, and altogether admirable in the courage and wisdom of your military decisions."

Ike wrote Marshall: "Since the day I first went to England, indeed since I first reported to you in the War Department, the strongest weapon that I have always had in my hand was a confident feeling that you trusted my judgment, believed in the objectivity of my approach to any problem, and were ready to sustain to the full limit of your resources and your tremendous moral support, anything that we found necessary to undertake."

He carefully prepared the V-E Day speech, writing four drafts in longhand and reading the final version to aides. "I have the rare privilege of speaking for a victorious army of almost five million fighting men," Ike said on May 4. "They, and the women who have so ably assisted them, constitute the Allied Expeditionary Force that has liberated Western Europe. They have destroyed or captured enemy armies totaling more than their own strength, and swept triumphantly forward over the hundreds of miles separating Cherbourg from Lubeck, Leipzig, and Munich."

In closing, Ike said he did not expect a hero's welcome in the United States. "When we are so fortunate as to come back to you, there need be no welcoming parades, no special celebrations. All we ask is to come back into the warmth of the hearts we left behind and to resume once more pursuits of peace—under our own American conceptions of liberty and of right, in which our beloved country has always dwelt." The Supreme Commander's words would not dim the enthusiasm of his admirers. Not since Charles A. Lindbergh in 1927 had there been such an authentically American hero, and a nation anxiously awaited Ike's return.

Chapter Twelve

THE FIRST PRESIDENT EISENHOWER

Milton Eisenhower was a popular appointment at Kansas State. He was liked immensely by undergraduates and could often be seen drinking milk shakes with students at a soda fountain in "Aggieville." He thrived on dialogue with students, sharing their concerns and listening to their ideas. No president in recent memory had been so open and accessible. Some faculty members deplored his lack of academic credentials, but his vast government experience was accepted by most as a more than adequate apprenticeship. Milton's strong views about modernizing the curriculum would encounter some hostility from old-line agricultural and mechanical school faculties. However, even his critics found him to be thoughtful and challenging. As the brother of the Supreme Commander and with his own record of public service, Milton brought Kansas State instant national recognition. If he bristled when newspapers referred to him as "Dwight's brother," Milton found that the family connection was an undeniable asset in his own career. His inaugural address was broadcast on a nationwide radio network. No other university president, not Conant of Harvard, Hutchins of Chicago, nor Butler of Columbia, had been given such attention in their first year.

"I could probably stay until I retired," Milton had told Dwight in April of 1943. "I think the college job would be interesting and

I believe I could do it well. If I were politically ambitious, it would be a good stepping stone." Indeed, his sponsors had been some of the most influential men in the state. Like them, he was a Republican and a member of an old Kansas family. With their support, he might win the governorship or a Senate seat. At Kansas State, some presidential aides thought Milton was vying for nothing less than the White House.

Milton struck up a friendship with Alf Landon, the former Kansas governor and 1936 Republican presidential nominee. Their conversations invariably turned to state and national politics. Landon later became critical of Milton's federal and United Nations activities. "There was a saying that they ought to raise the flag in celebration when Milton was on campus," Landon wryly observed.

Milton asserted that higher education should not be a "cloistered enterprise removed from the mainstream of life," but a part of the stream. His government service gave him the opportunity to match ideals with actions. The president of Kansas State was determined to launch educational innovations which would move the college beyond vocationalism. Milton thought the vocation-school concept of education was divorced from everyday realities and problems. By contrast, a liberal education could educate the "whole" man and force students to reach beyond a narrow specialty. In Washington, Milton had become disenchanted with rigid and petty bureaucrats whom he considered incapable of understanding other disciplines. He wanted more humanism, diversity, and a concern for the interdependence of divergent groups in education.

He explained his philosophy in a speech delivered at Colorado Agricultural and Mechanical College: "Education in a democracy must at all times be concerned with human values and human growth. It must emphasize a unifying force which enables each student to synthesize fragmented knowledge into broad understanding and help him arrive at sound judgments on a multitude of issues both inside and outside his field of specialization. . . . A college or university that is aimlessly neutral, skeptical, or cynical with respect to human values and moral concepts is essentially nothing more than a glorified information booth."

His inaugural address sounded the keynote for the educational revolution at Kansas State. He said the discovery of knowledge and its widest possible dissemination were "vital steps," yet by themselves "not enough." Although science and technology required more and more specialization, Milton said:

> Sound judgment in making decisions requires more and more integration. Judgment requires a careful fusing of facts from many disciplines. . . .
>
> Many of the educators who are thinking along these lines are concerned mainly with the liberal arts. It is necessary to start someplace, of course, and it is evident that the liberal arts can provide sequential subjects and teaching methods that will help students understand many basic relationships and will encourage them to become self-educative throughout life.
>
> But the technical schools and colleges have a responsibility, too. Perhaps theirs is the greater responsibility. For in our technical colleges we specialize in scientific disciplines and we therefore face the danger of encouraging a man to become a specialist within one discipline, and a dogmatist in affairs within other disciplines. And lack of understanding between men of varying disciplines is basically no different from lack of understanding between economic groups or nations. Most human understandings stem from a failure of the disagreeing parties to consider objectively the same set of relevant facts and then to reason from those facts toward an agreeable solution. . . .
>
> I conceive my function to be not that of dictating a program for the future but rather that of stimulating all who can help contribute the answers and of integrating their judgments into a useful, attainable program.

Ike received a recording of Milton's speech and wrote Helen that one element was missing. "Please tell him that I thought it was a masterpiece," Dwight said, "but I wish he would have referred to one other responsibility of the educator. It is the necessity of teaching and inculcating good, old-fashioned patriotism—

just that sense of loyalty and obligation to the community that is necessary to the preservation of all the privileges and rights that the community guarantees."

Milton was influenced by his brother's comments. With the aid of private funds, he was hoping to establish an Institute of Citizenship. Ike himself offered to donate $250,000 from a proposed Metro-Goldwyn-Mayer motion picture about his life to help Milton set up just such a program. When the film was not produced because of differences with the studio, Ike spoke to industrialist friends about donating to Kansas State. Dwight visited the campus in 1945, during his post V-E Day trip to the United States. After a brief talk, Ike was cheerfully told by a woman in the crowd: "Ike, you may be a great big general, but in this town you're just Milton's big brother." At a family reunion in Abilene, Ida Eisenhower was asked how she liked having her famous son at home. She gently replied, "Which one do you mean?"

The reorganization of Kansas State was a monumental undertaking. Milton organized the entire faculty into committees to review the existing curriculum and suggest revisions which would help him "put a broad liberal education into all 51 schools." Milton served as chairman of the steering committee and met weekly with representatives from each faculty committee.

Milton's efforts resulted in numerous innovations. A series of comprehensive courses were added with two-term courses in social studies ("Man and the Social World"), science ("Man and the Physical World" and "Biology in Relation to Man"), and humanities ("Man and the Cultural World"), designed to give students a broad education. With a $200,000 grant from the William Volker Foundation of Kansas City, he established an Institute of Citizenship. The institute offered courses such as "War, Peace and the World Community," "Freedom and Responsibility," and "The Journalist in a Free Society," with what Milton termed "its own and very different method of classroom procedure." The classes were mostly discussions and seminars, using original source materials instead of standard texts. A Great Books program was begun. The institute funded the Kansas Study of Education for Citizenship, and some twenty-five high schools launched their own innovative social studies programs in cooperation with Kansas State.

"I was most anxious that, at a time when complex social problems were crying loudly for citizen understanding and action," said Milton, "we should discover how a college could improve its training toward the goal of effective, participating citizenship."

If Milton brought educational changes to Kansas State, he also changed its physical landscape. During the 1930s, Harry Hopkins and his Works Progress Administration had constructed thousands of college buildings throughout the country. But F. D. Farrell, Milton's conservative predecessor, would not accept New Deal assistance. As a result, the college had problems handling its prewar enrollment of four thousand. Expansion became a critical problem when enrollment almost doubled at the end of the war.

Milton's skill in dealing with the legislature brought the college through this crisis. He persuaded legislators to adopt a special educational-building-fund tax at a rate of three-quarters of a mill. Suddenly, Kansas State had a building fund and tax-financed construction of a new library, a student union, and additional classroom facilities. A basketball fieldhouse and two new dormitories were already under construction, as was an All-Faith Chapel, for which Milton had conducted an intensive fund-raising drive. "It really should have been called an All-Protestant Chapel," said one Kansas State official. "There was no Star of David in the chapel and none of the Eastern religions were represented." By the time Milton's building program was finished, the campus had expanded by half. It was the largest growth in the college's history. "I suppose every college president in the country wished at the close of the war that he had at his disposal a plant twice the size of his actual one," Milton later recalled. "Fortunately, the tremendous increase in enrollment that was coming with the end of the war had been anticipated, and we had begun expanding the facilities of the college before the crest of enrollment was reached." To meet immediate demands of the postwar boom, Milton obtained trailers, hangars, dilapidated army barracks, and other military buildings. Some forty acres of temporary buildings were moved in and the college's daily schedule was expanded from eight to fifteen hours to accommodate the 7,500 students. "There were times when I wondered whether the faculty and students could possibly stand the rigorous program we were following," said

Milton. The faculty did not revolt over the longer hours since Milton was to raise their salaries by 75 percent.

He still found time to remain active in national and international affairs, carrying out numerous assignments at the request of President Truman. His off-campus activities drew some criticism, but Milton rationalized that he was performing a "national service" and "building prestige for the institution." In 1945, Truman offered to name Milton as a special assistant to the President or Undersecretary of Agriculture. He had replaced the inept Wickard at Agriculture and wanted Milton to assist the new secretary, Clinton P. Anderson of New Mexico, in merging the War Food Administration with the Department of Agriculture. Milton declined a formal title but agreed to commute between Washington and Kansas for three months on the condition that he work directly with Anderson. Secretary Anderson said then, "Milton knows the department from top to bottom. Personally, I believe him to be the best equipped man in the country to organize the department so that it may effectively carry out its programs and policies." Truman and Anderson went along with Milton's recommendations, and the new Administration commended his role.

Truman shortly afterward named Milton one of three members of a Fact-finding Board in the General Motors and United Auto Workers wage dispute. Since the war, national railroad and coal industry strikes had staggered the economy. Truman told Milton that an auto workers' strike would be disastrous and the UAW had already voted to strike. General Motors president Charles E. Wilson did not cooperate with the panel members, refusing to make financial data available. A 113-day strike followed. Early in January, Milton's board called for a pay increase of 17.4 percent, which was a compromise between the 11.6 offered by Wilson and Reuther's demand for 30 percent. Truman warmly endorsed their recommendation as noninflationary, noting that it would not require a price increase. Reuther, who had privately criticized the finding, gave it public praise. Wilson, later to serve as Defense Secretary in the Eisenhower administration, accused the board of making "unsound assumptions" and vetoed the recommended settlement. Two months later, General Motors and the UAW came to agreement for one cent less per hour than the panel had urged. Truman, impressed with Milton's patience and calm diplomacy, told the college official he would have future need of his services.

In March of 1946, Truman appointed him to the Famine Emergency Committee headed by former President Hoover. It was Hoover's first important government task since leaving the presidency thirteen years earlier. The New York *Sun* wrote that Milton was the logical appointment: "Maybe what's needed in the battle against national food shortages is another Eisenhower—he can tell you anything about agriculture from 'a' to 'e' because he knows his subject from the ground up." Actually, Milton found himself very much in Hoover's shadow. "He was the master," Milton recalled years later. "He needed very little help."

Milton had become deeply interested in the United Nations. As a college student, he had advocated American entry into the League of Nations. In his Kansas State inaugural address, Milton touched a responsive chord when he talked of the need for some international body. The UN came about largely as a result of the idealism and enthusiasm of the American public. It was founded in a San Francisco opera house in the closing days of World War II. Except for a cynical few, the American people somehow expected the new organization to prevent future wars and, in the process, solve most of the world's critical problems.

Milton was fully aware of the flaws which had brought down the League, yet he held great hopes for the UN. Secretary of State James F. Byrnes, the first speaker at the opening session of the UN's General Assembly, said, "I believe it will live because it springs from the impelling necessities of the age." Byrnes and President Truman asked Milton to become an Assistant Secretary-General. Trygve Lie of Norway had been elected Secretary-General and was to have eight assistant secretaries-general, each from a different nation. Milton was the choice of Truman and Byrnes and they urged him to accept the high UN position. They explained the importance of having an American "on the inside" and made reference to the United States' contribution of some 40 percent of the UN budget. Milton would have been interested in a UN trouble-shooting post, with the opportunity to move quickly and decisively in a world crisis, and devote his best efforts to the cause of peace and security. As a mediator and diplomat, he might be in contention for a Nobel Peace Prize and earn international prominence. But the post Truman and Secretary-General Lie wanted Milton to fill was that of a superadministrator, dealing with finance, personnel, and administration. Milton rejected the offer, explaining to Truman that he had been at Kansas State less than three years and could not "in good conscience" resign. Truman made an attempt to dissuade Milton, without success. "If it had been a policy-making position I might well have taken it," Milton said years later. "However, I didn't see any great contributions I could make to the United Nations in that particular job." Byron Price, director of the U. S. Office of Censoring during the war, took the job which Milton turned down and often served as Acting Secretary-General.

In November, Truman appointed Milton as a delegate to the first international conference of the United Nations Educational, Scientific and Cultural Organization in Paris. Earlier that fall Milton had been elected chairman of the U.S. National Commission for UNESCO. At the conference, he was vice chairman of the American delegation, as he would be for the next four years. Milton also became a member of UNESCO's executive board in Paris. "Here, I thought, was a unique opportunity to work for intellectual disarmament and the development of better understanding among nations and peoples," Milton said later. UNESCO became "a dominant interest" in his life. Milton's onetime OWI colleague, poet Archibald MacLeish, had written much of the UNESCO constitution and was an overwhelming favorite to win election as the organization's first Secretary-General. Milton and other American delegates were disappointed when MacLeish tearfully withdrew, declining the office because it would interfere with his writing. British scholar Julian Huxley was subsequently elected as Secretary-General. Milton was decidedly unimpressed with Huxley's judgment and leadership qualities. Milton's pet project at the initial UNESCO conference was a proposal for international freedom of information, an effort to end censorship of newspapers and periodicals and to drop tariffs on importation of international publications. The British, sensitive about rising nationalism in their Third World colonies, argued against the free flow of news and ideas. Milton's idealistic resolution was one of the casualties of the Paris sessions.

Such setbacks frustrated Milton, yet he remained enthusiastic about UNESCO. "UNESCO's job is to build that understanding among the peoples of the world which is essential to the successful functioning of the whole United Nations system," he said then. "Understanding will not in itself give peace; otherwise we wouldn't have civil wars. But neither can there be peace without understanding." Milton thought UNESCO could be instrumental in breaking down nationalistic and Hegelian concepts of education and replace them with one of interdependence and cooperation. As chairman of the national UNESCO commission, Milton advised the State Department on educational and cultural policies and served as official liaison between American organizations and UNESCO. He frequently made speeches before World Affairs councils and other civic organizations to promote UNESCO and was personally responsible for numerous local UNESCO movements. Kansas State became the first institution in the country to establish a student United Nations and a student UNESCO. When Milton emerged as an important force in UNESCO, the student UN was discontinued and the emphasis shifted to UNESCO. County UNESCO groups were organized throughout Kansas, and Milton took pains to visit as many of them as possible.

In spite of his UNESCO and federal activities, Milton did not give Kansas State short shrift. "He did the work of three or four people," recalled former assistant Lowell Brandner. "He worked terribly hard and took a great deal of work home each night. His staff and faculty members were damn glad when he left for a UNESCO conference. It gave them time to breathe. Except during working hours, I tried to avoid him. He expected you to work hard, but no one did as much as he did. I never saw another college president before or since who came close to handling as much work as Milton."

Dean of Administration Russell Thackrey said: "Milton had problems reconciling campus work customs with those of the federal government. In the president's office we kept fairly strict office hours, from eight to five, and Milton was distressed when he would call various administrators in late afternoon on fine days and find them not at the office—probably working in the garden or playing golf at the country club. He gradually became reconciled to the idea that college teachers may do a lot of their work at night or other odd hours, and that there are health and other values associated with outdoor recreation."

In his own home Milton was no less demanding. "Milton was very much a family man," Thackrey said. "He was perhaps a little hard on Milton, Jr. (Bud), in the sense of not appreciating how difficult it is for the son of a university head going to college where his father is president. Bud was a good though not a brilliant student—he maintained a creditable (B or so) average. But Milton, Sr., worried that he wasn't a top student."

At the time, Thackrey voiced concern about Milton's health. "He was having some problems with his eyesight," Thackrey recalled. "It was interfering with his relaxation and he had to give up golf. Some of us finally insisted that he take a month off because he was driving himself too hard." Milton took Thackrey up on the suggestion and went to Minnesota for a vacation, but when he returned threw himself back into his collegiate and off-campus activities with the same intensity. In November of 1947, while attending the second general conference of UNESCO in Mexico City, Milton again pressed for his resolution to reduce censorship barriers and quota restrictions. He became ill and missed some of the deliberations. Ike scolded Milton when he learned of the "siege of illness." He wrote, "I don't know why it is so difficult to make an otherwise intelligent man understand that his own efficiency and his own ability to render useful service depend upon his own good health. Activity must be paced to the capacity of the physical machine to support it and I don't know why you don't apply this simple truth to yourself. . . . I expect a return answer from you saying that you are taking immediately a week's vacation—even if you spend it in your bedroom reading. . . . After all, at this time of year you can take a little shotgun and go out into the fields of Kansas and see if you can shoot a few cottontails. Maybe you don't like to eat them, but there are plenty of people in the town that would like them. It's lots of fun and it provides a good, mild exercise in the tramping you would do through the fields."

Ike soothed his younger brother with a report of a recent visit with Sir John Maud, a British UNESCO delegate. "I must admit that Sir John's account of your performance was a glowing one," he wrote. "He is quite certain that you not only did a remarkable job but says that your retort in the final stages of the conference to the unwarranted Polish attack was a masterpiece. He thought that what you said and the way you said it were both worthy of the most brilliant statesman of any era."

Milton soon admitted that cutting such demanding activities as UNESCO would enable him to control his educational work and his health. In September of 1949, he gave up the UNESCO chairmanship. For all his work at international conferences Milton had disappointingly little to show for his effort. UNESCO's leadership had been too timorous to take a stand on his freedom-for-information proposals, and the organization was becoming increasingly paralyzed by conflicting pressures of member nations. Though satisfied that UNESCO's activities in science and education were of great benefit, Milton felt that more cooperative programs should have been enacted.

The UNESCO period had broadened Milton's perspective about civil rights and equality for blacks. Until then he had at times demonstrated a small-town parochialism and insensitivity that startled some of his liberal associates. He asked a youthful staff member whether he would "eat with a Negro" and seemed surprised when the response was affirmative. When civil-rights activist Bayard Rustin gave a speech on the campus he noted that blacks were not allowed to patronize "the Canteen," a popular soda fountain and restaurant located just off the campus. "I would rather see a whorehouse there," said Rustin. The earthy comment offended Milton, and the Kansas State president voiced his disgust. No action was taken against the business which depended so heavily on the college community.

Although Milton had blind spots, he was troubled by the institutionalized racial discrimination at Kansas State. Some observers felt that he was torn between his humanitarian UNESCO views and personal doubts about desegregation. However, he quietly abolished the college's old-fashioned racist policies. Blacks had been exempt from the mandatory freshman swimming examination and thus prohibited from using the college swimming pool. Milton ruled that all students must take the swimming test. Not long afterward blacks began organizing intramural sports teams. Encouraged by Milton the athletic department recruited black athletes. Big Six conference members Oklahoma and Missouri warned Kansas State that if their team brought black athletes to their campuses the games would be canceled. For Milton it was an acceptable risk and the conference rivals backed down. Blacks were admitted into college housing. One white parent wrote Milton: "I don't want my daughter to live in the same house with a black student." Milton replied tactfully: "I hope you will change your mind." Campus clubs and honor societies were warned that their charters would be revoked if they discriminated on the basis of race or religion.

Unlike his other reforms at Kansas State, there was no publicity about the removal of racial barriers. A series of forthright public statements and edicts would have strengthened Milton's national image and called attention to the widespread discrimination at other colleges and universities, yet he worried that thundering against racism would bring tension and possibly violence to the campus. The memories of the Kansas slave wars and John Brown still sharply divided the state, and Milton had little desire to reopen old wounds. He wrote Ike about discrimination in March of 1948: "At Kansas State I have moved very gradually against discriminatory practices and now, at the end of five years, I have got rid of most of them. A few still exist. I suppose this is the only sensible way to deal with the problem, as I'm sure you'll discover when you get to Columbia. But at the same time I think that steady, positive progress against un-American practices is imperative."

Milton's programs were well received by the student body. To the students, he was a folk hero, a larger-than-life figure whose efforts were making Kansas State a national showcase for state colleges. Despite his prominence, Milton still seemed to have time for the undergraduates. He dropped the ban on campus smoking, much to their delight. Student government was given broader and more substantive responsibilities, including membership on almost all faculty and administration committees. He authorized a student poll rating the efficiency of faculty members. "The students are doing a thorough job," Milton said, "of studying evidence, of formulating judgments, and of arriving at final recommendations." His popularity with students was such that crowds of undergraduates stood outside an auditorium to listen to his speeches. They were impressed that Milton was trying to open up the college and bring it closer to academic respectability. He was a citizen of the world and had brought a new dimension to the staid old campus. His standing-room-only audiences gave him rousing ovations and he reciprocated with a wave and the famous Eisenhower grin.

Though the adulation meant much to Milton, he was becoming restless. The presidency of Kansas State had helped further his career and reputation, but Milton sensed that it was time to make a move. He did not make the decision easily, but Milton had concluded that he would have a much greater impact at a larger college or university. Robert M. Hutchins offered him the vice presidency of the University of Chicago. The contributions which Hutchins had made in transforming American higher education were legendary and Chicago was then recognized as one of the two great universities in the country. Milton turned Hutchins down, explaining to a friend that he had outgrown the role of subordinate. He could best direct his energies at the presidential level. The University of Tennessee offered Milton the presidency, promising to double his Kansas State salary and provide a large expense account. Milton had little desire to move to the South. "I did not feel that I would be happy or effective in a southern state," he wrote Ike. "I would rather remain here and continue to build the educational level of Kansas State. Indeed, I am sufficiently contented with my work here that only an outstanding post elsewhere would cause me to change."

Milton briefly considered an offer to become executive director of the Boy Scouts of America at a board chairman's salary and with a luxurious New York office. "I finally said 'no' to the New York offer," he wrote Ike in March of 1948. "Two things checked me: Helen and I much prefer not to live in New York, and I don't want to move out of the field of higher education in which I've made something of a mark during the past five years." Milton had been approached about his availability for the presidencies of Penn State and the University of Michigan. Ralph Dorn Hetzel, the president of Penn State, had died in October of 1947, and a number of prominent alumni—among them University of Illinois president George Stoddard—had called for Milton's appointment. But James Milholland, a Pittsburgh lawyer and president of the board of regents, declared himself acting president of Penn State and moved into the presidential mansion. At Michigan, the president had not yet retired. "After five years at it, I believe I know how to do a good job of running a college or university," Milton wrote then. "If I give up most outside activities, such as UNESCO, I think I can control my work so that my health won't be unduly jeopardized. There is enormous satisfaction in working with university students, especially the less mature nonveteran students. One is fairly free to express himself in a nonpartisan way on major trends and issues; in other words, one can be honest with himself and at the same time be about as effective as one person ever can be in helping influence the currents of thought that shape our future."

With his options for advancement temporarily closed, Milton found himself courted by both Republicans and Democrats as a prospective political candidate. Senator Arthur Capper, at eighty-three, had decided to retire in 1948 at the end of five consecutive terms. Capper, who had been a leader of the Senate's progressive farm bloc in the 1920s and a Republican ally of the New Deal in the 1930s, watched Milton's meteoric rise with approval. In the summer of 1948, Capper and Alf Landon invited Milton to meet with them in Topeka. They offered to support him for Capper's Senate seat as the Republican candidate, and at the same time H. J. Yount of the CIO said the Democratic nomination was Milton's for the asking. Because of his unique status as a national figure and a native Kansan, Milton could have been the bipartisan choice for the Senate. Of all political offices, a Senate seat would have given him the opportunity to remain active in foreign affairs and national issues. However, Milton was hesitant to leave higher education for the political arena. He advised Capper, Landon, and

Yount that his work at Kansas State was not yet completed. Andrew F. Schoeppel, the lackluster and conservative governor, was subsequently elected to succeed Capper. Milton's political stock continued to rise as newspaper editors and politicians mentioned him favorably as a candidate for the governorship in 1950. National magazines listed him as a possibility for the presidency in 1952, particularly if Dwight remained aloof from politics. Holmes Alexander, writing in *Collier's*, predicted Milton's election to the governorship and offered this scenario:

"Milton Eisenhower will succeed Governor Frank Carlson, who in turn will succeed seventy-seven-year-old Clyde M. Reed in the Senate. After serving the traditional limit of two 2-year terms as governor, Eisenhower will replace Andrew F. Schoeppel, Kansas' junior U.S. senator, who is expected to retire gracefully. . . . The name of Milton Eisenhower (he's only fifty) will be industriously tossed around during the next two presidential seasons as a progressive Republican."

As an Eisenhower-for-Governor campaign quietly developed late in 1949, Milton issued a terse "no comment" when asked about the efforts of his supporters. If he stayed in Kansas, such a race would provide him with a new challenge. Both of the state's U.S. senators and the governor indicated they would support Milton's nomination and election. Organized labor and Democratic leaders were also friendly. Milton's staff was divided on what his decision would be, though publicly his spokesmen disclaimed any association with the political overtures.

In the meantime, Milton was finally in contention for the presidency of Penn State. For more than two years, Milholland had attempted to gain permanent appointment as college president. As president of the board of regents, he nullified early attempts to search for an academic administrator to succeed the deceased Hetzel. Milholland, an industrial lawyer, governed the college not unlike a factory. When the faculty pressed him for representation on the board of regents, he delivered what became known as the "pickle speech." Milholland imperiously asked the professors: "Can you imagine an employee of the H. J. Heinz Company electing a board of directors?" Milholland's relationship with the faculty steadily deteriorated, but he would not relinquish his claim to the college presidency.

The regents voted in Harrisburg, with Milholland still presiding, on January 21, 1950. Milton narrowly defeated the acting president. "Eisenhower was elected by the narrowest vote possible with the other candidate sitting in the chair," recalled Penn State counsel Roy Wilkinson. "So Milton was coming to Penn State under circumstances that could have made it very difficult if not impossible to function, for Milholland was still chairman of the board. As it turned out, Milton had him eating out of his hand." A subdued Milholland made the announcement of Milton's selection.

Kansas State was stunned by the announcement that Milton was leaving. "The town just can't seem to believe it," said Lowell Brandner, one of Milton's speech writers. "It was like a bombshell. We knew other colleges were interested in Mr. Eisenhower, but we didn't think he would accept another position. It took twelve calls to reach him at his home." Fred M. Harris, chairman of the Kansas Board of Regents, expressed regret at Milton's decision. "He has done a monumental job at Kansas State," Harris said. "Of course we cannot attempt to interfere with his personal progress, and we are proud that the eastern college selected our president."

Milton told the Kansas regents: "It is with considerable anguish that I've made a decision to accept the new offer." On January 30, he wrote Ike: "I made the decision largely on the basis of family—the Eakins in Washington and you and Earl not far away." There were other factors in his switch—his interests in national and world affairs had attracted him to the East, and Penn State was one of the largest colleges in the country. Moreover, it enabled Milton to return to the state where his ancestors had settled almost two hundred years earlier.

"Incidentally," Ike wrote Milton, "with your departure from Kansas, the only real connection the family will have with the State is through Roy's widow and one of the children. It seems odd, doesn't it?"

As Milton left Kansas State in July, he could boast of more achievements in his seven years than any three of his predecessors combined. Yet his success was resented by many faculty members and department heads. "Milton Eisenhower used democratic methods to achieve his dictatorial purposes," snorted one dean upon Milton's departure. Most of Milton's faculty detractors were from the technical schools and they came to dislike him when he kept speaking out about the dangers of specialization. His critics had opposed the comprehensives and the Institute of Citizenship and were indignant about the professors brought in by Milton with special privileges. Milton had misgivings about some of his department heads, but was careful not to humiliate them by removing them from office. In some instances, he created new administrative positions and put his own men above weak or slothful deans. Milton managed to push his amiable but bumbling dean of arts and sciences into the background without saying anything against him. He simply ignored him, and made most of the important decisions himself. He recruited scholars to upgrade liberal arts departments and appointed the first Ph.D. to the English faculty. As a result of Milton's selective hiring, Kansas State offered its students new intellectual challenges and received accreditation for more graduate programs. With each innovation, the anti-Eisenhower bloc became more resentful. Milton, whose only college degree had been his 1924 Bachelor of Science diploma in industrial journalism, had encouraged students and subordinates to address him as "Dr. Eisenhower" after William Jardine had presented him with an honorary doctorate in December of 1943. This affectation struck even friendly associates as a weakness and a vanity. In the spring of 1951, almost one year from his move to Pennsylvania, the Eisenhower critics at Kansas State got their revenge. The faculty senate defeated a proposal to award Milton an honorary doctorate.

"Milton may have stayed a year too long," a former aide recalled years later. "As an activist and mover he shook a lot of people up. The conflicts were all in the general education area. He had just about used up his bank account of good will. Yet he deserved all the national attention he received and we were damn lucky to have had him. He learned a lot and grew a lot here." Though some of his changes at Manhattan had been merely cosmetic, Milton had given Kansas State a vision for its future and transformed it from a small college to a major institution. "Milton was really one of the pioneers in the general education movement," said his successor at Kansas State, James McCain. "He had the structure pretty well established by the time I arrived in 1950." Milton was finally invited back to Kansas State to receive an honorary doctorate—in 1963—and a building now bears his name on the Manhattan campus. His perception and courage had been vindicated.

Chapter Thirteen

RETURN OF THE HERO

Nothing would ever be the same for Ike after V-E Day. At Churchill's invitation, he went to London on June 12. His welcome was one of the greatest ovations in the history of the English-speaking world. He rode through the ancient city in an open carriage drawn by white horses as millions cheered him. In a ceremony at the Guildhall, Ike was made a Freeman of the City of London. His speech, which he had spent hours drafting and redrafting, was a masterpiece of simplicity and idealism:

> Humility must always be the portion of any man who receives acclaim earned in the blood of his followers and the sacrifices of his friends. . . . The only attitude in which a commander may with satisfaction receive the tributes of his friends is in humble acknowledgment that, no matter how unworthy he may be, his position is a symbol of great human forces that have labored arduously and successfully for a righteous cause. . . . This feeling of humility cannot erase, of course, my great pride in being tendered the Freedom of London. I am not a native of this land. I come from the very heart of America. In the superficial aspects by which we ordinarily recognize family relationships, the town where I was born and the one where I was reared are far separated from

this great city. . . . Yet kinship among nations is not determined in such measurements as proximity of size and age. Rather we should turn to those inner things—call them what you will—I mean those intangibles that are the real treasures free men possess.

The city he had helped rescue from destruction was a proper setting for this personal triumph. One London newspaper printed his Guildhall address on the front page next to Lincoln's *Gettysburg Address*. Two days later, more than one million Parisians paid tribute as General de Gaulle presented Ike with a medal under the Arc de Triomphe. "There have been differences," said Ike, "you and I have had some. But let us bring our troubles to each other frankly and face them together. . . . Let's be friends."

His American homecoming on the hot morning of June 18 was no less extraordinary. Thirty thousand persons crowded into Washington's National Airport anticipating his arrival. As the Supreme Commander stepped from his plane, they chanted "Ike! Ike! Ike!" So loud and sustained were the cheers that the bands were drowned out. More than one million lined the streets of the capital city as Ike waved and grinned in an open car en route to Capitol Hill where he spoke before a joint session of Congress. That evening he dined with President Truman at a White House stag dinner. The next morning, Ike flew to New York and was paraded through thirty-seven miles of streets where some four million waved and cheered. Mayor Fiorello La Guardia, who had wanted a position on Ike's wartime staff, presented him with a Gold Medal and honorary citizenship of the city. "New York simply cannot do this to a Kansas farmer boy and keep its reputation for sophistication," Dwight said. At a dinner given in his honor at the Waldorf-Astoria, the Supreme Commander said "peace is an absolute necessity to this world." He added, "We should be ready to defend our rights, but we should be considerate and recognize the rights of the other man."

On June 21, Ike was feted in Kansas City and said: "This country here . . . has been called the heart of isolationism. I do not believe it. No intelligent man can be an isolationist, and there is no higher level of education anywhere in the world than in the

Midwest." He was overcome with emotion the next day in Abilene as twenty thousand people, more than four times the town's population, gathered in City Park to welcome him home. His four brothers had returned for a joyous reunion and the night before they had stayed together with their elderly mother in their modest boyhood home. "Through this world it has been my fortune, or misfortune, to wander at considerable distances," Dwight said then. "Never has this town been outside my heart and memory." He talked of boyhood fantasies of a hero's welcome from his home town and said, "That dream of forty-five years or more ago has been realized beyond the wildest stretches of my own imagination." His voice cracked as he asked his town to give all returning veterans the same warmth extended to him. "All of us are practically choked with emotion," he concluded. "Good luck, and God bless every one of you." The crowd roared in thunderous applause and cheers, overwhelming Ike once again. He struggled to hold back tears and managed to grin and wave. His series of triumphant personal appearances were without precedent in American history, but the return to Abilene had been the most satisfying of all. "If what I have seen today expresses the heart of America," he said, "I have no fear for the future of my soldiers." Ike said he was amazed and astonished at the outpouring of good will. He told friends and confidants that his position of prominence and trust would never be exploited for commercial gain, but he would speak out for international peace and understanding and continue to be a symbol for the principles of American democracy.

In July, Ike went back to Europe, dismantling SHAEF and serving as military commander of the U.S. occupation zone in Germany. A warm friendship developed between him and Soviet Marshal Georgi H. Zhukov, who served on the Allied Control Council and had been one of the most brilliant field commanders of the war. Zhukov was at Ike's side later that summer when Eisenhower was feted at a five-hour parade in Moscow's Red Square. "General Eisenhower is a very great man," Marshal Stalin told U.S. Ambassador Averell Harriman then, "not only because of his military accomplishments but because of his human, friendly, kind, and frank nature." Ike and Harriman disagreed about postwar relations between the Soviets and Americans, the Supreme Commander predicting an era of friendship and Harriman taking a more pessimistic view.

During that fateful summer of 1945, Stalin, Churchill, and Truman had gathered at Potsdam to divide the spoils of a conquered Germany and discuss the final campaign against Japan. In the middle of the conference, Churchill was displaced as Prime Minister by Clement Attlee when the Labour Party won a parliamentary majority. The Allied leaders called for Japan's unconditional surrender, and Truman confided that America had a new weapon, the atomic bomb which he was prepared to use against the Japanese. Secretary of War Stimson told Ike of the new weapon and the plan to use it. Ike had "a feeling of depression" and said that the United States would be scorned by world opinion for using something "as horrible and destructive" as the atomic bomb. What made this such an atrocity was that it was "completely unnecessary" to drop the bomb because Japan was already defeated.

Stimson hotly disputed Ike's remarks, but their conversation had no bearing on Truman's decision. The President had already authorized dropping the bombs on Hiroshima and Nagasaki on August 6 and 9. Japan surrendered on August 14, and the most destructive war in history was brought to a close. Ike would never lose his skepticism of the weapon and later referred to it as a "hellish contrivance."

At Potsdam, Truman made no effort to disguise his hero worship of Ike. During an automobile ride with Ike and Bradley, Truman began talking about the future of some wartime leaders. Ike's rejoinder was that he hoped for the seclusion of a quiet country home where it would be possible to live in semiretirement and "do what little I could" to promote the principles of world peace and interdependence. The plain-spoken Truman turned to face him directly and said: "General, there is nothing that you may want that I won't try to help you get. That definitely and specifically includes the presidency in 1948." On his recent visit to Abilene, Ike had testily disavowed all political ambitions when questioned about a future presidential race. Yet Truman's proposition was not so easily dismissed. A stunned Ike laughed and said: "Mr. President, I don't know who will be your opponent for the presidency, but it will not be I."

Truman called Ike back to Washington in November, appointing him to succeed Marshall as U.S. Army Chief of Staff. Although it was the highest position in the Army and the ultimate goal of nearly every American general, Ike had little enthusiasm for the promotion. He told Truman of his reluctance and wish to retire. Presiding over the demobilization of a wartime army was "frankly distasteful," he said privately.

Inevitably, the desk job was a letdown after the momentous events of the Supreme Command. Ike was restless and often irritable, a man of action confined to desk work and conferences. His office was in the Pentagon, which had opened three years before as the largest office building in the world, an ugly five-sided structure with seven and a half million square feet of space and a maze of endless hallways. Ike became lost in the miles of corridors on one occasion when he was returning to his office from the officers' mess. He was no less baffled by the building than a wide-eyed tourist.

His attitude about the job showed little change. In December he wrote John that he was "struggling away with the job that you and I used to talk about. Both of us then agreed that it was a sorry place to light after having commanded a theater of war. Far from changing my opinion, I am merely confirming the correctness of our conclusions." In a letter to Hazlett, he wrote: "For myself, there is nothing I want so much as an opportunity to retire. . . . The job I am taking now represents nothing but straight duty."

In the meantime, some British officials were proposing Ike as the first Secretary-General of the United Nations. Informal discussions took place with Secretary of State James F. Byrnes, who told British representatives that Dwight was committed to his job as Chief of Staff. The London *Daily Mail* said British leaders urged President Truman to convince Dwight to become available. The London *Daily Express* said in an editorial: "Where is a man who could fill the job? In America. His name is Dwight Eisenhower. . . . Time and again he proved in complex international councils of war that his genius was in the unifying of men. He has the shrewdest political intelligence, a personality not one man can speak of without affection."

His refusal to indicate any interest was in keeping with military tradition. Norway's foreign minister, Trygve Lie, was elected to the United Nations post. That the Eisenhower boom had started in Britain was another demonstration of his enormous popularity there. Later in the year, there were published reports that Truman was considering him as ambassador to the Court of St. James's.

The Chief of Staff was troubled by the country's demand for instant demobilization. Marshall had earlier promised that soldiers with two years of service would be discharged by March, and the separation rate soon reached one million a month. At the end of 1945, five million soldiers had been returned to their families. Ike later recalled that the Army "let its heart run away with its head." He went public with his protest, testifying before a congressional committee that dismantling American forces in Europe was nothing less than abandoning the "purposes for which we fought." President Truman concurred that the nation could not maintain commitments with a skeleton force and reduced the discharge rate to 300,000 a month in January. The plan to release all two-year veterans by March was suddenly dropped.

American occupation troops staged mass demonstrations in France, Germany, England, Japan, the Philippines, and Hawaii. Most of the soldiers were idle and bored, marking time until their discharges. The war was over and it seemed unfair that they were still in uniform.

Ike ordered an end to all GI demonstrations and said that he was doing everything possible to give the men who had "borne the brunt of battle a chance to go home." He directed all overseas theater commanders to send home "without delay all troops for whom there is no longer military need." Much of the unrest Ike blamed on the vocal "bring them home" sentiment in the United States. "This clamor to bring the boys home gets back to the soldier and has a very definite influence on his attitude and morale," he said at a news conference. "He thinks, 'Well, if everyone says bring us on home we must not have much to do over here.' . . . If the democratic Allies believe that a good solid occupation of hostile territory is necessary, it is up to us to keep our forces at reasonable strength."

He went to Capitol Hill and said the postwar occupation of hostile countries "cannot be obscured by emotion and near hysteria." His testimony pacified most of the congressmen, but on January 23 he was confronted at the Capitol by more than twenty angry servicemen's wives demanding that their husbands be sent home at once. The women, representatives of assorted "Bring Them Home" organizations, backed the Chief of Staff into a corner near a window and sharply questioned him for a half hour. Ike said that the encounter left him "emotionally upset." Years later, John Eisenhower said of the meeting, "They ought to have had their tails kicked."

In Ike's opinion, the rapid demobilization had been a disaster. He testified in March that the Army had been gutted to the point where there were no divisions in the continental United States fully trained and prepared for combat. "With respect to the operating efficiency of forces left in the United States, I should say it was very low," he told the House Military Affairs Committee. From his military point of view, Ike stood for unification of the armed forces and universal military training. Asked to name the army's greatest need, he said without hesitation: "Trained men."

He lived with Mamie at the chief of staff's official residence at Fort Myer and, for the first time in their marriage, had a full-time domestic staff. Ike began reading seed catalogs and planted his own garden. That summer he prepared sauerkraut from his own cabbages. His work day was often more than fourteen hours, and the strain and tension sometimes left him exhausted. As a concession, he trimmed the working day to eleven hours. Mamie accompanied him on a summer inspection trip to England and Europe. In Scotland, they spent a weekend as guests of the British royal family at Balmoral Castle. King George VI and Queen Elizabeth and their two daughters, Elizabeth and Margaret, were all present to meet their American visitors. The Eisenhowers were later received by Queen Mother Mary in London, described by Mamie as the most remarkable person she had ever met. Mamie said the aging queen struck her "as a great, unselfish mother who valued family love above all else." Ike and Mamie later traveled to Latin America, where he was cheered by adoring crowds in Rio de Janeiro, Panama, and Mexico City. "The cordiality of the welcome not only bordered on the hysterical, but it was sustained throughout our stay in each city," Ike wrote to a friend. After the eventful journey, he was so exhausted that an attack of indigestion hospitalized him.

Ike's role was all the more frustrating because two of his most trusted colleagues and advisers, Marshall and Smith, were far removed from Washington. Truman had asked Marshall to serve as a mediator between the Chinese Nationalists and Communists, and appointed Smith as ambassador to Moscow. "It was a blow to Beetle Smith when he was told that they wanted him to accept the Moscow job," Ike wrote a friend shortly after the appointment. "I know of no one better qualified for the job but of course his ambitions do not lie along diplomatic and political lines." Smith had been personally selected by Dwight to head the Operations Division of the War Department and his departure was a great disappointment.

The Chief of Staff continued to confide in Smith through correspondence. "Each day brings a succession of troubling and worrisome problems," he wrote on August 30, 1946. "There never seems to be a piece of good news. Such of these matters as are inescapable and inherent in current chaotic conditions, I can take in my stride. When they result from stupidity or negligence or complete lack of cooperation on the part of some of the other people with whom we have to deal, my patience and temper both give out. I will be more than delighted when the time comes that I can retire to a cabin somewhere and take it easy and let others worry about budgets and all the other things that are constantly on my desk."

As America's most popular war hero and highest-ranking soldier, Ike was in demand for speeches and public appearances. He was troubled that the wartime alliance had begun to disintegrate. Winston Churchill had made a ringing attack on the Soviet Union in his "Iron Curtain" speech at Fulton, Missouri, in March and Truman was taking an increasingly hard line. Ike was not blindly optimistic, but he still hoped that the Soviet-American wartime alliance could work in peacetime. At a news conference, he even made the observation that the nation's relations with the Soviet Union were improving. In a speech before the American Newspaper Publishers Association, delivered in New York a month after Churchill's belligerent "Iron Curtain" speech, Ike spoke of building a "universal and enduring peace" through "organized international cooperation, mutual international understanding, and progressive international disarmament."

He made twenty-six speeches in his first six months in the Pentagon, and his most important speeches were written in his study at Fort Myer. "One of my worst problems is how to decline a real flood of invitations that come from various associations, individuals, and patriotic bodies, all presenting altruistic or public-spirited purposes and all insisting that I could help them mightily by an appearance and a speech," Ike wrote an old friend. "Due to my very great desire to promote a few simple ideas in which I so earnestly believe, it is indeed difficult for me to say 'no,' except when I think I detect a mere desire on the part of a chairman or a secretary to use me for a little additional publicity for his meeting. The trouble is that in the vast percentage of cases I think the sponsors are really sincere and this of course awakens a desire on my part to help in my own feeble way. Nevertheless the whole thing is extremely wearing."

On the eve of his inspection tour of the Far East in May of 1946, Ike met with Truman at the White House. Truman told him of his growing dissatisfaction with Secretary of State James F. Byrnes, who had been trying to restrain Truman's hawkish foreign policy. The conversation turned to Marshall's efforts to achieve a viable compromise in China. Dwight was scheduled to visit Marshall in Nanking and wanted to know if Truman had any message for the wartime Chief of Staff. "One of you two are going to be my next Secretary of State," said Truman. The State Department had even less appeal for Ike than the Pentagon. On May 9, he lunched with Generalissimo and Madame Chiang Kai-shek and met shortly afterward with Marshall. Dwight amended Truman's message and said: "Mr. Truman says you're going to be his Secretary of State." Replied Marshall: "Hell, I'll take any job to get out of this place!" Marshall succeeded Byrnes in January of 1947, and Ike subtly avoided an unwanted appointment to an even more frustrating if prestigious position.

Speculation about Ike as a presidential candidate in 1948 had been widespread since his return from Europe. Truman might have offered him the State Department portfolio as a means of removing his most formidable opponent from consideration. For his part, Ike took pains to discourage all talk of a political career. The developing boom for the Chief of Staff threatened to interfere with his friendly working relationship with Truman. An old friend of Truman's was curtly ushered out of the Oval Office after tactlessly suggesting to the President that he could defeat anyone in 1948—except Eisenhower.

Ike told a visitor to his Pentagon office that he could make a more significant contribution to world peace as a symbol and spokesman for American idealism than as a political candidate or even as President of the United States. In March of 1946, he wrote one of his oldest friends: "When trying to express my sentiments myself I merely get so vehement that I grow speechless, if not hysterical. I cannot conceive of any set of circumstances that could ever drag out of me permission to consider me for any political post from Dog Catcher to Grand High Supreme King of the Universe." Yet on his Far Eastern trip, Ike found himself being urged to seek the presidency by his old mentor Douglas MacArthur. For nearly three hours, the five-star generals discussed the ultimate political race—each proposing that the other run. One of MacArthur's aides later said that Ike's erstwhile superior had been angling for an Eisenhower endorsement that night. But after disclaiming any interest in partisan politics, Ike was not about to jeopardize himself by making a commitment to anyone else. MacArthur, who fervently wanted the Republican presidential nomination, became bitter when Ike's popularity eclipsed his own.

A newspaper report from Washington in the winter of 1947 said that Ike had told some friends in Florida that he was considering running for President if the American people demonstrated that they truly wanted him. "It's a lie!" thundered Ike when he saw the published report while on a fishing trip. When he was introduced to an audience as "Our next President," he said: "There is no use denying that I'll fly to the moon because I couldn't if I wanted to. The same goes for politics."

At times, Ike renounced the presidency in the most explicit terms. During his 1945 Abilene visit, he had said: "In the strongest language you can command, you can state that I have no political ambitions at all. Make it even stronger than that if you can. I'd like to go further than Sherman in expressing myself on this subject." In 1884, Civil War hero William Tecumseh Sherman, then considered a likely bet for the Republican presidential nomination, stated that he would not accept the nomination, nor serve if elected. Ike's statement that he categorically opposed being swept into the presidency might well have silenced his supporters. But the Gallup poll indicated in August of 1947 that 35 percent of the American public favored his candidacy. He was annoyed by the persistent question, yet on a trip to Mississippi he asserted: "I wouldn't have the effrontery to say I wouldn't be President of the United States. No one has asked me." Hazlett wrote Ike asking whether he was becoming a candidate. On August 25, Ike responded:

> Please don't concern yourself about the possibility that I have "changed my mind." You may be certain that I have been absolutely truthful in every public statement I have made on the personal political question and you can be equally sure that I have not directly or indirectly given to anyone the right to represent my feelings and convictions differently at any place or at any time.
>
> It is difficult for many people—particularly those who have led a political life or are engaged in newspaper or radio work—to believe anyone who disclaims political ambition. Even though they may accept without the faintest hint of challenge any statement a man might make about any other subject in the world, on this one thing they maintain a position of doubt, not to say suspicion. . . . My own deepest concern involves America's situation in the world today. Her security position and her international leadership I regard as matters of the gravest concern to all of us and to our national future. Allied to these questions, of course, is that of internal health,

particularly maximum productivity. While there may be little that I can do about such matters, I do have the satisfaction of feeling that whatever I try to do is on a national and not on any partisan basis. Moreover, I flatter myself to believe that the people who listen to me understand that I am talking or working for all, not for any political party or for any political ambition. This is the attitude I hope I can preserve to the end of my days.

To avoid more political publicity, Ike established the ground rule that his press conferences be confined to military affairs. Exclusive interviews with reporters were declined. Former Interior Secretary Harold Ickes, who had begun a new career as a syndicated political columnist, sympathized with the Chief of Staff and wrote that Republicans were trying to force Dwight to foreclose all options. "I suggest that, in the interest of the country, General Eisenhower be let alone," wrote Ickes. "If the reporters continue to hound him, he should send them about their business in no uncertain tones." Ike lost his temper at a Chicago press conference when a reporter asked if the Army was attempting to direct national policy. "If," he snapped, "you can name one man in the Army who has any ideas of directing government policy just let me know and he won't be in the Army long." The "Reluctant Dragon" of American politics was finding it difficult to ward off sharp-edged questions with his celebrated grin.

Ike described his inner conflict to Smith, writing on September 17, 1947:

I do not believe that you or I or anyone else has the right to state, categorically, that he will not perform any duty that his country might demand of him. You did not want to become our ambassador to Moscow. There is no question in my mind that Nathan Hale accepted the order to serve as a spy with extreme reluctance and distaste. Nevertheless, he did so serve. Now in this matter of a political role the question naturally arises, "What circumstances could ever convince you or me that it was a duty to become a political candidate?" Certainly I do not see how anyone could obtain a conviction of

> duty from a deadlocked convention that should name him as a "compromise" selection after great portions of the delegates, representing equally large portions of the population, had failed to secure the naming of their own first choices. Under such circumstances I believe that instead of feeling a call to duty a man would have to consider himself merely a political expediency or political compromise. Consequently, as long as he should feel—as I do—that he does not want a political office and does not believe himself to be particularly suited for it, I think he would be perfectly within his rights to reject the suggestion.

Life magazine had published a scenario with Dwight emerging as the nominee following a fourth ballot Taft-Dewey stalemate. The notion of becoming a creation of a smoke-filled room was repugnant to Ike. A month later, he was even more distressed by a radio report which said Ike had held a clandestine meeting with Henry A. Wallace during which the former Vice President had tried to persuade the Chief of Staff to run against Truman for the Democratic presidential nomination. "Not only is the entire story fantastic," Ike wrote Milton, "but the implication that I had even countenanced people talking to me about a subject like this while I am still in the Army is very close to a challenge to a soldier's loyalty. . . . I believe that what irritates me more than anything else is the veiled, sometimes open, charge that I am being dishonest."

President Truman, with his political fortunes declining in public-opinion polls and the specter of a third-party challenge from the left led by Wallace, renewed his invitation to make Ike the 1948 presidential nominee of the Democratic Party. Through a friendly intermediary, Secretary of the Army Kenneth Royall, Truman advised his Chief of Staff that the nomination was his for the asking. As if to prove his sincerity, Truman offered to become Ike's vice-presidential running mate. The proposition was without precedent in American political history, yet Ike calmly rejected it. His own prospects, Ike told a friend, became remote when Wallace began the third-party initiative. It looked as if the Republicans could win the presidency with Dewey, Taft, Vandenberg, Stassen, or any prospective candidate. The need for nominating a popular war hero to capture the White House no longer existed. The nightmare of an Eisenhower ground swell had haunted Dewey and Taft for months. Ike hoped that his ordeal was over. "Personally I feel that there are a number of candidates in the field who would make acceptable political leaders," he wrote a friend, "and I cannot conceive of any set of probable circumstances that would ever convince me that it was my duty to enter such a hectic arena."

Remaining above the battle did not make him any less bewildered. "All of the so-called experts in the field of political analysis continuously point out that without artificial stimulus all these 'boomlets' for particular individuals sooner or later collapse," he wrote Hazlett. "I have been pinning my faith and my hopes on the correctness of this assertion—I have made my position very clear and still feel sure that I am not going to be faced with an impossible situation. It has been a most burdensome, not to say annoying, development. It has even resulted in bringing down on my naked head a lot of attacks from people who would ordinarily have no reason for concerning themselves about me one way or the other. But because they see me in some possible thwarting of their own purposes, they use the method of cursing anyone that gets in their way." Right-wing commentators such as Westbrook Pegler and Fulton Lewis, Jr., made Dwight their favorite target. He was described in the *American Mercury* as an incompetent Chief of Staff, and other reactionary publications portrayed him as an appeaser of the Soviets. Some of their propaganda claimed that Ike was Jewish and thus part of an international conspiracy. It was difficult to be immune to such vicious and mean-spirited abuse.

Still, Ike had not gone so far as Sherman had in his famous withdrawal of 1884. "I'm not going to give anyone the satisfaction of hearing me say I'm not going to run, either!" he said when asked to make an explicit statement. In January of 1948, Ike's longtime friend Harry Butcher wrote an article for a national magazine disclosing that during the war Eisenhower had said he would be honored to serve as President if nominated by both parties. "If the challenge is put to General Ike at the forthcoming Republican Convention," wrote Butcher, "he will accept, out of a sense of duty to his country. And maybe that's the big reason why I like Ike."

Confusion persisted about what Ike would do in such circumstances. By the middle of January, he was asking his Pentagon staff for advice, expressing concern about declining a prize that had not been won, and handling the touchy matter of a Chief of Staff's propriety. Furthermore, he was still bothered about his sense of duty. He gave his answer when Leonard V. Finder, publisher of the Manchester *Union-Leader* proposed to enter him in the New Hampshire Republican primary. The Chief of Staff wrote numerous drafts of his response over a two-week period, consulting with Secretary of Defense James Forrestal about the final version. The letter to Finder was released on January 22, 1948. Simultaneously came an announcement from the Pentagon that he would decline the nomination even if the convention chose him. Ike wrote Finder:

> I have hitherto refrained from making the bald statement that I would not accept nomination, although this has been my intention since the subject was first mentioned to me. . . . This omission seems to have been a mistake, since it has inadvertently misled sincere and disinterested Americans. But my reticence stemmed from cogent reasons. The first was that such an expression would smack of effrontery. . . . A second and even deeper reason was a persistent doubt that I could phrase a flat refusal without appearing to violate that concept of duty which calls upon every good citizen to place no limitation upon his readiness to serve in any designated capacity.
>
> It is my conviction that the necessary and wise subordination of the military to civil power will be best sustained, and our people will have greater confidence that it is so sustained, when lifelong professional soldiers, in the absence of some obvious and overriding reasons, abstain from seeking higher political office. . . .
>
> Politics is a profession, a serious, complicated, and in its true sense, a noble one. In the American scene I see no dearth of men fitted . . . for national leadership. On the other hand,

nothing in the international or domestic situation especially qualifies for the most important office in the world a man whose adult years have been spent in the country's military forces. At least this is true in my case. . . . In any case, my decision to remove myself completely from the political scene is definite and positive.

The Republican Eisenhower boom came to a sudden halt. A Herblock cartoon in the Washington *Post* showed "Mr. American Public" weeping at the headlines that Dwight would not run. Ike told a friend, "I feel as if I've had an abscessed tooth pulled. For the first time in months, I sleep at night." Ike wrote Milton that only the Kansas State president and two others among his inner circle had agreed with the Finder letter. In a January 26 letter to Hazlett, Ike wrote: "Now that it is done, I can at least devote my mind unreservedly to a number of other important things and will not feel like I am constantly on the 'witness stand.'"

In the meantime, he was preparing to leave the Pentagon. For months, he had complained about his problems as Chief of Staff. "Frankly, this job is even more irritating and wearing than I had anticipated," he wrote Smith on April 18, 1947. "We are still in the latter stages of destroying the greatest machine that the United States ever put together and at the same time trying to plan in orderly fashion to meet the needs of the moment as well as the longer range requirements of the future."

There had been offers to go into private industry and he had been interested in the possibility of becoming an executive with a book-publishing firm. Ike wrote Hazlett that a university offer did not seem quite right for one with his background and interests. "I would far rather attempt to write," said Ike.

However, the trustees of Columbia University persuaded Ike to accept an appointment as university president. "I told them that they were talking to the wrong Eisenhower," he recalled years later. Ike urged them to consider Milton, then president of Kansas State. According to a story circulated at the time and which has since become part of Columbia's folklore, a member of the Columbia presidential search committee had said: "What about Eisenhower?" Another member of the committee sent a letter after the meeting—to Ike, who accepted, while the rest of the trustees had anticipated that their president Eisenhower would be Milton. "The university would have been much better off with Milton," a Columbia University professor asserted thirty years later. "But the trustees wanted General Eisenhower."

Ike had been approached by Thomas J. Watson, chief executive of International Business Machines and head of Columbia's search committee. Dwight's reservations were made known—if not his brother Milton, the trustees should consider some other scholar or career educator. He might consider a college presidency, but in a much smaller school in a country setting. The very idea of Columbia University in New York City seemed intimidating to the man from Abilene. Watson and another trustee, Doubleday & Company president Douglas Black, argued that Ike's background in training young men, his firsthand knowledge of world affairs, and his rich administrative background gave him more than adequate preparation. In June of 1947, Ike met with Watson at West Point to further discuss the Columbia post. During the visit, he said that another drawback might be the social and entertainment aspects of the presidency. Mrs. Nicholas Murray Butler frequently gave receptions for more than one thousand people in the Morningside Drive presidential mansion. Her luncheons and dinners were on the grand scale and included many courses. Ike later reported that Watson "reassured me about the volume of social duties that might fall upon Mamie. He says that in New York particularly all of the entertaining is done either by one of the Trustees—each of whom I presume is a rich man—or by one of the deans. The president of the college is expected to entertain only when some very distinguished personage comes through the city and where it appears to the advantage of the college for prestige or other reasons to entertain the individual."

Ike reported to Milton: "Mr. Watson told me further that the matter has been one of lively discussion among all the trustees, and that the faint hope I gave them at West Point last week has gratified them all immeasurably. Of course this may be exaggeration, but it makes me feel a little bit more confident about going further with negotiations. . . . He [Watson] suggested to me also that because of my announced dislike for New York that he was getting some of the Board interested in providing a small country place in addition to one in town. I told him that I would discuss this matter with him when we got to New York, since I think I should actually like to start acquiring a small house of our own which we might one day leave to John."

President Truman had given Ike permission to accept the presidency if he so decided. Financially, Ike had many more lucrative offers than the $25,000-a-year Columbia presidency, yet by congressional act he was also entitled to a $15,000 annual government salary as General of the Army. So he could live very comfortably on the two incomes and maintain his dignity as a world figure. Following the Civil War, one of Ike's greatest heroes, General Robert E. Lee had begun a new career as a college president, although no American general had ever been selected to head an educational institution as prestigious as Columbia.

Late in the afternoon on Tuesday, June 24, Frederick Coykendall, chairman of the trustees, announced Ike's appointment. Columbia's president emeritus, eighty-five-year-old Nicholas Murray Butler, said: "General Eisenhower's great ability and remarkable character in dealing with world problems are precisely what the world needs today in the administration of a great university."

Raymond Moley, a former Columbia political science professor and onetime adviser to Franklin D. Roosevelt, wrote in his *Newsweek* column: "Eisenhower will need no apology in approaching an educational office. His interest in education is a trait that has been overshadowed by his more glamorous military career. . . . But it was as a massive public figure that Eisenhower attracted the Columbia trustees. The Columbia tradition demanded such a public figure."

In his first appearance at Columbia's Low Memorial Library, Ike received a chilly reception from the university's deans and administrators. "Nobody," he began, "is more keenly aware of my academic shortcomings than I am." By the end of his brief remarks, the atmosphere was friendly. Harry Morgan Ayres, director of the School of General Studies and a nationally prominent literary scholar, told some doubtful colleagues: "You have forgotten one thing, gentlemen—the Guildhall speech General Eisenhower delivered in London. I believe that to be one of the three greatest speeches ever made in the English language. Only a fine scholar could have written that."

Ike was somewhat more restrained in assessing his qualifications. He wrote Hazlett: "I know nothing about the workings of a great university and am certainly far from being an 'educator.' . . . With regard to the lack of scholarly attainment, the Board of Trustees insists that they want an organizer and a leader, not a professor." Dwight also wrote: "Mamie and I both hate New York City and recoil from the thought of living there permanently." In fact, he said they were looking for a "country place somewhere up in the Connecticut area and we confidently expect to live in such a place throughout the year."

Just as Milton had told the Kansas regents that he would continue his career as a presidential trouble shooter, so Ike advised the Columbia trustees that he would be in frequent demand as an adviser on national defense and military policy. In the letter to Hazlett, he wrote that an important factor in his acceptance was "their clear understanding of the point that I would never really separate myself from the uniformed services of the country. I explained to them carefully that I have lived 36 years in one idea and for one purpose and that as a result I have absorbed several simple conceptions and observations that would remain with me until the end of my days. From my viewpoint, going to Columbia is merely to change the location of my headquarters; perhaps it would be more accurate to say that I am changing the method by which I will continue to strive for the same goals." Ike, as he had advised Milton to do at Kansas State, would attempt to use the presidency as a forum for teaching the lofty principles of American citizenship and world responsibilities.

It would be almost a year before Ike assumed his new office at Columbia. Truman would have to name a successor as Chief of Staff, and Ike had responsibilities working for the unification of the military services under the new Department of Defense headed by his friend James V. Forrestal. Ike later said that the National Defense Act of 1947 brought about "too much form and too little substance." The effective coordination of the rival services had been Ike's great hope, yet he discovered that unification created greater wastes and inefficiencies than the old system.

Ike stepped down as Chief of Staff on February 7 and swore in his "good right arm" General Omar Bradley to succeed him. President Truman, who watched the ceremonies at the Pentagon, said: "Marshall to Eisenhower to Bradley—I think that's one of the finest exchanges I know." Two days earlier, in a farewell address to the National Press Club, the Washington press corps had given Ike a rousing ovation. The retiring Chief of Staff said he did not believe in the inevitability of another world war. He was "certain" that the Soviet Union "is in no position to fight a global war now" and did not want such a conflict. "You can be sure," he said, "that until her differential of strength becomes such as to lead her to think she might win quickly, Russia won't start any war deliberately." Ike said one danger was "the stupid starting of a stupid war." In his final official report as Chief of Staff, he spoke of the "profitless holocaust of the war." As the Army's ranking general, his tenure had been revealing about his political and moral philosophy. He had made the argument that the atomic bomb was not a basis for military policy. "I decry loose and sometimes gloating talk about the degree of security implicit in a weapon that might destroy millions overnight." Ike vigorously rejected the concept of equating military might with national security, writing in his final report: "National security does not mean militarism or any approach to it. Security cannot be measured by the size of munitions stockpiles or the number of men under arms or the monopoly of an invincible weapon. That was the German and Japanese idea of power which, in the test of war, was proved false. Even in peace, the index of material strength is unreliable, for arms become obsolete and worthless; vast armies decay imperceptibly while sapping the strength of the nations supporting them; monopoly of a weapon is soon broken. But adequate spiritual reserves, coupled with understanding of each day's requirements will meet every issue of our time."

There was no time for a vacation because Ike planned to use his immediate leave to write his memoirs. "This is the one chance in my lifetime to build security for my family," he said then. "The soldier leaves the Army as poor as he enters it." When Ike had bought an automobile earlier that winter he told Mamie: "That's the entire result of thirty-seven years' work since I caught the train out of Abilene." The battle among New York publishers to purchase his wartime memoirs soon made it clear that Ike would have more money than he ever imagined. Economic considerations were not decisive in his choice; he had turned down several proposals for a book and serialization, each for $500,000. Finally, Douglas Black of Doubleday and William Robinson of the New York *Herald Tribune* persuaded Ike that it was his duty to provide an account for historians and for his countrymen. He received a unique income-tax benefit on his memoirs when the Internal Revenue Service ruled that the $625,000 he received was not ordinary income, but a "capital gain." So he was permitted to keep $476,250 instead of paying a similar sum as straight income tax. Truman later said that he had ordered the IRS to make the ruling. The ruling was that Ike was an amateur writer and his book thus did not constitute property held by him "primarily for sale to customers in the ordinary course of his trade or business." In any event, the decision made Ike a modestly wealthy man and many observers thought it a just reward for America's most celebrated war hero. Congress later included a provision known as the "Eisenhower Amendment" to the Internal Revenue Code which required payment of income taxes on literary and other creative works.

Dwight wrote *Crusade in Europe* in seven weeks, on a schedule that he described as a "blitz." His files contained most of the book's source material—his wartime correspondence and his periodic diary entries. Ike had been embittered that his old friend and aide, Harry Butcher, who had collected and compiled the diary, sold *My Three Years with Eisenhower* to Simon and Schuster. The disturbingly intimate glimpses of Churchill's bad table manners had offended Dwight. So had the publication of Butcher's book. Because he did not type, Ike dictated the manuscript to secretaries. Two gifted editors, Kenneth McCormick of Doubleday and Joseph Barnes, foreign editor of the *Herald Tribune*, assisted the author. Dwight had no illusions about his literary capabilities and referred to himself as "a hack," but he was eager to produce a work that was both informative and readable. Although General Pershing's memoirs had won a Pulitzer Prize, Ike thought the volumes were mediocre. By contrast, he admired the simplicity and straightforwardness of General Grant's memoirs. *Crusade in Europe* was up to the standard of the Civil War classic. Richard Rovere was to describe Ike's book as "a document that sometimes comes close to splendor." Merle Miller, whose own book *Plain Speaking* gave Truman's salty opinions of Ike much publicity, reviewed *Crusade* for the Philadelphia *Inquirer*. Not only did Miller write that Ike's work was the most important and revealing volume to emerge from World War II, he added: "It is probably the best book ever written about any war by an active general, with the possible exception of Julius Caesar."

Having completed his book, Ike was now free to move to New York. The death of former Columbia president Nicholas Murray Butler in December, at eighty-five, meant that Ike and Mamie would be able to live in the presidential mansion. Columbia's trustees had earlier voted to permit Butler to occupy the residence at 60 Morningside Drive for the rest of his life. Butler had been Columbia's president for forty-four years and was instrumental in the building of the new campus at Morningside Heights. His nickname had been "Nicholas the Miraculous" and he was a remarkable administrator and fund raiser. During his early years as president, he attracted noted scholars from other leading universities. Columbia became the largest university in the world within his first ten years as president and it had the largest endowment of any American university. The campus was referred to in some journals as "the American Acropolis." Butler was also prominent in public affairs and in 1912 had been the Republican vice-presidential nominee. He had spurned repeated offers to run for mayor of New York or governor, but in 1920 made an unsuccessful bid for the Republican presidential nomination. Butler was a confidant to numerous presidents and such captains of industry as Andrew Carnegie. He was a legendary snob and once belittled a European monarch as "not very kingly." Students, particularly undergraduates, were regarded as a nuisance. Butler much preferred the company of fellow leaders in the Eastern Establishment.

In his last years at Columbia, Butler was deaf, blind, and increasingly senile. The university's trustees finally told Butler he had to resign. "It had become pathetic in the extreme," recalled a Columbia professor years later. "Butler literally would be led into a ceremony. Yet he would not resign." Columbia's endowment began diminishing as Butler's own health declined. The years of growth and expansion had ended, partly because Columbia had been without a functioning president since before the war. The trustees had sought a national leader, and in Dwight they were satisfied the university would be well served.

From the start, Ike attempted to conduct a less imperial presidency than Butler. His predecessor had been an autocrat given to dictating academic policy while Ike was inclined to delegate authority with the same system of decentralization that had served him at SHAEF and the Pentagon. Upon arriving on campus, Ike refused to work in Butler's office because it was on the second floor of Low Library and could only be reached by a private elevator. He wanted to be accessible to students and faculty, and moved to a less formal office downstairs. At a meeting with reporters, he spoke with refreshing candor. "I hope," he said, "to talk with various officials while I am here and possibly get some advance inkling of what a college president is up against. I know nothing about it." One of his first visitors was Harry J. Carman, dean of Columbia College. Carman found the new president to be somewhat solemn and uncomfortable.

"I need your help," said Dwight. "I'm awfully green at this job. Damn it, I don't even know what to call people around here. I find there are sixteen different schools here at the university and each one has a dean or director. What do I call these men? Dean? Director? Doctor?"

Carman tactfully explained that not all of them had doctorates, but that "dean" or "director" would be appropriate until he knew them and could address them on a first-name basis. "Good," said a relaxed Dwight. "From now on you're Harry and I'm Ike." A warm friendship developed between Carman and Dwight and in the months ahead the dean would accompany his new president on visits to classrooms and lecture halls. However, Dwight was to be as inaccessible to visitors as Butler had been. Two members of his Pentagon staff, Major Robert Schulz and retired Colonel Kevin McCann, were brought to Columbia as his administrative aides and quickly established themselves as the university president's palace guard. Their duty, as they saw it, was to protect and serve a five-star general. To the Columbia community, they seemed little more than a crude annoyance, hangers-on from the president's military past. But they succeeded in building a wall around him through which high university officials could not penetrate without their approval. "Even the deans couldn't get in," complained Roscoe B. Ellard of the journalism school, who enjoyed a social relationship with Ike. "McCann and Schulz were totally out of water in a university environment," recalled political science professor Herbert Deane. "It was a curious kind of entourage. McCann was a rough and ready Irishman, a stereotype of the old-fashioned newspaperman. Schulz had even less knowledge of academic affairs."

The feisty Schulz treated university administrators as if they were junior military officers. On one occasion when Deane was visiting with former political science colleague Grayson Kirk, who had recently been appointed university provost, Schulz came into the Low Library office and snapped: "The general wants to see you." Kirk responded evenly that he would be with the president in a few minutes. Schulz returned shortly afterward to repeat his message. "Schulz ordered him around like a member of the Army," said Deane. The military aide was informed that Kirk would see Ike as soon as his own visitor had left. Frank D. Fackenthal, acting president for the two years before Ike's appointment, had expected to be one of Ike's closest advisers. "I need you to help me," Ike told him. Fackenthal remained upstairs in the old president's office and was eager to assist the new administration. "The general didn't feel the need of my help at all," Fackenthal said years later. "The general never sent for me." Fackenthal was of the opinion that bringing Schulz and McCann to Columbia had been a serious mistake. Dwight's isolation from the faculty and students except for brief and formal occasions was to be one of his major disappointments at Columbia.

His personality and charm helped him secure some early triumphs. While Ike was still living at Fort Myer, some Columbia trustees informed him that football coach Lou Little had been offered the coaching job and athletic directorship at Yale. Little agreed to meet Ike at the Chief of Staff's residence to "talk it over." Little, a onetime All-America tackle at the University of

Pennsylvania, had been at Columbia since 1930. Some members of the Columbia faculty called him the best teacher on Morningside Heights. Though he had brought Columbia national prominence and a Rose Bowl championship, Little was respected within the university for the spiritual and moral standards he implanted among his athletes. In the 1950s, a national sportswriters' poll would name Little as the greatest coach of his era. There had been many opportunities to leave Columbia, including offers to serve as general manager and coach of a New York professional football team. Yale and Penn had spent years trying to lure him from Columbia. Finally, he had given in and was about to leave Columbia.

The meeting with Ike changed Little's plans. "Lou," Dwight began, "you cannot do this to me. You're one of the reasons I agreed to become president of Columbia." Ike reminded Little that they had met in 1924 as coaches of opposing teams—Ike with Fort Meade and Little as coach of Georgetown University. Little had not remembered the then obscure army coach whom his team had defeated, yet he was impressed that Ike could still recount in detail the football game from the distant past. Ike mentioned that he had read an article about Little's winged-T offense and asked how the backfield adjusted. By the end of their meeting, Ike had talked the coach into staying. "He nailed me in one interview," Little recalled later, "and without a raise in salary, either. He has that rare gift from God of making you feel appreciated, valuable—yes, inspired somehow." Ike demonstrated his gratitude by going to Baker Field to observe practice sessions which no Columbia president had ever done—Butler had in 1905 abolished the sport for ten years—and faithfully attending Columbia's home football games. Ike's intervention to retain Little won strong approval from alumni and the university community.

His first weeks on the campus were marked by a renewal of interest in his availability as a presidential candidate. The letter to the New Hampshire newspaper publisher had seemingly closed the door for 1948, but a coalition of Democrats did not accept Ike's withdrawal as final. For a variety of reasons, Truman was regarded as an almost certain loser in the November election. Organized labor and big-city Democratic bosses favored Ike as the one candidate who could assure a Democratic victory. Liberal New Dealers, who disdained Truman as a conservative usurper, urged Ike as a progressive alternative. It was no coincidence that President Roosevelt's three politically active sons—Franklin, Jr., James, and Elliott—all were working for an Eisenhower nomination. The liberal Americans for Democratic Action supported him, too, although Justice William O. Douglas was the favorite of some of its members. Southern conservatives joined the Eisenhower bandwagon because of disagreements with Truman's civil-rights policies. The Eisenhower movement included such Democrats as Strom Thurmond of South Carolina, Hubert Humphrey of Minnesota, Jack Arvey of Chicago, Mayor William O'Dwyer of New York, Richard Russell of Georgia, and Chester Bowles of Connecticut. A poll published by the New York *Times* indicated that Ike was within striking distance of the nomination and Truman's chances had dimmed. Though Truman had previously offered Ike the nomination, he was now eager to stay in power. If Ike's name was placed in nomination, Truman knew his own candidacy was doomed. Anxiously the President sent two mutual friends to ask Ike to make another disavowal statement.

Ike was irritated by the Truman-initiated pressure, but he conceded that another statement should be released. He wrote a memorandum to Robert Harron, Columbia's public information director, which Harron issued as a press release: "I shall continue, subject to the pleasure of the University Trustees, to perform the important duties I have undertaken as President of Columbia. I will not, at this time, identify myself with any political party, and could not accept nomination for any public office or participate in partisan political contest."

The "Draft Eisenhower" movement, having almost captured the nomination without an active candidate, continued on the proposition that their hero would never refuse the convention's call. Democratic boss John Bailey of Connecticut said Ike's participation in the fall campaign would not be necessary. Liberal Senator Claude Pepper of Florida resurrected Ike's own wartime scenario, a draft of Ike as a "nonpartisan" national candidate. Pepper intended to nominate Ike without the general's consent, but said the convention would adopt Eisenhower's principles in the platform. Weary of all political maneuvers, Ike sent Pepper a telegram asking the senator to cease all activities in his behalf: "No matter under what terms, conditions or premises a proposal might be couched, I would refuse to accept the nomination."

Ike's presidential boom was at last over. Some of his supporters then attempted to draft Justice Douglas, who gave them no more encouragement than Ike had. Truman won the nomination at the Philadelphia convention in the absence of an active and formidable opponent.

On Columbus Day, two days before his fifty-eighth birthday, Ike was formally installed as president on the university's South Court. Representatives from thirty-four foreign universities and some three hundred American institutions marched in the academic procession. Milton, as president of Kansas State, sat with other academicians and confided to some Columbia professors: "I don't know whether you men realize it or not, but in Ike you're getting the real scholar of the Eisenhower family."

As Ike spoke, his voice was dulled because of a head cold, but he managed to emphasize what he considered the major points of his inaugural address. He put particular stress on academic freedom. "There will be no administrative suppression or distortion of any subject that merits a place in this university's curricula," he said. While generally tolerant of the diverse intellectual opinions of Columbia's faculty, Butler had in the early years of his presidency dismissed a pacifist from a teaching position which precipitated the resignations of other professors. Ike showed no inclination to prevent students from organizing radical clubs or espouse nonconformist views on the campus, yet there were limits to his conception of academic freedom. When Teachers College dismissed a left-wing faculty member, he supported the action. In a letter to the university's alumni, Ike wrote: "Once in a while I have heard offhand remarks about 'pinkos' at Teachers College. . . . It has been my observation that those who shout loudest about the Reds in our schools have done little to inform themselves at firsthand or to make sure that we had good schools."

At a time when hate and hysteria prompted repressive measures by the Truman administration and state legislatures were suggesting loyalty oaths for teachers and professors, Ike opposed such measures. "We don't ask for special oaths from the parents," he said. "Then why ask for a special loyalty oath from the teacher?" With Eleanor Roosevelt, he took the position that Communists should not be permitted to teach at universities. "If I found he [an applicant] was a Communist, I would not appoint him," he said. "On the other hand, I certainly do not believe our faculty members should be subject to special loyalty oaths." His educational policies included the study of Communism "to help the present generation understand and value human rights." A professor of Polish history resigned in protest when Columbia accepted $30,000 from the Communist government of Poland to create an endowed chair in Polish studies. The resignation letter charged that the special professorship would be used for Communist infiltration of Columbia. Ike overruled the protests and held that the chair would indeed be established. In a letter accepting the resignation, Ike wrote: "If I ever find that the incumbent of this chair or of any similar chair steps aside from his academic assignment to infiltrate our university with philosophies inimical to our American system of government, the chair will be at once discontinued." He added: "A great deal of the trouble in the world today is traceable to a lack of understanding of the cultures of various countries. I intend to do all in my power to remedy this situation."

Ike saw the purpose of American education much as a high school civics teacher might, to teach the values for "effective citizenship." His view was simplistic and unsophisticated, yet it reflected a belief of a small-town boy who had risen to world prominence through the American system. To some academic dons, Ike's comments represented fatuous zeal. One distinguished scholar assured the new president that Columbia was preeminent in many fields and noted the over-all excellence of its graduate programs. "We have," he said, "some of America's most exceptional physicists, mathematicians, chemists, and engineers."

The president asked if they were "exceptional Americans."

"You don't understand," replied the scholar. "These are graduate students."

Ike burst into a rage, a large vein on his forehead throbbing as he said: "Dammit, what good are exceptional physicists . . . exceptional anything, unless they are exceptional Americans." He went on to say that every student who came to Columbia must leave it first a better citizen and secondarily a more learned scholar.

For years, Teachers College had been ignored by Butler as one of the least important branches of the university. Dean William Russell, who complained that the street separating his college from the main campus was the widest in the world, captivated Ike by outlining a Citizenship Education Study Project. Russell lamented that if only he had the funding, the college could demonstrate what citizenship really meant. Ike helped secure $450,000 from a foundation for Russell's patriotic enterprise.

Ike's ability to solicit contributions from the wealthy and the great foundations was said to have been a factor in his appointment at Columbia. On some projects such as the citizenship program, he was willing to call on people for financial aid. His friend Averell Harriman, largely because of Ike's connection with the university, donated Arden House, the historic estate of the Harriman family in Ramapo Hills, as the site for a favored Eisenhower project, the American Assembly. Ike did not like fund raising and was in some ways too proud and sensitive to throw himself into this aspect of the presidency. Although he had many friends among the wealthy and philanthropic, many of them already had long-standing commitments to other institutions and he was hesitant to ask them to shift their contributions to Columbia. Indeed, he refused to ask anyone flat out for a donation. Even his idolator Kevin McCann said, "He was almost certainly the poorest excuse for a fund-raising college president in the country." Ike himself said he was inadequate as a solicitor, and a 1949 letter to the alumni revealed a remarkably low-key sales pitch: "Some alumni and friends believe that Columbia is 'rich,' and some that it is 'poor.' Columbia is neither. It does have large assets, but it has equally large responsibilities. . . . Columbia is a gift-supported university." Expectations that Ike could have equal success as Butler had as a fund raiser "downtown" were quickly dispelled, yet Ike had never purported to be anything of the sort.

Ike told Columbia's trustees that it would take twenty years to master all the nuances of the university, but told them "I have no intention of undertaking that formidable task." In his seventh month at Morningside Heights, Ike wrote: "The job of running Columbia . . . is much too great for one man. It is a team effort of a high order." He went on: "One of the major surprises . . . is the paper work. When I left Washington, D.C., I thought I was leaving these mountainous white piles forever. From now on, I hoped, I would just handle policy matters. . . . One thing we have done, however, and that is to insist that most projects be stated in one typewritten page—except, of course, when the president writes a letter!"

There were other instances where Ike attempted to cut corners in the fashion of a Chief of Staff. In a university setting, such efforts often seemed counterproductive to other administrators. Provost Grayson Kirk was asked to preside over the University Council, the board comprised of deans and elected faculty representatives, traditionally to meet with the president. "On numerous occasions he would ask me to take over," Kirk recalled in 1977, "and he would say that he would try to come in at the end if he had time and sit on the sidelines. He wasn't entirely comfortable in that setting. I don't know whether he was timid or really very busy. It may have been good military form to send an aide."

When Ike was reminded of an upcoming meeting of the Association of American Universities by Brown University president Henry Wriston, also the association's president, Ike said he would send an aide. Wriston told him that was not acceptable and Ike became testy. It was explained that only presidents could attend such meetings under the association's rules. Ike went to the conference in Wisconsin and considered it worthwhile. In his enthusiasm, he proposed two colleges for membership in the association and his host Wriston gently explained that membership was restricted to universities and very prestigious ones at that.

Meanwhile, President Truman called Ike to Washington and asked him to serve informally as chairman of the Joint Chiefs of Staff. Ike asked the President if it was necessary to resign from Columbia and was assured that both Truman and Defense Secretary Forrestal would like him to stay at Columbia, but continue to advise them on unification of the armed forces. An informal leave of absence for "some seven or eight weeks" was granted in February of 1949 by Columbia's trustees who said Ike's appointment was in the university's tradition of public service. In announcing his temporary leave, Ike said: "It was, of course, understood between the Columbia trustees and me that urgent public business would always have first claim on my time." As it turned out, Ike was taking on too much responsibility, still attending some university conferences in New York and shuttling back to Washington for his defense chores. Ike had come in as Forrestal's physical and mental health were rapidly declining. Shocked at his old friend's condition, Ike encouraged Forrestal to take a leave and regain his health. When Forrestal mentioned the possibility of a resignation, Ike did nothing to discourage him. In early March, Forrestal did resign only to call Ike and argue that the resignation should be withdrawn. Ike was finally able to persuade him not to attempt to cancel the ceremony installing Louis Johnson as his successor, pointing out that he was far from a well man and would be exposed to public ridicule. Two months later, the driven and conflicted Forrestal committed suicide by jumping from a window of the top floor of Bethesda Naval Hospital. For Ike, it was nothing less than a national tragedy. He had liked Forrestal and regarded him as a selfless public servant in contrast to Secretary Johnson, whom he regarded as a calculating politician. Ike's own health deteriorated that spring as he was stricken with a painful attack of ileitis and confined to his bed in the Hotel Statler. After a week, during which he lost touch with everything, he was recovered enough to fly to Key West aboard President Truman's plane for three weeks of convalescence. His doctor ordered him to cut back his smoking from four packs of cigarettes a day to no more than one pack. Ike replied that he would have to quit cold turkey or not at all—and, with remarkable discipline, he gave up smoking. At Key West, he was gradually able to play golf, fish, and paint. On his return to Columbia, Ike's health seemed rejuvenated and he was ten pounds heavier, although it was May before he was able to resume his work full time.

Ike's happiest moments at Columbia were spent with its college students. If he was ill at ease with the faculty dons, Ike had no such inhibitions with young people. At a freshman-class stag dinner, he delighted the students with a candid talk, using "two damns and a hell," by their count. In his frequent visits to football practice sessions at Baker Field and in his Wednesday-morning visits to classrooms, Ike's warmth and sincerity invariably impressed the youthful audience.

Yet some strains developed between him and the student body, which were reflected in editorials of the Columbia *Spectator*. They were critical of his frequent absences from the campus for speaking engagements and other travels. The student newspaper referred to him as the general "who doubles as president of the university" and said that "perhaps in the near future our chief officer will have the time to meet some of us." When Ike spoke before the St. Andrew's Society of New York, he asserted that too much emphasis was being placed on security instead of individual liberty and said: "Possibly we have become too regardful of things we call luxuries. . . . Maybe we like caviar and champagne when we ought to be out working on beer and hot dogs." The *Spectator* commented: "Being content with beer and hot dogs has never been part of the American tradition we know. . . . We don't know, of course, but we are willing to bet beer and hot dogs weren't on the menu at the Waldorf-Astoria last Wednesday night, either." Publicly, Ike said that the editorial did not bother him and said the independence of the campus newspaper was essential to Columbia. However, his vein throbbed during private discussions of the incident and in a letter he complained that freedom of speech seemed to apply to everyone but him. So angered was he that Ike spoke of breaking precedent at Columbia and refusing to speak at commencement ceremonies. In time, he would laugh about the episode and say the student editorial amused him and the threat about boycotting commencement was forgotten.

Faculty members found Ike engaging in conversation and positively dazzling as an extemporaneous speaker. Members of the history faculty sat in rapt attention one afternoon as Ike sat in a room at Fayerweather Hall and confided some of his wartime burdens in the Supreme Command. In his visits to classrooms, he would compliment the professors, telling one lecturer that he had learned more about the occupation of Germany in fifteen minutes than in his own four years of experience with the occupation. When Nobel laureate Isidor Rabi was offered a position at the Institute for Advanced Study in Princeton, Ike told the physicist that his departure would leave a void which could not be filled and diminish Columbia's international stature in science. That Rabi remained at Columbia was in part Ike's accomplishment.

Socially, Ike and Mamie preferred the company of old army friends and their families to the university community. Few faculty members received invitations to the presidential mansion. One faculty member of Ike's circle, journalism's Roscoe Ellard, cherished the evenings of bridge at 60 Morningside Drive. He later described Ike as an extraordinary bridge player, who became more daring when he drank Singapore slings. "Ike was the sort of person who when he drank quite a bit would become more sweet and lovable," said Ellard, "and a more foxy gambler at bridge." Ellard refuted published rumors that Mamie was an alcoholic, saying that she seldom drank and had a low tolerance for alcohol. In a 1974 interview, Mamie told me that the rumors did not bother her because she and her friends knew they had no basis in fact.

In contrast to the public role played by Mrs. Nicholas Murray (Kate) Butler, Mamie sought privacy at Columbia. By previous arrangement with the trustees, Ike relieved Mamie of the formal social schedule which the Butlers had for many years maintained. The Eisenhowers extended their hospitality to important visitors, including some royalty, but as a couple they did not make their presence felt on the campus. Some friends described Mamie as sad and frail during the Columbia years. "She was kind of like a little girl who had not quite grown up," recalls one faculty member. "Ike went his own way and she had been left alone most of her life." An administrator who worked closely with Ike said: "Her role was really quite slight." Mamie insisted that Ike's Sundays be spent with her at the presidential mansion and observed, in 1950, that it was the only day he did not belong to Columbia and also happened to be the only day he ate breakfast. One weekend in the fall of 1950, Ike surprised her with a trip to central Pennsylvania and they bought a farm near Gettysburg as a country retreat.

Ike chafed at reports of his difficulties at Columbia. In a letter to Hazlett he confirmed that his responsibilities sometimes forced him "into a confusing, not to say almost nerve-wearing, kind of living. At such times . . . I unquestionably express myself in tones of irritation and resentment, and I have no doubt that a chance listener could interpret some of these expressions as irritation with my 'apparently' sole preoccupation. . . . If I were convinced that I had made a mistake in coming to Columbia, I am not so stupid as to fail to recognize the instant and obvious cure."

Late in 1950, Ike was asked to return to military duty as Supreme Commander of the armed forces of the North Atlantic Treaty Organization. President Truman phoned Ike, who was speaking at Heidelberg College in Tiffin, Ohio, to make the request. A friend had written Dwight to say it was his hope that Eisenhower would not be coerced into the NATO command. "I am a little astonished at your use of the expression 'talked into.' As you know, I am an officer on the active list on which I will always stay, by reason of a special Act of Congress," wrote Ike. "It is clear that my official superiors don't have to do any talking if they actually want me to take any military assignment." In fact, Ike was pessimistic about the NATO command and had little desire to go back into uniform. For all its pitfalls, the Columbia post had given him the aura of an elder statesman and that was precisely the role Ike told his son and others that he wanted to play. Upon his acceptance of the new Supreme Command, Ike submitted his resignation at Columbia but the trustees granted him an indefinite leave of absence. Though he cheerfully talked of coming back to Morningside Heights, Columbia's faculty hoped that this would not be the case. By naming Ike to NATO, some political observers said that Truman was removing his most threatening obstacle to reelection. New York's Governor Thomas E. Dewey, who had already endorsed Ike as his presidential candidate for 1952, chortled that the NATO experience would "increase his qualifications if that is possible." Grayson Kirk, named Columbia's acting president, thought Ike might be available. "My own hunch was that he would be receptive in 1952," said Kirk years later. "I didn't think he was very happy at Columbia."

Dewey's surprising 1948 defeat by Truman which was contrary to all public-opinion polls had overnight resurrected Ike as a presidential contender. Years later, John Eisenhower would ruefully describe November 2, 1948, as the darkest day in American history for the disruptive effect it had on his family. At Columbia, Ike had begun to go public with his political views, yet when a faculty member suggested that he ought to be President, Eisenhower responded: "I already am." The professor explained that he meant President of the United States. Ike replied: "You've got to be kidding."

Chapter Fourteen

THE MAKING OF A CANDIDATE

The job Ike faced in Europe was far different than his earlier Supreme Command, lacking the urgency of wartime and, in fact, little more than a holding operation. Secretary of State Dean Acheson had been instrumental in creating NATO as an extension of the Cold War Truman doctrine and its ideological battle to "stop Communism." With NATO, Acheson hoped to calm European rivalries and contain the Soviet bloc. The NATO treaty made it clear that a Soviet attack on any of the member nations would be considered an attack on the entire alliance. Years later, former State Department planner George F. Kennan described NATO as a "military defense against an attack no one was planning." On the surface, Ike reiterated his confidence in the defense of Western Europe, yet privately he showed anxiety. "He had an impossible job there," said John Eisenhower. "He was sitting there facing 175 Russian divisions and he didn't have the forces to fight their way out of a paper bag." Ike admitted to a congressional committee that almost nothing could be done to stop a Soviet attack if it came before the summer of 1951. As he saw it, his role was to "create a climate and a will for self-defense." That had been the mission of his three-week odyssey to twelve European capitals. In his first broadcast to nations within the alliance, he said: "I return to Europe as a military commander, but with no miraculous plans, no display of military force. I return with an unshakable faith in Europe—this land of our ancestors—in the underlying courage of its people."

If the odds were against repeating the conspicuous success of World War II, Ike's appointment raised the hopes and expectations of Western Europe. The leaders of the Grand Alliance were gone—Roosevelt dead and Churchill out of power—but Ike's return to Europe reaffirmed his position as the symbol of Western unity. The Korean War was said to have been only the first in a series of international Communist offensives and a popular theory was that Stalin would strike at Western Europe. *Newsweek* observed that Ike's job of lobbying Congress for a military buildup in Europe "will be one of the biggest Eisenhower or any other American has ever tackled. And on its success or failure the course of history for the next 500 years may well depend."

His meeting with senators and representatives took place on January 30, 1951, in the old auditorium of the Library of Congress. "I have one object in view," he said, "the good of the United States." Losing Western Europe, he argued, would mean yielding to the Soviet Union an industrial capacity second only to the United States and depriving American industry of vital natural resources. "We would suffer economic atrophy and then finally collapse," he said. On his recent trip, Ike said he found some "pessimism bordering on defeatism," yet he added there were at least some hints of "a rejuvenation . . . a spirit again to try to live the lives of free men, to do their part and to take the risk." The novelty of Ike's appeal as a citizen-soldier was evident in this presentation, for he asserted: "We are talking about what is in the hearts. . . . Nobody can defend another nation by itself. The true defense of the nation can be found in its own soul."

At the conclusion of his talk, the Eighty-second Congress applauded respectfully and many of its members had been visibly moved. Ike was far more effective than Truman or Acheson in convincing dubious congressmen that the West indeed had responsibilities in the postwar world. Still, there were some persistent and influential critics of American troop commitment to NATO and Ike hoped to persuade Senator Robert Taft of Ohio, the leader of this bloc, that there should be no fixed ceilings or arbitrary ratios. On domestic affairs, Ike had more than once expressed admiration in his correspondence for the courage and political convictions of the renowned "Mr. Republican." A clandestine meeting was arranged in the Pentagon between the two men and Ike was so optimistic that Taft would reach agreement with him on economic and military aid to NATO members that he had even drafted a statement announcing the Ohio senator's endorsement of collective security. However, the meeting produced no such results as Taft explained he was considering whether to vote for two, four, or six American divisions in Europe. From Ike's perspective, it seemed that Taft was playing politics with the future of the West, and the meeting ended on a chilly note. Had Taft agreed to the NATO commitment, Ike might well have renounced all efforts to draft himself for the 1952 Republican presidential nomination and given Taft a clear path to the prize which had so long eluded him. In the absence of bipartisan support for NATO, Ike made a conscious decision to keep his own options open and exercise his potential political strength to secure additional backing for the policy on Capitol Hill. Privately, he now referred to Taft as a very stupid man.

At SHAPE, near the village of Rocquencourt, some ten miles from Paris, Ike held responsibility for the Western Front from the Arctic to the Mediterranean, with authority over armed forces of nine countries. His Deputy Supreme Commander was Lord Montgomery, with whom there had been so many wartime differences, but they shared similar attitudes about the Atlantic Alliance. "Monty not only has a very fine reputation in this region as a soldier," Ike wrote a friend, "but *he is one*. Moreover, he is a very determined little fellow who knows exactly what he wants, is simple and direct in his approach, and minces no words with any soldier, politician or plain citizen when he thinks that that individual is not fulfilling his complete obligations to NATO. He is one man who clearly recognizes the truth of the assertion that Europe cannot forever depend upon America for military and economic aid and assistance." There was none of the at times petty animus which had separated the men during the war. "We became close friends," Montgomery recalled later. The Field Marshal noted, "He has the power of drawing the hearts of men towards him as a magnet attracts the bits of metal. He merely has to smile at you, and you trust him at once." Another familiar figure, General Alfred M. Gruenther, was Ike's chief of staff and handled most of the day-to-day details of SHAPE while the Supreme Commander was engaging in diplomacy and conferences. Gruenther had been a close friend since having served as Ike's deputy chief of staff in the Third Army in 1941. In addition to his widely recognized military abilities, Gruenther was regarded as one of the most skilled bridge players in America. Ike cherished their bridge matches even though he was usually beaten by his friend.

As Supreme Commander, Ike became a leading spokesman for a United States of Europe and drew frequent counsel from such advocates of a federated continent as Jean Monnet, the French statesman. When Ike was invited to make a speech before the English-Speaking Union in July, he vowed that it would be a strong and urgent appeal for a United Europe no later than 1952 and might even include a proposal for merging West Germany, Italy, France, Belgium, and Luxembourg into a single state. His speech did call for "a workable European federation," but was a far cry from the dramatic message he had pondered. Still undecided about a political career, Ike was fully aware of the dangers of being too far ahead of public opinion. It was to be Ike's only formal public speech on the issue.

Much of his time was spent in private conferences with European leaders. "I assure you that, as I go around to various capitals and meet with members of the several governments, I never let up for one single instant on pounding home some serious facts," Ike wrote Hazlett on June 21, 1951. "I insist that Europe must, as a whole, provide in the long run for its own defense. The United States can move in and by its psychological, intellectual, and material leadership help to produce arms, units, and the confidence that will allow Europe to solve its problem. In the long run, it is not possible—and most certainly not desirable—that Europe should be an occupied territory defended by legions brought in from abroad, somewhat in the fashion that Rome's territories vainly sought security many hundred years ago."

His popularity at home and prestige in Europe were undiminished. In a poll published and taken by *The Saturday Review*, Dwight was named the greatest living American, and in a

Gallup poll released in the winter of 1951 Ike had led President Truman by 31 percentage points as a hypothetical Republican candidate. By November, Gallup showed Ike increasing his margin by 5 points. However, a poll of Republican county chairmen indicated that Ike's nomination would be far from assured even if he returned to campaign—Taft was the choice of 1,027 while Ike was the favorite of but 375. The second Eisenhower presidential boom had started within moments of Truman's 1948 victory. It became a formidable political movement when Governor Dewey, titular head of the Republican Party, endorsed Ike on a nationally televised interview in October of 1950. "From then on," former Dewey press secretary James Hagerty recalled in a 1970 interview, "Governor Dewey threw all of his vast political resources behind Eisenhower. That made Eisenhower a significant factor in the Republican Party almost overnight." There had been published reports that Dewey had tried to persuade Ike to run for governor of New York in 1950 as a prelude to a presidential race, but, at Columbia, Eisenhower firmly vetoed the idea. Upon Dewey's formal endorsement of an Eisenhower presidential candidacy, Ike released a written statement: "I put my hand to do a job and do my best. I have no desire to go anywhere else if I can help to do what I want here at Columbia. This is the place for me. I don't know why people are always nagging me to run for President. I think I've gotten too old."

That Ike's attitude was softening about the presidency first became evident to John Eisenhower when his father returned from the three-week January 1951 European tour and confided, "Well, that's out, *now*." Before then, John had no indication that Ike would be any more available in 1952 than when he had written the Shermanesque letter as Chief of Staff. One popular theory had been that Columbia's trustees had given the university presidency to Ike as a means of promoting him for the White House and the idea is still debated at Morningside Heights. It was at Columbia that Ike emerged as a critic of social-welfare programs of the New Deal and the Truman administration and before a Texas audience had made the incredible statement "If security is all Americans want, they can go to prison." His political philosophy was a blend of Midwestern conservatism in domestic affairs and urbane internationalism. Ike identified with Taft and Herbert Hoover on most issues with the notable exception of NATO. Back in uniform, Ike could refrain from making potentially damaging political statements and resume the mantle of soldier-statesman. While Ike was at SHAPE, Churchill was asked by his physician, Lord Moran, if Eisenhower could be persuaded to seek the presidency. "Ike," Churchill replied, "has not only to be wooed but raped."

Reporters frequently called on Ike at NATO headquarters, but questions about politics and the presidency were prohibited. If an enterprising correspondent broke the ground rule, the interview was ended. With old newspaper friends, Ike allowed that he was disturbed how American politicians were captives of special interests and said he would like to see the citizenry discuss issues and exert their influence on Congress. His idealism was, in many ways, pure Frank Capra and so was much of the grass-roots "Draft Eisenhower" movement back in the United States.

Ike's party preference had been a carefully kept secret and made him something of a political double-threat. In 1948, he could have had either major party nomination for the asking and if the Republican race would be more difficult this time, Democrats seemed just as eager to embrace his candidacy again. At the 1951 National Governors' Conference, held at Gatlinburg, Tennessee, Ike won a poll of Republican governors and received a qualified endorsement from Adlai E. Stevenson, the freshman Democratic governor of Illinois. Stevenson pointed out that Ike was one of the architects of the Truman-Acheson foreign policy and would be well received by Democrats. "General Eisenhower's view on foreign policy is not the representative view of the Republican Party as a whole," said Stevenson. "Many leaders in the Republican Party . . . would be in sharp disagreement with Eisenhower as a party leader." Stevenson made the argument that Ike could defeat any Republican nominee, although he said the same of President Truman. If Ike sought the Republican nomination, Stevenson predicted a bloody and divisive GOP battle which would leave their party "as it hasn't been split since the Bull Moose days of 1912." A poll of congressional Democrats favored Ike while Republican congressmen chose Taft as their 1952 hope.

Republican or Democrat? His party affiliation was the biggest question in American politics. With some amusement, Ike told a visiting foreign service officer that *McCall's* had offered to pay him forty thousand dollars merely to confirm or deny that he was a Republican, yet he resisted making the commitment.

Ike had been for President Roosevelt, his Commander in Chief, in 1944, but had been against him in the three previous elections, especially the unprecedented third term. In 1948, he had favored a ticket of Michigan's Republican Senator Arthur Vandenberg for President and Harold Stassen for Vice President and discussed their merits with brother Milton, also a Vandenberg supporter. At Columbia, he had not registered as a Republican and declared no party preference. In the fall, Ike voted for Dewey over Truman, and the following year, in a special New York senatorial election, voted for Republican John Foster Dulles against the triumphant Democrat, Herbert Lehman. In 1950, he voted for Dewey's reelection as New York governor. The privacy of the voting booth had protected Ike's nonpartisan image although speculation continued.

By November of 1951, Ike had a form-letter response for inquiries about his party membership: "For me to admit, while in this post, a partisan political loyalty would properly be resented by thinking Americans and would be doing a disservice to our country. Such action on my part would encourage partisan thinking, in our country, toward a job in which the whole nation has already invested tremendous sums. The successful outcome of this venture is too vital to our welfare in the years ahead to permit any semblance of partisan allegiance on the part of the United States Military Commander in SHAPE." Still, Ike wrote Hazlett: "I believe that a bit of reflection will establish that there is no other possible course for me as long as I am in uniform. A man cannot desert a duty, but it would seem that he could lay down one in order to pick up a heavier and more responsible burden. So far as personal desire or ambition is concerned, there will *never* be any change for me. I could not be more negative."

Senator Henry Cabot Lodge of Massachusetts endorsed Ike for President in August of 1951 during an interview on NBC's "Meet the Press." Lodge added that it would be improper for Ike to become involved in any partisan campaign while on active duty in

Europe, but on September 4 he visited Ike at SHAPE and was sternly advised by military aides to stay "a very short time." For two hours, they talked about topics ranging from NATO to the presidency. Lodge had been among the seemingly endless political visitors at Columbia and his earlier effort to persuade Ike to run for President had been summarily dismissed. Ike had known Lodge since the middle 1930s on a casual basis and admired him for his resignation from the Senate to go into combat in World War II. Lodge at once began listing the reasons why Ike should consent to run for the Republican nomination and purported to speak for a broad coalition of organizations ready to forge a nation-wide campaign structure. "You are well known in politics," said Ike. "Why not run yourself?" Retorted Lodge, "Because I cannot be elected," and proceeded with his case.

Lodge was the grandson and namesake of the Brahmin Republican senator whose dislike of Woodrow Wilson had kept America out of the League of Nations. The younger Lodge was an internationalist and did not want Republicans to nominate a neo-isolationist, namely, Robert A. Taft. "The Republican party has lost five successive national elections," Lodge wrote in *Harper's*. "Its continuance as a viable organization is dependent on its winning in 1952."

Lodge was telling Ike that while nothing short of an Eisenhower candidacy would preserve the two-party political system, a Taft nomination might well mark the end of the Republican Party as a major political force in American life. The statement that Taft's nomination would be a certainty without Dwight was no doubt compelling, for Dwight had written a friend some months earlier that the election of Taft would nullify his own efforts in Europe. "You," said Lodge, "are the only one who can be elected by the Republicans to the presidency. You must permit the use of your name in the upcoming primaries."

Ike listened attentively and was noncommittal, but at the end of their meeting promised to "think the matter over." Years later, he would cite the conversation with Lodge as a turning point in his attitude about presidential politics. It would still be months before he would have to make a final decision, but that he was considering the possibility gave new hope to his supporters. As a student of history, Ike knew that the White House instead of a grand climax to a career might be an anticlimax and recognized that if Grant had shunned the presidency the Civil War hero's reputation would have been the better for it. "I think I pretty well hit my peak in history when I accepted the German surrender," he said.

Lodge had renewed his efforts for an Eisenhower candidacy, and on October 25 a front-page New York *Herald Tribune* editorial removed any doubt that Ike was the candidate of the Eastern Republican Establishment: "At rare intervals in the life of a free people the man and the occasion meet. . . . We believe that Dwight D. Eisenhower is the man." Just eleven years earlier the *Herald Tribune* had made the same kind of pitch for Wendell Willkie, giving the dark-horse Wall Street lawyer dramatic momentum. Taft, who had been overtaken by Willkie at the 1940 convention and an also-ran to Dewey at the 1948 convention, was starting early, trying to secure the nomination by the spring. By October 16, when Taft made his candidacy official, the Ohio senator was advised by his inner circle that no less than 400 of the 604 delegates required to nominate were firmly in his corner. Shy and reticent, with a stiff, awkward manner, Taft was too colorless to attract broad political appeal. With his old-fashioned rimless glasses, protruding teeth and half-bald head, he looked distinctly unpresidential. Although prominence had come to him as the son of President William Howard Taft, he quickly impressed Senate colleagues as an intelligent, hard-working, and often courageous leader. He was clearly the most powerful Republican senator of his generation and since 1939 had been the voice of his party on Capitol Hill and in the nation at large. Some political critics stereotyped him a reactionary for his isolationism, his demands for a more limited national government, and his economic views, but Taft was, in fact, a thoughtful conservative who had introduced legislation for federal aid to education, public housing, and public health programs. On civil liberties, Taft had challenged the legality of the Nuremberg war trials and President Truman's legality to draft striking workers. In foreign affairs, Taft was more of an anti-interventionist than an isolationist. His role in writing the Taft-Hartley labor law, designed to define unfair union practices, earned him the lasting enmity of organized labor. Despite strong union opposition, Taft had won reelection to his Senate seat by an overwhelming margin in 1950. One year older than Ike, at sixty-two Taft recognized that 1952 was his last and best chance to capture the presidency.

Most of the delegates to the Republican Convention would be chosen not in the sixteen presidential primaries, but at state conventions in the other thirty-two states where Taft's long-standing ties with regional party leaders would work to his obvious advantage. If the public-opinion polls gave Ike a higher rating, Taft could take some comfort in an NBC radio poll which indicated he led Eisenhower by more than 2 to 1 among delegates chosen in late 1951. Still hopeful that Ike would not seek the nomination, Taft spoke kindly when asked about the NATO commander.

In November, Ike returned to Washington, at Truman's request, to discuss NATO business. As it turned out, during a two-hour meeting in the Oval Office, Truman again offered to help make Ike President and expressed a willingness to step aside in his behalf. The proposition was reported at the time by Arthur Krock of the New York *Times*, who said that Ike made his differences with the Democratic Party clear enough for Truman to drop the matter. Ike said he supported the Taft-Hartley Act, which Truman had vetoed and Congress had overridden. What else happened at this meeting between the two men was never told. On December 18, 1951, some six weeks after this session, Truman wrote Ike a handwritten letter: "The columnists, the slick magazines and all the political people, who like to speculate, are saying many things about what is to happen in 1952. As I told you in 1948 and at our luncheon in 1951, do what you think best for the country. My own position is in the balance. If I do what I want to do, I'll go back to Missouri and *maybe* run for the Senate. If you decide to finish the European job (and I don't know who else can) I must keep the isolationists out of the White House. I wish you would let me know what you intend to do. It will be between us and no one else. I have the utmost confidence in your judgment and your patriotism."

What Ike was thinking remained a mystery beyond his most intimate circle of friends, but there now appeared to be a strong chance of an affirmative answer on the presidential question. The Eisenhower brothers had strong reservations about Dwight attempting a political transition. In 1948, their counsel had been unanimous against Dwight's candidacy, particularly on the Democratic ticket. During the Democratic Convention, Edgar wrote Ike that he would campaign against him though he hoped it would not be necessary. Arthur, noting that Ike was receiving eleven thousand letters daily urging him to take the Democratic nomination, said his letter urged him not to change his decision. As the second Eisenhower boom developed, the brothers were again skeptical. Milton's position was that Ike was already a world figure and did not need the presidency to retain his international stature. When a Michigan Young Republican leader called on Milton at Penn State, the visitor said Ike owed it to the nation to return home and seek the presidency, or at the very least make a statement that he would be open to a convention draft. Milton replied, "It's really very significant that you feel the general owes it to his country to run for President. Tell me, will you vote for him if he runs on the Democratic ticket?" According to Milton, the Young Republican's jaw dropped and then Milton scolded: "You mean he owes it to the Republican Party."

In a similar vein, Edgar had been approached by Republicans and Democrats who urged Ike's candidacy yet said they would vote against him should he choose a political party other than their own. Such encounters disgusted the crusty Tacoma lawyer, and he advised Dwight that his influence on the country would be far greater at Morningside Heights than in the White House. Edgar wrote: "If I thought that sacrificing you on the altar of politics would restore our internal government to a sound basis . . . I would probably be willing to make the sacrifice, but I am so convinced that it would be useless because of the other elements within our country, that I am not in favor of putting you up as the sacrificial lamb for the benefit of a lot of selfish, unthinking, greedy, crooked and vulturous politicians."

Although Arthur had long opposed Ike's presidential candidacy, his attitude seemed to be mellowing. Writing Ike in October that he would make no attempt to influence the decision, Arthur pledged his full support whatever it was to be.

Because Milton was the closest to Ike, he was the one brother whose movements and public statements might suggest the NATO commander's true position. At Penn State, he was visited by numerous Republican officials seeking clues about Ike's leanings. In June of 1951, Milton went to Philadelphia to receive an honorary degree from Jefferson Medical College and met with two nationally prominent Republicans, Congressman Hugh Scott of Philadelphia, a former chairman of the Republican National Committee, and Harold Talbott, an executive with the Chrysler Corporation and formerly the chief fund raiser for the Willkie and Dewey presidential campaigns. Scott and Talbott predicted that Ike could win the nomination without campaigning for it if only he would not issue a repudiation of their efforts.

Milton replied that his own influence was limited and he had always opposed a political career for Ike, hoping instead that his brother might retire peacefully to Columbia or Gettysburg. "I have not seen my brother since his last visit to Washington," said Milton to his visitors, "and even then we did not discuss politics in any way. However, I can say positively that, so far as his personal inclinations are concerned, he has had and still has a violently negative attitude toward this political question." Scott was not discouraged by the meeting and, in fact, said publicly that Ike would probably become a candidate, giving the impression that his authority was the president of Penn State. Milton, who was never accused of having a thick skin, was indignant that Scott had violated the confidence of a private talk and was misrepresenting what Milton had told him. The indefatigable Scott had been leaking "inside" information to *Newsweek* and other publications which said that Milton confirmed Dwight's Republicanism. Though Milton respected Lodge, Pennsylvania Senator James H. Duff, and Kansas Senator Frank Carlson, the leadership of the "Draft Eisenhower" movement, he questioned Scott's ethics in a letter to Dwight. From London, Ike wrote: "As for all the rest of the things that are worrying you, I went through it all a long time ago. I refuse to fret any more. My advice to you is to develop a good laugh when such questions are put to you, and merely make some facetious remark of the character, 'If you ever find anyone who can speak authoritatively for that brother of mine, I should like very much to meet him.' This or anything else of a like character would serve."

As always, Milton dutifully followed Ike's instructions. In the meantime, Scott visited Ike twice in France to ask for the general's permission to state that he was indeed available for the nomination. Ike referred Scott to a newspaper article which said Eisenhower would accept the convention's call, but would not actively campaign for the nomination. Scott was disappointed that Ike would not go public with any such statement, yet brightened when Ike said he did not like the prospect of a Truman-Taft race. On Scott's return to the United States, the wily Philadelphian continued to tell Republicans that Ike would be responsive to their draft.

Milton was himself coming to the viewpoint that Ike was the only Republican who could win the presidency and felt a new administration, after twenty years of Democratic rule, would be good for the nation. By October, Milton was advising his brother that "without a good candidate in opposition," Taft would be nominated, leaving party moderates with "no place to go." He added: "When I realize how very dirty the coming presidential campaign is going to be, I just pray that you will in no way be identified with it. But, on the other hand, the possibility that the American people must choose between Taft and Truman is so terrifying that I think any personal sacrifice on the part of any honest American citizen is wholly justified." In the middle of October, William E. Robinson of the *Herald Tribune* flew to State College for a luncheon meeting with Milton. Robinson had traveled to Europe often in connection with the foreign edition of the *Herald Tribune* and was frequently Ike's house guest. In their conversations, Robinson persistently argued that Ike should run. His words carried much weight, and Ike finally agreed that a small group of his close friends should hold private meetings to keep him advised of the political situation. When Ike arrived in Washington for his meeting with President Truman, he summoned Robinson, Milton, and General Lucius Clay to his suite at the Statler for a briefing.

At a press conference in Washington, Ike for the first time in public seemed receptive to a presidential race. Asked about Senator James Duff's "Draft Eisenhower" campaign efforts, Ike said he had not seen Duff in a "long, long time." He then replied: "If I have friends that have been my friends so long they know how I would act and react under given circumstances, that's their own business and I have never attempted to interfere with any man exercising his own privileges as an American citizen." Privately, he told Clay that he would accept though not seek the nomination.

It was on this same Washington visit that Ike firmly rejected the Democratic presidential nomination and almost certain election, although he still refused to acknowledge that he was a Republican. Later in November, Lodge officially became Ike's campaign manager and spokesman for the Draft Eisenhower movement. The selection of Dewey for such a post would have been anathema to party conservatives who regarded him as the personification of "me-tooism" and New York bossism. Milton suggested that Dewey's role be in the background and the New Yorker came to the same conclusion. Even Dewey's lieutenants—Brownell and Hagerty—would work behind the scenes.

To Lodge and other leaders of the Eisenhower campaign, it was obvious that Taft was far in front in the race for the nomination and Ike's mere availability might not be enough. On December 3, 1951, Lodge wrote Ike requesting that he attend a January meeting of the Republican National Committee in San Francisco where all the other presidential contenders were scheduled to speak. Ike replied on December 12: "I accept, without reservation, your observations and comments on the political scene at home; you fully convince me of the impracticability of nominating an individual who, for any reason, must remain inactive in the political field prior to the National Conventions. From my viewpoint, this is an entirely new factor in the problem; and, since my current responsibilities make pre-convention activity impossible for me, the program in which you and your close political associates are now engaged should, logically, be abandoned. To this, I assume you agree. Under no circumstances should friends, whom I admire and respect, continue to work on a project involving me when they have become convinced that my personal convictions condemn their efforts, in advance, to futility and defeat."

Ike went on to suggest several explanations the group might use to justify the dismemberment of the Draft Eisenhower organization, stressing that for an absentee candidate to win the nomination was probably impossible. He assured Lodge that it had been an honor to have been considered for the presidency by such a "distinguished group of Americans," but the only concession he would make would be to avoid repudiating their efforts.

The tall, broad-shouldered Lodge, who had won six battle stars and the Bronze Star in World War II, would not accept Ike's withdrawal and chose to continue the campaign on the basis that his efforts would not be repudiated. In a quickly written response to Ike, Lodge expressed confidence that the nomination could still be won. While public-opinion polls attested Ike's popularity, Lodge and his group were determined to demonstrate the Eisenhower voter appeal in presidential primaries.

On the surface, Ike was as evasive as always when asked about his political future. In a lengthy December 11 conversation with C. L. Sulzberger of the New York *Times*, Ike said that once he entered politics his opponents might create scandals and disrupt his family life. His greatest ambition, said Ike, was to be an elder statesman devoid of political ties. Sulzberger, an occasional luncheon and golfing companion, was a trusted confidant and had long known that Ike was a Republican, yet the NATO commander said for his political affiliation to become known would damage the Atlantic Alliance and jeopardize bipartisan American support of NATO. Although he had strong misgivings about Taft and opposed his nomination, Ike strongly reiterated that he would do nothing to influence the convention.

Over the Christmas holidays, *Herald Tribune* publisher Robinson stayed with the Eisenhowers at Marne Lac Coquette and managed to persuade Ike to let him, Robinson, disclose that Eisenhower had voted Republican in the 1950 New York elections. "Why do I have to do this thing?" Ike grumbled, but did nothing to prevent Robinson from making the announcement. As Robinson was leaving, Mamie glared at him and said: "Bill, what are you trying to do to us? I don't think I should ever speak to you again." Even more than Ike, Mamie was against a presidential race, for it would mean her cherished privacy would be gone forever. She was comfortable living in their two-story French chateau, which overlooked a man-made lake and acres of green parklands. The elegant house, which had served as a residence for such eminences as Napoleon III and later Louis Pasteur, had been redecorated by the French Government for the Eisenhowers, and Mamie had made but one change, ordering a wall in their bedroom to be covered with mirrors. The bedroom served as Mamie's office and she later recalled answering hundreds of letters asking her to use her influence to help Ike become President. Her unfailing response was that she was as much in the dark as the rest of the country for the decision was Ike's alone.

On Sunday, January 6, 1952, Lodge called a news conference at the Shoreham Hotel in Washington to make the announcement that Ike was a Republican and his name was to be entered in the New Hampshire presidential primary. "I will not be repudiated," said Lodge. "Go ahead and ask the General." At SHAPE, Ike burst into a rage upon learning details of the Lodge news conference and sent a stern message to General Clay complaining that they had gone too far. The following day, Ike released a statement confirming that Lodge had given "an accurate account of the general tenor of my political convictions and of my Republican voting record." Ike added: "Under no circumstances will I ask for relief from assignment in order to seek nomination to political office and I shall not participate in the pre-convention activities of others who may have such an intention with respect to me."

The Draft Eisenhower forces were still plotting to push Ike into an open candidacy for the nomination. Given Ike's romantic concept of answering the will of the people, they arranged for a mass rally following a Friday-night boxing match at New York's Madison Square Garden. Some fifteen thousand cheering supporters attended the midnight Eisenhower rally and the proceedings were filmed and flown to France for Dwight's viewing. It was for Ike "a moving experience" to see and hear the massive crowd chanting "I Like Ike" and he later claimed to be "profoundly affected" by the motion picture. A week later, on February 16, Ike was in London for the funeral of King George VI and arranged to meet Clay and two other close friends, George Allen and Texas oil millionaire Sid Richardson. At this meeting, Clay said bluntly that unless Ike came home Taft could not be beaten. If Dwight wanted the presidency, he would have to fight for it like any other aspirant. Much to the delight of his friends, Ike tentatively agreed to do just that, although he was not certain of his timing.

New Hampshire's primary had become complicated with another candidate, University of Pennsylvania president and former Minnesota governor, Harold E. Stassen, vying for Granite State delegates. Stassen had been the political sensation of 1948, sweeping most of the Republican primaries that year until an ill-advised radio debate with Thomas E. Dewey led to his defeat in the Oregon primary and cost him the nomination. Franklin D. Roosevelt had talked favorably about Stassen as a future President and had even considered naming him to a wartime cabinet position, but Stassen chose to go on active duty with the Navy and became Chief of Staff to Admiral William F. "Bull" Halsey. Stassen did return from the Pacific to help write the United Nations charter and after his military discharge began campaigning for the presidency. At Penn, Stassen pondered his near-miss in 1948 and began planning what he hoped would be a successful comeback. The Eisenhower strategists encouraged Stassen, hoping that he could bruise Taft in the primaries and make Ike's nomination inevitable. Stassen in November of 1951 had recommended that Taft suspend his candidacy in favor of Eisenhower and a month later the onetime "boy wonder" met with Ike at SHAPE. On his return, Stassen declared his candidacy and gave the impression that Ike would not run. Stassen's presence in New Hampshire, where Ike's name was on the ballot, troubled the Eisenhower camp. Lodge bristled when some overzealous Eisenhower supporters boasted to reporters that New Hampshire was "in the bag."

As it turned out, Lodge's worries were groundless. Ike won all fourteen delegates and won the primary with 46,661 votes to Taft's 35,838, Stassen's 6,574, and MacArthur's 3,227. The Eisenhower campaign had a spectacular send-off with their candidate's vote greater than all three opponents combined. In Paris, Ike said he was "deeply touched."

One week after the New Hampshire race came the Minnesota primary, which all political observers and presidential hopefuls had conceded to Stassen. The Minnesota legislature had scheduled an early primary to give Stassen's candidacy an expected boost and wary Eisenhower operatives obtained a court order withdrawing a slate committed to Ike. Defeat could tarnish the myth of Ike's political invincibility.

Trudging to the polls through a cold, near-blizzard day, more than 108,000 Minnesotans wrote Ike's name on their ballots. Stassen, who had never lost an election in his native state, edged the write-in general by but 20,000 votes. It was termed the "Minnesota Miracle" and Ike said he was "astonished." The Minnesota vote had put Stassen out of the running and the unprecedented wave of write-in votes removed any doubts Dwight might have had about his decision to come home.

On the Democratic side, there were developments no less surprising. President Truman had been upset in the New Hampshire primary by Senator Estes Kefauver of Tennessee, an appealing populist underdog. Though Truman had confided to associates that he would probably not seek reelection, the defeat was unexpected and humiliating. At the end of a Democratic dinner speech on March 29, Truman announced his political retirement. Ike was said to have been moved by Truman's abdication and no doubt was relieved that he no longer faced the dilemma of having to run against his Commander in Chief and benefactor.

Ike's candidacy became official with the April 11 announcement by the White House that his request for relief from his NATO duties had been granted, effective on June 1. To friends, Ike spoke of the dangers of military men becoming politically involved and seemed troubled about his own situation. Once made, however, the decision was irrevocable. In the primaries, Taft won in Wisconsin and Nebraska and continued to attract state convention delegates. However, Eisenhower landslides in Massachusetts, New Jersey, Oregon, and Pennsylvania gave Ike momentum. Taft maintained his delegate lead with primary victories in West Virginia and in South Dakota, where his margin over Ike was 800 votes.

SHAPE had been transformed into a political campaign headquarters as Ike concluded his NATO tour. "General Eisenhower feels that he is in a fight," explained an aide, "and no man likes to lose a fight once he gets into it."

In a farewell press conference in Paris, Ike was asked to comment on Taft's isolationist philosophy. "I most certainly would not," he snapped. "I'm still in uniform." As for NATO, he said: "My confidence in free men and their ability to defend themselves and protect themselves are greater than ever. I know we can do it."

When he left Paris, he was NATO's Supreme Commander, but Dwight was a candidate for President of the United States upon his arrival in Washington. It was still General of the Army Eisenhower, too, for Ike would not resign his commission unless nominated and told one friend that he would not be terribly disappointed should that happen. Yet it was apparent that Ike was no longer an unwilling candidate and was ready to throw himself into the battle at Chicago.

Chapter Fifteen

AMERICA LIKES IKE

Dwight David Eisenhower was a decided underdog for the Republican presidential nomination when he returned to Abilene, Kansas, for a second homecoming celebration on June 4, 1952, to formally launch his drive for the White House. Not only did Taft have almost 100 more delegates than Ike, but his primary-vote total had exceeded Eisenhower's by 670,000 votes. In primary states where both organizations had fielded active campaigns, Ike overpowered Taft by more than 2 to 1. *Newsweek,* analyzing Dwight's return in a cover article, said: "Although recognized by sight and called 'Ike' by almost everybody in the United States, the country knew surprisingly little about him—what he was like, what he thought about the problems facing the nation and the world, and what sort of President he might make. Millions already had rallied to his support because they knew that, as a soldier, he had led Allied troops to victory in Europe, demonstrating a talent both for diplomacy and leadership. . . ."

Although his uniform and five stars were left behind in Washington, Ike's military demeanor was not easily modified. As he descended from his airplane at Kansas City, he was taken aback when Colorado Governor Dan Thornton, a folksy politician wearing cowboy boots and a ten-gallon hat, slapped him across the shoulder and said: "Howya, pardner!" General Ike glared menacingly and stood erect, then smiled and said, "Howya, Dan." The transition to a political candidate had indeed begun.

The Abilene appearance was a carefully staged media event, for his real homecoming had been held seven years earlier. Milton asked Ike if his presence there was really necessary and the older brother assured him that it was. Arthur and Edgar also came to watch Ike trowel the cornerstone of the Eisenhower Museum, a $100,000 enterprise funded by the citizens of Kansas. Speaking to a shirt-sleeved crowd in a field of wild grass, behind his boyhood home, Ike recalled his early life. "I found out in later years that we were very poor," he said, "but the glory of America is that we did not know it then." In the afternoon, the Eisenhower brothers and Mamie watched a parade of floats and bands commemorating Ike's life and times. Dwight hugged Mamie when the "marriage float," with two Kansas children on pink clouds in front of a heart, passed the reviewing stand.

His first political address was a disappointment to a national radio and television audience as well as the rain-drenched crowd at Abilene Stadium. Thunder clouds opened up shortly after the parade and for several hours the downpour continued, leaving the streets flooded and the fields surrounding the stadium a sea of mud. Local organizers had talked confidently of a crowd of some forty thousand, but the grandstands in the twenty-eight-hundred-seat stadium were half empty as a result of the storm. The rain was still falling at five o'clock when Ike splashed through the mud to the outdoor platform. On television, he gave the appearance of a tired old man. His speech was dull and ponderous, the product of many hands, yet lacking any meaningful theme. He was against disunity, inflation, excessive taxation, bureaucracy, and Communism. "One party has been in power too long in this country," he said. Ike blamed the Truman administration for losing China "in one of the greatest international disasters of our times."

The speaker might have been a conservative Midwestern senator. "Mr. Eisenhower has stated his views," said the liberal *New Republic*. "They are superficial and inadequate. The best that can be said for them is that they were no sillier than those voiced by another pragmatic man, Franklin Roosevelt, in 1932." The pro-Taft Chicago *Tribune* dismissed Ike's speech as "five-star generalities." The *Wall Street Journal* noted the similarity between his views and Taft's and Eisenhower's sharp break with President Truman. Doris Fleeson said Ike's approach "is a little too much like raising hell about a fire without telling exactly where it is, who started it, and how to put it out."

If the prepared speech was a disaster, Dwight's press conference the following morning was a virtuoso performance. James Reston of the New York *Times* said the reaction of the national press corps was that Eisenhower may have surpassed Franklin Roosevelt as the master of the press-conference technique. "He has that easy grace that marks a great athlete," said Reston. "He has the most expressive face and hands in American public life, and yet there is a restrained toughness in his expressions and his gestures that appeal to the intellectual and the worker alike. . . . He is direct, and what is equally important, he seems to be more direct in his answer to some questions than he actually is." When asked about Senator Joseph R. McCarthy, the witch-hunting anti-Communist demagogue, Dwight said: "Any kind of Communistic, subversive or pinkish influence [must] be uprooted from responsible places in our government. . . . On the other hand, I believe that can be done under competent leadership . . . without besmirching the reputation of any innocent man or condemning by loose association or anything else."

At a press conference two days later in New York, one Emanuel M. Josephson, author of a right-wing book called *Rockefeller, Internationalist: The Man Who Misrules the World*, asked irreverently: "General, how do you justify your association with Alger Hiss?" Reporters shouted Josephson down as Dwight frowned and snapped, "What's that you say?" He then said, "Ladies and gentlemen, I do not believe that it is necessary for me to defend myself against Communism or Fascism in any form." Confirming that he had met Hiss once while visiting the Carnegie Endowment for International Peace, he said, "I never saw him before or since." (Hiss, a former American diplomat and temporary Secretary-General of the United Nations, had been convicted of perjury and accused of passing State Department documents to the Soviet Union.)

Near the end of this meeting with the press, Ike said: "When I put my hand to any plow, I know only one rule: To work as hard as I possibly can. I am certainly going to try to work honestly, honorably, and in keeping with what I really believe the American people would like me to do. . . . I don't want to lie to you and say that I love all this. I do say that I'm in it now with heart and soul."

In Abilene, a newsreel cameraman had asked: "Did you ever dream when you left Abilene that you would come back and run for the presidency of the United States?" Replied Dwight: "I don't know what dreams crowd the head of a young boy, but I think that before I left it was whether to try to be a Honus Wagner or a railroad conductor. I remember that both of them were very important."

Walter Lippmann, the nation's most influential political analyst, wrote that Ike's adjustment from soldier to candidate was "something to marvel at," noting "that he took it all in his stride without being rattled in the least or breaking down into phoniness." Lippmann saw in Eisenhower a modern Washington who had the potential to unite the country and overcome seemingly insoluble problems.

Throughout June, Ike actively campaigned for the nomination. With the advice of Milton, he strenuously courted Pennsylvania Governor John Fine, who controlled the largest bloc of uncommitted delegates. A bald, jowly little man, Fine was receptive to the Eisenhower overtures and talked wistfully to friends about exchanging his support for the promise of a cabinet post. The Pennsylvanian was shrewd enough not to confront Dwight directly with such an unseemly proposition. "I have no political debts," said Ike at the time. "I am strictly a no-deal man." Indeed, some of the candidate's political advisers were astonished when Ike told a Midwestern delegate to "vote your conscience" on a potentially critical issue due to come before the Credentials Committee. Ike's low-key delegate pitch added to his appeal. No one could challenge him when he asserted: "I have never asked a single person to place me first in his preference list, and I never shall. My first and great obligation is to the American public . . . to explain my convictions and myself as well as I can." Eisenhower's tough-minded inner circle did not necessarily have to follow such idealistic guidelines. When a Taft boomlet started in New York, Governor Dewey reminded its organizers that he could cut their patronage, and Ike's support held firm.

Fully aware of the almost comic failure of his first political speech, Ike was uncomfortable with the warmed-over clichés and platitudes written by the committee of ghost writers. As his campaign train moved through Michigan, he summoned advisers to his private car. Holding a text which had gone through no less than eight drafts, Ike said, "I'm not going to deliver this speech. It doesn't sound like me. What's more, there are parts I can't understand. And if I can't understand them, the American people won't." They argued that it was too late to prepare another speech and urged him to reconsider. There was nothing more to discuss, snapped Ike, summarily dismissing them.

The next morning Ike told a breakfast audience in Detroit: "All my prepared talks are thrown out the window. . . . If I make blunders, I know my friends will excuse it." His modest and self-deprecating manner once again proved far more effective than any political pose. When he told a breakfast of farm editors in Denver that he knew almost nothing about the problems of agriculture, but would value their advice, his ignorance suddenly became a virtue. In a meeting with the pro-Taft Nebraska delegation, Ike emphasized the need for a rejuvenation of the nation's moral leadership and suddenly departed from his normally genial pitch to cite France as an example of "moral degeneration." The liberator of Occupied France and leader of NATO, who had long been a popular hero to the French, complained to the Nebraskans that half of France was agnostic or atheists. Though his remarks were informal and off the record, they soon became public and provoked bitter commentaries from the French press. American journals gave the incident scant attention, for the most influential publishers and columnists were committed to Ike—*The Saturday Evening Post*, Henry Luce's *Time*, *Life*, and *Fortune*, the New York *Times*, New York *Herald Tribune*, and Washington *Post*, all had endorsed his candidacy.

An unprecedented hate campaign was being waged against Eisenhower by right-wing and anti-Semitic organizations. In their pamphlets, Ike was variously represented as being a Communist, a Jew, a German, a Swede, and an appeaser. After seeing some of this crude literature, Dwight informed aides that he did not want to be shown any more. The smear brochures alluded to gossip about Kay Summersby and Ike's alleged affair; and stories were circulated that Mamie was an alcoholic, and Ike suffered from a disease which one newspaper columnist said was cancer. The most prolific of the anti-Ike pamphleteers was Joseph P. Kamp of Wichita, Kansas, whose tabloid called *Headlines* depicted Jews with Nazi-like caricatures and carried such headlines as "IKE BACKED TRAITOROUS FRONT," "WOULD GENERAL IKE TRY TO ABOLISH THE UNITED STATES," "REDS, NEW DEALERS USE IKE IN PLOT TO HOLD POWER" and "IKE CODDLED COMMUNISTS WHILE PRESIDENT OF COLUMBIA UNIVERSITY." Taftite Republicans distributed *Headlines* in primary states and Taft himself did nothing to discourage his more primitive supporters.

In the struggle for the nomination, Taft still maintained his lead of one hundred delegates and took control of the most important Republican Convention machinery. Taft's partisans dominated the Republican National Committee and it followed that the convention plums went to conservative stalwarts. Walter Hallanan, Taft's manager in West Virginia, was designated temporary chairman to preside over the first days of the convention; House Minority Leader Joseph Martin, a Taft ally, was named permanent chairman; and Colorado Senator Eugene Milliken, a vociferous Taft supporter, was chairman of the Platform Committee. When Oregon's national committeeman, Ralph Cake, one of Ike's strategists, called for a keynote speaker not identified with either of the candidates, he was ruled out of order. General Douglas MacArthur, a Taft supporter, was chosen by an overwhelming voice vote. Taft made it known that MacArthur was his probable vice-presidential candidate and added they would form "quite a ticket."

Meanwhile, Taft's steamroller went out of control in Texas, giving Ike the dramatic issue he needed to close the margin. The Eisenhower forces, led by Houston oilman Jack Porter, had soundly beaten Taft at precinct and county conventions, and public-opinion polls indicated that native Texan Ike might well win the Lone Star State in the fall. Henry Zweifel, a Fort Worth businessman and boss of the state Republican organization, refused to allow the pro-Eisenhower delegates to participate in the state convention at Mineral Wells, saying that the precinct meetings had been swamped with Democrats and Independents and did not represent the party. A thirty-eight-member pro-Taft delegation was picked by Zweifel at Mineral Wells and the pro-Eisenhower majority then elected its own slate, forcing the Chicago convention to decide the issue. Eisenhower headquarters immediately denounced the "rape" and "steal" of the Texas delegation. Ike himself came to Texas and said the "rustlers stole the Texas birthright instead of Texas steers." In Dallas, he spoke bluntly about the minority status of the Republican Party. "Some people do not seem to be impressed by these facts," he said. "The truth is, we seem to have this year a new kind of party bolters on our hands. They are the ones who try to bolt the doors of entrance into our party to keep our disturbed and disillusioned Democrats. The only sound Republican policy is an open-door policy. We Republicans must stage a nation-wide political revival that will bring a lot of Democrats through that open door." In Texas, he said there was no real Republican Party, but "a small clique . . . who look upon our party as their fenced-in political preserve." If Taft's claim to Texas was upheld, the nomination was his. When Taft suggested a compromise: twenty-two delegates for himself and sixteen for Eisenhower, Ike privately deemed the offer acceptable. Lodge, arguing that moral issues cannot be compromised, rejected the proposal. There were also disputes over the Georgia and Louisiana delegations and Eisenhower's people correctly sensed that a convention showdown on the contested delegations could produce a roll-call majority and give Ike enough momentum to take the nomination.

On the eve of the convention, Taft was still ahead but the outcome was very much in doubt. The New York *Times* said Taft was within 75 votes of nomination. A Gallup poll indicated Taft was favored by 61 percent of Republican county chairmen, and a *Newsweek* poll of fifty leading political writers forecast a Taft nomination. Tom Lawson McCall, a Pacific Northwest radio commentator, said Eisenhower was so clearly the popular choice that if defeated at Chicago he should run as an Independent.

Among Republicans, Ike led Taft by 9 percentage points in the Gallup poll. But more importantly, Eisenhower led all Democratic contenders by large margins in Gallup surveys while Taft ran behind, and among Independents, Eisenhower led Taft by 7 to 1. For three days, the New York *Times* published editorials headlined "TAFT CAN'T WIN," and the theme dominated Eisenhower efforts to convert wavering delegates. Having suffered five consecutive presidential defeats, the party's survival seemed a legitimate question.

As expected, Taft's contested southern delegates were recognized by the Republican National Committee and the Credentials Committee. Moreover, the contested delegates would be permitted to vote on their own fate on the convention floor. At the Republican Governors' Conference in Houston, three pro-Eisenhower governors—Dewey, Adams of New Hampshire, and Douglas McKay of Oregon—gained the unanimous support of all twenty-five governors in condemning the practice of allowing disputed delegates to vote on seating themselves.

The first session of the convention at the air-conditioned International Amphitheater opened on the afternoon of July 7. Senator John Bricker of Ohio called for adoption of the rules of the previous convention in an attempt to end debate on the disputed delegates. Governor Arthur Langlie of Washington quickly rose to offer the "Fair Play" amendment which said that contested delegates could not vote on credentials matters. After acrimonious debate, Ike's forces won this first test, 658 to 548. When President Truman heard this vote, he said wryly, "I am afraid that my favorite candidate is going to be beaten." Taft's position as the front runner had been put in serious jeopardy by subordinates who allowed a roll-call vote without a floor majority.

In the event of a deadlock between Ike and Taft, a legendary soldier was eager to fill the void. General MacArthur had been available in the past, but always before he had been on active duty in the Pacific. MacArthur's 1951 firing by President Truman because of the general's open defiance of Korean War policy, brought a storm of protest in the United States and the general returned for a series of welcome-home celebrations and speaking tours. To conservatives, MacArthur was America's most singular hero and a symbol of rugged individualism. MacArthur considered himself a man of destiny, a twentieth-century Caesar, and had talked with friends about the inevitability of his election to the presidency. That his former aide, Eisenhower, had emerged as a serious contender for the White House was bitterly resented. MacArthur said ruefully that "Eisenhower was the best clerk I ever had," and later added that his onetime subordinate was "the apotheosis of mediocrity." For his part, Ike volunteered that he "took dramatic lessons under MacArthur for nine years." The rift between the celebrated generals became public in the spring when MacArthur declared a preference for Taft. With Taft's early convention setback, it was considered a possibility that MacArthur's speech would be the turning point of the convention. The seventy-two-year-old general was considered a great orator and if anyone seemed capable of influencing delegates it was MacArthur. At past national conventions, dramatic and personally magnetic speakers had made the most of such opportunities. In 1896, William Jennings Bryan's "Cross of Gold" speech against the gold standard was the key factor in his own nomination for the presidency at Chicago. As MacArthur made his entrance, there was excitement and pandemonium and a rousing ovation. MacArthur's confident smile betrayed his ambition to be President and to upstage his former junior officer. On the podium, MacArthur acknowledged the cheers and the spotlights accentuated his Olympian profile. Like Napoleon and Caesar, MacArthur believed his fate and the nation's had at last arrived.

MacArthur's keynote speech was widely interpreted as dreadful—a far cry from his "Old Soldiers Never Die" address to Congress. It was a Bible-thumping, conservative speech, notable chiefly for its clichés and verbosity. Though his command of the English language was superb, MacArthur was a captive of a nineteenth-century political philosophy. In an act of personal spite, he attacked the general (without naming him) who "foolishly permitted" Soviet forces to capture Berlin. MacArthur charged the Democratic administration with "discarding victory as the military objective and thereby condemning our forces to a stalemated struggle of attrition." There was strong applause at the conclusion of his speech, but no more than for any party functionary, and it quickly diminished. MacArthur may have realized that like the old soldier of the army ballad, he was indeed fading away.

Two other hopefuls still thought a Taft-Ike stalemate might catapult one of them to the nomination: perennial candidate Stassen and California Governor Earl Warren, the 1948 vice-presidential nominee. However, an Eisenhower nomination was beginning to look probable as the previously uncommitted Michigan and Pennsylvania delegations shifted to the general, and Eisenhower's forces scored a clean sweep in a second confrontation on the disputed southern delegates, winning floor votes after another bitter debate. Ike received another boost when Governor Theodore McKeldin of Maryland, a favorite-son presidential candidate, withdrew and agreed to nominate Eisenhower.

On the morning of July 11, Ike and his four brothers watched the presidential balloting on television in the Eisenhower suite at the Blackstone Hotel. Mamie, bedridden with an infected tooth and an allergic reaction to her medication, was in the next room and Ike gave her periodic reports on the proceedings. After the first roll call, Ike had 595 votes, Taft 500, Warren 81, Stassen 20, and MacArthur 10. The Stassen and Warren organizers had tentatively agreed to call for a recess after the first ballot, to exploit the impending deadlock. Yet Stassen's position was vulnerable for his Minnesota delegation was in rebellion. Senator Edward Thye shouted for recognition: "Mr. Chairman, Mr. Chairman, Minnesota wishes to change—" and the galleries roared in expectation as the house organist began playing "The Minnesota Rouser." Thye then declared: "Minnesota wishes to change its vote to Eisenhower." This simple vote change made Dwight David Eisenhower the Republican presidential nominee, giving him 614 votes, 10 more than was needed. Stassen had tearfully pleaded with his delegates not to desert him, but he had fallen out of touch with reality and was ignored. As soon as his nomination became official, Ike hurried into Mamie's bedroom to give her the news.

Ike telephoned Senator Taft to ask if he could come across the street to visit him at the Conrad Hilton, a break from the tradition of waiting for the vanquished to call on the party's standard-bearer. Brother Arthur had urged him not to violate that precedent. As Ike walked through the crowded lobby, he was booed by

Taftites, and the crowd chanted, "We Want Taft!" Security men escorted him to Taft's room where he met the senator and his three sons. Ike's eyes were moist and he appeared somewhat ill at ease, while Taft, having already written a concession statement, was poised and reconciled to his defeat. Ike well understood that Taft, not he, represented the philosophy and hopes of a majority of the convention's delegates and but for the maneuvering of the "Fair Play" amendment his rival would have been the nominee. Admitting that he was tired, Ike told the senator that he hoped they could be friends and work together. "My only problem for the moment," replied Taft, "is that for the twenty minutes it took you to get over here I have been bombarded by requests from photographers for a picture. Would you be willing to have one taken?"

As the two Republicans stepped into the high-ceilinged hallway, the crowd resumed its cheering for Taft. The senator graciously asked them to stop in deference to the party's candidate. General Eisenhower looked passive and shy, somehow out of place in this carnival setting. "You'll get used to it," said Taft. Ike's rejoinder was that he had just told Mamie about a nightmare when he was both nominated and elected. Mr. Republican told Ike that his election was as certain as anything could be.

"I came over to pay a call of friendship on a great American," said Ike. "His willingness to cooperate is absolutely essential to the success of the Republican Party in the campaign and of the Administration to follow."

With more than a few of the crowd openly weeping, Taft said: "I want to congratulate General Eisenhower. I shall do everything possible in the campaign to secure his election and to help in his administration."

Returning to the Blackstone, Ike wrote a telegram of resignation as General of the Army. It was a wrenching moment for the forty-year soldier and the Eisenhower brothers wept under the extraordinary circumstances.

The selection of a running mate was a matter Ike left to his political advisers. Among the leaders of the Draft Eisenhower movement, Ike would have welcomed Lodge, Dewey, or Clay as his vice-presidential candidate. However, it would have appeared somewhat incestuous for a close associate to have been named, and Dewey had long ago ruled himself out, Lodge was seeking reelection to the Senate, and Clay as a military man could hardly be considered for a ticket headed by another general. Some party leaders talked wistfully of an Eisenhower-Taft "dream ticket," but it seemed unlikely that Taft would consider the vice presidency, having rejected such opportunities at past conventions. A group of twenty-five Eisenhower friends and party leaders met in a room at the Hilton to examine the field of prospective candidates. Eisenhower said Senators Richard Nixon and William Knowland of California; Governors Dan Thornton of Colorado, Arthur Langlie of Washington, and Alfred Driscoll of New Jersey; and Congressmen Charles Halleck of Indiana and Walter Judd of Minnesota were all perfectly acceptable. Dewey reportedly proposed Nixon to the group and a Westerner, Ralph Cake, gave the Californian a glowing endorsement. According to insiders, Dewey viewed Nixon as "a respectable McCarthy," a political gut fighter who could rally conservatives behind Eisenhower and heal the wounds from the bitter Eisenhower-Taft fight. Several months before Dewey had invited Nixon to New York and advised him of this possibility.

Nixon, then thirty-nine, was an ambitious, faceless, rootless, thoroughly amoral man who had won his congressional seat in 1946 by portraying the Democratic incumbent, Jerry Voorhis, as a dangerous radical supported by Communists. In Congress, Nixon gained a measure of prominence for his role in the unmasking of Alger Hiss. Nixon made his reputation as a political knife man in his 1950 Senate campaign by using anti-Communist smear tactics against his Democratic opponent, Helen Gahagan Douglas, whom he denounced repeatedly as "The Pink Lady." Nixon had national aspirations, but since California's Governor Warren was planning another bid for the presidency, his own efforts had to be subtle if not clandestine to avoid an embarrassing split in the state party organization. When Dewey made his initiative, Nixon worked behind the scenes to advance Eisenhower's candidacy and undermine Warren, to whom he was legally bound as a California delegate. For good measure, Nixon spread the word that Taft would be a weak nominee. Upon learning of Nixon's activity, Taft described Nixon as "a little man in a big hurry" with a "mean and vindictive streak." On the eve of the convention, Nixon mailed out a much-publicized questionnaire to California Republicans, asking them to select "the strongest candidate the Republicans could nominate for President." Eisenhower led this unscientific poll, which served the purpose of diminishing Warren's claim as California's "favorite son." Nixon's efforts to undercut Warren were perhaps most successful on the Fair Play amendment, where he helped persuade a majority of the delegation to take the Eisenhower position. Though Warren never commented publicly on Nixon's pursuit of the vice presidency, his son, Earl Warren, Jr., later said that Nixon "wronged my father and the whole state" by using "back-door tactics" undertaken "for political gain for himself." The Eisenhower people, including Dewey, were kept well informed of Nixon's subterfuge within the California delegation. In the meeting at the Hilton, it was pointed out that Nixon would bring the ticket geographical balance as a Westerner and that his youth might attract young voters. "When we reached an agreement—and everyone thought Nixon's selection was a good idea, a call was made to Eisenhower who agreed to put Nixon on the ticket," recalled Ralph Cake in an interview years later.

Eisenhower and Nixon and their wives appeared before the convention that evening and received a thunderous ovation. The general praised the vice-presidential candidate, whom he had met briefly when Nixon visited NATO headquarters, and said his running mate "has a special talent and an ability to ferret out any kind of subversive influence wherever it may be found, and the strength and persistence to get rid of it." The choice of Nixon dismayed some of Ike's earliest supporters. Senator Wayne L. Morse, during a conversation with political analyst Tom Lawson McCall, said: "How could they do it? This Jew baiter, this Red baiter, this labor baiter. How could they try to foist him upon the American people? Why couldn't it have been a progressive Republican like Leverett Saltonstall?" Ohio Senator John Bricker refused to make a seconding speech for Nixon and it was with some misgivings that California Senator William Knowland placed his junior colleague's name in nomination. Joseph McCarthy was enthusiastic and told reporters: "I think Dick Nixon will make a fine Vice President."

Accepting the nomination, Dwight said: "Ladies and gentlemen, you have summoned me on behalf of millions of your fellow Americans to *lead a crusade*—for freedom in America and freedom in the world. I know something of the solemn responsibility of *leading a crusade*. I have led one. I take up this task, therefore, in a spirit of deep obligation. Mindful of its burdens and of its decisive importance, I accept your summons. *I will lead this crusade.*"

Some political observers questioned whether Ike really could lead an American crusade. Max Lerner said Eisenhower's years in military service had left him wholly unfamiliar with civil rights, tidelands oil, federal aid to education, and other critical issues of the day. "Ike has won," wrote Lerner, "but in victory he emerges a prisoner. He is a prisoner of his own career, with its lack of American experience. He is a prisoner of a party torn by civil war, where he is torn between appeasing the Taft forces and appealing to independent liberals."

I. F. Stone, noting that Ike had been absent from the United States for most of the preceding twenty years, said, "Eisenhower, with his uniform off, seems more and more like a very uninformed Rip Van Winkle come back to civilian life as the naïve tool of the Chase National Bank crowd. . . . The more he talks the more poorly equipped for the job he appears." Stone predicted that a vigorous Democratic campaign could defeat Eisenhower. "The Democrats can defeat Ike if they want to," said Stone.

Two weeks after the Republican Convention, Democrats gathered in the same building to choose their candidates. There was some speculation that President Truman might change his attitude and run again himself, but he resisted the temptation to run against his onetime Chief of Staff. Kefauver, who had defeated Truman in New Hampshire and added a string of primary victories, was the front runner when the convention opened, yet he was too much of an independent to attract a majority. His much-publicized organized crime investigations had linked some big-city Democratic bosses to the Mafia and they took their revenge at Chicago. Vice President Alben Barkley, at seventy-four, said he was still vigorous, youthful, and available, but Truman and top organized labor leaders gently told him he was too old. Two powerful Senate conservatives, Richard Russell of Georgia and Robert Kerr of Oklahoma, were at best regional candidates with little hope of nomination. Averell Harriman, Truman's foreign-aid administrator and former Secretary of Commerce, was well liked at the White House, but Truman sensed that voters would find him less appealing than the world leaders with whom Harriman was accustomed to working. Harriman possessed great self-confidence and thought he was the most qualified and liberal of all the contenders, the rightful heir to the legacy of the New Deal and the Fair Deal. As an old friend of Eisenhower's, Harriman thought Ike was charming but politically naïve. Several weeks before the convention, Harriman received an endorsement of sorts from Governor Adlai Stevenson of Illinois. Though men of power liked him, Harriman was unable to pick up enough delegates to make a serious challenge.

The most attractive Democratic leader was Stevenson, who that spring had turned down Truman's offer of the nomination. What was mistaken for coyness was in reality a driving ambition. Stevenson's reluctance to seek the presidency in 1952 had nothing to do with his capacity for the job, for he wanted to be President. But he did not want to risk his political career against a seemingly unbeatable war hero. Throughout the summer and well into the convention, Stevenson kept saying that he wanted only to run for reelection as governor. A "Draft Stevenson" movement was organized and quickly gained strength. On the third ballot he was nominated. General Eisenhower, who admired Stevenson as an internationalist and an urbane, civilized political leader, told his son, John, "I would have stayed in uniform if I had known the Democrats were going to run Stevenson."

In the aftermath of his convention triumph, Ike took a vacation in Colorado, where he and Mamie stayed at the Brown Palace Hotel in Denver. More than eight thousand people had cheered him at the Denver airport on his arrival, and everywhere he went he was trailed by throngs of newsmen, photographers, and admiring fans. A campaign headquarters and suite of offices were opened at the Brown Palace and the candidate sought the counsel of such advisers as Senators Lodge, Dirksen, Frank Carlson of Kansas, and James Duff of Pennsylvania. To demonstrate his willingness to campaign for Republican candidates, Ike released his telegram to Illinois Congressman Edward H. Jenison, promising every "sector of Republicanism" would receive his "wholehearted support."

In Denver, Ike and Mamie said farewell to John, who had received orders to go to Korea. "If you're captured," Ike had told his son in an earlier conversation, "I suppose I would just have to drop out of the presidential race." John told him that there was no cause for his parents to worry, but he later admitted that the possibility did haunt him and the only solution would have been to fight Chinese or North Korean soldiers to the death rather than put his father in a vulnerable position in dealing with the Communist nations. Ike presented John with an alarm clock at the Denver airport and said good-by.

For relaxation, Ike retreated to the 1,900-acre ranch in the Colorado Rockies owned by his friend Denver businessman Aksel Nielsen. There, Ike took his folding easel, paintbox, and canvases along with his fishing gear. When the Eisenhower press entourage came to take photographs and gather color for their articles, Ike was hip-deep in St. Louis Creek and casting a dry fly. Still unaccustomed to sharing private moments with outsiders, Ike was pensive and for more than an hour did not get a bite. Finally, when he caught a small trout, the newsmen left and Ike said frankly he preferred the company of fish.

Meanwhile, the job of uniting the bitterly divided Republicans remained. Nixon was already actively campaigning and trying to woo disgruntled Taftites. Yet Ohio's Republican National Committeewoman Katherine Kennedy Brown said Taft Republicans could not possibly get behind Eisenhower until the general disassociated himself from Dewey. Eisenhower, on the advice of brother Milton and his own instincts, was keeping the controversial New Yorker in the background, but had no intention of repudiating his most influential supporter. Ike was, however, perfectly willing to cut all ties with President Truman, whom he had served so long and with notable success. In mid-August, Truman invited Eisenhower to the White House for a briefing from former Ike aide Walter Bedell Smith, followed by a luncheon with Truman and his cabinet. Dwight replied: "In my current position as standard-bearer of the Republican Party and of other Americans who want to bring about a change in the National Government, it is my duty to remain free to analyze publicly the policies and acts of the present Administration whenever it appears to me to be proper and in the country's interests. . . . Consequently I think it would be unwise and result in confusion in the public mind if I were to attend the meeting in the White House to which you have invited me." Truman, a proud and sensitive man, was hurt and angered by Ike's wired response and wrote in longhand a letter expressing regret that the general had "allowed a bunch of screwballs" to come between them and reiterated his friendship. The Democratic President received an apologetic note from Dwight, but the damage had been done and Truman could take little comfort when Stevenson, writing to Tom Humphrey of the *Oregon Journal*, referred to the mess in Washington.

Ike's political education was at times unpleasant and he was downright cynical about the elaborate strategies prepared by some of his own professionals. "Dad didn't like politics and he wasn't crazy about politicians," John Eisenhower recalled years later. "There were a lot of things about the Republican Party he didn't care for." Ike was clearly annoyed after a meeting at the Brown Palace Hotel with Republican leaders. "All they talked about was how they would win on my popularity," he told Governor Sherman Adams of New Hampshire. "Nobody said I had a brain in my head."

For six weeks following the convention, Ike seemed content to make bland policy statements. Like most centrist candidates, he was playing it safe. At Boise, Idaho, he said he had adopted "the middle way," which he also termed "that straight road down the middle." Ike accepted the "social gains" of the New Deal and Fair Deal, but with more efficient administration. On August 25, he made his first major campaign appearance in a "nonpolitical" address before the American Legion Convention in New York. "Fifty years ago," he said, "America was the wonder of humanity. . . . We shall make it that again." Though he had been welcomed by a long and intense ovation by the Legionnaires, his speech had only been interrupted by mild applause. Two days later, Stevenson was interrupted by applause no less than thirty-six times.

One reporter covering Eisenhower quipped, "He just crossed the thirty-eighth platitude." A number of Ike's supporters feared that he was repeating the mistake of Thomas E. Dewey in 1948 in failing to carry the fight to the Democratic opposition. On the same day of his American Legion speech, the Scripps-Howard newspaper chain published front-page editorials in nineteen newspapers under the headline: "IKE, WHEN DO WE START?"

The editorial said: "We trust Dwight Eisenhower doesn't think what he has been doing and saying this last month can classify as campaigning for office. . . . We still cling to the hope that when he does start campaigning he will come out swinging. . . . If he doesn't, he might as well concede defeat and go back to the cloisters of Columbia University or the tranquillity of his Pennsylvania farm. . . . Ike is running like a dry creek."

His greatest problem, *Newsweek* said, was "how to make such a moderate position dramatic and exciting enough to the millions of independent and Democratic voters the Republicans must enlist if they are to win." Ike huddled with his advisers about the pessimistic press reports. After the meeting, at Ike's headquarters at the Hotel Commodore in New York, Henry Cabot Lodge said: "We are not trying to win a popularity contest in August. We are trying to win an election in November." The Gallup poll showed Ike leading Stevenson by 9 percentage points, but the same poll had picked Dewey in 1948. A September survey of fifty prominent Washington correspondents predicted a close race, with Stevenson the favorite.

What made Ike's chances somewhat uncertain was the question of Robert A. Taft. His considerable following still viewed Taft, not Eisenhower, as the party's true leader and those who had fought for his nomination were not willing to transfer their loyalties until Taft gave them a clear signal. Taft had retreated to his summer home in Murray Bay, still bitter about his convention defeat. When Ike sent a telegram seeking Taft's advice, the senator replied that he would meet with him after his vacation. Through intermediaries, Taft sent Ike his terms for active support of the ticket. The concessions included a guarantee that the Cabinet would include an equal number of Taft people, and veto power over the appointment of Dewey to a Cabinet position. Moreover, Taft wanted a firm commitment to the Taft-Hartley Act and assurances that an Eisenhower administration would not bring a Republican New Deal. When he did not get a quick response, Taft grumbled about the heavy-handed tactics used against him at Chicago and even talked about organizing a conservative third party for 1956. In late August, Taft told a visiting Chicago newsman that he would not encourage his supporters to back Eisenhower until Ike met his demands.

That Ike was politically flexible was revealed in a June 20 letter to foreign-policy adviser John Foster Dulles, discussing the Republican foreign policy plank: "There are innumerable instances of method, detail and procedure on which I am always ready to accept almost any revision of my own views." To gain Taft's support, Ike was more than willing to negotiate a political settlement. A breakfast meeting with Taft was arranged at Ike's Columbia University residence on September 12. Taft had sent the general a seven-page statement the night before, but Ike did not read it until their meeting. Dwight found Taft's demands far more moderate than had been indicated, with no restrictions about possible appointments or substantial changes in campaign policy. In the "unity statement," which Taft read at a news conference after the meeting, they conceded "differences" in foreign policy, endorsed Taft-Hartley, and said the major issue of the campaign was liberty against the creeping Socialism of the Fair Deal.

Ike had solved the Taft problem and taken a major step toward unifying the party. Taft's supporters, particularly in the Midwest, went to work for Eisenhower. There was, to be sure, some backlash from liberal Republicans. Senator Wayne Morse of Oregon, already miffed by the Nixon selection, denounced the "Surrender at Morningside Heights" and said he would not campaign for Ike. Stevenson said, "Taft lost the nomination but won the nominee." The Democratic candidate added that the "great crusade" had become the "great surrender."

On September 18, Ike's campaign was jolted by revelations that a group of conservative California businessmen had given Nixon an eighteen-thousand-dollar secret fund. The New York *Post*, which broke the story, headlined its front page: "SECRET RICH MEN'S TRUST FUND KEEPS NIXON IN STYLE FAR BEYOND HIS MEANS." Until then, Eisenhower and Nixon had piously campaigned against Democratic corruption. Nixon typically said the newspaper article was a left-wing smear, part of the persecution he had endured "ever since I took part in the investigation which led to the conviction of Alger Hiss."

Nixon could not cover up the scandal because some of the fund's donors confirmed its existence. The New York *Herald Tribune* and the Washington *Post*, two strongly pro-Eisenhower newspapers, called for Nixon's resignation from the ticket. Democratic National Chairman Stephen Mitchell called for Nixon to step aside. Milton Eisenhower, no admirer of Nixon, quietly suggested that it was a matter for the Senate to investigate. Dewey and General Clay were for dumping Nixon and Harold Stassen wired Nixon a suggested statement of resignation. Ike's inner circle had come to the painful conclusion that Nixon must go. Press secretary Jim Hagerty reported to Ike that the newspapermen on the campaign train had voted 40 to 2 against Nixon.

In an emotional meeting with the newsmen, Ike said he assumed that Nixon had not been guilty of unethical or illegal behavior, but he added: "I'm taking my time on this. Nothing's decided, contrary to your idea that this is all a setup for a whitewash of Nixon. Nixon has got to be as clean as a hound's tooth."

Nixon, angered by Eisenhower's remark, vowed to fight to stay on the ticket. When the general called him, however, Nixon offered to withdraw if it was Eisenhower's wish. Instead, Dwight suggested that Nixon go on national television and make full disclosure of his finances. Nixon was less than eager to go public with his personal expenditures and asked Ike if there would be an endorsement after the speech. Ike replied that he was not about to be rushed and Nixon snapped: "There comes a time when you have to piss or get off the pot!" Nixon's outburst did nothing to enhance his position and the senator agreed to make a televised statement. California's other senator, William F. Knowland, was summoned to the Eisenhower campaign train from Hawaii and became the odds-on choice to replace Nixon. Ike told Adams: "If

Nixon has to go, we cannot win." Still, there seemed to be substance to the conflict-of-interest charges, and Dewey bluntly advised Nixon that Eisenhower's high command wanted his resignation.

Defending himself, Nixon went on television immediately following the Milton Berle show, to deliver what became known as his "Checkers Speech" because of a gratuitous reference to his cocker spaniel. It was estimated that fifty-five million Americans watched or listened to the speech. Nixon's talk was pure political soap opera, which, when viewed more than a quarter century later, seems unbearably unsophisticated. In many ways, though, the speech was Nixon's greatest political triumph, transforming him overnight from a potential political corpse into a martyred hero. He discussed his personal finances—his 1950 car, the mortgage on his house, debts to another bank, and a life-insurance policy. His wife did not have a mink coat, but a "respectable Republican cloth coat" and, he scolded, she did not work on his office payroll like the wife of Democratic vice-presidential candidate John Sparkman. Nixon pointed to revelations that Stevenson, too, had a political expense fund, and then called for Stevenson and Sparkman to make their finances public. Ike, watching the telecast in a backstage office at a Cleveland auditorium, instantly recognized that Nixon was forcing him into a corner. Ike's income-tax returns would show the special treatment he had received for *Crusade in Europe* and give Democrats a perfect issue. To compound this transgression, Nixon made a daring power play to ensure that Ike would not control his fate. On Dewey's instructions, Nixon was to ask viewers to send telegrams to Los Angeles where Nixon's staff would take responsibility for the massive clerical work of handling the telegrams. Eisenhower, far removed from the scene, would make his own decision. Nixon instead said the Republican National Committee would decide and urged the audience to write or wire their recommendations.

The conservative national committee had been behind Nixon prior to the speech and with their support he could defy Eisenhower should the general try to force him off the ticket. Ike burned at Nixon's impudence, yet understood that he was powerless. Nixon had outflanked the old soldier and taken his appeal to a more sympathetic authority. Mamie and her mother, Elvira Doud, in the room with Ike, wept as they watched Nixon, and in the auditorium, men and women tearfully applauded the vice-presidential candidate. Ike's emotional response was more controlled and he acted quickly to bring Nixon to heel. Putting aside a prepared speech, Ike hurriedly wrote his public answer to Nixon. "I have seen many brave men in tough situations," he said. "I have never seen any come through in better fashion than Senator Nixon did tonight. . . . When I get in a fight, I would rather have a courageous and honest man by my side than a whole boxcar full of pussyfooters." Despite this fulsome praise, Ike refused to give Nixon what really counted: his endorsement. "It is obvious that I have to have something more than one single presentation," he said. "I am not ducking any responsibility, I am not going to be swayed by my idea of what will get the most votes. . . . I am going to say: Do I myself believe this man is the kind of man America would like to have for its Vice President?" In conclusion, Dwight disclosed that he had summoned Nixon to meet him in Wheeling, West Virginia, the next day. Nixon got the message—he would have to grovel properly to get Ike's vote of confidence.

"What more does he want?" Nixon asked an aide. "I'm not going to crawl on my hands and knees to him." Nixon then dictated a letter of resignation which an aide promptly destroyed.

Nixon was against going to Wheeling and sent word to Ike that he was resuming his campaign schedule in Montana. An open break was avoided when Eisenhower promised a full endorsement if Nixon came to West Virginia as instructed. The senator's plane landed late in the evening and Ike himself was there to meet Nixon. "Dick," said the general, "you're my boy." Nixon's eyes filled with tears and he broke down and wept on Knowland's shoulder. For the moment, Nixon had salvaged his political career but in so doing he had alienated the one figure to whom his future was constitutionally linked. Ike would in later years torment Nixon with subtlety and cunning, leaving his Vice President with an even greater sense of inferiority and resentment.

Ike's earlier commitment to support the Republican ticket was perfectly consistent with his position as the party's titular leader.

Yet after the convention he denounced the smear tactics of witch-hunting anti-Communists, meaning Republican Senators William Jenner of Indiana and McCarthy of Wisconsin, and at a Denver press conference defended General Marshall against their attacks: "If he was not a perfect example of patriotism and a loyal servant of the United States, I never saw one. If I could say more, I would say it, but I have no patience with anyone who can find in his record of service to the country anything to criticize." In terms of political principle, it would have been understood had Ike refused to make joint appearances with either Jenner or McCarthy, both seeking reelection. Jenner had called Marshall, Eisenhower's mentor, "a living lie" and "a front man for traitors." McCarthy said Marshall was part of a "conspiracy" to betray America to Communism.

In September Ike did urge the reelection of Jenner during a campaign swing through Indiana, though he did not mention the senator by name. Jenner, trailing Democratic Governor Henry Schricker, his opponent, in the polls, chose to ignore the snub and resourcefully managed to get himself photographed embracing Ike. During Eisenhower's speech at Butler University in Indianapolis, Jenner repeatedly clasped Ike's shoulder and smiled for cameramen. Ike, his vein throbbing, turned and left the stage in disgust. "I felt dirty from the touch of the man," he later confided to an aide. The incident revealed Ike's contempt for the cynicism and hypocrisy of politicians, although his private comments hardly erased the image of public solidarity with Jenner.

A month later, Ike himself seemed to have submitted to the ultimate in political expediency when he embraced McCarthy at a rally in Milwaukee and deleted from his prepared remarks a rebuke to McCarthy and a defense of Marshall. That Eisenhower was even considering such a moralistic and dramatic gesture was refreshing to some of his idealistic young associates. Taft, on most issues a man of high principle and an often courageous defender of civil liberties, had praised McCarthy and came close to endorsing McCarthyism, in his campaign for the presidential nomination. Ike was violently upset on learning that he had been scheduled to campaign in Wisconsin and then proposed the tribute to Marshall "right in McCarthy's back yard." Wisconsin Governor

Walter Kohler pleaded for the general to avoid a confrontation with McCarthy and the possible loss of Wisconsin by going through with the planned rebuke.

McCarthy had made the same request before Ike at a Peoria, Illinois, hotel, where the presidential candidate was staying the night before going to Wisconsin. The brash senator told the general that Communist infiltration of the government was the overriding issue of the campaign and threatened the very future of the nation. Kevin McCann, who witnessed the meeting, later recalled: "Hardly had he [McCarthy] gotten into his statement when Dwight Eisenhower broke in that he had come, not to hear a lecture, but to make his own position crystal clear. Then, coldly, savagely, he stripped from the senator all his pretensions of dedication to American security . . . of any sincerity of purpose or of effectiveness in performance." McCann said he had never seen Eisenhower so angry. Ike told McCarthy that he revered Marshall. After his reprimand, the general cut McCarthy short with a "good night" and left the room.

If McCarthy's crude advance was rebuffed, the same appeal from Governor Kohler, a respected moderate, received a sympathetic hearing. The governor had been privately critical of McCarthy and told Eisenhower that he agreed with the principle of defending Marshall. His bottom line was that the Marshall reference in the Milwaukee speech would disrupt Wisconsin politics and possibly cost Ike the state. To help Kohler retain the governorship and preserve party unity, Eisenhower struck out the controversial passage. It was a classic act of political caution which tarnished Ike's reputation as a crusader for democratic principles.

Ike gave McCarthy cool treatment during their joint appearances. In Green Bay, he emphasized the "differences" between McCarthy and himself, yet said they differed on "method" rather than objectives. Governor Kohler recalled that McCarthy's expression was dark when Ike spoke and that the senator kept shaking his head in disagreement. At the Milwaukee Arena, Eisenhower managed to avoid mentioning McCarthy in his endorsement of the state party ticket and said: "We would have nothing left to defend if we allowed ourselves to be swept into any spirit of violent vigilantism." Wisconsin party leaders may have been pleased with Eisenhower's compromise, but Ike found the whole episode distasteful and later praised Marshall in no less than three campaign speeches. Still, the impression lingered that he had given McCarthyism his tacit endorsement, and although General Marshall would not comment on the incident, Mrs. Marshall disclosed that her husband had spent many evenings listening to the radio waiting for Ike to repudiate McCarthy.

President Truman had in the meantime come forth as Ike's most fervent critic, charging that his former Chief of Staff was being "shoved around" by "special interests" and was little more than their "tool." Truman said Ike was "showing the nation—he has certainly shown me—that he's not the man we thought him. He doesn't measure up." Truman's folksy "give 'em hell" technique degenerated into a strident and vicious ad hominem attack on Eisenhower. He accused Ike of adopting the Nazi theory of a "master race," of shirking his military responsibilities, and other crimes and misdeeds. Truman had been waiting to denounce Ike since his refusal of the August luncheon invitation and his frustrations were compounded by his rift with Stevenson, who had attacked corruption in the Truman administration and established his national campaign headquarters in Springfield, Illinois, in an effort to put a distance between himself and Truman. Stevenson was too high-minded for slashing personal rhetoric and had promised to "talk sense to the American people." Truman could not lambast his own party's nominee so he vented his rage on Eisenhower.

The charges of anti-Semitism stung Ike more than any other, for his hatred of Nazism had been an obsession and his shock on learning of their death camps profound. Leaders of Zionist and Jewish organizations counterattacked Truman's violent crack. "Much is permitted in a campaign," said Rabbi Abba Hillel Silver of Cleveland, "but the attempt to identify a man like General Eisenhower, whose humanity and broad tolerance are known all over the world, with anti-Semitism and anti-Catholicism is just not permissible even in the heat of a campaign."

Ike had been forthright on civil rights and equality for blacks and during his southern tour said: "Unless we protect the rights of our neighbor, whatever the color of his skin, we are going to lose our own rights." In Chicago, he promised not to appoint anyone who held "a reactionary view about the basic tenet of our Constitution, that we are created equal, regardless of race or religion or anything else." Herman Talmadge, the segregationist Georgia governor, accused Ike of selling out to Harlem, yet his position on the issue had been consistent with his wartime efforts to integrate the combat forces.

While Eisenhower and Stevenson debated lofty issues of state, Nixon and McCarthy joined Truman in the political gutter. Both Republican senators linked Stevenson with "Communism." Nixon ripped "Adlai the appeaser," whom he said had been "duped by Communist Alger Hiss" and was thus untrustworthy to deal with the Soviet Union. McCarthy referred to Stevenson as "Alger" and incorrectly stated that the American Communist Party was working for Stevenson's election. Nixon's performance as a campaign hatchet man further damaged his chances of winning Dwight's confidence and in later months Eisenhower would attribute some of Nixon's shortcomings to immaturity.

In the home stretch of the campaign the Korean War overshadowed all other issues. Truman's escalation of the war in the small Asian nation was not unlike Lyndon Johnson's later buildup in Vietnam: A distant conflict represented as a threat to America which enabled Truman to resume his favorite role as wartime Commander in Chief. The Korean General Assembly had wanted to unite with North Korea, but unpopular South Korean leader Syngman Rhee wanted to preserve his regime and provoked an attack from the north. Rhee secured the backing of Truman and Chiang Kai-shek. The United Nations Security Council, in emergency session, called for member nations to assist South Korea in bringing an end to hostilities. With the Soviet Union boycotting the debate the resolution passed unanimously. Truman thus sent American forces to Korea without congressional authority but with United Nations sanction. Over the next three years American casualties were to include more than 177,000 killed, wounded, or captured by Communist armies. In early October of 1952, Ike said that Korea was "a useless war" and stressed that it was an Asian conflict. Speaking at the Cow Palace in San Francisco on October 9, Ike said: "I pledge full dedication to the job of finding an intelligent and honorable way to end the tragic toll of American casualties in Korea. No one can pledge you more. Nor can there be a more solemn pledge. For this war is reaching tonight into the homes of hundreds of thousands of American families. I do not believe that Korea must forever be a part of our American daily life."

The climactic moment of the campaign came in Detroit on October 24 when Ike attacked "the false answer . . . that nothing can be done to speed a secure peace," and said "the old administration cannot be expected to repair what it failed to prevent." If elected, Ike promised to "concentrate on the job of ending the Korean War . . . until that job is honorably done. That job requires a personal trip to Korea. I shall make that trip. Only in that way could I learn how best to serve the American people in the cause of peace. . . . I shall go to Korea." From any candidate a peace initiative would have been a welcome gesture, but coming from the Supreme Allied Commander of World War II and NATO, the Korean proposal was a lightning bolt. His background gave the commitment to end the war far more authority than an ordinary campaign promise. Its impact on the nation's consciousness had been stunning, and Truman was predictably angered. Stevenson weakly responded that Ike's speech was a "proposal for a quick and slick way out of Korea" which invited a "Munich in the Far East with the probability of a third world war not far behind." America's war hero was the dove and the diplomat-governor had become the hawk. Indeed, Stevenson said he would rather lose the presidency than play politics with war and peace.

Ike observed privately that his "I will go to Korea" speech might win or lose the election for him, but made no forecast. After their near-unanimous prediction of a Dewey victory in 1948, public-opinion pollsters were understandably cautious. The day before the election the New York *Times* headlined its front page analysis: "ELECTION OUTCOME HIGHLY UNCERTAIN." The Gallup poll, which had long demonstrated Ike's phenomenal popularity in its "trial heats," had Ike leading Stevenson 47 to 40 percent with 13 percent undecided. To protect himself, Gallup reported late gains by Stevenson and said if the Democratic candidate received a 3 to 1 margin in the undecided vote he could repeat Truman's 1948 comeback. On the Korean issue, Gallup's surveys found that voters thought Ike could find a better conclusion than Stevenson by 67 to 9 percent.

On Tuesday morning, Ike and Mamie voted in their Upper West Side precinct and spent the rest of the day at the Columbia presidential residence. At Columbia, there had been some complaints that Ike was still using the mansion and running his campaign from there. Indeed, several hundred Columbia faculty members had sponsored a full-page advertisement in a New York newspaper endorsing Stevenson and the Columbia *Spectator*, the student newspaper, also backed Adlai.

The Eisenhowers went to the Hotel Commodore early in the evening for the victory celebration at Citizens for Eisenhower campaign headquarters. The mood was one of excitement, confidence, and expectation as Ike appeared at the party. Early election results, while highly encouraging, were by no means conclusive and Ike took a ninety-minute nap at 10:30 P.M. At that time CBS television predicted a narrow Eisenhower win on the basis of a projection by their Univac computer. When Ike awoke around midnight, the dimensions of his victory were clear—an electoral landslide and the largest popular vote total of any candidate up to then, a plurality of 6.5 million votes over Stevenson, and the electoral votes of thirty-nine states with 442 electoral votes including four states in the Democratic South. Ike's first phone call as President-elect was to Herbert Hoover, the last Republican President. As the results became more apparent, including the realization that his coattails had elected a Republican Congress, Dwight became impatient waiting for Stevenson's concession statement and snorted, "What is the matter with that monkey?" Stevenson made a graceful and touching speech at 1:40 A.M., hailing Ike as a "great leader in war" and "a vigorous and valiant opponent." Shortly afterward, Ike appeared in the Commodore ballroom and raised his arms in the familiar World War II V-sign. "I recognize clearly the weight of the responsibility you have placed on me," he said, "and I assure you that I shall never in my service in Washington give short weight to those responsibilities."

Chapter Sixteen

COMMANDER IN CHIEF

On November 29, less than one month after the election, Ike kept his promise and went to Korea. President Truman had further alienated his erstwhile friend and adviser by offering Ike the presidential airplane "if you still want to go." This questioning of his sincerity stung Ike no less than Truman's fierce campaign rhetoric and the President-elect voiced doubts that he could "stand sitting next to him" during the January inaugural ceremonies. In the meantime, Seoul was preparing a hero's welcome. Huge archways, built of wood and paper, were erected along every block and smiling posters of Eisenhower hung beside such signs as "Unification of Korea under Freedom" and "Disband the puppet North Korean Army." South Korean President Rhee planned to impress Ike with a show of unity and strength, and elaborate drills were held daily for the "spontaneous" demonstration. Rhee, alarmed by Ike's election pledge to withdraw American troops where Koreans could hold off Communist forces, wanted increased American and United Nations military support.

Because of the risks of the Korean trip, extraordinary security measures were taken that were reminiscent of the deception tactics used by the Allies before D-Day. Ike left his Columbia University residence at 5:30 A.M. in darkness and freezing weather. For security purposes, the cover story was that Ike was spending the weekend at 60 Morningside Drive while deliberating on several Cabinet appointments. In the afternoon, Secretary of State-designate John Foster Dulles announced from Eisenhower's front porch that in a conference with the President-elect, they had chosen Henry Cabot Lodge as United Nations ambassador. Over the next few days, the appointments of Sinclair Weeks as Secretary of Commerce, Martin Durkin as Secretary of Labor, and Winthrop Aldrich as ambassador to England seemed to indicate that Ike was actively filling the remainder of his team. Milton Eisenhower, Nelson Rockefeller, and Arthur S. Flemming, Ike's three-member committee on government reorganization, emerged from the Columbia mansion after a three-hour meeting. Not until Henry Kissinger's clandestine 1971 mission to China would an American statesman's visit be shrouded in such secrecy and mystery. The other members of the Eisenhower party had left their homes in the dark and without advising family or friends of their destination.

Ike's visit was not made public until December 5, when he was safely out of the war zone following his three days in Korea. If Rhee thought Eisenhower could be persuaded to make a greater American commitment to the stalemated war, the Korean leader soon found that he had underestimated the President-elect. As a military man, Ike recognized that the stalemate could only be broken by an all-out offensive against China and he was against such a course because world opinion would have been shocked. And Ike would not risk war with China to appease Rhee. Ike declined Rhee's invitation to address the National Assembly and through adroit maneuvering also managed to avoid the military review. In freezing weather, Ike donned his old battle jacket and spent most of the three days visiting American units around the battle lines, meeting with commanders, and observing North Korean and Chinese lines. For Ike, the high point of his visit was the opportunity to spend time with John, then on active duty with the 15th Infantry, which the senior Eisenhower had commanded years earlier at Fort Lewis. Ike ate pork chops and sauerkraut with enlisted men from his old command and heard firsthand testimony about the pain and suffering endured by the soldiers in the unpopular war.

Within a few days, one of Ike's luncheon companions was killed in action.

On his return to New York, Ike said, "This journey marks not the end but the beginning of a new effort to conclude honorably this phase of the global struggle. This is not the moment to state more than that resolve. For we face an enemy whom we cannot hope to impress by words, however eloquent, but only by deeds—executed under circumstances of our own choosing."

There would be no global crusade in Asia under Eisenhower because, he determined, the price was too high: countless American lives and isolation from the international community. Ike accepted Douglas MacArthur's invitation to discuss a proposed settlement of the Korean War, while President Truman fumed that any plan to end the war should come to the White House. MacArthur, then serving as board chairman of Remington Rand was still the hard liner, called for nuclear attacks on the Chinese if they did not leave Korea. Diplomatically, Ike explained that the war would not be extended. Enough was enough, and the American people were tired of nearly three years of a fruitless war. On MacArthur's advice, however, Ike did make veiled warnings about using atomic weapons against the Chinese and North Koreans if a peace settlement was not reached. As Commander in Chief, Ike meant to cut American losses at the Thirty-eighth parallel, and he called upon the Soviet Union to help bring about the peace.

To demonstrate that the nuclear threat was real, Ike that spring had atomic weapons shipped to Okinawa. Happily, the peace talks were resumed, and if Ike carried a big stick, he was speaking softly. On March 28, Communist leaders agreed to a mutual exchange of sick and wounded prisoners. Two days later came a significant truce offer from Chinese Premier and Foreign Minister Chou Enlai with the proposal of an exchange of prisoners of war, with the additional agreement that prisoners refusing to return could be handed over to a neutral state. For the next two months, terms of the armistice were negotiated at Panmunjom. Ike publicly established his quest for peace in a memorable speech in mid-April:

> Every gun that is fired, every warship launched, every rocket fired signifies, in the final sense, a theft from those who hun-

ger and are not fed, those who are cold and are not clothed. . . . The cost of one modern heavy bomber is this: a modern brick school in more than thirty cities. . . . We pay for a single fighter plane with a half million bushels of wheat. We pay for a single destroyer with new homes that could have housed more than eight thousand people.

This is not a way of life at all, in any true sense. Under the cloud of threatening war, it is humanity hanging from a cross of iron. These plain and cruel truths define the peril and point the hope that come with this spring of 1953. . . . A world that begins to witness the rebirth of trust among nations can find its way to a peace that is neither partial nor punitive. . . . The first great step along this way must be the conclusion of an honorable armistice in Korea. This means the immediate cessation of hostilities and the prompt initiation of political discussions leading to the holding of free elections in a United Korea. . . . We seek, throughout Asia as throughout the world, a peace that is true and total.

Eisenhower's speech was at once courageous and profound. Though some congressional partisans of the "China Lobby" dissented, the response from the American public and the world was overwhelmingly in favor of Ike's peace initiative. A Korean settlement, Ike said, could be a prelude to disarmament. "The government is ready to ask its people to join with all nations in devoting a substantial percentage of the savings achieved by disarmament to a fund for world aid and reconstruction," said Ike. "We are ready, in short, to dedicate our strength to serving the *needs* rather than the *fears*, of the world."

Rhee, the Harvard- and Princeton-educated South Korean President, was recalcitrant toward the emerging settlement, and he bitterly opposed any armistice that would leave Korea divided and recognize the Communist regime in North Korea. At seventy-eight, Rhee stubbornly and unrealistically wanted total victory. In a blunt letter to Rhee, Ike wrote: "The enemy has proposed an armistice which involves a clear abandonment of the fruits of aggression. The armistice would leave the Republic of Korea in undisputed possession of substantially the territory which the Republic administered prior to the aggression, indeed this territory will be somewhat enlarged. . . . It is my profound conviction that under these circumstances acceptance of the armistice is required of the United Nations and the Republic of Korea. We would not be justified in prolonging the war with all the misery that it involves in the hope of achieving by force the unification of Korea."

Although Ike promised economic aid to South Korea and a mutual security pact between the United States and South Korea, Rhee was unyielding. Indeed, the South Korean desperately tried to break up the peace talks by releasing more than twenty-seven thousand anti-Communist Chinese and North Korean prisoners. Rhee's action did not mean the collapse of negotiations, but Communist leaders did charge that the United Nations had "connived" with the South Korean. "This thing is so foolish as to be fantastic," Dwight said at his June 19 cabinet meeting. The aging South Korean backed down in early July when an American diplomat made it clear that Eisenhower was going through with the truce. Ike secured a peace and reduced world tensions when the armistice was signed on July 27, 1953. His campaign pledge had been fulfilled, and the fighting had ended. "The war is over," Ike said to a photographer, "and I hope my son is going to come home soon."

In his speech on television that announced the armistice Ike said that what had been gained was "an armistice on a single battleground, not peace in the world." The end of the Korean conflict brought none of the wild celebrations that had followed both World Wars, yet there was an enormous sense of relief that the nightmare was over. "I am deeply thankful to see an end to the bloodshed," Ike wrote newspaper publisher Leonard Finder, "although there is no real assurance . . . about a satisfactory solution for the long term."

Truman, Acheson, and MacArthur might have presided over more bloodshed, but Eisenhower had reversed their hawkish military policies. Right-wing Republicans complained about a "Munich in the Far East," yet there was no national remorse at the "peace without victory." The dictatorial Rhee would eventually be ousted by a popular rebellion in South Korea. Eisenhower's decision to fold the war was common sense, yet his three immediate successors would not learn from his example and sought military adventure in Asia with catastrophic results.

Ike had decided early that he could do without the regal trappings of the presidency much as he had rarely flaunted his military decorations. The presidential retreat at Key West was sold and the Shangri-la, the presidential hideaway in the Catoctin Mountains of Maryland, was renamed Camp David for his father and grandson. "Shangri-la was just a little too fancy for a Kansas farm boy," Ike wrote a friend. As part of his effort to do away with costly luxuries, Ike had the presidential yacht *Williamsburg* put in mothballs. "I am committed to an administration of economy, bordering on or approaching austerity," he explained in a letter to Hazlett. "I felt that the very word 'yacht' created a symbol of luxury in the public mind that would tend to defeat some of the purposes I was trying to accomplish."

His announcement that he would not wear the traditional cutaway coat and silk top-hat at the Inauguration had caused a stir among social arbiters. When Ike said he would wear a club coat without tails and a Homburg hat, the Inauguration became the most informal in modern history. It followed then that the most memorable part of his inaugural speech was not the formal address prepared by many hands through numerous drafts, but a prayer written in less than ten minutes that morning on a hotel scratch pad. Ike had read the prayer to John and Barbara Eisenhower, who gave instant approval.

By the time Ike had finished his hastily written prayer, he and Mamie were due at the White House to meet the Trumans for the drive to the Capitol. Ike had refused the departing President's invitation for lunch and Truman said, years later, that Eisenhower had snubbed him by not coming into the White House. On the basis of Truman's vulgar accusations against him in the 1952 campaign, Ike was not of a mind to show deference to the feisty Missourian. There was little conversation between them during the limousine ride to the ceremonies. At one point, Ike said: "I did not attend your inauguration in 1948 out of consideration for you, because if I had been present I would have drawn attention away from you."

Truman hotly replied, "You were not here in 1948 because I

did not send for you. But if I had sent for you, you would have come." While the two Presidents were sitting in a gilded suite in the Capitol, waiting for the program to begin, Ike asked Truman who was responsible for ordering John home from Korea and mentioned that his son had been concerned about the appearance of favoritism. "Tell him the contrary old man in the White House did it," said Truman. Though Ike expressed appreciation to Truman then for the special order and in his letter of January 23 repeated his thanks, in later years Truman would complain that the Eisenhowers had not shown proper gratitude.

The skies had been leaden and foggy for most of the morning and rain and thundershowers had been forecast for the afternoon. Only moments before Ike walked through the rotunda to the Inaugural platform, the sun broke through the dark clouds. A crowd of 140,000 covered the east plaza as an unusually solemn Ike took the presidential oath. Truman stared at the floor, Senator Taft's expression was frozen, and Mamie wept. His prayer reflected his hope, and idealism:

> *"Almighty God, as we stand here at this moment, my future associates in the executive branch of government join me in beseeching that Thou will make full and complete our dedication to the service of the people in this throng and their fellow citizens everywhere.*
>
> *"Give us, we pray, the power to discern clearly right from wrong, and allow all our words and actions to be governed thereby, and by the laws of this land. Especially we pray that our concern shall be for all the people regardless of station, race, or calling.*
>
> *"May cooperation be permitted and be the mutual aim of those who, under the concepts of our Constitution, hold to differing political faiths; so that all may work for the good of our beloved country and Thy glory."*

Following his speech, Ike turned and kissed Mamie. Some 750,000 people lined the streets to get a glimpse of the Eisenhowers during their procession to the White House. When they reached their destination, the inaugural parade began and for more than five hours, Ike stood soldierlike as patriotic and school floats passed. John Eisenhower recalled that his father almost lost patience with the festivities when an obscure California television cowboy named Monte Montana lassoed Ike.

Two days later, on January 22, Ike wrote a diary note: "My first full day at the President's Desk. Plenty of worries and difficult problems. . . . The result is that today just seems like a continuation of all I've been doing since July '41—even before that."

Ike had observed his two immediate predecessors from close range and had for more than a decade been dealing with world leaders. More than any newly elected President of the twentieth century, Ike was an international figure and yet he quickly discovered the enormous difference in holding the nation's highest office. The revelation came in a telephone call from General Omar Bradley, one of Ike's oldest friends and then chairman of the Joint Chiefs of Staff. "He called me Mr. President, and I have known Brad all my life!" said Ike.

In the summer of 1953, Ike wrote another friend: "I found to my amazement—once I was actually sitting behind this desk—that I became somewhat of an embarrassment to many of my old friends. They didn't want to call me openly—or at least in front of others—by my nickname, and this embarrassment apparently carried over in some cases into their letters. They used all kinds of dodges to avoid extremes of informality and formality, and I soon found that it seemed better to fall in, at least partially, with their own ideas than it was to engage in a long and fruitless argument. One or two of my former correspondents have even cut me off their list—I think for no other reason than they felt somewhat embarrassed in addressing me by a formal title and yet they could not quite practice the informality that once characterized their friendships."

After twenty years out of power, Republicans controlled both the White House and Congress. Although the party's true believers had been against the social revolution of the New Deal and longed for a return to the days of McKinley, Ike declared, "We are not going to turn the clock back." His philosophy, which he would later describe as "modern Republicanism" and "dynamic conservatism," was more humane and flexible than the rigid dogma of the Republican right.

Ike's closest confidant and adviser was Milton Eisenhower, who brought to the White House his vast experience in government and education. Though Milton and Ike agreed that it would be improper for the younger brother to hold a Cabinet post in the Eisenhower administration, there was never any question that the president of Penn State was destined to fill a unique role in the history of the American presidency. Indeed, only one other presidential brother, Robert F. Kennedy, can be compared to Milton, yet the differences were significant for Kennedy did accept a position in his brother's cabinet and had been campaign manager of John F. Kennedy's 1960 presidential race. It can be argued that Milton's contributions during the Eisenhower years helped make it possible for President Kennedy to appoint his brother to the Cabinet.

President Eisenhower's military background and his remarkable success at building command structures in World War II made a chief of staff system at the White House inevitable. Ike's staff chief would carry the rank of "assistant to the President." Ike might have picked one of three former deputies—Generals Walter Bedell Smith, Lucius Clay, or Alfred Gruenther, yet they were never considered. Although each knew Eisenhower well and understood his definition of lines of authority, Ike was sensitive about the possible image of excessive military influence in his administration. Only two men were in the running: defeated Senator Henry Cabot Lodge of Massachusetts and Governor Sherman Adams of New Hampshire. Lodge, who had been dealt a stunning upset by thirty-five-year-old John F. Kennedy, was more interested in international affairs than time-consuming administrative chores and was appointed United Nations ambassador, with cabinet rank. Sherman Adams thus became "assistant president."

For the next five years, Adams was to exercise such power and influence that some political commentators would suggest that he, not Ike, was the real President. Ike explained Adams' role this way: "A man like that is valuable because of the unnecessary detail he keeps away from the President. A President who doesn't know how to decentralize will be weighed down with details and won't have time to deal with the big issues." Adams had served as chief of staff in the 1952 campaign and had been an early passenger on the Eisenhower presidential bandwagon, the man behind Ike's important victory over Taft in the New Hampshire primary.

The thin, angular, silver-haired Adams was a descendant of the Quincy, Massachusetts, family which had produced two Presidents—John and John Quincy Adams, and like his famous ancestors he could be waspish, short-tempered, and abrupt. However, he also possessed some of their virtues—courage, efficiency, and an indefatigable appetite for hard work.

Adams was born in a Vermont hill village not far from the community where Calvin Coolidge had been raised. After serving in the Marine Corps during World War I, Adams attended Dartmouth and earned a Spartan reputation by once hiking eighty-three miles in twenty-four hours. His first job was as a lumberjack in Vermont, and in the late 1920s he returned to New Hampshire as general manager of a lumber company. In 1940, Adams was elected to the New Hampshire legislature and within two years was chosen House Speaker. His meteoric rise continued with his election to Congress in 1944, but stalled in 1946 in his first attempt to win the governorship as the incumbent edged him by 157 votes in the Republican primary. Two years later, the persistent Adams was elected governor and at Concord he consolidated more than eighty administrative departments into forty-three in the most comprehensive reorganization ever undertaken in New Hampshire.

Adams often worked eighteen-hour days and once skied and snowshoed more than five miles after a blizzard to get to the capital. "He drives himself endlessly and has found contentment in working hard at a job he liked," wrote Mrs. Adams in a biographical sketch of her husband, "and for less remuneration than he could have had at a job away from his beloved mountains and his simple country life. With him it has always been the job that counts, not the salary." Mrs. Adams also disclosed that "Sherm" had the socially unorthodox, but "reasonable" habit of going to bed when he thought it was appropriate, even if they had guests. As a fiscal conservative, Adams had much in common with Robert A. Taft, yet he doubted whether Taft could win the presidency and viewed Eisenhower as a more pragmatic candidate.

For his key part in securing Ike's nomination and election, Adams figured prominently in speculation about appointments in the new Administration. Eisenhower liked Adams, appreciated and returned his loyalty, and admired his administrative capability. Friends confided that Adams wanted nothing more than to become ambassador to Canada. If it was a relatively powerless office, Adams might have considered Ottawa a natural place to end his public career, for he had long been familiar with Canada through his years in the lumber industry and regional politics. Adams could have had the appointment for the asking, but he could not refuse Eisenhower's offer to become the President's chief deputy. Adams would run the White House staff, help in the formation of Administration policy, and would handle political matters, including patronage. "The one person who really knows what I am trying to do is Sherman Adams," said Ike. Because of his wide authority, Adams had more influence than any presidential assistant of his era and a popular joke of the 1950s had the punchline: "What if Sherman Adams died and Ike became President?" At a session with reporters, Ike said: "No subordinate of mine, including Adams, can possibly make a decision without getting my general approval or a decision which is inconsonant with the general policies laid down by me." At all times, Adams was Ike's deputy—"my right hand" as Eisenhower termed him—and Ike made the truly important decisions while Adams contributed his counsel and handled the political maneuvering.

Along with Adams, Secretary of State John Foster Dulles was the most visible of Eisenhower's lieutenants. As soon as Governor Dewey removed his own name from consideration for the Cabinet, Dulles was assured of the appointment. Ike's own favorite is said to have been John J. McCloy, an old friend who had served as Assistant Secretary of War and as postwar high commissioner for Germany. McCloy was, as Richard Rovere would later describe him, "Chairman of the Board of the American Establishment," and yet he was unacceptable to Taft Republicans because his service had been in Democratic administrations. By contrast, Dulles had the backing of Taft and Dewey, his longtime associate. As a compromise, Ike proposed to name Dulles as Secretary and McCloy as Undersecretary with the understanding that Dulles would eventually move into the White House as foreign-policy adviser and McCloy would be promoted to Secretary. The crafty Dulles readily accepted and volunteered to make the approach to McCloy. So it was that Dulles explained that he would remain the authority and presidential adviser on foreign affairs. McCloy had enough knowledge of foreign policy to recognize that a formidable White House adversary could sharply reduce the influence of the State Department and he declined any such arrangement. Dulles shrewdly chose another Eisenhower favorite, General Walter Bedell Smith, as Undersecretary in a master stroke, for the appointment created a vacancy in the directorship of the Central Intelligence Agency and Dulles persuaded Ike to name his younger brother, Allen Dulles, as CIA director. Although Smith told Eisenhower that it might be unwise to have the nation's intelligence network and the State Department being run by brothers, Ike said that Foster had given him assurances that there would be no conflict.

Dulles turned sixty-five during his first month as Secretary and he possessed from youth a keen interest in world affairs. His grandfather had been Secretary of State under Benjamin Harrison and his uncle had been Secretary of State under Woodrow Wilson. With his grandfather, he had attended The Hague Peace Conference in 1907, and worked as secretary to the Chinese delegation. As an undergraduate at Princeton, Dulles studied ethics from Wilson and as a young lawyer, he served on President Wilson's staff at the Versailles Peace Conference. Dulles was to be the most durable of all the Wilsonians. At Wilson's request, he stayed in Europe beyond the conference as the chief delegate to the reparations commission and his performance helped make his reputation. As a partner in the prestigious Wall Street law firm of Sullivan and Cromwell, Dulles had frequent international assignments. His long and highly beneficial association with Dewey began in 1937 when Dulles attempted to recruit the young racket buster as a law partner, a position which Dewey readily accepted, then declined in favor of a political career. Dulles thus became Dewey's chief sponsor and promoter, working for him in three presidential campaigns. Wendell Willkie, who was trounced by Dewey in his bid for the 1944 Republican presidential nomination, blamed his defeat on the long-forgotten John W. Foster, Dulles' grandfather. Dewey was simply a vehicle for Dulles to regain his grandfather's eminence, wryly observed Willkie. In 1948, Dewey made no secret of his plan to designate Dulles as Secretary of State, and national magazines published lengthy and highly favorable profiles about the next Secretary. Dewey said that Dulles was the "world's greatest statesman" and though their ambitions were dashed by Truman's surprise victory, Dulles received numerous consolations. Dulles' stature in world affairs peaked again in the 1940s as the Republican spokesman for internationalism. With Secretary of State Cordell Hull, Dulles had discussed his Wilsonian hopes for a United Nations. As a result of that meeting, Dulles was later named a senior adviser to the American delegation at the San Francisco Conference and was a principal architect of the United Nations. Dulles was a U.S. delegate to the UN from 1946 through 1949 when Governor Dewey appointed him to the United States Senate. Campaigning as a Republican and criticizing Truman's policies, Dulles was beaten by Democrat Herbert Lehman in a special election in November of 1949. Truman took the Dulles campaign rhetoric personally and was reluctant to give him another diplomatic assignment, but Secretary of State Dean Acheson urged such an appointment to give the Administration bipartisan support. Truman charged Dulles with negotiating a peace treaty with the Japanese, a task that Dulles had long coveted. For a full year, Dulles traveled between Tokyo and Washington, working out the details of the treaty. When the treaty was signed in September of 1951, Dulles received the credit. Dulles finished fourth in a 1952 *Saturday Review* poll for President, yet he recognized that he could not aspire to the top because he was less appealing to the public than he was to national leaders. Though he had been handsome as a young man, in later years Dulles projected a grave, stern public personality with his drooping mouth and thin-rimmed glasses.

His 1949 Senate race had been a bitter setback and Dulles vowed never again to run for political office. In 1952, he was the odds-on favorite to become Secretary of State in the event of a Republican victory. At the convention, Dulles drafted the party's foreign-policy plank that was approved by both Ike and Taft.

Dulles continued his campaign for Secretary of State with a lengthy and somewhat confusing article about foreign policy for *Life*. In the magazine article, he criticized the Truman-Acheson "containment" policy toward Communism and called instead for "liberation" of Communist bloc countries. Later in the year, Ike gently scolded Dulles for his hard-line rhetoric and made the suggestion that Dulles explain that liberation could be achieved through peaceful methods. There was remarkably little contact between Ike and Dulles during the 1952 campaign and, according to some observers, Eisenhower found the veteran diplomat a bore. Once Dulles had been appointed Secretary of State, however, they began working closely together and Ike developed genuine respect for Dulles. In a rare burst of hyperbole, Ike predicted that they would become the most successful team in history and he later hailed Dulles as the greatest of all secretaries of state. The prominent role Dulles played in the Administration and as a leader of the Western Alliance gave some observers the impression that he, not Eisenhower, was directing American foreign policy. Ike told Emmet Hughes, his assistant, that he valued Dulles for his expertise: "The fact remains that he just knows more about foreign affairs than anybody I know. In fact, I'll be immodest and say that there's only one man I know who has seen more of the world and talked with more people and knows more than he does—and that's me." For all of the Dulles bluster about "brinkmanship" and confrontation with the Communists, with nuclear weapons as a potential tool, it would be Ike's proposals for disarmament that captured the popular imagination.

Ike's choice for Secretary of Defense, Charles E. Wilson, had been president of General Motors for twelve years, and he symbolized the "business administration" of Eisenhower's Washington. Wilson was known as "Engine Charlie" because he was often confused with the president of General Electric, the other Charles E. Wilson, who was nicknamed "Electric Charlie." The latter Wilson was a Democrat and had served as defense production chief during World War II. "Engine Charlie" battled "Electric Charlie" for more steel and aluminum for General Motors and during one of their disputes said, "He's Control Charlie. I'm Decontrol Charlie."

In appearance, speech, and mannerism, Wilson resembled the Colonel Blimp caricature of a fat-cat industrialist. Born in Minerva, Ohio, Wilson believed in the old-fashioned virtues of the heartland. At the age of eighteen he was the youngest man to graduate from Pittsburgh's Carnegie Tech and shortly afterward he designed the first Westinghouse auto starter. He was thirty-eight in 1928 when he came to Detroit as vice president of General Motors. Thirteen years later, Wilson was president of GM and one of the preeminent industrialists of his generation. His struggle with Walter Reuther, dynamic leader of the United Auto Workers, was a mismatch, but Wilson learned from their exchanges. Indeed, there were signs that the quintessential capitalist had acquired a social conscience for he sold the UAW a five-year contract with a cost-of-living escalator, which was then a radical formula for averting a strike.

Wilson and Ike became acquainted while Eisenhower was Chief of Staff. Although Wilson did not take a public role in the presidential campaign, he was an Eisenhower man. General Clay recommended him to Ike for the Pentagon, and the President approved. Wilson was less than eager to enter government and accepted the appointment only after a long session with Ike. This meant Wilson was giving up an annual income of more than $500,000 for a $22,500 salary. Wilson said that Dwight was the "only man in the world" for whom he would leave General Motors, but in his Senate confirmation hearings there appeared to be some doubt as to whether Wilson was willing to cut his corporate ties with the firm which had provided more than $12 billion in armaments during World War II. His refusal to sell more than $2.5 million in General Motors stock struck the Senate Armed Services Committee as a conflict of interest and placed his nomination in jeopardy. Wilson's ill-chosen statement that he thought "what was good for our country was good for General Motors, and vice versa" was widely distorted into "What's good for General Motors is good for the country," by Eisenhower critics. Ike was prepared to withdraw the nomination should Wilson insist on remaining a General Motors stockholder, but Wilson agreed to liquidate his holdings.

In Cabinet meetings, Wilson acquitted himself well, and his

penchant for the unorthodox made him at times refreshing. During discussion of the Korean War at an early Cabinet session, Wilson proposed recognition of Red China as part of the settlement package. The China initiative was promptly vetoed by Ike, who was having enough trouble selling a Korean armistice to the Republican right. Wilson's indiscreet remarks about the unemployed as "kennel-fed dogs" went against Ike's earlier plea for his industrialist Cabinet secretaries to show humanity and demonstrate an interest in "the little fellow." Ike was also disappointed that Wilson had not taken stronger hold of the Pentagon where the spirited rivalries between the armed services continued.

George Humphrey, the new Secretary of the Treasury, had been recommended by Wilson's sponsor, General Clay, and, like the Defense Secretary, had worked his way from employee to chief executive officer of a major corporation—in Humphrey's case, the M. A. Hanna and Company, a Cleveland-based investment and operating company that controlled, among other things, the world's largest coal producer, Pittsburgh Consolidation Coal, and National Steel, one of the nation's great steel firms. For years Humphrey had been a powerful man while maintaining a low public profile. He was little known even in Ohio except among the power elite. Over the years he had been a financial supporter of Robert A. Taft and shared much of the senator's conservative philosophy, but Humphrey had never sought an active political role. Indeed, his main interests were horses and hunting and, whenever possible, Humphrey escaped to "Milestone," his three-thousand-acre estate near Thomasville, Georgia.

In their first meeting, Ike looked at the balding Humphrey and said, "I see you part your hair the same way I do." An instant rapport developed between them and no Cabinet officer was to enjoy such a personal relationship with Eisenhower. On the cruiser *Helena*, returning from Ike's historic Korean trip, Humphrey astonished Ike by matching his own performance at skeet shooting. They would later hunt together on Humphrey's Georgia estate. His personality, demeanor, and temperament were remarkably similar to Ike's.

"In Cabinet meetings I always wait for George Humphrey to speak," said Ike. "I sit back and listen to the others talk while he doesn't say anything. But I know that when he speaks up he will say just what I am thinking." In domestic affairs, Humphrey was the dominant force within the Administration and he was to exercise influence over foreign and defense policies. Humphrey favored bringing the Korean War to a quick conclusion because he viewed the war as too much of a drain on the American economy. He also advocated cutting the defense budget by a third, and Eisenhower agreed that military spending had become wasteful. Humphrey sought nothing less than a balanced budget and he compared his job to taking over the wheel of a runaway truck as it rolled down an icy hill. When the Administration failed to reach a balanced budget by 1957, Humphrey criticized what he termed excessive spending. Yet there was no break with Ike, who continued to count him as a friend and adviser. Milton Eisenhower thought that Humphrey had overreached by speaking out against Administration policy, but the President's brother had never been an admirer of the Treasury Secretary, whom he considered too rigid and unyielding in policy matters and "much too certain of his own infallibility." The reflective Milton and the nonintellectual Humphrey were opposites. When Humphrey was asked if he had read Ernest Hemingway's book *The Old Man and the Sea,* he said: "Why would anybody be interested in some old man who was a failure and never amounted to anything anyway?" As a voracious reader and as the president of one of the nation's largest universities, Milton could hardly approve of such provincialism.

Milton and Humphrey were to clash more than once, yet their differences did little to harm their respective positions with Ike. Humphrey prevailed over Milton in the controversial decision over the St. Lawrence Seaway. Milton argued against American partnership with Canada because, he said, the project might well damage the already troubled American railroad industry and also because the seaway would have to be heavily subsidized. Humphrey, a leading force behind the development of iron ore in Canada, countered that Canada's natural resources would yield enough tonnage to justify the seaway. For military reasons, Ike had favored a seaway project in the past and Humphrey's economic arguments were probably decisive. The Humphrey influence went beyond his responsibilities at Treasury.

Though Humphrey was the Administration's most stalwart conservative, Taft had disapproved of the appointment. Taft knew and admired Humphrey, but he had recommended Senator Harry F. Byrd, Virginia's fiscally conservative Democrat, and he was irritated that as the senior senator from Humphrey's state, he had not been consulted. If Taft did not like the handling of the Humphrey appointment, he violently objected to the appointment of Martin Durkin, a plumbers' union president and a Democrat, as Secretary of Labor. Durkin's opposition to the Taft-Hartley Act was understood by Taft; as he was a labor leader, it was expected. For Eisenhower to appoint Durkin to the Cabinet, however, Taft considered a repudiation. Privately, Taft questioned Ike's intelligence and competence; and there was public speculation about Taft breaking with Ike even before the Inaugural.

Taft was pondering a race for Senate Majority Leader and it was with some concern that Eisenhower's inner circle discussed this possibility, for a hostile party floor leader could effectively obstruct Administration programs. Senator Styles Bridges of New Hampshire, who had been the Minority Leader in 1952, was the Administration's favorite to become Majority Leader. The fleshy-faced Bridges was an internationalist on foreign policy and a conservative in domestic affairs. His relationship with Ike was friendly, and with Sherman Adams, Bridges had long-standing ties. Bridges, however, would not challenge Taft because he wanted the chairmanship of the Senate Appropriations Committee. When Taft approached Ike through a mutual friend, Eisenhower tacitly endorsed the Ohio senator. Ike had acted shrewdly, for Taft would have been the most powerful senator with or without the floor leadership and his cooperation on important issues might well be the difference between victory and defeat.

Walter Lippmann wrote that Taft was functioning as an American version of a British prime minister: a man dedicated to carrying out the programs of his party and serving the head of state. Taft, despite some misgivings about Eisenhower appointments, was largely responsible for the early confirmation of the Cabinet. In March, Taft defended Ike's appointment of career diplomat Charles E. Bohlen as ambassador to the Soviet Union against vicious attacks from McCarthy and Democratic Senator Pat

McCarran of Nevada. Styles Bridges, too, alleged that Bohlen was an appeaser and a security risk. Bohlen had served as an aide to Roosevelt at the 1945 Yalta Conference, and at his own confirmation hearings he defended the results of the World War II meeting. Taft's endorsement was credited with saving Bohlen's nomination and Ike's prestige.

Had Taft not been Majority Leader, there is reason to believe that he would have joined those fighting the Bohlen appointment. But Taft had assumed responsibility for the Administration's men and policies and whenever possible he would assist Eisenhower. In late April, Taft reacted angrily when Ike advised him that the budget for 1954 would have to include a deficit of more than $5 million. "You're taking us down the same road Truman traveled," shouted Taft. "It's a repudiation of everything we promised in the campaign." The proposed budget was later amended to provide for a tax reduction in 1954.

Ike did his best to cultivate a friendship with the aloof Taft. James C. Hagerty recalled in a 1970 interview that Eisenhower told Taft in one of their early meetings that the senator was to have total access to the President and that included walking into the Oval Room while another meeting was in progress. If Taft wanted to confer with Eisenhower, he was advised that the formality of asking for an appointment need not be bothered with. The White House staff understood that Taft was to be treated with the same deference accorded Eisenhower. Ike and Mamie attended a reception at Taft's Georgetown house in the spring, one of the rare social engagements they accepted. Taft accompanied Ike on a weekend golfing trip to Augusta, Georgia, in April and in a friendly match Eisenhower edged his former political rival by several strokes. "Senator Taft and I are becoming right good friends," Ike noted that April in his diary. "The relations between the Executive Branch and Republican leaders in Congress are getting better and better." Eisenhower appointed Taft's son William Howard Taft III ambassador to Ireland and a distant Taft cousin, Ezra Taft Benson, Secretary of Agriculture. Both appointments delighted Senator Taft and helped to ease his doubts about the influence of Dewey and the Eastern Republican Establishment at the White House.

To be sure, there remained strong differences between Ike and Taft on foreign policy. Taft was skeptical about NATO and other costly mutual-security programs, and in the Korean War he called for the bombing of Manchuria. Still, Taft worked to prevent right-wing Republican senators from launching a full-scale offensive on Ike's foreign policy. On domestic matters, Ike later recalled that Taft was "really much more liberal than me." Indeed, Ike said that Taft recommended federal aid to education, public housing, and increased Social Security benefits. Eisenhower declined to press for any of the Taft suggestions. "Dad was not a social reformer in any sense," recalls John Eisenhower. "He had a feeling that if he could work his way up, anybody could." So it was that Ike's belief in the American dream closed his mind to social-welfare proposals.

Eisenhower did move to centralize the existing social-welfare agencies into a centralized department so that services could be better coordinated. Milton Eisenhower, Arthur Flemming, and Nelson Rockefeller had recommended a "Department of Welfare" to administer the human programs. Flemming approached Taft on Ike's behalf and was advised that Republican conservatives would never agree to a cabinet-level department with such a name. Several moments later, Taft suggested that it be called the Department of Health, Education, and Welfare. Flemming liked the idea as did the President. Taft's standing among the party's conservatives was unchallenged and he pushed through the Administration's bill creating the department.

Richard H. Rovere, writing in *The New Yorker*, noted that "there has never been a Congress in which one man has the kind of authority that Senator Taft now wields."

As it turned out, Taft was suffering from terminal cancer and in June he "temporarily" resigned the floor leadership. On July 31, after a painful two-month ordeal, Taft died. Ike and Mamie called on Taft's widow within minutes of hearing the news. Eisenhower had tears in his eyes as he consoled Martha Taft and said, "I don't know what I'll do without him—I don't know what I'll do without him."

With Taft's death, Eisenhower lost his most indispensable ally on Capitol Hill. No other Republican senator or congressman could replace Taft as the Administration's "prime minister," speaking for the party with the power and authority of a national leader. Franklin D. Roosevelt had intervened in the selection of a Senate Majority Leader in the late 1930s, supporting New Deal loyalist Alben Barkley of Kentucky over conservative Pat Harrison of Mississippi. Roosevelt won that particular battle, but his involvement in Senate affairs was resented and helped forge a coalition between Democratic conservatives and Republicans. Eisenhower, in a similar position, was urged by some to help a party moderate win the floor leadership. "I want to say with all the emphasis at my command that this Administration has absolutely no personal choice for a new Majority Leader," he said. "We are not going to get into their business."

Taft had already designated a successor—California's William F. Knowland who was then serving as "Acting" Majority Leader. Leverett Saltonstall, the moderate Majority Whip, would have been far more acceptable to Eisenhower than the bull-necked Knowland, an outspoken conservative. For his vigorous support of Chiang Kai-shek, Knowland had earned the nickname of "The senator from Formosa." At an embassy dinner, Knowland had toasted "Back to the Mainland." During the negotiations toward a Korean armistice, Knowland had warned against a "Munich in the Far East." Eisenhower kept his promise of nonintervention in the leadership vote, and Knowland, at the age of forty-five, became Majority Leader. In 1952, Knowland had been on Ike's list of possible running mates and was the back-up choice when it appeared that Nixon would resign from the ticket. Nixon and Knowland had been competing for years as youthful, ambitious Republican comers. While their voting records were similar, the men were different. Nixon was flexible and devious. Above all else, Knowland was a man of integrity with unflinching commitment to his old-fashioned political philosophy. Knowland's refusal to compromise dismayed Eisenhower more than once. "Bill is about as subtle as a Sherman tank," said one of Knowland's colleagues. In 1954, when the Majority Leader thought Eisenhower was becoming more amenable to the admission of Communist China into the United Nations, Knowland thundered that he would resign as the party's Senate leader and devote the rest of his life to pulling the United States out of the UN. On another occasion, Knowland called for a congressional investigation of the foreign policy of John Foster Dulles.

Eisenhower found himself relying more and more on the more liberal Democratic leadership—Minority Leader Lyndon B. Johnson in the Senate and Minority Leader Sam Rayburn in the House of Representatives. *Congressional Quarterly* reported that the Democrats provided Eisenhower with the margin of victory fifty-eight times in 1953. Republican conservatives scuttled Eisenhower's foreign-aid bill in the summer of 1953.

In his frustration with his own political party's narrow partisanship, Eisenhower talked with some associates about organizing a new American political party dedicated to what he termed progressive policies. Franklin D. Roosevelt had, in 1944, communicated with liberal Republican Wendell Willkie about building a third-party movement, and Ike in 1953 thought for a brief period that such a realignment of the political system might be necessary. Eisenhower recorded in his diary, however, that he would first attempt to work within the Republican framework.

Of all the challenges to Eisenhower's policies, the Republican right made its strongest showing with the Bricker amendment that would have limited presidential treaty-making authority. The legislation had been introduced by Republican Senator John Bricker of Ohio in protest of such Democratic administration treaties as the 1945 Yalta agreements. Had the amendment simply called for two-thirds Senate approval of international treaties, Eisenhower would have acknowledged their constitutional obligations. However, Ike charged that the "which" clause would force a return to the Articles of Confederation, thereby giving every state government veto power over treaties. *Time* said Bricker's legislation had produced "one of the basic constitutional debates of this century."

The sponsor of the amendment was John William Bricker, a tall, handsome, white-haired Ohio senator. "An honest Harding" was Alice Roosevelt Longworth's acid description. During three terms as governor of Ohio, Bricker built a reputation as an economizer by starving some essential state services to make possible a huge budget surplus. In 1944, he was a serious contender for the presidential nomination and was picked by Dewey as the vice-presidential candidate. Elected to the Senate two years later, Bricker became sharply critical of the international agreements of the Yalta Conference and of the Truman-Acheson foreign policy. On a personal level, Ike regarded Bricker as friendly and attractive if somewhat vain, and in 1952 Bricker had been among those discussed as potential running mates on an Eisenhower ticket. Because of Bricker's stature, he could not be dismissed as easily as a McCarthy or a Jenner, and when Bricker presented his amendment at the Hotel Commodore before the Inaugural, Ike referred it to subordinates for study.

Bricker enlisted sixty-three cosponsors for his amendment which he introduced in January of 1953, including some moderate and liberal senators. But the most vocal proponents of the measure were conservatives and old-line isolationists determined to limit presidential treaty power. In the beginning, Bricker had some reason to hope for Eisenhower's support because Ike had criticized Roosevelt and Truman for extending the power of the executive branch and had talked about restoring the constitutional balance of government. Ike's early misgivings, however, were reinforced by his conferences with Dulles and Brownell within the Administration and with two of America's most celebrated lawyers, John W. Davis and John J. McCloy, namely, that its passage would give most state legislature responsibilities in foreign policy and severely cripple presidential authority in international affairs. Eisenhower, hesitant about dueling with the legislative branch, offered Bricker several compromises that would have reiterated the constitutional intent. Bricker was offered the chairmanship of a federal commission to study treaty making and make recommendations. When Bricker spurned Ike's personal efforts to settle the issue, Eisenhower asserted his leadership and massive prestige.

In so doing he confronted an intensive lobbying effort by such conservative organizations as the U.S. Chamber of Commerce, the American Medical Association, the Daughters of the American Revolution, the Veterans of Foreign Wars, the American Legion, and the American Bar Association. A right-wing group called the Vigilant Women for the Bricker Amendment presented petitions with more than 500,000 signatures to the Senate. Seattle lawyer Frank E. Holman, a former president of the American Bar Association, orchestrated much of the pro-Bricker campaign. Holman, whom Ike referred to as a man obsessed with saving the nation "from Eleanor Roosevelt," had developed the amendment for Bricker. Holman was friendly with Edgar Eisenhower, who practiced law in nearby Tacoma, and they had worked together in bar association activities. Edgar supported Holman's crusade against the United Nations Covenant on Human Rights and the United Nations Genocide Convention, telling Ike that they endangered personal liberties in the United States. Edgar had never tried to conceal his mistrust of international agreements and his advocacy of the Bricker amendment was predictable.

For much of the next four years, the correspondence between Edgar and Ike dealt with the Bricker amendment, with the elder brother lecturing the President on the fine points of American law and Ike responding that the Constitution was an adequate safeguard against presidential abuse. Throughout their debate, the brothers retained good humor but each kept insisting that the other was wrong. In March of 1953, Edgar warned Ike that he was receiving "bad advice," and cautioned further that the Senate Foreign Relations Committee would give Eisenhower's cabinet "a very rough time" in debates over the amendment. For good measure, Edgar also criticized Ike's appointment of Bohlen as ambassador to the Soviet Union and boasted of his friendship with Styles Bridges, the leading critic of the Bohlen nomination. On the amendment and the need for a check of presidential treaty-making power, Edgar wrote: "I don't care if his name is Dwight Eisenhower or Franklin Roosevelt—the very thing that happened at Yalta and these other meetings between Roosevelt, Churchill, and Stalin ought to be enough to scare the pants off of any clear-thinking individual who has any respect for our form of government."

Dwight replied: "There is nothing that has taken place in any of the so-called war conferences and meetings that has binding effect upon the United States or upon any one of our citizens. If a President presumed, on his own authority, to commit our country to such an obligation, then he would, in my opinion, be acting unconstitutionally." He also wrote: "I cannot agree that merely because one President desperately tried to arrogate to himself greater power than contemplated in the Constitution, that the Constitution should be changed so as to limit the legitimate powers of the President."

With Bricker rejecting a compromise drafted by the Senate leadership and Eisenhower's staff, the debate continued into 1954. On January 12, Ike wrote Edgar: "A basic principle of treaty-making is that each of the representatives engaged in drawing up the agreement represents *one* nation. If either of these representatives attempts to represent [as Ike said the Bricker amendment "which" clause would do] forty-eight included states or governments, his efforts to produce agreements that will advance the interests of his own side, will be hopelessly handicapped. . . . I realize that the President has no official role in amending our Constitution. But he can fight them—to the bitter end. That, in the case of certain aspects of what is now proposed, I will do. . . . People who hysterically fear that some such organization as the United Nations is going to take over the United States and control its internal affairs are some of the best creators of bogy men that I have yet encountered."

Later that month, Edgar wrote Ike that he was being pressured to make a public break with the Eisenhower administration on the amendment, but he assured his brother that he would confine his views to their private correspondence. As a lawyer, Edgar had been making the argument that he had a better grasp of constitutional matters than Ike. "Whether or not my legal argument is exactly correct, the principle on which I stand will, I hope, be apparent to you," Ike wrote in a longhand postscript.

The Bricker amendment's chances seemed bright in the Senate for there had been few defections among the original sponsors of the measure and Eisenhower's opposition had seemed less than firm in the early weeks of 1954.

On January 25, Ike told the nation that he was "unalterably opposed to the Bricker amendment." In a letter to Senate Majority Leader Knowland, he said: "We cannot hope to achieve and maintain peace if we shackle the Federal Government so that it is no longer sovereign in foreign affairs. The President must not be deprived of his historic position as the spokesman for the Nation in its relations with other countries.

"Adoption of the Bricker Amendment in its present form by the Senate would be notice to our friends as well as our enemies abroad that our country intends to withdraw from its leadership in world affairs."

For another month, the debate and maneuvering continued with intensive lobbying by both sides. On February 26, the measure fell four votes short of the requisite two-thirds majority. Despite the narrow margin, it was a signal victory for President Eisenhower. Years later, Bricker said that his constitutional amendment had been blocked by Eisenhower "and nobody else." The Old Guard and nationalist forces would not get a second chance at revising presidential authority in foreign affairs.

Ike found himself under attack from another Republican senator: Joseph R. McCarthy of Wisconsin. The senator was "Fighting Joe" to his legions of admirers, a symbol of the crusade against world Communism, yet to his detractors McCarthy was the most dangerous man in America. McCarthy was described as the nation's most gifted and successful demagogue and for three years he had demonstrated a remarkable flair for dramatizing himself and appealing to the darkest of American prejudices and hates.

McCarthy, a husky, black-haired man with a heavy beard and drooping jowls, won election to the Senate in 1946 by campaigning as "Tail-gunner Joe," a self-styled combat hero of World War II. Actually, McCarthy had been an intelligence officer and the nickname was a McCarthyesque invention as were the combat wounds he later claimed. By embellishing his record, McCarthy secured a Purple Heart for injuries sustained when he fell down a flight of stairs, and in the Senate he demanded and was awarded, the Distinguished Flying Cross. In Washington, McCarthy's chief notoriety came from his unsavory connections with lobbyists for assorted special interests. He was reputed to be on the take from real estate firms and, true to form, he battled public housing. For his service to a soft-drink company, McCarthy acquired the nickname of the "Pepsi-Cola Kid." Outside of Washington, he was almost unknown and by January of 1950 McCarthy was concerned enough about his lack of stature to seek out several friends and ask them to help find him an issue that would give him a national identity. McCarthy's suggestion of a hundred-dollar-a-month pension for the elderly was dismissed by his conservative advisers as too inflationary, but one member of the group offered an alternative—Communist infiltration in government. McCarthy seized upon the issue at once and vowed to "hammer" away at "Reds." In point of fact, the nightmare decade had begun in March of 1947 when President Truman issued Executive Order 9835, providing for loyalty tests of civil servants and inviting the doctrine of guilt by association. Truman in 1951 issued another such order and authorized the dismissal of federal employees if there was "reasonable doubt" about their loyalty.

So Truman had institutionalized McCarthyism long before the Wisconsin senator began Red-baiting. Truman's hard line and the subsequent blacklisting and character assassination had already ruined numerous lives and created an anti-Communist hysteria reminiscent of the "Red scare" that followed World War I. In Truman's case he was trying to rally support for his Cold War foreign policy and alert the nation to the threat posed by the Soviet Union. His war-scare tactics and crisis measures proved to be counterproductive when McCarthy began charging that Truman was "soft on Communism." A series of events had already undermined confidence in Truman: the detonation of an atomic bomb by the Soviets; the triumph in China of Mao Tse-tung's Communists; and the perjury conviction of longtime State Department official Alger Hiss relating to charges that he had been a Soviet spy. On February 9, 1950, McCarthy was scheduled to give a Lincoln Day address in Wheeling, West Virginia, and decided to test his new issue. Waving a piece of paper and his voice rising in indignation, McCarthy told the West Virginia Republicans that he held a list of 205 Communists who were known to be working in the State Department. McCarthy later confided to a friend that his celebrated paper was "an old laundry list." McCarthy repeated his charges later that week in Salt Lake City and in Reno, although he reduced the number of State Department Communists to 57. McCarthy's speeches brought him more publicity than he had ever imagined and from then on, almost everything he said would make headlines.

A Senate committee was appointed to investigate the McCarthy charges and concluded that they represented "the most nefarious campaign of half-truths and untruths in the history of the Republic." Democratic Senator Millard Tydings of Maryland was chairman of the committee, and McCarthy retaliated by accusing him of pro-Communist sympathies. McCarthy campaigned against Tydings and, in Illinois, against Senate Majority Leader Scott Lucas and they were defeated. If McCarthy had been unable to unmask any Communists in government, he demonstrated that he was a formidable political force. In 1952, McCarthy played a role in the defeat of another Senate adversary, William Benton of Connecticut. No less than eight senators were said to have owed their election to McCarthy's rough-and-tumble campaigning. In June of 1951, McCarthy went gunning for General George C. Marshall, who was described by President Truman as the "greatest living American." McCarthy made the fantastic allegation that Marshall was part of a conspiracy to betray America to Communism and published the speech as a book, entitled *America's Retreat from Victory: The Story of George Catlett Marshall.* McCarthy's reckless attack drove Marshall from public life, for the five-star general resigned as Secretary of Defense. Secretary of State Dean Acheson became another McCarthy target and felt threatened enough to spend much of his time denying charges of Communist influence in the State Department. Truman and Acheson were inhibited by McCarthyism, and Walter Lippmann observed that the government was paralyzed as never before. Lippmann and other commentators suggested that the election of a Republican administration in 1952 could remove the specter of McCarthy.

With the election of Eisenhower and a Republican Congress, McCarthy became chairman of the Senate Committee on Government Operations, a previously innocuous position but one that McCarthy quickly converted into a powerful forum. Majority Leader Taft denied McCarthy membership on the Senate Internal Security Committee, which concerned itself with hunting subversives, and Taft said that McCarthy could do little damage with Government Operations. Yet within a few weeks McCarthy was back in the limelight as chairman of his committee's Permanent Subcommittee on Investigations with subpoena power and the authority to investigate whatever he wanted.

From the vantage point of his committee chairmanship, McCarthy shifted his fire to the Eisenhower administration. The senator contended that there were still Communists in the State Department and accused Secretary of State Dulles of lying. Partly to appease McCarthy, Dulles named former FBI agent Scott McLeod as the department's security chief and the foreign service became subjected to the agony of threats and, in many cases, ruined lives. Dulles, fearful of McCarthy, seemed more interested in remaining Secretary than in protecting career diplomats. Almost seven thousand "security risks" lost their government jobs during McCarthy's tenure as committee chairman, although none were charged with any crime or subversive act. In March of 1953, McCarthy announced that he had negotiated an agreement with Greek shipping interests that would halt their trade with Communist nations. Ike not only refused to reprimand McCarthy, but undercut foreign-aid director Harold Stassen who had condemned McCarthy's involvement.

Eisenhower's inner circle was divided about how the President should handle McCarthy. Milton Eisenhower, C. D. Jackson, Emmet John Hughes, and Jim Hagerty deplored the senator and at various times suggested that Ike vigorously denounce McCarthy. Urging a more conciliatory approach were Vice President Nixon, Republican National Chairman Leonard Hall, and presidential assistant, General Wilton Persons. Eisenhower argued that such a confrontation would elevate McCarthy to the same level as the presidency, noting that Acheson had erred in matching the senator blow for blow. "I will not get into the gutter with that guy," said Ike. Milton, whose opinion counted heavily, agreed with the President.

Oddly enough, the most outspoken McCarthy critics in the Eisenhower family were Ike's more conservative elder brothers—Edgar and Arthur. In an April 1953 letter to Ike, Edgar wrote: "I condemn McCarthy's actions in making any kind of agreement with any group of people in a foreign country, whether it is with Greek ship owners or Russian generals. . . . If my name were different from what it is, I would take a blast at McCarthy for what he has done."

In July, Kansas City banker Arthur Eisenhower went to Las

Vegas for a meeting of the board of directors of Trans-World Airlines. During a luncheon interview Arthur said, "When I think of McCarthy, I automatically think of Hitler. . . . He wants to keep his name in the papers at all costs. He follows the old political game which is 'Whose name is mentioned the most in politics is often selected for the highest office.'" Arthur called McCarthy a "rabble rouser" and a "menace to America."

Of McCarthy's treatment of witnesses called before his subcommittee, Arthur said: "He is a throwback to the Spanish Inquisition. He calls in people and proceeds to make fools of them by twisting their answers. What chance do they have? They have no rebuttal because they have no recourse. . . . It is Nazi-like and what makes it all so much more of a fiasco is that he has never been responsible for the conviction of one Communist."

In the meantime, McCarthy began investigating the State Department's overseas libraries and claimed that they were stocked with "pro-Communist" books. McCarthy's list of forbidden authors included Archibald MacLeish, W. H. Auden, Stephen Vincent Benet, John Dewey, Henry Steele Commager, Bernard DeVoto, Theodore Dreiser, Sherwood Anderson, Dashiell Hammett, Brooks Atkinson, NAACP director Walter White, and historian Foster Rhea Dulles, the cousin of the Secretary of State. Books were removed from shelves and, in some cases, burned by timid officials. Reports about the book purge produced shock waves in Europe and Ike was enraged by McCarthy's assault on the libraries.

On June 14, 1953, Ike received an honorary degree at Dartmouth and in extemporaneous remarks he warned students about McCarthyism. "Don't join the book burners," he said. "Don't think you are going to conceal faults by concealing evidence that they ever existed. Don't be afraid to go to your library and read every book, as long as that document does not offend your own ideas of decency. That should be the only censorship."

Eisenhower's "book burning" speech seemed to be a turning point in his struggle with McCarthy, but Ike would still not make a direct attack on the Wisconsin senator. Three days later, at a news conference, Merriam Smith of United Press asked him if the Dartmouth speech was indeed an anti-McCarthy statement.

"Now, Merriam," said Ike, "you have been around me long enough to know that I never talk personalities."

Swede Hazlett sent Ike a letter congratulating his old friend for getting "ready to crack down on McCarthy" and adding that "I have always known that you feel about him much as I do." In a July 21 letter, Ike responded that Swede had correctly guessed his view of McCarthy, but misinterpreted his strategy.

> It is quite clear that whenever the President takes part in a newspaper trial of some individual of whom he disapproves, one thing is automatically accomplished. This is an increase in the headline value of the individual attacked.
>
> I think that the average honorable individual cannot understand to what lengths certain politicians would go for publicity. They have learned a simple truth in American life. This is that the most vicious kind of attack from one element always creates a very great popularity, amounting to almost hero worship, in an opposite fringe of society. Because of this . . . Huey Long had his idolators. Every attack on him increased their number (an expression of the underdog complex) and enhanced the fervor of his avowed supporters.
>
> When you have a situation like this, you have an ideal one for the newspapers . . . to exploit, to exaggerate and to perpetuate. In such a situation, I disagree completely with the "crack down" theory. I believe in the positive approach. I believe that we should earnestly support the practices of American principles in trials and investigations—we should teach and practice decency and justice. We should support—even militantly support—people whom we know to be unjustly attacked, whether they are public servants or private citizens. . . .
>
> Persistence in these unspectacular but sound methods will, in my opinion, produce results that may not be headlined, but they will be permanent because they will earn the respect of fair-minded citizens—which means the vast bulk of our population. To give way in anger or irritation to an outburst intended to excoriate some individual, his motives and his methods, could do far more to destroy the position and au-

thority of the attacker than it would do to damage the attacked.

Without mentioning McCarthy, Ike did speak out against McCarthyism when the senator gave him an opening. In the summer of 1953, a McCarthy aide wrote in the *American Mercury* that Protestant clergymen were the largest group supporting Communism. In a telegram to the National Conference of Christians and Jews, Ike said: "Generalized and irresponsible attacks that sweepingly condemn the whole of any group of citizens are alien to America." In November, on a national television broadcast, McCarthy challenged Ike's statement that Communism in government would not be an issue in the 1954 congressional elections. Ike had expressed hope that anti-Communist rhetoric would be "a matter of history and memory."

McCarthy's popularity seemed to be at a peak in January 1954 when the Gallup poll reported that 50 percent of the American public rated him favorably, and 29 percent unfavorably. As an Irish Catholic, McCarthy had a large following among his religious and ethnic brethren, but he also had much support from Protestant fundamentalists and Eastern European ethnics who were anti-Communist zealots. Historian Richard Hofstadter wrote that McCarthy "received a measure of support disproportionate to their numbers in the general population from Catholics and from the ill-educated, but also from Republicans, Irish-Americans, the lower classes, and the aged." National magazines speculated about McCarthy as a potential presidential candidate against Ike in 1956. Adlai Stevenson stung Ike by observing that the Republicans were "a political party divided against itself, half McCarthy and half Eisenhower." Eisenhower replied sharply that Stevenson's remark was "nonsense," yet he was disturbed by the McCarthy threat.

Still, Ike would not shift his strategy and he remained "convinced that the only person who could destroy McCarthy was he himself." Ike understood the subtleties and nuances of power far better than most of those who criticized him for lack of political acumen or moral courage. By the end of 1954, McCarthy was finished as a political force and had fallen into disrepute.

McCarthy's investigation of Communist influence in the Army

marked the beginning of the end of his reign of terror. When McCarthy accused Secretary of the Army Robert T. Stevens of coddling Communists and concealing evidence of espionage at Fort Monmouth, New Jersey, the Army countercharged that McCarthy had attempted to secure preferential treatment and a commission for G. David Schine, one of his aides who had been drafted and was an army private. Out of this dispute came the Army-McCarthy hearings which lasted for five weeks in the spring of 1954, and the television coverage made it possible for much of the nation to observe McCarthy in action, and for a time school children were shouting "point of order" in playgrounds in imitation of McCarthy. The senator came across as a street fighter in his exchanges with colleagues and a harassed Secretary Stevens, but his coarse and boorish behavior was clearly visible on the television screen. Representing the Army was Joseph L. Welch, a wily Boston lawyer with courtly manners, whose wry rejoinders exposed McCarthy's vulnerability. Welch's cross-examination of McCarthy revealed that the senator had falsified evidence during the hearings and had received stolen and classified government documents, yet the most devastating blow came when McCarthy slandered a young member of Welch's law firm as a Communist sympathizer and the counsel responded in a choked voice: "Until this moment, Senator, I think I never really gauged your cruelty or your recklessness." Though the hearings were inconclusive, Senator Ralph Flanders of Vermont introduced a motion of censure against McCarthy for "conduct . . . unbecoming a member of the United States Senate." A select committee headed by Utah Republican Arthur Watkins recommended McCarthy's censure and in December McCarthy was "condemned" by a 3-to-1 margin.

"The McCarthy-Army argument, and its reporting, are close to disgusting," Dwight had written in an April 27 letter to Hazlett. "It saddens me that I must feel ashamed for the United States Senate." In December, following the McCarthy censure, Ike wrote in a letter to Clifford Roberts: "McCarthy is operating at the same old stand. I see that he picked up a statement of mine in which I expressed admiration for the statesmanlike and dignified way in which Arthur Watkins conducted the nastiest job that any man ever had, to let go an outburst against me. He apologized to the country for supporting me in '52. The answer to that is that I apologize also for his support. But the incident shows that he at least is completely determined to hold on to every headline he has."

McCarthy's influence suddenly vanished and with the Democrats regaining control of the Senate and House in the 1954 elections, he lost the committee chairmanship. His speeches were ignored and he was shunned by other senators. The Eisenhower administration, which had feared him, could reject his nomination for postmaster of his home town in Wisconsin. McCarthy called for Republicans to nominate FBI director J. Edgar Hoover for President in 1956, but nobody was listening. With the political decline came a physical decline. Always a heavy drinker, McCarthy turned more frequently to alcohol and was sick much of the time. His weight fluctuated from week to week and he would appear fleshy and rotund and then become gaunt. On May 2, 1957, McCarthy died at Bethesda Naval Hospital.

In world affairs, Ike faced the thorny problem of the Indochina war and, as a student of history, he well understood that the European colonial empires that had been superimposed upon that region could not repress a nationalist, democratic movement. Churchill resisted an Eisenhower suggestion that Britain renounce colonialism, making the argument that "dependent peoples" were a British responsibility. Churchill's attitude, which Dwight described as "Victorian," was reminiscent of the "white man's burden" of Rudyard Kipling, and in the decade after World War II, the colonial powers more than ever symbolized the racialism of a bygone era. Franklin Roosevelt had voiced reservations about French wishes to reclaim Indochina from the Japanese at war's end, but with Roosevelt's death, France asserted its claim, and the Truman administration made no objection. Ho Chi Minh, the tenacious and idealistic leader of the Vietnamese nationalist movement, had since youth worked in the anti-French cause and in 1919, at the Versailles Peace Conference, he made an unsuccessful attempt to petition the great powers for freedom for his homeland. In Europe, Ho became captivated by liberal democratic and Marxist philosophy and joined the French Socialist Party, and in 1920 he helped found the French Communist Party when the Socialists failed to support national liberation for colonial areas. On his return to Indochina, he organized the Indochinese Communist Party and in 1940 forged a coalition of nationalists and revolutionaries into the Viet Minh, also known as the League for the Independence of Vietnam. That same year, the Vichy government of France agreed to Japanese occupation of Indochina, and Ho's Viet Minh emerged as the most effective guerrilla units against the foreign invaders. Ho received American supplies and military advisers.

In 1945, the Viet Minh formed the Democratic Republic of Vietnam with Ho as president. Ho was a scholar of American history and in writing the Vietnamese Declaration of Independence he was deeply influenced by Thomas Jefferson's declaration of 1776. Ho's document began with familiar words: "All men are created equal. They are endowed by their creator with certain inalienable rights, among these are Life, Liberty and the pursuit of Happiness." From the fall of 1945 through the winter of 1946, Ho made no less than eight appeals to President Truman for American and United Nations intervention against the French, but none were answered.

The French, with British and Japanese troop support, took Saigon and southern Vietnam. Though France recognized Ho as the head of state of the Democratic Republic (North Vietnam) and agreed to a referendum in South Vietnam on unification, the promise was not carried out. The French, instead, restored Bao Dai, the playboy emperor who was living in Hong Kong with his mistresses, as head of a puppet government and they declared that he was sovereign of all Vietnam. American policy shifted from neutrality to open support of the French when Mao Tse-tung won the Chinese Revolution in 1949 and established a Communist regime in Peking. From a 1950 grant of $10 million, American aid to the French peaked at $1.1 billion in 1954, nearly 80 percent of the counterrevolutionary war chest. Ho Chi Minh would often express puzzlement at the inconsistency of an American government, born in revolution, siding with European colonial interests. America's foreign-policy mandarins had become so obsessed with anti-Communism that the nation's traditional commitment to freedom and against despotism and injustice was sometimes forgotten. Morally, the French position in Vietnam was indefensible and yet there were economic as well as political considerations. In 1953, Ike said: "Let us assume we lose Indochina. The tin and tungsten that we so greatly value from that area would cease coming. So when the U.S. votes $400 million to help that war, we are not voting a giveaway program. We are voting for the cheapest way to prevent the occurrence of something that would be of the most terrible significance to our power and ability to get certain things we need from the riches of Indochina."

By 1954, after nearly eight years of jungle warfare in Vietnam, the French were tiring of occupation and French Premier Joseph Laniel said his government would accept "any honorable" settlement and would not seek the unconditional surrender of the Viet Minh. Within the Eisenhower administration, American intervention in Vietnam was seriously considered. The National Security Council in August of 1953 had concluded that any negotiated settlement would "mean the eventual loss to Communism not only of Indochina but of the whole of Southeast Asia" and therefore "critical to the security of the U.S." The most forceful advocates for direct intervention were Secretary of State Dulles and Admiral Arthur W. Radford, then chairman of the Joint Chiefs of Staff. Vice President Nixon, a stalwart hawk, publicly suggested that "if to avoid further Communist expansion in Asia and Indochina, we must take the risk now by putting our boys in, I think the Executive has to take the politically unpopular decision to do it." With Radford, Nixon recommended American bombing of the Viet Minh when the nationalists launched a strong assault against the French fortress at Dien Bien Phu in northwest Vietnam.

Ike ruled out any such action. As he later explained: "There were grave doubts in my mind about the effectiveness of such air strikes on deployed troops where good cover was plentiful. Employment of air strikes alone to support French troops in the jungle would create a double jeopardy: it would comprise an act of war and would also entail the risk of having intervened and lost."

Eisenhower urged France to request United Nations military assistance in Indochina and refused to permit American forces to intervene without UN sanction, noting prophetically that such a precedent could mean involvement in numerous other Asian wars. In April of 1954, he wrote: "For more than three years I have been urging upon successive French governments the advisability of finding some way of 'internationalizing' the war; such action would be proof to all the world and particularly to the Vietnamese that France's purpose is not colonial in character but is to defeat Communism in the region and to give the natives their freedom. The reply has always been vague, containing references to national prestige, constitutional limitations, inevitable effects upon the Moroccan and Tunisian peoples, and dissertations on plain political difficulties and battles within the French Parliament. The result has been that the French have failed entirely to produce any enthusiasm on the part of the Vietnamese for participation in the war. . . .

"The French have used weasel words in promising independence and through this one reason, as much as anything else, have suffered reverses that have been really inexcusable." Eisenhower and General Matthew Ridgway were cautious about entering the war. Ike had been critical of Truman's intervention in Korea without congressional approval and he sensed that Congress was against going it alone into another distant war so soon after Korea.

In Eisenhower's view, the French had made a major blunder in moving fifteen thousand men into Dien Bien Phu because the odds favored the attacking Viet Minh. The French had used the same cordon defense successfully against "Black Flag" Vietnamese guerrillas in 1885 in consolidating their hold on Indochina, but the Viet Minh were much more disciplined and were well armed and supplied under the direction of General Vo Nguyen Giap. Indeed, Viet Minh antiaircraft artillery shot down sixty-two French planes and prevented air drops into the besieged fortress. On April 27, Dwight wrote about Dien Bien Phu: "It still holds out and while the situation looked particularly desperate during the past week, there now appears to be a slight improvement and the place may hold on for another week or ten days. The general situation in Southeast Asia, which is rather dramatically epitomized by the Dien Bien Phu battle, is a complicated one that has been a long time developing."

On May 7, 1954, after fifty-five days of intense battle, the Viet

Minh captured Dien Bien Phu and effectively shattered France's hold over its longtime colonial territory. In the meantime, an international conference at Geneva resulted in a negotiated cease-fire and the temporary partition of North and South Vietnam with the provision that national elections would be held in 1956 to unify the nation under a central government. To Eisenhower and Dulles, the Geneva accords were a disaster, for Ike readily conceded that in a national election Ho Chi Minh would receive 80 percent of the vote against the weak, pleasure-loving Bao Dai. The United States refused to sign the Geneva agreements, and Ike promised only that Americans would not use force to disturb the settlement.

During the negotiations, Dulles was reported to have hinted that the United States might use nuclear weapons to help France retain Indochina. Murray Kempton later wrote, "There is no evidence that he would have dared transmit that suggestion to a President who plainly would not have trusted him with a stick of dynamite to blow up a fish pond."

In November, Dulles established a Southeast Asia Treaty Organization that he envisioned as an anti-Communist alliance in the NATO mold and its charter members were the United States, Britain, France, Australia, New Zealand, Pakistan, Thailand, and the Philippines. However, SEATO was largely a ceremonial body, for member nations were bound only to consult and made no military commitment. A decade later, President Lyndon B. Johnson attempted to justify his escalation of the United States military effort in Vietnam by citing the SEATO pact as a binding treaty, yet New York *Times* columnist C. L. Sulzberger was more precise in describing SEATO as "the alliance that never really was." Eisenhower's decision against intervention had meant the end of the first Indochina war in 1954 and his calm judgment had prevailed over such hawkish cold warriors as Dulles, Nixon, and Radford. At the same time, his administration gave massive economic aid to the South Vietnamese regime headed by Ngo Dinh Diem—$3 billion during the next four years—that enabled Diem to consolidate his hold on the South and, in defiance of the Geneva agreements, block national elections. The Pentagon Papers were to conclude that "South Vietnam was essentially the creation of the United States." Diem's parochial betrayal of the Geneva accords and American disregard of political forces within Vietnam were to have tragic consequences.

Shortly after the Indochina cease-fire came another Far Eastern crisis as Communist China began shelling offshore islands held by the Chinese Nationalists in the Formosa Straits. Mao Tse-tung had made known Peking's intention of liberating Taiwan from Chiang Kai-shek, the deposed ruler of China who had fled to the island province with more than two million of his followers, making it the effective territory of the Republic of China. Truman at first ruled out intervention and military aid to Chiang, but with the outbreak of the Korean War in 1950 his policy changed and he ordered the Seventh Fleet into the Formosa Straits to restrain Chiang's forces from attacks against the mainland and to protect Taiwan against Communist invasion. With the pro-Chiang "China Lobby" exploiting American hysteria over the "loss of China to Communism" and maintaining its political pressure in Washington, U.S. policy continued to favor the Nationalists. In 1953, Dwight announced the "unleashing" of Chiang by removing the prohibition against a Nationalist attack on the mainland, while assuring Taiwan of further protection from the Communists. "Any invasion of Formosa would have to run over the Seventh Fleet," said Ike. To the most adventurous of the hard liners, the Communist shelling of Quemoy seemed a glittering opportunity to make war against Red China. Admiral Radford called for the defense of the offshore islands and American bombing of the mainland in collaboration with an invasion by South Korean and Nationalist Chinese armies. Senate Majority Leader Knowland urged a naval blockade of the Chinese coast, which Eisenhower immediately vetoed as a belligerent act that would be counterproductive. As for the Radford hard line, Ike said that it might well bring World War III and that the offshore islands were not worth the price.

Chiang longed for another world war as his best hope of ousting Mao and resurrecting himself as leader of all China. "Our plan for fighting Communism and regaining the mainland will necessarily form," said Chiang, "an important link in the general plan of the free world to combat worldwide Communist aggression."

In World War II, Chiang had joined Roosevelt, Churchill, and Stalin as a member of the "Big Four," as a full partner in the great alliance. Western intervention in Korea and Indochina gave Chiang hope that his old allies might help him reconquer China.

His attitude was unrealistic, for among the Western allies only the United States still recognized his claim to the Middle Kingdom and Taiwan had been deliberately excluded from the SEATO treaty to gain the support of other Asian and European nations. Eisenhower himself had reservations about the commitment to Chiang and said that his escalation of troops on the offshore islands was "a thorn in the side of peace." Former British Prime Minister Clement Attlee, an Eisenhower friend and wartime associate, bluntly suggested the abandonment of Taiwan. In maneuvering to ease tensions, Ike held that the United States would not be committed to "full-out defense" of the offshore islands and yet would repel any assault on Taiwan. Under a mutual defense treaty with Taiwan, Ike reiterated the commitment to defend Taiwan but not the Tachen islands, and in exchange for this assurance, Chiang conceded that his soldiers would not attack the mainland without the permission of the United States. In January, Eisenhower submitted a resolution to the Senate for authorization by the President to "employ the armed forces of the United States as he deems necessary" in order to protect Taiwan. By overwhelming margins, the Senate and House approved the resolution and Dwight had a congressional mandate to intervene in Taiwan and its region at his discretion. Though the People's Republic of China considered Taiwan part of its territory, there were signs that Peking wanted a peaceful and long-term solution rather than a possible confrontation with the United States. "Conditions permitting, the Chinese people are ready to seek the liberation of Taiwan," said Premier and Foreign Minister Chou En-lai. "Provided that the United States does not interfere with China's internal affairs, the possibility of peaceful liberation of Taiwan will continue to increase."

Eisenhower had quietly but forcefully used his influence to achieve peace in Asia, and the stalwart hawks were effectively rebuffed. Ike wanted the Cold War with the Soviet Union to thaw and if the differences between the superpowers were inherent in their philosophies, the dangers of a nuclear confrontation gave a new urgency to détente. The death of Premier Joseph Stalin on March 5, 1953, had come a month after the Soviet marshal had talked hopefully about a summit conference with Eisenhower. In such an atmosphere, the Soviet Union seemed ready to begin an era of peaceful coexistence in foreign policy for its sphere of influence extended into Central Europe and domestic stability had been accomplished through bloody purges and the world war. Stalin's heir apparent, Georgi Malenkov, talked of coexistence in his eulogy at the dictator's funeral. Lavrenti Beria, Stalin's secret police chief and the most feared of his possible successors, was slain in June as Malenkov made his bid for supreme power. Within the Kremlin, fierce infighting persisted which culminated in the resignation of Malenkov early in 1955.

Another Stalin protégé, Marshal Nikolai Bulganin, became Premier. Following Stalin's death in 1953, Churchill had proposed and Ike rejected an East-West summit conference. Eisenhower was ready for such a conference in the summer of 1955 and, although Dulles was skeptical, Ike agreed to a July meeting in Geneva with Bulganin, British Prime Minister Anthony Eden, and French Premier Edgar Faure. The Soviet withdrawal of troops from Austria and the signing of the Austrian State Treaty in the spring of 1955 had broken a diplomatic stalemate and demonstrated to Eisenhower that a conference on other issues might be worthwhile. "Personally I do not expect any spectacular results from the forthcoming 'Big Four' Conference," Ike wrote Hazlett on June 4. "Nevertheless, I should think that Foster and I should be able to detect whether the Soviets really intend to introduce a tactical change that could mean, for the next few years at least, some real easing of tensions. If we do not obtain some concrete evidence of such a tactical change, then, of course, the effort must be to determine the exact purpose of recent Soviet suggestions for conferences and easing of tensions and so on."

Eisenhower's mood seemed more optimistic as he prepared to board the presidential plane, the *Columbine*, for the historic journey, and he said, "a new dawn may be coming." No peacetime President since Woodrow Wilson had gone to Europe, and the stage was set for an international drama. On the first day of the conference, Ike presided and said: "We meet here for a simple purpose. We have come to find a basis for accommodation which will make life safer and happier not only for the nations we represent but for people elsewhere. . . . We cannot expect here, in the few hours of a few days, to solve all the problems of the world that need to be solved. . . . Nevertheless, we can, perhaps, create a new spirit that will make possible future solutions of problems which are within our responsibilities. And, equally important, we can try to take here and now at Geneva the first steps on a new road to a just and durable peace."

On the fourth day of the conference, Nelson Rockefeller, then serving as presidential assistant for national security, came up to John Eisenhower, who had come to Geneva at his father's invitation. "You have got to be in the conference this afternoon," said Rockefeller. "Your dad is going to throw a bombshell. He's going to do a great thing." At the conference, John sat behind Rockefeller and when President Eisenhower's turn to speak came, Rockefeller told the President's son: "Hold your hat, here we go now!"

Speaking in the elaborate council chamber of the defunct League of Nations' Palais des Nations, Ike made a disarmament proposal that was at once bold and radical. "I should address myself for a moment principally to the Delegates from the Soviet Union, because our two great countries admittedly possess new and terrible weapons in quantities which do give rise in other parts of the world, or reciprocally, to the fears and dangers of surprise attack.

"I propose, therefore, that we take a practical step, that we begin an arrangement, very quickly, as between ourselves. These steps would include: To give to each other a complete blueprint of our military establishments, from beginning to end, from one end of our countries to the other; lay out the establishments and provide the blueprints to each other. Next, to provide within our countries facilities for aerial photography to the other country—we to provide you the facilities within our country, ample facilities for aerial reconnaissance, where you can make all the pictures you choose and take them to your own country to study, you to provide exactly the same facilities for us and we to make these examinations, and by this step to convince the world that we are providing as between ourselves against the possibility of great surprise attack, thus lessening danger and relaxing tension. Likewise we will make more easily attainable a comprehensive and effective system of inspection and disarmament, because what I propose . . . would be but a beginning."

French Premier Faure responded, "I wish the people of the world could have been in this conference room to hear the voice of a man speaking from great military experience. Had this been possible they would believe that something had changed in the world in the handling of this question of disarmament. I am sure that this conference has scored its first victory over skepticism."

The Soviets, caught by surprise, were less enthusiastic about the "Open Skies" proposal, although Premier Bulganin said that it had merit and would be studied. As the session adjourned, the great powers seemed to be closer to détente than at any time since World War II. The warmth of the cheerful Soviet Premier gave Eisenhower a moment of triumph. However, Ike walked to the postconference reception with Nikita Khrushchev, the general secretary of the Communist Party. "I don't agree with the chairman," said Khrushchev sternly. Eisenhower instantly recognized that Bulganin had been shouldered aside by the tough-minded Khrushchev. "After that exchange going down the hall," Ike told John Eisenhower, "I didn't pay any more attention to Bulganin."

If Eisenhower's attempts to persuade Khrushchev to accept the Open Skies plan were unsuccessful, his remarkable gesture produced the impression that he was really a world statesman. *Le Monde* of Paris, a traditionally anti-American journal, said: "Eisenhower, whose personality has long been misunderstood, has emerged as the type of leader humanity needs today." As Ike returned home, the Gallup poll showed that 74 percent of the American public approved of his performance.

In a larger sense, the "spirit of Geneva" had advanced American-Soviet relations beyond the unbending hostility of the postwar decade and given hope to a world, all too weary of war, that the great powers might settle their differences peacefully. "It is my judgment that the prospects of a lasting peace with justice are brighter," said Ike on his last day in Geneva. "The dangers of the overwhelming tragedy of modern war are less." Though the Open Skies proposal would be discussed by Eisenhower in correspondence with Soviet leaders for more than three years after Geneva, they would not consent to its adoption.

For some months prior to Geneva, Ike had been discouraging speculation about his candidacy for reelection in 1956. "I shall never again be a candidate for anything," Ike wrote a friend in December of 1953. "This determination is a fixed decision (subject to modification *only* in the case of some world-wide cataclysm that I cannot now foresee and which would make political change at such a moment almost catastrophic for our country). Of course I realize that American politics demands that a President keep his intentions secret in this regard; otherwise, it is assumed that his whole influence on the political scene would disappear and he could not possibly lead in the development of a legislative program."

In the aftermath of the Democratic victory in the 1954 congressional elections, Republican leaders carried their appeal to the White House: Only Dwight D. Eisenhower could hold the presidency in 1956. General Lucius Clay told Ike, "I am ready to work for you at whatever sacrifice to myself because I believe in you. I am not ready to work for anybody else that you can name." Eisenhower cut him short with the statement that he would make a decision later, but in his diary Ike said his attitude about 1956 was "wholly adverse."

Eisenhower noted in a June 4, 1955, letter to Hazlett that "No man has ever reached his 70th year in the White House" and added, "No one has the faintest right to consider acceptance of a nomination unless he honestly believes that his physical and mental reserves will stand the strain of four years of intensive work."

Three weeks after the Geneva summit, Ike flew to Denver for a vacation with Mamie and her mother, Elvira Doud. On August 15, he wrote Hazlett with reference to his own age: "Normally the last person to recognize that a man's mental faculties are fading is the victim himself. . . . I have seen many a man 'hang on too long' under the definite impression that he had a great duty to perform and that no one else could adequately fill his particular position. The more important and demanding the position, the greater the danger in this regard."

In Colorado, Ike rode horseback and fished at the Rocky Mountain retreat of his wealthy friend Aksel Nielsen and played golf at the exclusive Cherry Hills Country Club. It was the kind of vacation that he liked best and he kept official business to a minimum. When Republican state chairmen came to Denver for breakfast at the Brown Palace and endorsed Eisenhower for a second term, Ike said the party should not be dependent on one man. "Humans are frail and they are mortal," he said. "Never pin your flag so tightly to one mast that if a ship sinks, you cannot rip it off and nail it to another."

On the morning of September 24, Eisenhower awoke in the second-floor bedroom of his mother-in-law's Lafayette Street house with an agonizing pain in his chest. He was flushed and perspiring and could not speak. Sensing that something was wrong, Mamie called General Howard Snyder, Ike's doctor. Clay and others had questioned whether Snyder was competent to care for a President of the United States, but Eisenhower had been Snyder's patient for a decade and showed no inclination to change. Arriving at the Doud house, Snyder quickly tested Eisenhower's pulse, blood pressure, and heartbeat. Within three minutes came Snyder's diagnosis—Eisenhower had suffered a heart attack. Through the early morning, Snyder administered medication to dilate the arteries and to prevent further clotting, and additional medication to ease the shock.

The nation was jolted as it had not been since the death of Franklin D. Roosevelt ten years earlier. Eisenhower had become a symbol of world peace and national unity and yet until the heart attack many Americans had not fully realized their dependence on him. Ike had seemed so vigorous and active that the news from Denver was almost incomprehensible.

Three days after the heart attack, it was disclosed that Ike had pulled through his crisis. He would survive, although his recovery would be long and frustrating. That he was no longer in danger came as an enormous relief to the nation and the world, but the speculation about a second term had for the moment ceased. "Today I am walking a few steps," Ike wrote Hazlett on October 26. "The doctors say my progress follows the normal pattern. . . . Apparently there is a period of some four months before they can make an accurate prognosis of the level of activity a heart victim can sustain without incurring any damage. By that time a lot of factors that now appear doubtful or uncertain should definitely crystallize."

Chapter Seventeen

AN EISENHOWER ALTERNATIVE

When Ike was stricken with the heart attack, the national political spotlight fell on possible contenders for the presidency. On the assumption that Ike would not run for a second term, Democrats were suddenly optimistic about their chances in 1956. Adlai Stevenson was the early front runner, but Governor Averell Harriman of New York and Senator Estes Kefauver were also seeking the nomination. If Ike was to be replaced, many Republican leaders were less than certain about their party's choice. Chief Justice Earl Warren had broad appeal, yet he declared that under no circumstances would he leave the Supreme Court. Vice President Nixon, then only forty-two, was popular within the congressional wing of the party and had conducted himself with dignity during Ike's incapacitation. Nixon, however, had been an outsider at the White House and his slashing political style had earned him the contempt and loathing of intellectuals and liberals. In Gallup poll trial heats for 1956, Nixon ran behind both Stevenson and Kefauver, and most political observers agreed that he could not win against either Democrat. The New York *Herald Tribune* singled out Milton Eisenhower as a Republican who had a very good chance of retaining the presidency for his party. Only two days after Ike's attack, the Chicago *Sun-Times* endorsed Milton as "a worthy successor" and "the most promising candidate the

Republican Party could offer in 1956." New York's Congressman Adam Clayton Powell, a Democrat and the most charismatic black leader of his generation, said, "If the President's brother gets the Republican nomination, no Democrat can win."

Three Republican governors—Theodore McKeldin of Maryland, Walter Kohler of Wisconsin, and Charles Russell of Nevada—spoke out for Milton and a poll of Republican state chairmen indicated surprising strength for his candidacy. "If we can't have one Eisenhower to win for us," said one Republican leader, "why not try with another?" Missouri's state chairman Perry Compton and Oregon's state chairman Wendell Wyatt named Milton as their preference. Explaining the Milton phenomenon, Oregon State Senator Mark Hatfield, an early organizer of the "Draft Ike" movement in 1952, said: "Milton represents the more enlightened wing of our party and he probably has more profound knowledge of government than Ike."

Time magazine publisher James A. Linen predicted that Milton would be a formidable candidate. For weeks, the speculation continued and Milton's chances were assessed in the public prints. William Lambert, a reporter for *The Oregonian,* interviewed Edgar Eisenhower, who said: "I've had all the damn presidents in my family I want to. I've been bothered to death and I want to live a peaceful life for the years I have left. I'm not interested in another member of my family serving in the presidency."

In the meantime, Milton was maintaining a discreet silence at Penn State. The idea of his presidential candidacy was not a new one. As early as 1949, a national magazine had described him as presidential timber. At NATO headquarters, Ike had in 1951 told a visiting delegation of Republicans that they should be supporting Milton, not himself, for the presidency. In the White House, Ike still considered his youngest brother to be of presidential stature. On December 24, 1953, he wrote Hazlett: "As I have more than once told you, the man who, from the standpoint of knowledge of human and governmental affairs, persuasiveness in speech and dedication to our country, would make the best President I can think of is my young brother, Milton. Under no circumstances would I ever say this publicly because, in the first place, I do not think he is physically strong enough to take the beating. In the second place, any effort to make him the candidate in 1956 would properly be resented by our people. So he is out as far as I am concerned." But Milton was not so easily eliminated from presidential politics and Ike's much-publicized tributes did more than anything to generate enthusiasm for his brother.

Milton's role as confidant, adviser, and trouble shooter was unprecedented for a presidential brother. Only Robert F. Kennedy would hold comparable authority, but he was a brilliant political technician and later Attorney General in the Kennedy Cabinet. Though Ike had seriously discussed appointing Milton to the Eisenhower Cabinet, they mutually decided that it would be inappropriate. Following the death of Milton's wife, Helen, efforts were made to change Milton's mind about a Cabinet-level appointment. At the urging of Secretary of State Dulles, Ike suggested that Milton become United Nations ambassador or ambassador at large. However, Milton held that appointment to a full-time position would create the impression of a family dynasty and preferred to continue in his unofficial but important capacity as Ike's most trusted confidant. "It just happens that my brother and I have very much the same philosophy," said Milton in a 1967 interview. "We began working together intimately in the 1930s, a working relationship which both of us enjoy in mutual respect, and it's a cooperation of a very close order that persists to this moment."

So it was that Milton played a major part in the Eisenhower administration. "I did not work for him," said Milton, "I was not subservient to him. To me, he wasn't even the President of the United States; he was a brother whom I respected and loved very deeply. Therefore, he could think out loud with me, raise questions, provide his own answers, with no suspicion that this would ever be disclosed to anyone else, or that I would myself make an expression different from my own honest convictions merely because he was the President. And I think anyone who occupies this lonely spot needs someone; it might be his wife, which I think it probably might have been in the case of Franklin Roosevelt, or it might be a very intimate friend, but it just happens that our relationship had been such that I think perhaps I filled this need of his, perhaps better than anyone else could have."

With Nelson Rockefeller and Arthur Flemming, two old

friends, Milton served on the Committee on Government Reorganization and had been partly responsible for the creation of the Department of Health, Education, and Welfare, the United States Information Agency, the Small Business Administration, the Agency for International Development, the Federal Aviation Agency, and the National Aeronautics and Space Agency. Milton's impressive background in government made him indispensable to Ike, who was unfamiliar with many of the programs that he had suddenly become responsible for. He was reticent about his dealings with Ike and would flatly refuse to lobby for friends in the Oval Office. Rockefeller once approached Milton in the White House staff dining room and said, "I'd like you to bring up something with your brother."

"Why don't you do it, Nelson," responded Milton.

"I can't get in to see him," he said.

"Well, I'm not going to mention this to him," said Milton. "I never initiate a subject, but I express an opinion on anything he asks me about. If you're having trouble seeing him, I'll arrange for you to see him."

The episode demonstrated Milton's strict adherence to his understanding with Ike: He was a forceful advocate and a sharp critic, but within the privacy of the presidential bedroom or office. "Dr. Milton had a very high regard for the office of the presidency," said a longtime aide. "He had a rather formal feeling about it. I learned this quickly and never intruded or asked." At Penn State, a direct telephone from the White House was installed in Milton's office. "We all got out of the room when it rang," said the aide. Every Friday, an army plane would take Milton over the ridges of the Black Moshannon Forest and south to Washington. On weekends, he would stay at the White House in the upstairs Red Room and work in an office in the Executive Office Building. In the presidential living quarters, Ike would often relax with a scotch and soda and Milton with a martini while the conversation ranged from weighty matters of state to personal hobbies.

When Ike became a presidential candidate, Milton asked the trustees of Penn State to grant him a leave of absence to assist in the campaign. "They were quite unfriendly to such a suggestion," said Milton, "but said it would be perfectly appropriate for me to help in the campaign and also carry on my work at the university." As the Eisenhower campaign train rolled across the country, Milton was there to give his brother counsel. There were limits to his participation in the election drive. Following the convention, he did not campaign in Pennsylvania and later, when Ike was President, he declined an invitation to a one-hundred-dollar-plate dinner for Ike at Hershey. "You can pretend it's a party for the President of the United States," said Milton to a friend. "But it's not. It's a fund raiser for the Republican Party and I won't go as long as I'm president of Penn State."

Over Ike's first months in office, Milton developed a system with the approval of his trustees that he would spend four days a week working for Penn State and three days for his brother. Milton's closeness to the President of the United States added to his reputation and that of the university, but his own accomplishments at Penn State had been considerable and he was nationally recognized as a leader in higher education. In 1950–51, his first year as president of Penn State, Milton traveled more than sixty thousand miles throughout the Keystone State. "I met with industrial, agricultural, and labor groups, getting their views on what the university should be to the state and interpreting the university to them," said Milton.

From the start, Milton set high standards at Penn State. "I am certain that citizens of William Penn's state want their land-grant college to be one of the truly illustrious educational and research institutions of the nation," he said in his 1950 inaugural address. He raised faculty salaries 35 percent, built five massive new buildings with a ten-million-dollar state grant—including the three-million-dollar Hetzel Student Union—and he enlarged the library and seven other buildings. As he had done at Kansas State, Milton raised the liberal-arts requirements for technology students and in so doing raised the academic standards. Under his direction, the Penn State Foundation was organized to solicit private funds for development of the college and within two years had secured more than $800,000 in gifts. In 1953, Penn State officially became a university and Milton received most of the credit for transforming the institution from an isolated state college to national prominence.

"Penn State got to be accepted as a university and Milton Eisenhower had a lot to do with it," said Philip S. Klein, a distinguished historian who served as chairman of the history department. "It went much deeper than changing the name from college to university. Dr. Eisenhower brought in an academic atmosphere and a hell of a lot more. His predecessor had looked at Penn State as a factory and did not have Eisenhower's broad look. Dr. Eisenhower took what had been an engineering and agricultural college and gave it a national image and made Penn State significant in a large way."

Robert Bernreuter, a veteran Penn State administrator, said, "When Dr. Eisenhower came here, we sort of considered Penn State as number two or three among the colleges in Pennsylvania. But when he left, we thought of it as number one."

There were occasional disputes with the faculty as Milton broadened the curriculum, but the opposition never became vitriolic as had been the case at Kansas State. M. Nelson McGeary, a political science professor, said, "Eisenhower had a battle with a group of faculty members, yet it was not a knock-down, drag-out kind of fight. He was very impressive and convincing. By the end of the meeting, I'm not sure that everybody agreed with him, but they did respect him. There was a great deal of genuine affection for him." Milton's innovations at Penn State were more carefully planned and faculty support was more actively sought than in his earlier presidency. "Dr. Milton learned his lesson at Kansas State," said a longtime associate. "He had been a strong activist in revising and expanding programs. But the moment he left, they began to undo what he had done. At Penn State, he was pragmatic and laid the groundwork first."

It was a turbulent period in higher education as domestic anti-Communism dominated American politics. Since Truman's 1947 executive order creating a Loyalty Security program had come the rise of Joseph McCarthy and his charges of softness on Communism in government and in the nation's universities. In Pennsylvania, long a stronghold of Republican conservatism, McCarthyism was a potent political force, and legislation was introduced requiring loyalty oaths at all state universities. The presidents of Temple University and the University of Pittsburgh testified that if the state appropriated funding, the loyalty oaths were proper. Speaking last, Milton opposed the loyalty oaths, saying that it would be appropriate for the presidents to certify that "to the best of his knowledge all faculty members were loyal," and offering to take such an oath himself. A law, however, was adopted and as president Milton circulated a questionnaire among three thousand employees to comply with the act. Wendell Scott McCrae, a veteran of World War I and the publications production manager of the Department of Information, was fired for defying the procedure. Milton said there was no evidence that McCrae was "subversive." However, he explained, "Since it is manifestly not possible to permit each employee to determine for himself how the college shall comply with the loyalty act; since the procedures followed were adopted with the approval of an overwhelming majority of the staff and accepted in practice by all but Mr. McCrae, and since I could not otherwise make to the Governor the certification required by the act, I have no alternative but to terminate Mr. McCrae's employment."

In December of 1952, Milton drafted with Rockefeller and Flemming a memorandum for revamping the federal loyalty program: "We note the fact that in order to be effective, subversive individuals need not necessarily be numerous, provided that they are able to infiltrate important echelons of the government and remain undetected.

"Many good citizens are alarmed, not only by the phenomenon of such disloyalty among their fellow citizens but also by some of the methods which have been pursued in attempting to combat the condition—methods which it is felt, in certain instances, may involve an invasion of our basic liberties which should not be jeopardized even temporarily unless all other avenues of self-defense have been closed to us."

Milton perceived seeds of repression and anti-intellectualism in McCarthyism and urged Ike to openly denounce the Wisconsin senator. "McCarthy was such an evil and penetrating force in our society that I wanted the President, in the strongest possible language, to repudiate him," Milton recalled years later. Though disappointed at the time, Milton said that later events confirmed Ike's shrewdness in avoiding a confrontation. In the spring of 1955, McCarthy publicly attacked Milton as the "unofficial President of the United States" and blasted his ties with Nelson Rockefeller and past Democratic administrations, and stopped just short of calling Milton pro-Communist. As always, Ike was more concerned about the criticism of a family member than the senator's frequent attacks against him. In a telephone conversation with Milton, Ike suggested that his brother tell Penn State's trustees they are familiar with his philosophy, but if they believed McCarthy's charges, he might have to resign. Ike said Milton might also tell them that he was complimented, as was his brother, by McCarthy's enmity. McCarthy's free-swinging body punches had lost much of their sting and Milton was far from fearful of the demagogue's assault. Indeed, the opposition of McCarthy made Milton all the more attractive to the academic community much as Spiro Agnew's 1970 diatribe against Kingman Brewster enhanced the Yale president's reputation as a national educational leader. The day after McCarthy's attack, Milton and his daughter, Ruth, were vacationing in Land O' Lakes, Wisconsin, and were guests at a dinner party at a resort hotel. By coincidence, Senator McCarthy and his wife were having dinner across the room. Much to Milton's disgust, McCarthy embraced him, shook hands, and said that he was glad to see Milton in Wisconsin. Although Milton could not conceal his feelings and pointedly refused to introduce the senator to the other dinner guests, McCarthy went down the table and spoke with everyone. Beneath McCarthy's bluff aggressiveness was self-doubt and naïvete, for he could never understand why his verbal targets treated him with such hostility.

It did not take long for politicians in Harrisburg to test Milton's flexibility. For generations such old-fashioned political bosses as Matthew Quay and Boies Penrose had operated state institutions as personal fiefdoms and maintained tight control over patronage and contracts. Though civil service and other reforms had taken some of the political element out of state institutions, the backrooms were still prospering when Milton came to Pennsylvania. The governor's office attempted to pressure Milton into appointing a crony of Republican Governor John S. Fine to a staff position at Penn State. Milton despised statehouse patronage and rejected the job seeker as unqualified and undeserving of the minimum salary of the university pay scale. Shortly afterward, "Dunk" McCallum, Fine's administrative assistant, protested that "with all the millions in state funds you receive, can't you find one little job for the governor's friend?"

"This is not a state hospital," said Milton. "This is an educational institution."

If Milton would not conform to the old pork-barrel ways of Harrisburg, his sense of responsibility and integrity made a strong impression on legislators of both parties. In 1955, they provided him with some $20 million—nearly double the appropriation that Penn State had received in his first year—and $1 million more than he had requested. "Dr. Milton had a keen understanding of the political process," said Keith Spaulding, a New York *Herald-Tribune* editor who became Milton's assistant at Penn State. "He never inflated a budget to ask for more than he needed. He always went into legislative hearings with an absolutely defensible budget. This was a great change in style for Pennsylvania politics and Penn State."

Ultimately, Milton was approached about running for the governorship or the Senate. Despite a voter registration advantage of more than 900,000 the Republicans had lost the governorship in 1954 when the jowly, lackluster lieutenant governor, Lloyd Wood, was upset by Democratic State Senator George Leader, in the gubernatorial election. Under the state constitution, a candidate for governor was required to have been a resident of Pennsylvania for seven years and Milton would have been eligible for the 1958 election. Philadelphia *Inquirer* columnist John M. Cummings, an influential journalist in state political circles, wrote that Milton "might pull the Republican elephant out of the bog in which it has been mired since election day."

Milton had been avidly courted by the Old Guard conservatives allied with the Pennsylvania Manufacturers' Association and it was of no small significance that his first major speech after the Penn State appointment was before a PMA dinner in Philadelphia, February of 1950. Joseph Grundy, the eighty-seven-year-old president of PMA, was a symbol of exploitive capitalism and reaction, who said that Robert Taft was the greatest American since William McKinley. Though Milton actively worked behind the scenes to help Ike win the Pennsylvania delegation in 1952 and the PMA forces supported Taft, the presidential race did not end his relations with the PMA faction. Indeed, G. Mason Owlett, Republican National Committeeman and Grundy's longtime PMA deputy, later offered to support Milton for either the governorship or the Senate. Republican state chairman George Bloom, Republican finance chairman Philip Sharpless, and PMA mandarin Roger Rowland also indicated that Milton would have organization support. It was not unusual for such old-line bosses to put forward a reformist moderate like Milton, as Grundy had sponsored liberal Gifford Pinchot in the 1920s and the machine would back patrician William W. Scranton in the 1960s. Social philosophy and ideology were less important than winning elections and aiding business and in Milton the stalwarts considered that they had an almost certain winner.

In the meantime, Milton and Ike were encouraging youthful moderates and progressives from the "Citizens for Eisenhower" clubs to become more active in Pennsylvania Republican politics. With his friend Roy Wilkinson, a lawyer and Penn State's counsel, Milton arranged for a select group of promising young Republicans to attend a stag dinner at the White House. After cocktails in the presidential study and dinner in the state dining room came a lively discussion in the Blue Room. Ike told the ambitious Pennsylvanians: "You've got to remember, you don't just knock off the top of the party. You've got to start at the grass roots." When one of the guests responded, "Mr. President, when you were in Europe and a bad decision was made, did they replace the privates or the generals?" Ike retorted, "Damn it, they didn't elect generals." Within a decade, a member of the group was elected governor of Pennsylvania, another was appointed attorney general, and two became judges. But their ascendancy was delayed by party elders.

"Unfortunately," Milton later recalled, "the then leadership of the Republican Party in Pennsylvania, despite the President's assurances, felt that this was a threat to their leadership, and they therefore not only ignored it, but tended to shun the very young and promising leaders that he had brought in for consultation."

In Senator James H. Duff's mind the purpose of the stag dinner was to promote Milton as an alternative to his renomination in 1956. Known as "Big Red," Duff had begun his political career as a Bullmoose Progressive in 1912 and in 1946 was elected governor. Duff had been a progressive governor, pushing through environmental and tax reforms against the opposition of the PMA mountebanks. In 1950, Duff was elected to the Senate and became a prime mover in Ike's preconvention campaign, with Dewey and Lodge, gaining national stature in the process. Duff's strong personality was more suited to executive than legislative leadership and he had become restless in the Senate, where his record was notable chiefly for his high absenteeism.

Philadelphia's reform mayor, Joseph S. Clark, had declared as the Democratic challenger for Duff's seat and his candidacy was regarded as a serious threat. If Milton became the Republican nominee, Clark's chances were considered less promising. The PMA stalwarts, who planned to cut Duff, would campaign vigorously for Milton as would the "Citizens for Eisenhower" moderates and progressives. "There were a lot of people, including myself, who said that Duff could not be reelected," recalled Roy Wilkinson years later. "To an extent, Milton was blamed when I said that Duff would be a weak candidate. I was sorry that Duff lost—but when he ran behind Ike by 400,000 votes—it proved my point." (Clark was elected by 18,000 votes of more than 4 million cast.)

As the momentum for Milton's Senate candidacy gained strength in 1955, Wilkinson made repeated overtures to his friend on the Penn State campus. "May I say that you would consider running if Duff withdraws?" asked Wilkinson.

"No you may not," said Milton. "The day after Jim Duff says he will not run, then I will give it some thought. It would be completely inappropriate to cause trouble for my brother. How could he pick between Duff and me? How could I put him in that position?"

That Duff had been an Eisenhower loyalist weighed against those supporting Milton. "I never considered running against Jim Duff," Milton said in a 1977 interview, although he confirmed that the Senate would have been his preference over the governorship. "The talks about running for governor went pretty far," he said. "A lot of political leaders approached me and, with reference to our family's history in Pennsylvania, they said that I certainly would not be a carpetbagger."

Milton decided against leaving higher education for the rough-and-tumble of Pennsylvania politics. Under the state's constitution, a governor was limited to one four-year term, and for years the chief executive had been less powerful than durable legislative chairmen and floor leaders. In addition, the problems of highways and taxation were much less stimulating than the national and international issues which Milton dealt with in his brother's administration.

To the students of Penn State, Milton was the symbol of their university's newfound prominence and an accessible friend. On his first visit to the campus after his 1950 appointment, Milton was spontaneously welcomed by several thousand students on the front steps of the Old Main Building. "The board of trustees can appoint a president," said a skeptical editorial in the *Daily Collegian*, "but only the students can make him 'prexy.'" Ten months later, the student newspaper said that Milton had earned the title traditionally bestowed only on Penn State presidents who had won the affection and respect of the campus. In the summer of 1950, Milton established the Penn State student encampment and met with one hundred student leaders with the message that his administration would include students in the decision-making process and wanted the dialogue to begin at once. "All I can say about students is bad," said an elderly administrator. Even the progressive counsel, Roy Wilkinson, said that the student encampment was "playing tennis without a ball." But the experiment gained Milton a firsthand knowledge of student concerns and established a two-way communication that he valued greatly. Milton became a regular dinner guest at fraternities and encouraged students to visit his home for evening "bull sessions."

He was seen everywhere, from visiting with ailing students at the infirmary to shouting encouragement on the sidelines at a preseason football scrimmage. In 1950, Charles A. "Rip" Engle became head football coach and the Nittany Lions were soon a nationally ranked power with such stars as Lenny Moore and Roosevelt Grier, and Milton rarely missed a home game. He was an all-around sports enthusiast and he also attended basketball, baseball, track, wrestling, and gymnastic events. Gene Wettstone, the Penn State gymnastics coach who also coached the United States Olympic gymnasts, said that Milton became so expert that he could score an exercise as well as veteran officials. Charles Speidel, who coached Penn State's national wrestling championship team, said the president mastered his knowledge of complicated holds and could anticipate a fall. For his own exercise and relaxation, Milton often fished in the clear streams of Centre County, sometimes with his older brother. Milton said, "Ike was a purist and only used dry flies. But on one occasion he wasn't catching anything. I went downstream and caught some trout with wet flies, so he came down, switched to wet flies, and caught a three-and-a-half-pound brown trout. He was so disgusted, he ripped out the fly, threw the trout back in the water, and went back to using dry flies."

Milton's most significant contribution to Penn State—transforming it from a college into a university—led to a town-and-gown dispute with the borough of State College. In a letter to Chamber of Commerce president Herbert R. Imbt, Milton wrote, "The town has always honored the institution by bearing its name. Now, unfortunately, the name State College constantly misstates the situation to the world." To avoid confusion, Milton suggested that the borough did not need to be named for the university. Among the names discussed were Nittany and University Park, but local residents voted against the name change in a 1954 referendum. "People said that it was bad enough when students tried to run things, but when the president tries to interfere, then it's time to put our foot down," said Roy Wilkinson. In the winter of 1955, Milton achieved a compromise of sorts by opening a University Park Post Office in the Student Union Building, and gaining official recognition for University Park.

Helen, the president's wife, was charming and gracious, and actively involved in the university community. Her favorite project was the planning of an All-Faith Chapel and she worked on it with Milton and other university officials. She accompanied Milton on his 1953 diplomatic mission to Latin America, and they made frequent trips to Washington to be with Ike and Mamie and Helen's parents. One of the great blows of Milton's life came on July 10, 1954, when Helen died of cancer, at the age of forty-nine. For Milton, who would never remarry, it was a devastating loss. "She made my life easy and wonderful," he said. "She had a great talent for never permitting unpleasant situations to bother me at home." In 1955, Ike came to Penn State and helped dedicate the All-Faith Chapel in Helen's name. "A lot of us were very touched and moved when Dr. Eisenhower's wife died and the response of everyone showed the affection the university felt for them," said a veteran liberal-arts professor more than twenty years later.

The morning after Helen's funeral, Milton sat alone for breakfast in the dining room in the presidential mansion. A moment later, his daughter, Ruth, entered the room and sat in Mrs. Eisenhower's empty chair. "Good morning, Father," she said with affection, and Milton said that his daughter was of enormous comfort during this troubled period. "I probably would have stayed at Penn State and retired there if my wife hadn't died," said Milton in a 1976 interview. "I was all right for the next year when Ruth was with me, but when she went to Swarthmore I was all alone in that big house. It's strange how you can have a latent reaction. I found myself distracted and losing interest and began finding fault with students, faculty, and trustees. I didn't think it was fair to the university for me to stay."

Milton resigned for "personal reasons" in June 1956. In his letter to the trustees, he said: "When my family and I came to Penn State, it was our intention to remain here permanently. Mrs. Eisenhower, our children, and I developed a deep and abiding fondness for the institution that could not possibly be exceeded by that of the most loyal and devoted alumnus. Then, the greatest loss that can come to any man visited my household."

His friends sensed that Milton would be able to contribute significantly to national and world affairs by moving to Washington and working for and being with Ike, where the void created by Helen's death could be filled in part by the companionship of his brother. Secretary of State Dulles told Ike that Milton had unique qualifications to become ambassador at large, with responsibility for Latin America, or United Nations ambassador. Ike told Milton that the UN appointment did not imply dissatisfaction with Henry Cabot Lodge, but that Dulles thought Milton's qualifications were "unique" and another position could be found for Lodge. With Milton's years of experience as a UNESCO delegate and his obvious influence with Ike, the appointment would have probably been well received. Still, Milton thought it best to decline a cabinet-level or ambassadorial office in his brother's administration.

Milton's service as Ike's special envoy to Latin America in 1953 and beyond was fascinating and enjoyable to one who had so long been absorbed with international affairs. Because Secretary Dulles was primarily involved in Europe, the Middle East, and Indochina, Milton's role in Latin-American relations was all the more significant. Prior to his five-week good-will trip, Milton had thought in terms of traditional foreign aid for development but his views changed sharply. "All the briefings that I underwent before I went to Latin America, also as a result of all the study that I had done from 1946 to 1953, had convinced me that the great need of Latin America was development capital, for industry and for agriculture as well as for social services," said Milton years later. "Further, in all of the discussions that I had in those early years with the leaders of Latin America, they never once mentioned to me the need for social change. . . . But as I traveled around and saw the situation, namely, a few and a very few fabulously rich people in a country, small if any middle class, and oceans of poor, miserable, illiterate people living constantly at the starvation level, I became exceedingly worried, and felt that orthodox aid would do no more than strengthen the prevailing order, which might make some people better off, but would leave the masses just as deprived, just as poor as they were." Despite an exhaustive five-week schedule that included wreath layings and protocol visits and official banquets, Milton was able to spend many hours in conference with South and Central American leaders and observe firsthand the social and economic schism in most of the nations. "In the long view," wrote Milton in his report, "economic cooperation extended to help the people of Latin America raise their level of well-being and further their democratic aspirations will redound to their benefit and to ours."

Milton's report became the major basis for Latin-American policy and Secretary of State Dean Rusk later credited Milton as the real father of the Kennedy administration's "Alliance for Progress." After studying the report, Ike wrote Milton: "I feel a bit diffident about complimenting anyone on a task where his competence in the particular field is so clearly superior to mine. In your knowledge of South America and your ability as a writer, I would not be bold enough to claim equality with you. . . . Finally, how does anyone go about the writing of a commendation for his own brother; that is, for a man who knows all the writer's failings, foibles, idiosyncrasies, and even stupidities?

"After all this, I still think it is completely proper for me to say that I am deeply grateful . . . and to express my belief that you have performed, again, a distinct and valuable service to your country."

The personal and philosophical bond between Milton and Ike was widely known and with President Eisenhower's heart attack in 1955, the advocacy of Milton's candidacy for 1956 seemed logical to the Citizens for Eisenhower forces. "I don't pretend to know what influences other voters," a politician told journalist Roscoe Drummond. "But I know what would influence me. I ask myself: Who is President Eisenhower's closest, most trusted, most influential adviser and I know the answer is Milton Eisenhower. If Milton Eisenhower were President, who would be his closest, most trusted, most influential adviser? The answer is that it would be Dwight D. Eisenhower. I would like that very much. I think many other voters might, too."

For Milton, the presidential boomlet was an embarrassing dilemma. On October 23, 1955, he sent Sherman Adams a letter to be given to Ike in the Denver hospital:

> This letter will be given to you by Governor Adams when your physicians permit.
>
> Before you learn it from some other source, I want to tell you that midst all the theorizing about what Republican might be nominated for the Presidency in the event you later

decided not to be a candidate for re-election, my name is occasionally being mentioned.

This is of course an expression of confidence in you.

But I am embarrassed, for each trip I make to Denver, in my natural desire to be of some small assistance, is accompanied by additional political speculation, though certainly not of stunning proportions.

You know that such little help as I have been able to give you in these recent years has been non-partisan, and devoid of personal political purpose. You know, too, that I have never considered running for political office, and would not now or later trespass upon our relationship, which is precious to me, by condoning even a modest movement in my behalf for the Republican nomination for the Presidency.

A public statement by me about this would smack of effrontery. So for the time being, I'll do no more than refrain from making additional trips to Denver, hoping that the talk about me will cease. If it does not, and if, when you go to Gettysburg, you still want me to help with the more personal phases of your work, I shall, provided of course you concur, risk the appearance of effrontery and make a brief, emphatic statement or find some other way, possibly through Jim Hagerty, of putting a durable stop to the speculation.

On October 25, came Ike's reply:

Dear Milton:

Today Sherman Adams showed me your letter of the twenty-third. Don't you know that long before I became President, you were my favorite candidate for that office?

Chapter Eighteen

THE EISENHOWER ERA

As Ike rallied from the seizure and learned that he had indeed suffered a heart attack, he had the perfect reason for retiring from the presidency in 1956. "At least," said Ike, "this settles one problem for me for good and all." In a letter to a friend in March of 1956, Ike said he probably should have issued a brief statement the preceding October "to the effect that I would determine as soon as possible whether it was physically possible for me *to finish out this term, but that I would thereafter retire from public life.*"

For five weeks, he was shielded from newspapers and news broadcasts because his doctors did not want him troubled by reports and speculation about his health, politics, and other potentially bothersome subjects. When Milton came to Denver for a weekend, he helped Ike work crossword puzzles. During this period Ike listened to such favorite records as "Stardust," "Clair de lune," and "The Merry Widow" and read Western potboilers for relaxation. Mamie, staying in a hospital room next to Ike's, was in the process of answering more than eleven thousand "get well" messages to the President. Sherman Adams went to Denver and served as Ike's chief deputy, handling policy decisions and scheduling visitors that included Vice President Nixon and Cabinet members. Press secretary James Hagerty and Ike had previously agreed that in the event of a serious illness there would be full disclosure. President Woodrow Wilson's crippling stroke in 1919 had provoked a constitutional crisis about presidential disability, and the White House had been controlled by Edith Bolling Wilson, the First Lady, and Admiral Grayson, the presidential physician.

"All of us," said Milton, "were very conscious of the severe criticism that had been leveled at Mrs. Wilson for having assumed, apparently, a good deal of authority during the President's illness. And all of us who surrounded the President were determined not to give the slightest indication, either in reality or in appearance, that I or anyone else was trying to assume such a role." Hagerty said that Ike had cited Wilson's isolation from the public during his convalescence and said, "Jim, don't let that happen to me."

Hagerty saw to it that comprehensive daily reports of Ike's condition were made available and the public even learned about his bowel movements. Dr. Paul Dudley White, a distinguished heart specialist from Boston, was called to Denver to treat Ike. White found his famous patient to be stable and in high spirits and said that within two weeks Ike could have conferences. The physician was so optimistic that he said it was conceivable that Ike would be able to run for reelection in 1956. As Ike recovered, he wrote in an October letter that he hoped Republicans would nominate a moderate who would carry out the Eisenhower programs and who could win the election. "This is the tough one," wrote Ike. Among the possible standard-bearers, Ike could approve of Milton, Deputy Defense Secretary Robert B. Anderson, Cabot Lodge, Nixon, Attorney General Herbert Brownell, and General Lucius Clay. When Ike returned to the White House on November 11, nearly 90 percent of the capital press corps predicted that he would not seek another term. Three days later, on Mamie's birthday, Ike and Mamie drove to their Gettysburg farm for further rest, and the political guessing game continued.

At his farm, overlooking the historic Civil War battlefield, Ike "had a letdown feeling that approached a sense of frustration." Though he had talked often and in definite terms about retirement, Ike now found such a prospect boring and depressing. "You know," Ike later confided to Sherman Adams, "if it hadn't been for that heart attack, I doubt if I would have been a candidate again." Within the family, Milton and John were against a reelection campaign because of the obvious strains of an election marathon and another four years in the White House, yet Mamie worried that Ike would find the winding-down process so painful and wrenching that retirement might prove more damaging to his health than a second term. Republican National Chairman Leonard Hall and General Clay argued that Ike should seek another term to assure that his policies would be continued. Senate Minority Leader William F. Knowland was making known his availability and planned to announce his candidacy in late January. If Milton or Chief Justice Warren would not campaign for the nomination, the conservative Knowland or Nixon became the main contenders. Ike told aide Emmet Hughes that Nixon had not grown in office and was not "presidential timber." With that, Ike seemed hesitant to have Nixon as a running mate again, much less support him as the presidential nominee in 1956.

In January, Ike flew to Key West for a two-week vacation that included much walking and golf in the sun. A tanned if somewhat thin Ike said, "I feel very much better—stronger—and much more able to get about." When asked about his political plans, Ike said, "All of the considerations that apply to such things are complicated. Naturally I want to confer with some of my most trusted advisers. I would say that the presidency is probably the most taxing job on earth—as far as tiring of the mind and spirit, but it also has, as I have said before, its inspirations."

On January 13, Ike hosted an informal dinner at the White House for a group that included Adams, Dulles, Lodge, Brownell, Hall, Hagerty, Humphrey, Summerfield, and Milton. Following the meal, they went to the presidential study on the second floor for a discussion about Ike's options. "Dad knew Milton's attitude," John recalled years later. "I didn't feel as strongly about it as he did. Milton wasn't given a chance to say anything that night. The other men in the room said, in all seriousness, 'You owe it to your country to help keep the finest group of people ever seen in government. It'd be a shame for the country to lose their services.'" Dulles stressed Ike's importance as a peacemaker and Lodge emphasized Ike's contribution to restoring national unity.

"I didn't know you'd all be against me," Milton said smilingly. When the others had spoken, Milton was asked to summarize the arguments for and against a second campaign, but the group had already reached a consensus. Most of the advisers left the White House optimistic that Ike would soon declare for reelection. The following week, John sent his father a four-page letter, recommending that he not make the race. Suggesting that Ike could support Warren, Humphrey, Milton Eisenhower, Nixon, Adams, or Dewey, John said, "This man would have about a 45 percent chance of election." As a son, John did not want to see his father risk another heart attack and remembered all too vividly Ike's comment, "Hell, this job killed Wilson." Yet John said his opposition to another campaign would be soothed if Ike's doctors gave their approval.

The problem of presidential disability still concerned Ike. On January 23, he wrote: "I do think people ought to give a little more thought to what the failing health of a President might do to the office and to the cause for which a whole Administration could be working.

"We well know that when advancing years and diminishing energy begin to take their toll, the last one that ever appreciates such a situation is the victim himself. Consequently, he can slow up operations, impede the work of all his subordinates, and by so doing, actually damage the cause for which he may even think he is giving some years of his life."

Washington and the nation awaited the decision of Ike's physicians. Major General Howard Snyder said on February 13 that Ike would "prefer to die with his boots on," but cautiously said that the President was not yet ready to determine his physical fitness. Dr. Paul Dudley White announced his final medical report the next day: "The President has made a good recovery. . . . Medically the chances are that the President should be able to carry on an active life satisfactorily for another five to ten years."

Two weeks later, Ike announced his decision in the presence of Mamie and their longtime friends Lucius and Marjorie Clay. He was indeed a candidate for a second term. The announcement became official on February 29 at Ike's morning press conference when he said that an affirmative answer had been reached and would be explained that night on television and radio. "I have decided," said Ike, "that if the Republican Party chooses to renominate me I shall accept the nomination. Thereafter, if the people of this country should elect me I shall continue to serve them in the office I now hold."

In a March 2 letter to Hazlett, Ike wrote:

> The whole business of making up my mind to bow my neck to what seemed to be the inevitable; of then deciding how and when to make my announcement as to a second term; and finally the intensive work of preparing notes from which to speak to the American people, has so occupied my mind and days that I simply had no chance to carry out my hope of writing to you in advance to tell you all about it.
>
> Even the giving of my consent, in 1952, to stand for the Republican nomination was not as difficult as was the decision to lay my name again before that convention. I suppose there are no two people in the world who have more than Mamie and I earnestly wanted, for a number of years, to retire to their home—a home which we did not even have until a year or so ago. . . .
>
> I wish I could tell you just exactly what finally made me decide as I did, but there was such a vast combination of circumstances and factors that seemed to me to have a bearing on the problem—and at times the positive and negative were delicately balanced—that I cannot say for certain which particular one was decisive.
>
> One—and this has been mentioned to no one else—had to do with a guilty feeling on my own part that I had failed to bring forward and establish a logical successor for myself. This failure was of course not intentional. To the contrary, I struggled hard to acquaint the public with the qualities of a very able group of young men. . . . But the evidence became clear that I had not been able to get any individual to be recognized as a natural or logical candidate for the Presidency.
>
> Parenthetically, I have just about decided that a first-term President—unless he has been publicly repudiated from the

beginning of his term—can scarcely get his own party to think in terms of a candidate other than himself.

Though Ike's renomination was a certainty, the fate of Vice President Nixon suddenly was very much in doubt. Ike offered Nixon a Cabinet position—Secretary of Defense—instead of a second term and said publicly that he had asked the Vice President "to chart out his own course." In a conversation with Nixon, Ike had cited recent public-opinion polls and expressed disappointment that Nixon had trailed Earl Warren for the Republican nomination and Stevenson in a hypothetical presidential election. A shaken Nixon said he would consider the matter, but he recognized that Ike considered him expendable. Only a few weeks before Nixon had been a prominent contender for the presidency and the previous September the nation came to realize just how close Nixon was to becoming President. An earlier Vice President, John Nance Garner, had observed that the office "isn't worth a pitcher of warm spit." However, Nixon relished the Cabinet meetings, his participation in the National Security Council, and his much-publicized tours to exotic foreign capitals where he met heads of state. To Ike, Nixon had a certain usefulness as his liaison with state and congressional Republicans and as the knife man against Democrats and even Nixon's onetime ally, Joseph McCarthy. In the 1954 election Nixon's rhetoric had been particularly strident as he attacked Democrats as the "party of treason" and swung away at Truman and Stevenson, whom he suggested were soft on Communism. Stevenson described Nixon as "McCarthy in a white collar" and House Speaker Sam Rayburn said, "His name is mud up here." When Nixon praised Earl Warren in a speech as a great *Republican* Chief Justice, Ike himself took issue with the Vice President's partisanship.

Since the 1952 fund scandal, Nixon had lost the confidence of Ike's inner circle and his sly innuendoes and campaign-circuit half truths served to remind them of the "Tricky Dick" image. Milton Eisenhower felt that Nixon was devoid of statesmanlike qualities and overly political. His reservations about Nixon were well known in political circles, and one national news magazine published an article with the title "Will Ike's Brother Stop Nixon?"

Another of Ike's confidants, General Clay, opposed Nixon and vetoed an effort to change the Citizens for Eisenhower to the Citizens for Eisenhower and Nixon. During the past four years, Nixon had been treated as an outsider and had never been invited to the parlor floor of the White House, and at a Republican picnic on the Gettysburg farm Ike chortled at Nixon's comment that he had never been inside the farmhouse. Ike's faith in Nixon was wavering and he was giving serious thought to Deputy Defense Secretary Robert B. Anderson as Nixon's replacement. Anderson was a conservative Texan and a former Democrat who had been a highly successful lawyer and oil executive before joining the Eisenhower administration. Young (forty-five), a skilled administrator, and a presidential favorite, Anderson shared Ike's distaste for politics, which made him all the more attractive. On April 9, a Gallup poll was published that underscored Nixon's weaknesses: only 19 percent said Nixon would help the Republican ticket and 32 percent said he would hurt. On a related question, a majority of independents told Gallup interviewers that Nixon would not make a good President. There had been numerous precedents for incumbent Presidents to drop their running mate in a second campaign: Lincoln, in 1864 had replaced Hannibal Hamlin with Andrew Johnson; and in 1944 Franklin Roosevelt permitted an "open convention" to choose Senator Harry Truman over controversial Vice President Henry Wallace. A humiliated Nixon, embarrassed by Ike's public vagueness about his future, had decided against accepting a Cabinet portfolio and was interested in two high-salaried job offers from the private sector. With some bitterness, Nixon told friends that he was about to announce his retirement from politics.

Republican National Chairman Hall, a Nixon supporter, urged the Vice President to postpone any such action. Conservative senators and congressmen endorsed Nixon's renomination and in the New Hampshire primary Nixon received a heavy write-in vote. On April 26, Nixon went to the White House and told Ike that he wanted another term as Vice President. Given Nixon's support from the party's conservative wing, and Hall's prediction that Nixon's dumping would split the party, Ike responded warmly and expressed delight with the decision. Nixon said later that the

New Hampshire vote was a turning point in his ordeal and his spirits were further lifted by an impressive write-in vote in the Oregon primary.

In the meantime, Stevenson had been knocked back from his position as Democratic front runner when he was upset by Kefauver in the Minnesota primary. The race for the Democratic nomination was the most vigorously contested in memory with a bruising series of primaries between Kefauver and Stevenson with both men fighting hard. Stevenson's victories in the climactic Oregon and California primaries eliminated Kefauver from contention, but New York Governor Averell Harriman remained a candidate and won the endorsement of former President Truman. "It never occurred to me that I could have beaten Eisenhower," Harriman told me in a 1976 interview. "But I had more vigorous ideas about the Democratic Party than Stevenson. Stevenson was very popular and a delightful man, but not as vigorously liberal on the issues."

The presidential campaign changed suddenly on June 9 when Ike became seriously ill and underwent major surgery to relieve an obstruction of the small intestine. With his second major illness in less than a year, Ike demonstrated his own mortality and there was renewed speculation that he would decide not to run. The second illness, ileitis, seemed less troublesome to the public than the heart attack, yet one of Ike's surgeons said that it was a grave, sometimes fatal illness. Hagerty did not make Ike's doctors available for public comment and did his best to minimize the severity of the presidential condition. To a remarkable degree, Hagerty succeeded, and Ike's renomination was never seriously threatened.

"I don't want to complain unduly," Ike wrote on July 12, "but the first days after the operation were really uncomfortable. . . . Now that I am here at Gettysburg and can detect a daily increase in strength and vitality, I am ready to put the whole nasty business behind me."

On August 1, a lean and somewhat gaunt Ike held his first press conference in two months and discussed his health in detail. Chicago *Daily News* correspondent William McGaffin told Ike that his friends and neighbors in Gettysburg revered him but hoped he would not run because they feared Ike would not live out a second term. "Frankly," said Ike, "I don't think it is too important to the individual how his end comes, and certainly he can't dictate the time. What we are talking about here is the importance to the country, and it happens that at this moment the Republican Party apparently thinks I am still important to them and to the country. Since I believe so much in the Republican Party, and I believe that it needed rebuilding so badly—an effort which I have been making, as you well know—I said I would continue to try. This is a decision that the American people are going to have to face. I am flattered by what you tell me about my friends and neighbors at Gettysburg, but I have made up my mind this is the thing I should try, and we will see what the American people have to say about it."

Ike's illness reopened the debate about Nixon's executive capabilities and a second "Dump Nixon" movement began with its leader, Harold Stassen, taking a leave of absence as White House disarmament adviser. In conversations with such associates as Arthur Larson and Emmet John Hughes, Ike expressed no regret over Stassen's anti-Nixon activity. "I told Harold he should feel entirely free," Ike told Hughes, "so long as he did not purport to speak in my name." Ike noted that Nixon "just hasn't grown" and told Hughes that a Cabinet secretaryship would be more appropriate for Nixon than the vice presidency. To Larson, Ike mentioned a New York *Times* report that Nixon was unpopular with younger people and quoted a veteran politician as telling him that Nixon might cost Eisenhower 4 percent of the vote. If Eisenhower had reservations about Nixon, he would not go public with them: The party would determine its vice-presidential candidate.

Stassen urged the nomination of Governor Christian Herter of Massachusetts and sent a seven-page letter to all delegates recommending an Eisenhower-Herter ticket. California Governor Goodwin Knight eagerly came out against Nixon and such Eisenhower stalwarts as former Colorado Governor Dan Thornton and Maryland Governor Theodore McKeldin began angling for the vice presidency. Stassen's activity, however, had been loosely organized and the reaction on Capitol Hill was swift and harsh. Twenty members of Congress called for Stassen's resignation from the Administration and he, not Nixon, became the center of controversy.

Meanwhile, Leonard Hall and Sherman Adams deprived Stassen of his candidate by persuading Governor Herter to nominate Nixon at the San Francisco convention with the promise of a high State Department appointment.

At the convention, Stassen seemed a quixotic figure tilting at windmills. He was barred from Ike's suite at the St. Francis Hotel until an ultimate humiliation: agreeing to drop the "Dump Nixon" campaign and to second the Vice President's nomination.

Eisenhower and Nixon were renominated at the Cow Palace one week after the Democrats had nominated Stevenson and Kefauver in a turbulent convention in Chicago.

Although the presidential candidates were the same, the men were different. Stevenson was the attacker and Ike was defending his social-welfare domestic policies and his firm but noninterventionist foreign policy. In a letter, Ike said that "the Stevenson-Kefauver combination is, in some ways, about the sorriest and weakest we have ever had run for the two top offices in the land."

Stevenson's campaign lacked the style and eloquence of his brilliant 1952 speeches and the candidate seemed at times as sluggish as a punched-out club fighter. Searching for a theme, Stevenson lacked consistency and could be hawkish in urging a greater defense capability and blaming the Administration for losing Southeast Asia to Communism, and dovish in calling for a nuclear test ban and the end of the peacetime military draft. On issues of war and peace, Eisenhower maintained his unique advantage and retorted that a nuclear test ban without international supervision would be a disaster and that abolishing the draft would be letting down America's allies. Stevenson's most effective blows were against Nixon, whom he described as "shifty," "rash," and a "man of many masks." And referring to Ike's uncertain health, Stevenson asked, "Are we seriously asked to trust the decision over the hydrogen bomb to Nixon?" On Ike's instructions, Nixon was campaigning on a "higher level" and projecting the image of a "new Nixon," more mature and responsible than the street fighter of campaigns past. Surprisingly, the most reckless smear of the campaign was made by Stevenson in September when he accused Milton of assuming "special responsibility" for "appeasing" Argentine dictator Juan Perón and enabling the South American to deposit more than $100 million in Swiss banks. Though Ike had refrained from mentioning Stevenson's name, this attack on Milton enraged him as nothing else had. By comparison, the attack by Joseph McCarthy on Milton was insignificent, for the Wisconsin senator lacked Stevenson's stature. Milton had taken pains to avoid dealing with such Latin-American despots as Fulgencio Batista, Rafael Trujillo, "Papa Doc" Duvalier, and Perón. His 1953 visit to Argentina had not involved any secret treaties or loans with Perón, but Milton had negotiated the restoration of American press rights that the dictator had suspended. The day after Stevenson's charge, Ike responded that the Truman administration had made $130 million in loans to Perón and that the attack on his brother was unjustified. For the rest of the campaign, Ike continued to refer to the Stevenson blunder. In a telephone conversation with Milton, Ike asked his younger brother if he should follow the advice of Hall and Adams in getting even tougher with Stevenson for the criticism of Milton. Though Stevenson had done him a disservice, Milton told Ike that it was a dead issue and no further mention should be made. Twenty years later, Milton was less passive about the Stevenson incident. "He was a goddamn liar," said Milton. "When he learned it was a lie, he never admitted it. He never had the decency to withdraw the charge. He was getting desperate. He couldn't stand up to President Eisenhower so he had to attack Milton Eisenhower. . . . I was disappointed. I think on the whole he was a smart man with sound intellectual qualities. Someone may have misinformed him. But when he knew the charge was untrue he didn't do anything about it."

In the closing days of the campaign, world affairs diverted the attention of most Americans. For months, tensions had been building in the Middle East as Egypt's dynamic new leader, Gamal Abdel Nasser, turned to the Soviet Union for military weapons that were being used against Israel. The Eisenhower administration, which had spurned earlier requests for Egyptian military aid, offered to help fund a billion-dollar high dam at Aswan on the Nile that would irrigate more than two million acres for agricultural development. Dulles suddenly withdrew the loan in July, distrusting Nasser's Soviet ties and doubting Egyptian ability to repay the loan. Angrily denouncing the United States, Nasser vowed to build the dam by nationalizing the Anglo-French-controlled Suez Canal and using the Canal's revenues for the Aswan project. British and French leaders reacted sharply to Nasser's seizure of the Canal and they informed Ike that force might be required to regain their holdings. British Prime Minister Anthony Eden, who had been Churchill's longtime foreign secretary and one of the heroic voices against Fascism in the 1930s, remembered the appeasement policy of Neville Chamberlain at Munich and compared Nasser to Hitler. Ike gave Eden no encouragement and suggested that his wartime associate was overreacting. "I personally feel sure that the American reaction would be severe," Ike wrote Eden on July 31. "Permit me to suggest," Ike wrote the Prime Minister on September 8, "that when you use phrases in connection with the Suez affair, like 'ignoble end to our long history' in describing the possible future of your great country, you are making of Nasser a much more important figure than he is." Ike and Dulles called for the organization of a users' association to guarantee the operation of the Canal, with payment to Egypt for its facilities.

After three months of stalemate, Britain and France had grown impatient by late October. That the British were no longer consulting with him about military intervention gave Ike hope for a peaceful solution, and he said that "a very great crisis is behind us." But Britain, fully aware of Ike's opposition, was planning its last great military adventure with the gamble that he would be a friendly neutral.

The Suez war exploded on October 29 when Israel invaded the Sinai Peninsula followed by British and French invasion of the Canal Zone. Ike wrote a friend on November 2:

> The Mideast thing is a terrible mess. Ever since July twenty-sixth, when Nasser took over the canal, I have argued for a negotiated settlement. It does not seem to me that there is present in the case anything that justifies the action that Britain, France, and Israel apparently concerted among themselves and have initiated. . . . The real point is that Britain, France, and Israel had come to believe—probably correctly—that Nasser was their worst enemy in the Mideast and that

until he was removed or deflated, they would have no peace. I do not quarrel with the idea that there is justification for such fears, but I have insisted long and earnestly that you cannot resort to force in international relationships because of your fear of what might happen in the future. . . .

I think that France and Britain have made a terrible mistake. Because they had such a poor case, they have isolated themselves from the good opinion of the world and it will take them many years to recover. . . .

All these thoughts I communicated to Eden time and again. It was undoubtedly because of his knowledge of our bitter opposition to using force in the matter that when he finally decided to undertake the plan, he just went completely silent. Actually, the British had partially dispersed some of their concentrations in the Mideast and, while we know the trouble was not over, we did think that, so far as Britain and France were concerned, there was some easing of the situation.

Ike appealed to the United Nations for a cease-fire which Britain and France vetoed in the Security Council. The Soviets, capitalizing on the split among the Western allies, proposed joint Soviet-American operations against the British and French, a suggestion that was described by Ike as "unthinkable," and he warned Moscow that Russian intervention would be met with force. On November 2, the UN General Assembly voted overwhelmingly for a cease-fire and within four days the British and French had agreed. The Suez crisis would soon bring the resignation of an aging and sickly Anthony Eden as Prime Minister, thus ending a long and distinguished career, but for Britain it also marked the end of five centuries as a major world power. France's defeats in 1940 and 1954 had similarly diminished its position as a world power. For Ike, the peaceful settlement was a signal triumph: a dramatic repudiation of gunboat diplomacy and Victorian imperialism that reiterated his credentials as a peacemaker. The temporary rift with Britain had troubled Ike and he wrote Churchill: "I shall never be happy until our old-time closeness has been restored."

During the same week of the Suez crisis, Soviet tanks withdrew from Budapest and Moscow announced a willingness to withdraw all troops from Hungary in the wake of a popular revolution. When the new regime announced Hungary's withdrawal from the Warsaw Pact—its alliance with the Soviet Union—Khrushchev ordered his Russian soldiers to return and the young, bold government was deposed and Premier Imre Nagy and some thirty thousand Hungarians were to be slain. "Poor fellows, poor fellows," said Ike to New York *Times* columnist C. L. Sulzberger, "I think about them all the time. I wish there were some way of helping them." But assistance to the Hungarian "freedom fighters" would have risked another world war and Ike's foreign policy was calculated to avoid any such catastrophe. Thus American opposition to the Soviets was confined to the United Nations where the General Assembly voted 50 to 8 for Russian withdrawal from Hungary only to be vetoed by the Soviets at the Security Council.

On November 6, while Suez and Hungary were still in the headlines, the nation voted. Ike had been supremely confident and laughed at John's comment that the outcome might be in doubt. If Ike was reasonably certain of victory, he wanted his last election to be nothing less than a landslide. "Unless I win by a comfortable majority (one that could not be significantly increased or decreased in the next few days by any amount of speaking on either side), I would not want to be elected at all," Ike wrote a friend on November 2. "Since by the Constitution this is my final term, my influence in these next four years with my own party is going to be determined by their feeling as to how popular I am with the multitudes. If they feel that I am a rapidly 'waning' star, then they would be disposed to take the bit in their teeth regardless of my opinions. . . . In almost every project some Democratic help will be absolutely necessary to get it accomplished. Again this strength can be marshaled on both sides of the aisle, *only* if it is generally believed that I am in a position to go to the people over the heads of the congressmen—and either help them or cause them trouble in their districts.

"For these two reasons I think that my only opportunity for doing anything really worthwhile is to win by a comfortable majority. This belief, incidentally, was an additional reason for my deciding to do a bit of traveling in the campaign. It also offered me a chance to prove to the American people that I am a rather healthy individual."

On election night, it was soon apparent that the tense international situation had added to Ike's already massive appeal. He won the largest popular vote in American history—35,590,472 votes—a plurality of 9.5 million, winning 41 states with 457 electoral votes. Ike received surprisingly large support from blacks and Catholics, blocs that traditionally voted Democratic, and he became the first Republican in nearly a century to win Louisiana. Watching the returns in the presidential suite of Washington's Sheraton Park, Ike became impatient waiting for Stevenson's concession and again referred to his opponent as a monkey. When the defeated candidate finally conceded, Ike made his triumphant appearance in the ballroom with his arms raised in his trademark victory salute. "With whatever talents the good God has given me, with whatever strength there is within me," said Ike, "I will continue to do just one thing: to work for 168 million Americans here at home—and for peace in the world."

Though his popular mandate was greater than his 1952 landslide it was even more of a personal victory, for the Republicans had failed to recapture either house of Congress. In Oregon, where Ike had campaigned for his former Interior Secretary, Douglas McKay, the voters had chosen maverick Democrat Wayne Morse for the Senate. In Washington, Eisenhower stalwart Arthur Langlie lost the Senate race to incumbent Warren Magnuson. Edgar Eisenhower had written Ike that both McKay and Langlie were trailing and that a presidential campaign swing probably would not make much difference. Ike went to the Pacific Northwest despite his brother's advice and the election results confirmed that Republican candidates needed more than a hero's coattails to oust entrenched Democratic senators. "Frankly, I think if I had known that we were going to get a Democratic Congress, I probably would have refused to run on the theory that it would have been better to have a Democratic President and have the responsibility fixed," Ike confided to Senator Styles Bridges in the spring of 1957.

In fact, Ike's relationship with Democratic Senate Majority

Leader Lyndon Johnson and House Speaker Sam Rayburn had been friendly and generally cooperative. The Republican leadership—Knowland and Martin—was less congenial and Ike did not enjoy his meetings with them. John Eisenhower, years later, would say that Knowland had been a particular thorn. "I think my party ought to trust me a little bit more when I put not only my life's work, but my reputation and everything else on the line," Ike snapped during a meeting with Senator Bridges.

As his second administration began, Ike stood uneasily at the center of the civil-rights revolution. Blacks had shown a new militancy in their struggle for equality and justice. In 1956, a charismatic twenty-six-year-old minister, Martin Luther King, Jr., emerged as a symbol of the movement with his inspiring leadership in the boycott of segregated public buses in Montgomery, Alabama. So effective was the boycott that the bus company's revenues declined 65 percent and downtown stores were similarly devastated. King and other boycott leaders were convicted by a Montgomery court of violating an antilabor law that prohibited boycotts and the city also demanded and received an injunction that forbade blacks from using car pools. In November, just when King was beginning to lose hope, the Supreme Court declared that the "Jim Crow" segregation laws were unconstitutional. The boycott had been won. Under Chief Justice Earl Warren, the Court had entered the most activist period in its history with profound social consequences. In 1954, Warren himself had written the opinion in the landmark school desegregation case *Brown* v. *Board of Education of Topeka* which overturned the "separate but equal" doctrine. "We conclude that in the field of public education," wrote Warren, "the doctrine of 'separate but equal' has no place. Separate educational facilities are inherently unequal."

Ike's appointment of Warren may have been his greatest contribution to the advancement of social justice and civil rights. In later years Ike said privately that the Warren appointment was "the biggest damfool mistake I ever made" though he conceded that Warren would probably be remembered favorably by history. The academic community had denounced the Warren appointment in 1953 and conservatives were vitriolic in their opposition. Edgar Eisenhower had written Ike that naming Warren would be "a tragedy." In a letter to his older brother, Ike wrote: "I wonder how often you have met and talked seriously with Governor Warren. This I have done on a number of occasions, because, from the very beginning of my acquaintanceship with him, I had him in mind for an appointment to the high court—although, of course, I never anticipated an early vacancy in the Chief Justice position. To my mind, he is a statesman. We have too few of these. Many people condemn him because of a particular medical plan he advocated for California. On this point, I would have, of course, disagreed with him, but I find that, at least, he never advocated such a thing nationally.

"Well—here is a man of national stature . . . of unimpeachable integrity, of middle-of-the-road views, and with a splendid record during his years in active law work."

Warren's judicial activism astonished Ike and the President later decided not to appoint anyone to the high Court without previous service on a lower federal court or a state supreme court. In Warren's memoirs published posthumously in 1977, the Chief Justice said that Ike had personally lobbied for the segregation states during the Brown case by inviting Warren to a White House dinner which the counsel for the states, John W. Davis, also attended. According to Warren, Ike had fulsome praise for Davis and on one occasion took Warren by the arm and said, "Speaking of the Southern segregationists: These are not bad people. All they are concerned about is to see that their sweet little girls are not required to sit in school alongside some big overgrown Negroes."

When the Court made its historic decision, Warren said he became *persona non grata* at the White House. Ike privately thundered that the decision had set back racial progress fifteen years and might well lead to social disintegration. On a personal level, he was disappointed that such old friends as South Carolina Governor James F. Byrnes, the former U.S. Supreme Court Justice and Secretary of State, were no longer speaking to him because of their bitterness over the Brown decision. "I personally think the decision was wrong," Ike told his assistant Arthur Larson. Despite his misgivings about the decision, Ike would not publicly defy the Court as his Republican successors Richard Nixon and Gerald

Ford would do in the 1970s over the volatile issue of school busing. Indeed, Ike took considerable pains to conceal his resentment of the decision and to observe the separation of powers. In June of 1957 Ike was distressed by published reports that he was at odds with Warren. On June 21, Ike wrote the Chief Justice: "I was told this morning that some enterprising reporter has a story that at a private party I severely criticized the Supreme Court, expressing anger. I have no doubt that in private conversation someone did hear me express amazement about one decision, but I have never even hinted at a feeling such as anger. To do so would imply not only that I knew the law but questioned motives. Neither of these things is true.

"So while resolving that even in private conversations I shall be more careful of my language, I do want you to know that if any such story appeared, it was a distortion."

In 1957, Ike pushed the first Civil Rights Act since Reconstruction through a reluctant Congress. A year earlier, southern senators had stalled the Administration's proposal that would have outlawed statutes that prevented blacks from voting in national elections. Senate Majority Leader Johnson had weakened the bill by adding an amendment that permitted jury trials in contempt cases, but Ike held that such a compromise would nullify the new law, and the Administration negotiated further with Johnson to break the stalemate. Johnson agreed to a compromise that left the question of jury trials in voting rights cases up to the regional federal judges. The Civil Rights Act of 1957 established a Civil Rights Division in the Justice Department and an independent Commission on Civil Rights with subpoena powers.

During the debate over the civil-rights law, Ike wrote Hazlett:

> I think that no other single event has so disturbed the domestic scene in many years as did the Supreme Court's decision of 1954 in the school segregation case. That decision and similar ones earlier and later in point of time have interpreted the Constitution in such fashion as to put heavier responsibilities than before on the Federal government in the matter of assuring to each citizen his guaranteed Constitutional

rights. My approach to the many problems has been dictated by several obvious truths:

a. Laws are rarely effective unless they represent the will of the majority. In our prohibition experiment, we even saw local opinion openly and successfully defy Federal authority even though national public opinion then seemed to support the whole theory of prohibition.

b. When emotions are deeply stirred, logic and reason must operate gradually and with consideration for human feelings or we will have a resultant disaster rather than human advancement.

c. School segregation itself was, according to the Supreme Court decision of 1896, completely Constitutional until the reversal of that decision was accomplished in 1954. The decision of 1896 gave a cloak of legality to segregation in all its forms. As a result, the social, economic and political patterns of the South were considered by most whites, especially by those in that region, as not only respectable but completely legal and ethical.

d. After three score years of living under these patterns, it was impossible to expect complete and instant reversal of conduct by mere decision of the Supreme Court. The Court itself recognized this and provided a plan for the desegregation of schools which it believed to be moderate but effective.

The plan of the Supreme Court to accomplish integration gradually and sensibly seems to me to provide the only possible answer if we are to consider on the one hand the customs and fears of a great section of our population, and on the other the binding effect that Supreme Court decisions must have on all of us if our form of government is to survive and prosper. Consequently the plan that I have advanced for Congressional consideration on this touchy matter was conceived in the thought that only moderation in legal compulsions, accompanied by a stepped-up program of education, could bring about the result that every loyal American should seek.

I think that some of the language used in the attempt to translate my basic purposes into legislative provisions has probably been too broad. Certainly it has been subject to varying interpretations. This I think can be corrected in the Congress.

But I hold to the basic purpose. There must be respect for the Constitution—which means the Supreme Court's interpretation of the Constitution—or we shall have chaos. We cannot possibly imagine a successful form of government in which every individual citizen would have the right to interpret the Constitution according to his own convictions, beliefs and prejudices. Chaos would develop. This I believe with all my heart—and shall always act accordingly.

Ike's failure to intervene in 1956 when the University of Alabama expelled Autherine Lucy, a black student who had been admitted under court order, gave some comfort to segregationists. So did his aloofness when the high school in Mansfield, Texas, defied a federal court order to desegregate. In 1957, however, Governor Orval Faubus of Arkansas so brazenly defied the Constitution that Ike could no longer stand passively above the battle. Little Rock's Central High School was to be integrated in September following the orders of the local federal district court. The school board and the mayor favored the plan and it was anticipated that the nine black students would be admitted quietly and without incident. But Orval Faubus decided otherwise and correctly predicted that his action would "divide this state and eventually divide the nation." Oddly enough, Faubus had never been a race baiter and was elected governor as a political moderate. What Faubus was doing had little to do with his feelings about blacks, which had previously been friendly. The little governor from Greasy Creek recognized that a confrontation with the federal government might be exploited for his own political gain and work to his advantage in his coming bid for reelection. When the White Citizens Council began a campaign against Little Rock's desegregation plan, Faubus joined the white supremacists. The day before schools would open, Faubus said there would be violence if the federal plan were carried out. He called up the Arkansas National Guard, sending soldiers with bayonets to keep the black students from attending Central High School.

In July, Ike had made clear that he did not want to use federal force to desegregate schools. "I have been informed by various lawyers that the power does exist," he said. "But . . . I can't imagine any set of circumstances that would ever induce me to send Federal troops into a Federal court and into any area to enforce the orders of a Federal court, because I believe that the common sense of America will never require it. Now, there may be that kind of authority resting somewhere, but certainly I am not seeking any additional authority of that kind, and I would never believe that it would be a wise thing to do in this country."

Ike and Mamie were on a working vacation in Newport, Rhode Island, when the Little Rock crisis began and instead of a leisurely golfing holiday President Eisenhower soon found himself with the gravest challenge to federal authority since the Civil War. Anxious to avoid a collision with Faubus, Ike agreed to meet with the governor at Newport. During their meeting, Faubus was properly deferential and said he would make clear his respect for federal law. For his part, Ike said prompt action should be taken to allow the black students to attend school. When Faubus left, Ike had reason to be optimistic; yet within minutes he learned from an Arkansas congressman that the governor's position was unchanged. The Guardsmen were staying. Ike had been embarrassed by Faubus, a onetime fruit tramp, in full view of the nation and world. In Little Rock, angry mobs threatened the young blacks and classes were canceled when a federal injunction removed the Arkansas troops.

Faubus committed his most serious blunder in turning a political controversy into a military confrontation. In all his years in military command and the presidency, Ike had never been a moralist. If left to his own inclinations, Ike would have avoided the dramatic Little Rock confrontation. But when Faubus dispatched armed troops against the authority of the federal government and the Constitution, it transcended politics and became a direct challenge to Ike's leadership. The law must be enforced, Ike told his brother and Milton strongly agreed.

As Commander in Chief, Ike acted decisively, calling for the mob "to cease and desist" and warning that force would be met with greater force. When the white harassment persisted the next morning, Ike federalized the Arkansas National Guard, bringing all ten thousand members under his command, and ordered a thousand United States paratroopers to occupy the high school. The black students finally were able to attend classes and the troops remained until December to protect them.

Ike's assertion of federal authority brought heated protest from some southern leaders, including Senator Richard Russell of Georgia. On September 27, Ike wrote Russell: "Few times in my life have I felt as saddened as when the obligations of my office required me to order the use of force within a state to carry out the decisions of a federal court. My conviction is that had the police powers of the State of Arkansas been utilized not to frustrate the orders of the Court but to support them, the ensuing violence and open disrespect for the law and the Federal Judiciary would never have occurred. The Arkansas National Guard could have handled the situation with ease had it been instructed to do so. . . . When a state, by seeking to frustrate the orders of a Federal Court, encourages mobs of extremists to flout the orders of a Federal Court, and when a State refuses to utilize its police powers to protect against mobs persons who are peaceably exercising their rights under the Constitution as defined in such Court orders, the oath of office of the President requires that he take action to give that protection. Failure to act in such a case would be tantamount to acquiescence in anarchy and the dissolution of the union.

"I must say that I completely fail to comprehend your comparison of our troops to Hitler's storm troopers. In one case military power was used to further the ambitions and purposes of a ruthless dictator; in the other to preserve the institutions of free government."

Most of the nation supported Ike's intervention in Little Rock. A Gallup poll published shortly afterward reported that 64 percent of the American public thought that Ike had done the right thing—only in the South did a majority (53 percent) oppose him

—and outside the region 74 percent said that the troops should have been sent in. Adlai Stevenson said Ike had acted correctly and the former governor expressed hope that the President would appeal to the nation's consciousness and inspire new attitudes about race relations. Stevenson was offered a presidential appointment as a member of the new Civil Rights Commission, but after much discussion with his advisers, he turned it down.

To the black community, which had given Ike more than 40 percent of the vote in both presidential campaigns, Eisenhower's intervention demonstrated that segregation might indeed be on the way out. Martin Luther King, Jr., congratulated him: "I wish to express my sincere support for the stand you have taken to restore law and order in Little Rock, Arkansas. In the long run, justice finally must spring from a new moral climate, yet spiritual forces cannot emerge in a situation of mob violence. You should know that the overwhelming majority of Southerners, Negro and white, stand firmly behind your resolute action. The pen of history will record that even the small and confused minority that oppose integration with violence will live to see that your action has been of great benefit to our nation and to the Christian tradition of fair play and brotherhood."

The following year Governor Faubus closed Little Rock's high schools to prevent further desegregation, but a federal court ruled his action as unconstitutional and Little Rock police maintained order when integration was finally implemented. The governor's demagoguery and subterfuge brought him national notoriety and made him something of a folk hero to rabble-rousing southern whites. Not only did he win a third term in 1958—with 69 percent of the vote—but he was to ride his Little Rock prominence to four more two-year terms. His success in Arkansas was not lost on other regional politicians, and Alabama's George Wallace would challenge federal authority during the Kennedy administration in an unsubtle effort to repeat the Faubus triumphs.

The Eisenhower administration had made two historic breakthroughs: the first civil-rights law in eighty-two years and the establishment of integration as a constitutional right. No President since Lincoln had such opportunity to give inspired leadership on racial relations, but Ike was neither a social philosopher nor a social innovator and the initiative for further change would have to come from others. Yet Ike did not miss the significance of the coming civil-rights revolution, particularly in the South. In May of 1960, he defended the movement in a letter to Lucy Eisenhower—the blond, right-wing, matronly wife of Edgar—whose politics went beyond her husband's constitutional conservatism to embrace neoracism. She had written her brother-in-law that the lunch counter sit-ins in the South were minor incidents undeserving of attention and that the NAACP was a Communist-front organization. "I think you are mistaken," wrote Ike, "if you think that Southerners are completely unaware of these incidents [sit-ins]. Within the last weeks I have been in Florida and Georgia at least three times. I have heard the matter discussed by my friends in those areas. . . . I think most Southerners agree that we must make some progress toward achieving political and economic equality among all individuals regardless of race."

The space age officially began on October 4, 1957, when the Soviet Union launched Sputnik I, the first man-made satellite, and a month later put a much larger satellite in orbit that carried a live dog. America and the West were startled and a crisis in national confidence resulted. In addition to the wounded pride, there were fears that the balance of power had shifted in the Cold War and that the Soviets now controlled the skies. Nuclear scientist Edward Teller, the Dr. Strangelove prototype, whose technological brilliance had contributed to the development of the hydrogen bomb, said America had lost "a battle more important and greater than Pearl Harbor." Senate Majority Leader Johnson said, "We have got to admit frankly and without evasion that the Soviets have beaten us at our own game—daring scientific advances in the atomic age." Clare Boothe Luce, a prominent Eisenhower Republican, said, "The beep of the Russian sputniks is an outer-space raspberry to a decade of American pretensions that the American way of life is a gilt-edged guarantee of our national superiority."

The sudden inferiority complex baffled Ike. "No one ever suggested [a satellite] to me as anything of a race," he said, "except, of course, more than once we would say, well, there is going to be a great psychological advantage in world politics to putting the thing up. But that didn't seem to be a reason, in view of the real scientific character of our development, for just trying to grow hysterical about it." According to John Eisenhower, his father had been briefed about the probability of the launching of Sputnik, but did not anticipate American reaction. "Where his difficulties came was that he did not evaluate the psychological impact that this thing would have on the American people," John recalled years later. "It was a mystery to him then. . . . He never for a moment regarded this as a race and he underestimated the shock it caused when the Sputnik went up."

Public discontent heightened after the 1,100-pound Sputnik II blasted into orbit in November. After consulting with scientists, Ike attempted to calm the nation with a presidential address on the post-Sputnik world. There was, he said, no cause for panic.

Calling the Sputniks "an achievement of the first importance," Ike was quick to add that "earth satellites, in themselves, have no direct present effect upon the nation's security." There was, however, military significance in the launchings, for Ike conceded that "the Soviets are quite likely ahead in some missile and special areas, and are obviously ahead of us in satellite development." But, he said, "As of today the over-all military strength of the free world is distinctly greater than that of the Communist countries."

Near the end of his talk, Ike announced the appointment of Dr. James Killian, president of the Massachusetts Institute of Technology, as special assistant to the President for science and technology. "This man, who will be aided by a staff of scientists and a strong advisory group of outstanding experts reporting to him and to me, will have the active responsibility of helping me follow through on the program of scientific improvement of our defenses." The challenge of Sputnik, Ike said, would be better met by better and more intensive education than larger defense appropriations. "Defense today is expensive, and growing more so. We cannot afford waste. . . . Certainly, we need to feel a high sense of urgency. But this does not mean that we should mount our charger and try to ride off in all directions at once."

To regain lost prestige, top priority was given to escalating America's own satellite program. There were some embarrassing setbacks—delays, postponements, and, in December, the Vanguard satellite crashed and burned on its Cape Canaveral launching pad. On January 31, 1958, almost four months after Sputnik I, Explorer I was launched by a Jupiter rocket and America was finally competitive in space.

On November 25, 1957, Ike met King Mohammed V of Morocco at National Airport, escorted him to Blair House, and then returned to the White House. While sitting at his Oval Office desk, Ike suddenly became dizzy, his vision blurred, and a pen slipped from his hand. As he called his secretary, Ann Whitman, Ike found that he could not express himself clearly. Mrs. Whitman and General Andrew Goodpaster, a presidential assistant, convinced him to go upstairs to his bedroom. Ike had suffered a stroke—his third critical illness in little more than two years—and it had come at a time of grave national and world crises. Sherman Adams soberly apprised Vice President Nixon of Ike's condition, and it was arranged that Nixon would preside at the state dinner for King Mohammed that evening. John Eisenhower, then stationed at the Pentagon, rushed to the White House when notified by Goodpaster and spent the evening with his father. Ike mentioned the forthcoming NATO summit conference in Paris scheduled in early December and said that he would have to resign if he could not attend with the other heads of state. The next morning, Ike became so frustrated in trying to regain his speech that he threw a tantrum and pounded the bed with his fists. In the meantime, there were rumors that he was incapacitated, that he was dying, that he would resign. Adams had told Nixon that he might shortly have to assume the presidency. Senator Wayne Morse, for one, suggested that Ike resign. Walter Lippmann made the proposal that Nixon assume Ike's duties for the duration of the President's convalescence. Later that week Ike determined that he would attend the NATO Conference as a test of his capability to continue in office. His family and doctors argued that it was reckless and would put too much of a strain on Ike after the stroke. Having made a remarkably quick recovery, Ike overruled them and went to Paris, arriving there on December 14.

The streets of Paris were crowded as thousands turned out to welcome the erstwhile Supreme Commander. Ike seemed genuinely moved by the outpouring of affection. British Prime Minister Harold Macmillan wrote in his diary that Ike "had a great reception from the people of Paris. He stood up in the open car, waved his arms to the crowd and generally delighted them all with his manner." The next day Ike and Macmillan, his wartime political aide, met privately at the American Embassy and the President disclosed that he would have resigned if his physicians had forbidden him from making the European journey. Because of the close bond between Ike and Macmillan, Anglo-American relations that had been shattered during Suez had been fully restored. A highlight of Ike's visit was a sentimental return to SHAPE, where he had presided over NATO in its formative years. John, who accompanied his father to Paris, was concerned that this side trip might be too much for the sixty-seven-year-old President and his anxieties were not eased when it was discovered that a formal ceremony had been arranged. Despite the cold and damp weather, Ike removed his hat and gave an impromptu talk.

In a letter to Hazlett, Ike wrote: "As for my recent physical mishap, never at any time did I feel ill, so I don't deserve any special commendation for making the Paris trip. My only apprehension was about the formal speeches I knew I would have to make, and, to some extent, concerning the informal conferences with the various heads of government. But all in all, the experience was pleasant and I think all to the good. I especially got a kick out of my visit to my old SHAPE headquarters.

"With reference to the illness itself, apparently months will be needed to complete the full cure. But the only symptom I notice now is a tendency to use the wrong word—for example, I may say 'desk' when I mean 'chair.' But that tendency seems to be decreasing and people who haven't seen me for months say, honestly I think, that they notice a much improved condition in this ailment."

Ever since the heart attack, Ike had been considering the question of presidential disability and possible contingencies. Haunted by the memories of the Wilson tragedy, he did not want his Administration to become paralyzed if critical illness struck him again. Wilson had been crippled by a severe stroke in 1919 and Ike's stroke, however rapid the recovery, could not be dismissed. In February, following consultation with Dulles and Deputy Attorney General William Rogers, Ike wrote to Vice President Nixon suggesting the conditions for him to serve as "Acting President" in the event of presidential disability. Nixon agreed and the White House soon disclosed the unprecedented provisions:

"1. In the event of inability the President would—if possible—so inform the Vice President, and the Vice President would serve as Acting President, exercising the powers and duties of the Office until the inability had ended.

"2. In the event of an inability which would prevent the President from so communicating with the Vice President, the Vice President, after such consultation as seems to him appropriate under the circumstances, would decide upon the devolution of the powers and duties of the Office and would serve as Acting President until the inability had ended.

"3. The President, in either event, would determine when the inability had ended and at that time would resume the full exercise of the powers and duties of the Office."

Without success, Ike had attempted to get congressional approval of the presidential disability pact. The arrangement was thus a personal one between a lame-duck President and his upwardly mobile Vice President.

Throughout his presidency Ike's foreign policy reflected his keen understanding of the world and the balance of power. Following the Suez crisis, he determined that the United States would have to fill the void left by the discredited European powers in the Middle East and in early 1957 announced the Eisenhower doctrine that authorized economic and military aid to Middle Eastern nations requesting such assistance and the use of American forces to protect any nation in the region "against overt armed aggression from any nation controlled by international Communism." In April of 1957, Ike had moved the Sixth Fleet into the eastern Mediterranean when the young King Hussein of Jordan reported that leftist forces were attempting to overthrow his regime. In July of 1958, the region became tense as a revolutionary coup d'état overthrew Iraq's monarchy and the governments of Lebanon and Jordan seemed to be threatened. Britain sent paratroopers into Jordan and Ike, responding to a desperate appeal from Lebanon's President, sent fourteen thousand marines into Lebanon.

"The basic mission of United States forces in Lebanon was not primarily to fight," Ike wrote in *Waging Peace*. "Every effort was made to have our landing be as much of a garrison move as possible. In my address I had been careful to use the term 'stationed in' Lebanon. . . . The geographic objectives of the landings included only the city of Beirut and the adjoining airfield.

"The decision to occupy only the airfield and capital was a political one which I adhered to over the recommendations of some of the military. If the Lebanese Army were unable to subdue the rebels when we had secured their capital and protected their government, I felt we were backing up a government with so little popular support that we probably should not be there."

With his knowledge of military strategy and power, Ike had assessed the Lebanon landing and made certain that it would not mean that the United States would become trapped in a self-defeating quagmire. Though the Soviets and Nasser condemned Ike's "imperialism," there was no counterthrust and civil order was restored in Lebanon. In August, an Arab resolution passed the UN General Assembly that said Arab states would respect the independence of other nations in the Middle East. Having demonstrated his commitment to the Eisenhower doctrine and its promise of defending American allies, Ike withdrew American troops in October.

In the meantime, there were renewed tensions in the Formosa Straits as the Chinese Communists shelled the offshore islands of Quemoy and Matsu, and Chou En-lai reiterated Peking's claim to liberate Taiwan. Ike added aircraft carriers and destroyers to the Seventh Fleet and persuaded Chiang to reduce his troops on the islands of Quemoy and Matsu. If Chiang hoped to bring about a war between the United States and the People's Republic, he was bitterly disappointed, but the Americans had shown their commitment to the protection of Taiwan.

In the summer of 1958, Ike was deeply troubled by revelations that his assistant, Sherman Adams, had received expensive gifts from Boston textile tycoon Bernard Goldfine that included a vicuña coat and paid hotel bills. In addition, there were allegations that Governor Adams had pressured the Securities and Exchange Commission and the Federal Trade Commission on Goldfine's behalf when Goldfine was to face charges for violation of federal regulations. Not since the 1952 Nixon fund scandal had such a conflict-of-interest case exploded into a major political issue. Adams admitted receiving the gifts, but denied using improper influence to help his industrialist friend. What Ike learned about Goldfine's less-than-savory reputation confirmed that Adams should have known better. Democrats and many congressional Republicans demanded Adams' resignation. On June 18, Ike defended his chief of staff: "I personally like Governor Adams. I admire his abilities. I respect him because of his personal and official integrity. I need him. Admitting the lack of that careful prudence in this incident that Governor Adams yesterday referred to, I believe with my whole heart that he is an invaluable public servant doing a difficult job efficiently, honestly, and tirelessly." But like President Jimmy Carter's spirited 1977 defense of his friend and budget director, Bert Lance, Ike's endorsement was not enough to overcome the grave political implications of the Adams affair. The Gallup poll reported that Republicans, Democrats, and independents favored an Adams resignation in light of the scandal. Air Force Secretary Harold Talbott had been forced to resign in 1955 for using his position for personal gain.

There would be no cover-up of damning information, for Ike had set a precedent by saying that Nixon must be "as clean as a hound's tooth" or be dropped from the ticket. Nothing would so demonstrate the essential differences between Eisenhower and his Vice President as Nixon's taped commentary on the Adams case during Watergate. "I can't let you go down," Nixon told John Mitchell. Adams had made mistakes, Nixon said, "but he shouldn't have been sacked. . . . And, uh, for that reason, I am perfectly willing to—I don't give a shit what happens. I want you to stonewall it, let them plead the Fifth Amendment, cover up or anything else if it'll save it—save the plan. That's the whole point." Where Ike was a man of ideals, concerned with doing the right thing, Nixon was without any such convictions. "It's unfair—Haldeman and Dean," said Nixon. "That's what Eisenhower, that's all he cared about—Christ, 'be sure he was clean.' Both in the fund thing and the Adams thing. But I don't look at it that way. And I just— That's the thing I'm really concerned with. We're going to protect our people if we can."

Adams could not survive the charges of impropriety and his efforts to rally support among congressional Republicans were futile. 1958 was an election year and Adams was considered even more of a liability than the recession. Maine's September election brought the defeat of Republican Senator Frederick Payne, another beneficiary of Goldfine's largesse, and increased the demands for Adams' resignation. Ike had already concluded that Adams must go. On September 22, Adams resigned with a kindly testimonial from Ike but with his reputation so seriously tarnished that his public career would never be resumed.

Getting rid of Adams did not seem to end Ike's domestic troubles. The economic recession that had begun in late 1957 had worsened and more than five million Americans were unemployed. Democratic campaigners scored points by blaming the Administration for the nation's economic ailments while Republicans in such industrial states as Ohio and California alienated the blue-collar vote by campaigning passionately for "right-to-work" laws. Nixon, still the party's most prolific campaigner, spoke out against "radicals" and contrasted Democratic "appeasement" with Republican strength. In the last month of the campaign, Ike campaigned for party candidates with uncharcteristic partisanship as he ripped into the Democrats as left-wing extremists and reckless spenders. His strongest appeal was made in California where Senate Minority Leader Knowland was running for the governorship with presidential aspirations clearly evident. Knowland lost to Democrat Edmund G. "Pat" Brown by more than one million votes. Nationally, the Democrats won their greatest victory since the high-water mark of the New Deal, gaining thirteen new senators and forty-eight congressmen. Democratic candidates received 5.7 million more votes than Republicans. Pollster Samuel Lubell reported that the recession, inflation, the right-to-work amendments, and a loss of confidence in Ike all worked against the Republicans.

Among the few bright spots for the minority party were the election of three new senators from New York, Pennsylvania, and

Maryland where Ike's appearances had helped Republicans win close contests. Two politically attractive Republican moderates bucked the Democratic landslide to oust popular Democratic governors: Nelson Rockefeller in New York and Mark Hatfield in Oregon. Rockefeller, Ike's former assistant for national security, suddenly was a legitimate contender for the presidency in 1960. On the Democratic side, Senators John F. Kennedy of Massachusetts and Stuart Symington of Missouri had won impressively and were being touted as possible Democratic standard-bearers along with Senate Majority Leader Johnson, Senator Hubert Humphrey of Minnesota, and the durable Adlai Stevenson.

Though his party had been repudiated and much of the public interest was shifting toward the 1960 elections, Ike was not ready to assume the mantle of elder statesman. For the first time, the Republican congressional leadership was to be directed by men who were openly Eisenhower's men on Capitol Hill: Everett Dirksen of Illinois succeeded Knowland as Senate Minority Leader, and Charles Halleck of Indiana deposed the aging Joseph Martin as House Minority Leader. As a result, Ike became less dependent on the bipartisanship of Democrats Rayburn and Johnson, and with Dirksen's help he was able to blunt Democratic social-welfare legislation on such programs as federal aid to education, medical care for the aged, and federal housing programs. Introducing Ike at the 1960 convention, Dirksen would say: "It has been my privilege to be a part of his team. It has been my privilege to help carry the flag for his program."

At the White House the departure of Sherman Adams had left a void that would be partially filled by press secretary James Hagerty, whose shrewd public-relations instincts and political flexibility were undeniable assets. During the Goldfine controversy it was revealed that Hagerty, too, had received free hotel rooms from the Boston industrialist, but unlike Adams he had not used his White House influence on Goldfine's behalf.

In October of 1958, Major John Eisenhower was transferred from the Pentagon, where he had been an army staff member of the Joint War Plans Division, to the White House where he became assistant staff secretary. Ike had written Hazlett that during his first term John would walk through the White House "wide-eyed," but the elder Eisenhower had much respect for his son's judgment and intellect and often confided in him about secret matters. Just as Ike had brought John to Europe to witness the Normandy campaign, so he wanted his son to participate in the events of the Eisenhower presidency. John's first assignment at the White House had been for a month in 1954 just before attending the Army Command School at Fort Leavenworth.

"Dad and I'd always talked about the possibility of my getting a little education by working in the White House and there was no reason to stay an extra month in Benning," John recalled years later, "so I went on temporary duty." In 1957, when White House staff secretary Andrew Goodpaster was scheduled for a three-week leave, Ike told John, "Goodpaster's going on leave, take a week to get familiar with his job and you're *it* for the time he's gone." At the Pentagon John occasionally found himself in conflict, with strong loyalties to his father and to the Army, whose old-line militarists resented Ike's "New Look" defense policies and budget cutting. "I think the Army suffered under my dad's administration," said John. "But their positions were always trying to prove how we [the Administration] were falling on our face and I found a very decided conflict of loyalties there."

On one occasion John asked a superior to take his name off a report when the officer "jazzed it up" to discredit the Eisenhower administration. "I don't want to be responsible for this paper," said John. "It's gone too far." Happily, for John, the colonel struck Eisenhower's name from the document. By the time of his 1958 White House appointment, John had been with his father through two critical illnesses, the Suez crisis, and the 1956 presidential campaign. "I seem to have been drawn into this thing like a whirlpool," he said, "and was more and more involved in the White House all the time." Still, there was some anxiety about joining Ike's staff. "Working in the White House is pretty heady stuff," he said, "being so close to the throne and not having to go through twelve great minds to get your boss your ideas." Two decades later, John would describe his White House staff years as the most stimulating and rewarding period of his life.

Mamie Eisenhower found the White House almost peaceful after years of living in "a goldfish bowl," as she put it. Before moving into the White House, Ike and Mamie had moved twenty-five times—seven times in one year. The plump and feminine Mamie still enjoyed shopping for clothes, and she required storage rooms in addition to her dressing room because she never threw away old clothes. Mamie was a frugal housekeeper and frequently read food advertisements in Washington newspapers and would clip coupons for the White House staff to hold down the presidential food budget. To the White House staff, there was never any question about her authority in running the executive mansion. Chief Usher J. B. West said years later: "Underneath that buoyant spirit, there was a spine of steel, forged by years of military discipline. As the wife of a career army officer, she understood the hierarchy of a large establishment, the division of responsibilities, and how to direct a staff. She knew exactly what she wanted, every moment, and exactly how it should be done."

As a small-town girl, it seemed almost like a fairy-tale dream for Mamie to be First Lady. "I never drove up to the South Portico without a lump coming to my throat," Mamie recalled in a 1974 interview. In discussing vandalism by tourists, she became indignant and expressed astonishment that Americans would desecrate a national treasure. Mamie worked to make the White House more of a historical showcase by launching efforts to recover antique furniture and china, for she had been disappointed at the lack of authentic presidential antiques. Ike once observed: "I personally think that Mamie's biggest contribution was to make the White House livable, comfortable, and meaningful for the people who came in. She was always helpful and ready to do anything. She exuded hospitality. She saw that as one of her functions and performed it, no matter how tired she was. In the White House, you need intelligence and charm—to make others glad to be around you. She had that ability."

Mamie took several steps to ensure the family of more privacy than previous presidential families. The White House social season was trimmed down; staff members were put under a strict no-talking rule; and her visits outside the mansion were unpublicized. There were no press conferences or public speeches. "I think Ike speaks well enough for both of us," she said. Much of her time and energies were devoted to helping charitable causes and philanthropic organizations such as the Heart Fund. "The only thing I ever asked of the Cabinet wives was that they help support charities, and nearly all of them were cooperative," she told me in 1974. "When I was offered free tickets to charity benefits, I always told them, 'I'm no deadhead. I pay my own way.'"

One of the few rules of her marriage, she said, was that "Ike took care of the office—I ran the house." Political issues were rarely discussed, she said. "When Ike came home, he came home." From time to time, Ike did seek her advice on political personalities. "Mamie is a very shrewd observer," he once said. "She has an uncanny and accurate judgment of people with whom she was well acquainted. I got it into my head that I'd better listen when she talked about someone brought in close to me." It had done Treasury Secretary George Humphrey no harm that Mamie liked his wife; and Vice President Nixon, treated cavalierly by Ike, had a friend and defender in Mamie. On budget matters and economic problems, Ike would on occasion consult with his wife. During a White House conference on the cost-of-living index, Ike interjected, "Let me try this out on Mamie, she's a pretty darn good judge of things."

Mamie's favorite vacation stop was Elizabeth Arden's Maine Chance health and beauty resort near Phoenix, Arizona, and she would also visit her mother periodically in Denver. In Washington, Mamie's most frequent companions were her sister, Frances "Mike" Moore, and Barbara Eisenhower, her attractive daughter-in-law. For health reasons, Mamie did not like to travel in airplanes and thus did not accompany Ike on his 1959 and 1960 good-will tours. So Barbara, traveling with John, became the ranking woman at state affairs on Ike's journeys.

At the beginning of 1959, the Soviet Union threatened to use military force against the Western powers if West Berlin was not declared a free city by May. Khrushchev's ultimatum was designed to crack the Western Alliance, and Britain seemed willing to bend. Secretary of State Dulles went to Europe for conferences with British Prime Minister Macmillan, French Premier Charles de Gaulle and West German Chancellor Konrad Adenauer. John Eisenhower recalls that his father "blew his stack" when the British ambassador reported that his government might go along with the

Russian demand. "Dad picked up the phone, while I was sitting there, and called Dulles," John recalled, "and Dulles was able to report that this particular piece of news had been refuted by Macmillan, and also that the heat was off for the moment." Dulles was terminally ill with cancer, and the Berlin trouble-shooting mission was to be his last European trip. In March, when Macmillan and Ike visited Dulles at Walter Reed Hospital, the Secretary of State told the Prime Minister: "If appeasement and partial surrender are to be our attitude, we had better save our money." So ravaged was Dulles by the cancer that in April he resigned and a month later he was dead. Former Massachusetts Governor Christian Herter succeeded Dulles as Secretary, but Ike himself would govern the nation's foreign affairs.

In the spring, Ike briefed congressional leaders on the Berlin crisis and its implications for the West. House Speaker Rayburn, who shared Ike's views on the conservation of military force, said, "We want to make sure we do all the talking we can before we fight." By contrast, Senate Majority Leader Johnson insisted that Ike should reverse plans to cut back army personnel and increase the armed forces because of the Berlin threat. "I've got enough military forces to take care of this situation," Ike responded. To get enough troops to "fight the Russians on the ground," Ike said, would mean "we're going to go to a garrison state." Senator Richard Russell, chairman of the Armed Services Committee, was "the really outstanding figure of the group" in John Eisenhower's opinion. As Ike explained various possibilities, he told the group that he would first seek congressional approval. "If you have to act, Mr. President," said Russell, "you go ahead and act, don't come to us." Flashing a grin, Ike said, "Oh, I certainly intend to. In case of an emergency, I will act before I come to you. But if there is time, I'll always consult with you."

The May deadline passed without incident as the Soviets withdrew their threat. "After Khrushchev became convinced that we would stand up to him, he began a very, very clever retreat and muddied the waters," recalled John Eisenhower. Though Ike's firmness and the cohesiveness of the Western Alliance had deterred the Soviets, the situation remained too volatile for celebrations. "The boss was very careful not to ever give indication to

Khrushchev of 'we told you' or 'we knew you'd back down,' or anything like that," said John. "We made it easy for him to back down."

For some months Khrushchev had been interested in visiting Ike both to improve his image as a world statesman and to see firsthand the American people and their diverse cultures. As the Berlin tensions eased somewhat Ike authorized an invitation to the Soviet leader pending some progress on the question of German reunification at the foreign ministers' conference in Geneva. Through a misunderstanding, Undersecretary of State Robert Murphy—Ike's wartime political aide—invited Khrushchev with no restriction.

"Dad was furious," said John Eisenhower, "and he gave him [Murphy] a little lecture about how he used to operate with Dulles. But he was now stuck and the Khrushchev visit was on. In other words, Dad was sort of pushed down toward this summit meeting."

Khrushchev had hosted an American delegation that included Nixon and Milton Eisenhower in the summer of 1959. At an American exhibition in Moscow, Nixon and Khrushchev engaged in the celebrated "kitchen debate." Years later, John Kenneth Galbraith would write of Khrushchev: "He seems to have sensed, if he did not fully know, that millions of Americans would believe that anyone who argued with Nixon could not be wholly wrong." The Soviet leaders recognized that Milton was the American representative closest to Ike and dealt with him as such. "I got to know Khrushchev very well," Milton recalled. "I think they may have put me in a position of privilege partly because I was a brother of the President's." Milton's conversations with the Soviet Premier provided Ike with valuable background before the Khrushchev visit.

As the world awaited Khrushchev's American pilgrimage, Ike went to Europe for meetings with Allied leaders. There had been some resentment and uncertainty about the Khrushchev invitation and Macmillan was particularly angered, for it meant that his hopes of a four-power summit conference would be further delayed. Macmillan blamed American "stupidity, naïvete and incompetence" for the open terms of the Soviet Premier's visit. To reassure America's Western allies, Ike planned a trip to West Germany, England, and France for consultation about the upcoming Soviet talks.

Making the arrangements for the presidential odyssey was John Eisenhower. "I started getting into the trip business," he said years later. "I was sort of the henchman in charge." Ike's instinctive response to the Khrushchev acceptance was to erase Allied misunderstanding. "He didn't want to give the impression that he was speaking for the West," said John. "He did want to make sure that he was consulting with them before he talked, then assured them that he was talking only for the United States when he was talking to Khrushchev. This was his way of trying to pull the chestnuts out of the fire that had resulted from this misunderstanding."

It was a brilliant gesture and huge crowds cheered Ike throughout the European tour. A banner, "We Like Ike and Konny," [Adenauer] welcomed him to West Germany, and Ike said: "In my country, the name of Adenauer has come to symbolize the determination of the German people to remain strong and free. In the implementation of that determination, the American people stand by your side." Adenauer received what he wanted—an assurance that Ike would not yield on Berlin. In England, there were reunions with Churchill, Montgomery, and Queen Elizabeth, but the real business was conducted in private sessions with Macmillan, who still was pressing for a summit conference. At Chequers, the Prime Minister's country residence, the old friends golfed and later dined; the Queen sent grouse for their dinner. Macmillan had visited Khrushchev in Moscow and gave Ike additional insights about the Soviet Premier. On Ike's departure, Macmillan noted the enthusiasm of "the hundreds of thousands, almost millions" of people who greeted him and said: "You will have realized the affection which we have for you personally . . . and you will have known how from the real hearts of the people has gone out their affection. We also hope that in the course of your visits to three European capitals and your proposed interchange of visits with Mr. Khrushchev, we may be able to set out upon a road which will be fruitful for the world, and bring us that of which we spoke together two nights ago: peace and justice."

"For me," said Ike in response, "there is always a bit of sadness in my heart when I leave this country. I have had many experiences here, in war and peace. I have formed some of the most valued friendships that I have. . . . I would like for all of you to remember, and on our side of the water I should hope that we always remember, the value of these relationships."

From London Ike went to Paris for meetings with another wartime comrade, French President Charles de Gaulle. It was to be their first meeting in years and French newspapers hailed the talks as the "Old Soldiers' Summit." De Gaulle was a larger-than-life figure physically and intellectually and in many ways the most impressive political figure of his generation. As the leader of the Free French during World War II he had demonstrated vision and courage. From the ashes of postwar France he wanted to build through his towering personality a modern world power. "France cannot be France without the grandeur," said De Gaulle. When he disapproved of France's constitution that was passed in a 1946 referendum, he retired from public life. In June of 1958, with France threatened with a civil war over the question of its Algerian colonial holdings, De Gaulle returned to power. His political resurrection sent shock waves to Washington and London. Roosevelt and Churchill heartily disliked De Gaulle and their alliance was often hostile. With Ike, De Gaulle got along well and Eisenhower would later list De Gaulle as one of the five greatest men of his lifetime. When John Eisenhower said, "De Gaulle's return to power was awful," Ike responded: "I think it's a good thing." De Gaulle had already asserted his independence by withdrawing the French fleet from NATO's jurisdiction and declaring that French troops were autonomous from NATO. Shortly after assuming power, he had suggested the reorganization of NATO and a Western European Confederation under his leadership. Although Great Britain would not go along with the idea, West Germany began a new relationship with France. De Gaulle talked of establishing direct relations with the Soviet Union and of developing France into a nuclear power. As Ike left for France, the Manchester *Guardian* warned: "There he will have to tackle the thorniest of his allies and, although again his own warmth and charm cannot fail to help, the duration and domesticity of his stay in Britain may itself prove something of a handicap."

De Gaulle was, John Eisenhower remembered, "the most interesting part of the trip . . . very much of an unknown quantity to us. I'm not sure that Dad had seen him since World War II or shortly thereafter. . . . He certainly was a different personality, much more benign-looking, much more self-confident-looking than he had been in '45."

Ike's reception in France was reminiscent of the crowds that had cheered him as the liberator of Europe. "It was obvious that the Franco-American brotherhood-in-arms, of which our visitor was the most glorious symbol," said De Gaulle, "was very much alive in the minds of our people." When Ike asked De Gaulle how many persons had lined their parade route, the French President said there had been "at least" one million. "I did not expect half as many," said Ike, visibly moved.

In their talks, Ike disagreed with De Gaulle about France's ambitions to be a nuclear power but won no concessions. De Gaulle said that he, too, wanted to see Khrushchev before any four-power summit conference. Though there were differences, John Eisenhower said that they were discussed in "the most friendly and reasonable tone of voice."

With obvious emotion, De Gaulle said, "I find in him, with the most profound joy, the good, warm, the loyal companion beside whom I have marched in difficult times along the road of history. Which is why, to all of you, I can say that between us all has gone very well."

During a banquet toast Ike paid tribute to the French President: "Unless we have the stubbornness, the courage, the resolute persistence of General de Gaulle, we shall not win. I think that with that kind of courage, we shall never fail. I would call him stubborn, but as long as he is stubborn in support of principle and right and peace, this is a powerful inspiration for all of us."

On September 7, Ike brought a positive message when he returned to Washington. "Every troublesome little problem has been talked out, and I am quite certain that for the moment, at least, everything is going splendidly." Khrushchev's arrival was eagerly anticipated by a curious nation, for a Soviet premier had never visited the United States.

Khrushchev was the most colorful and flamboyant leader on the world scene: a onetime miner and peasant who retained the common touch on his rise through the Soviet hierarchy. "Khrushchev's humor was typically folksy and thus often almost crude," said Yugoslavian writer Milovan Djilas, "but it was lively and inexhaustible. He was the only one of the Soviet leaders who delved into details into the daily life of the Communist rank and file and the ordinary people. He did not do this with the aim of changing the system, but of strengthening and improving things under the existing system." Having visited the Premier in Moscow, Macmillan wrote Ike a brief character sketch, describing Khrushchev as much more humane than Stalin although nonetheless a very clever political leader. "As the memories of revolution and civil war die away," wrote Macmillan, "Khrushchev is anxious less to be regarded as the odd man out in international affairs and more as the responsible leader of a great bloc of countries."

Chairman Khrushchev's silver plane landed at Andrews Air Force Base on September 15 and Ike and his entire cabinet were on hand for the historic meeting. "Just as I hope that I may later visit and learn more about your people," said Ike, "I know that you seek better understanding of our system, of our people, and of the principles which guide and motivate them. I assure you that they have no ill will toward any other people, that they covet no territory, no additional power. Nor do they seek to interfere in the internal affairs of any other nation. . . . After all, our common purpose should be, always, a just, universal, and enduring peace."

For twelve days Khrushchev toured the United States, visiting Eleanor Roosevelt at Hyde Park, addressing the United Nations, inspecting such varied enterprises as a Pittsburgh steel mill, Iowa farm, and a Hollywood studio where Frank Sinatra and Shirley MacLaine were filming *Can Can*. At Los Angeles, Khrushchev threatened to leave in a rage when Norris Poulson, the mountebank mayor, insulted him in a speech. But Khrushchev continued his tour and responded warmly to the large crowds that turned out to see him. "The plain people of America like me," the Chairman told Henry Cabot Lodge. "It's just those bastards around Eisenhower that don't."

After the sightseeing, Khrushchev met Ike at Camp David for three days of talks and such pleasant diversions as watching a movie Western and flying to Ike's Gettysburg farm where the Soviet Premier was introduced to Barbara Eisenhower and the Eisenhower grandchildren. "He certainly had my kids mesmerized," said John Eisenhower. Khrushchev expressed admiration for Ike's Black Angus cattle and Ike insisted that the Premier accept a prize member of the herd as a gift. To reciprocate, Khrushchev arranged to have a planeload of Russian birch trees sent to the Eisenhower farm. During their working sessions, the two leaders talked about their mutual frustrations at military expenditures and the necessity for an arms limitation agreement between the superpowers. There was tough talk about Berlin and Khrushchev finally said, "The ultimatum is lifted." John Eisenhower said the Soviets were fully aware of Ike's Abilene heritage and the influence of the Old West on his character. "When Dad said, 'You step across the line in Berlin and I'll shoot,' I think Khrushchev believed him," John said. "I think Khrushchev believed him more because of his background out here in 'Wild Bill Hickok' country." In his memoirs, dictated near the end of his life, Khrushchev said that he "always admired Eisenhower for his modesty, his common sense, and his many years of experience."

Khrushchev's visit had been a turning point in the Cold War and the optimism of the period was reflected in what was termed "The spirit of Camp David." Peaceful coexistence seemed more than a slogan, but a realistic hope for a generation that had been through the bloodiest of all wars. Ike's demonstration that he was his own Secretary of State had strengthened his image at home and abroad.

In December, Ike embarked on the most spectacular diplomatic tour ever undertaken by an American President; in nineteen days he visited eleven nations on three continents in such exotic settings as Rome, Casablanca, Athens, Madrid, and New Delhi. His visit to India was of special political significance, for Dulles had been hostile to neutral powers. Ike had always been more understanding and sympathetic toward India's policy of nonalignment.

During a meeting with a conservative Republican senator, Ike had said: "Suppose India said, 'We take our stand with the West.' Consider where we are—right up against an eighteen-hundred-mile border against China. How much have we got to put into India to make it reasonably safe for them even to exist?" Indian Prime Minister Jawaharal Nehru had long admired Ike, and the multitudes that cheered "Welcome, the Prince of Peace" and almost smothered Ike in flowers were more vast than his World War II victory celebrations. "Freedom, as Gandhi said, is the gift of God," said Ike, "and God's gift cannot forever be kept from his children. But immediately we must search out with all free nations more effective and practical ways to strengthen the cause of peace and friendship in freedom. . . . One reason I came to India is to tell you that America wants to join with all free men in advancing this cause."

At the Élysée Palace, Ike spent a weekend with De Gaulle, Macmillan, and Adenauer to set the agenda for the summit with Khrushchev in the spring of 1960. There was still disagreement between Ike and De Gaulle on NATO and no real compromise emerged from their talks, but the four chiefs of state settled on a mid-May summit with Khrushchev in Paris.

Something happened on the morning of May 1 that would disrupt the summit and result in the withdrawal of Ike's invitation to visit Russia. An American reconnaissance aircraft, the U-2, was hit by a Soviet rocket over the Russian city of Sverdlovsk in central Russia. As early as 1956 Ike had told John Eisenhower about the secret spy flights over the Soviet Union and the detailed surveillance that they made possible. The Soviet rejection of the Open Skies plan was the justification for the spy missions by the U-2s, and Allen Dulles, director of the Central Intelligence Agency, gave Ike absolute assurances that no pilot would be taken alive. On that fateful morning in 1960, only four people at the White House—including Ike and John—were familiar with the U-2. Goodpaster and John lamented the apparent death of the pilot. A cover story was released claiming that due to an equipment failure the missing plane had violated Soviet air space. But the Administration was caught in a lie when the Soviets disclosed that they had captured U-2 pilot Francis Gary Powers. "Once he was taken alive, then we were in the soup," said John Eisenhower, who felt that Dulles and the CIA had let his father down. Senator J. William Fulbright, among others, urged Ike to disclaim responsibility for the flights. Throughout World War II Ike had been willing to take the blame for military setbacks and his reaction to this diplomatic crisis was consistent with his wartime attitude. Because of the overpowering evidence, Ike said that denials would have been ineffectual. "No one wants another Pearl Harbor," said Ike. "This means that we must have knowledge of military forces and preparations around the world, especially those capable of massive surprise attacks. Secrecy in the Soviet Union makes this essential."

Ike and Khrushchev went to Paris for the summit meeting with the Western European heads of state. They met in the Élysée Palace and Khrushchev excoriated Ike as a "thief caught red-handed in his theft" and said that the U-2 affair doomed the summit conference to failure. Finally, the Soviet Premier said Ike's trip to the Soviet Union that had been scheduled for June should be postponed. Ike responded that the flights were suspended on his orders and that the conference should proceed, a position endorsed at once by De Gaulle and Macmillan. Khrushchev and his entourage walked out and it was announced that he would continue the summit only if Ike apologized for the U-2 incident. A day later, on May 17, Khrushchev left for Moscow, where he said substantive questions such as Berlin would be discussed with the next American President. That Eisenhower would be unable to make his pilgrimage to the Soviet Union shattered the hope of ending the Cold War and achieving détente. In a 1976 interview, Averell Harriman said that the cancellation of Ike's trip prevented what might have been a significant breakthrough in Soviet-American relations. "It was a tragedy that Eisenhower didn't get to go to Russia," said Harriman. "He was a hero of the Russian people. He would have been received as no one has been received anywhere. Détente might well have started then."

As if the breakdown of the summit was not enough, Ike's June visit to Japan was canceled following widespread demonstrations against the United States, and in the midst of a Far Eastern good-will trip that included a homecoming to the Philippines where he had served twenty years earlier and a visit to Taiwan to meet with Chiang Kai-shek. The sudden collapse of the Japanese tour was a major embarrassment, for Japan had just signed a new military treaty with the United States.

It was an election year and Democratic politicians capitalized on the foreign-policy setbacks with charges that American prestige was declining. Democratic presidential candidate John F. Kennedy's campaign theme was the necessity "to get this country moving again," with the unmistakable implication that America had been without leadership during the Eisenhower years. Though Kennedy in private conversation would hold Ike responsible for the national drift, he accepted the political truth that President Eisenhower was far too popular to criticize publicly or by name. Kennedy instead focused on Republican candidate Richard Nixon and on such unappealing symbols of GOP conservatism as William McKinley, Calvin Coolidge, and Herbert Hoover. Many political experts had predicted that the Democratic Convention would select a Stevenson-Kennedy ticket, but Stevenson's luck and timing were bad. That he wanted a third nomination was clear enough to Stevenson's friends, and his supporters cheered wildly at the convention, yet he had not campaigned for the nomination and Kennedy had been actively seeking the presidency for nearly four years. In the two most important primaries, Wisconsin and West Virginia, Kennedy won impressively against Minnesota Senator Hubert Humphrey; and in the Oregon primary Kennedy handily defeated maverick Wayne Morse. Former President Truman supported Missouri Senator Stuart Symington, and Senate Majority Leader Johnson himself was a candidate, hoping for a deadlocked convention that would turn to him as its compromise. Kennedy, however, was too far ahead to be deterred at Los Angeles and was nominated on the first ballot. As his running mate, Kennedy selected Lyndon Johnson.

Looking much younger than his forty-three years, Kennedy was an attractive and articulate representative of the war generation—a war hero and Pulitzer Prize historian—he was also the first Roman Catholic nominated for the presidency since the 1920s, and if his candidacy alienated some Protestant right-wingers, it also promised to attract many Catholics who had supported Ike. Johnson's place on the ticket was a master stroke which bolstered Democratic strength in the South where Ike had run strongly. In 1956, Ike had written that a combination of Johnson and Kennedy would have been his most formidable opposition, and both senators had gained stature in the intervening four years.

Republican ingenuity had deprived their party of its strongest candidate in 1960. Stung by Franklin Roosevelt's four smashing victories, the Republican-controlled Eightieth Congress in 1947 initiated the Twenty-second Amendment that placed a two-term limitation on the presidency. Years later, Harry Truman gleefully chortled that Eisenhower would have easily defeated Kennedy in 1960 but for the amendment. Fully recovered from his ailments and still vigorous and alert, Ike would have been prepared to campaign much more actively than had been the case in 1956. Without the constitutional limit, John Eisenhower is of the opinion that his father would have run for a third term for the same reasons that he ran for a second. "The comedown is always pretty hard when you leave the presidency," said John in a 1974 interview. "I think Dad would have been a candidate again."

There is much evidence that Ike did not necessarily view Nixon as his inevitable successor. Behind the closed doors of the White House, Ike pointed out Nixon's shortcomings to some of his own assistants. Although Ike said that his Vice President had matured, he qualified the compliment with the comment that Nixon was too political. His uncertainty about Nixon in 1956 had been no charade and Ike had been ready to dump him as early as the fund scandal. In an undated handwritten list of prospective 1960 candidates, Ike gave Treasury Secretary Robert B. Anderson, Ambassador Henry Cabot Lodge, Kentucky Senator Thruston Morton, White House chief of staff Sherman Adams, Chicago businessman Charles Percy, and White House economic adviser Gabriel Hauge higher marks (A+) than he gave Nixon, Attorney General Brownell, New Jersey Senator Clifford Case, and Connecticut Senator Prescott Bush (A). On the same piece of paper, Ike noted that Milton was "disqualified" because of their family ties and that Adams "possibly" would be eliminated because of age, and General Gruenther because he was a Catholic. Secretary Anderson was the most frequent beneficiary of Eisenhower praise.

In a December 8, 1954, letter to Hazlett, Ike had written: "One of these old Democrats but now a Republican—Bob Anderson of Texas—is just about the ablest man that I know anywhere. He would make a splendid President of the United States, and I do hope that he can be sufficiently publicized as a young, vigorous Republican so that he will come to the attention of Republican groups in every state in the union." Three years later, in a conversation with Emmet John Hughes, Ike stated that Anderson was the most experienced of all candidates and one that Eisenhower would be willing to "fight for." Anderson was reluctant to seek the presidency and without an aggressive campaign could not hope to win the nomination. Another and even more remote possibility suggested by Ike was Arthur Larson, the former dean of the University of Pittsburgh Law School who had served him as Undersecretary of Labor, director of the United States Information Agency, and as special assistant to the President. Larson's 1956 book, *A Republican Looks at His Party*, became the manifesto of what Ike termed "modern Republicanism," a political philosophy that embraced fiscal conservatism and social liberalism. "It is a type of political philosophy," said Ike, "that recognizes clearly the responsibility of the federal government to take the lead in making certain that the productivity of our great economic machine is distributed so that no one will suffer disaster, privation, through no fault of his own. Now, this covers the wide field of education and so on. We believe likewise in the free enterprise system." Described in Larson's book as the architect and embodiment of a new political movement, Ike in turn said that Larson would make an admirable Republican standard-bearer in 1960. By 1959, there was only one promising alternative to Nixon—Nelson Rockefeller. Although Rockefeller had served Ike as special assistant, Undersecretary of HEW, and chairman of the committee on reorganization, Ike had not included his name on laundry lists of possible successors. It was through Milton, an old friend, that Rockefeller came into the Administration. While Ike gave Nelson high responsibility, Rockefeller's emergence as a presidential contender came only after he left Washington and was elected governor of New York. Handsome, wealthy, ambitious, with nearly two decades of Washington experience under three Presidents, Rockefeller struck many as the most dynamic and forceful candidate the party could nominate and the most likely winner against Kennedy. Rockefeller's best chance against Nixon was in the primaries, but in December of 1959 the governor conceded that the Vice President held a wide lead among party leaders and announced his own withdrawal as a candidate. Nixon's nomination was all but assured with the Rockefeller announcement and Ike would do nothing to obstruct his Vice President's preconvention campaign.

In the late spring Rockefeller said that he would accept a convention draft and he blasted Eisenhower administration policies on a range of issues from civil rights to the defense budget, demanding that Nixon address the same issues before the Chicago convention. Nixon met with Rockefeller in New York and in a scene not unlike the one at Morningside Heights eight years earlier worked out a compromise statement. Rockefeller's repudiation of the Eisenhower administration displeased both Ike and Milton. "I have always assumed," said Milton, "that he [Rockefeller] felt he had to have a platform different from Nixon's in order to forward his candidacy because all of the pressures were moving so clearly toward a Nixon nomination." Milton said the salvos were an "unhappy event" for him and Ike because they admired Rockefeller. Ike blamed "half-baked advisers" for selling Rockefeller on the proposition that the defense budget should be increased by more than $3.5 billion. When Rockefeller asked Ike, in early June, whether he should become an active candidate, Eisenhower said bluntly that it would be a mistake and people would regard the governor as indecisive. Fully acknowledging Nixon's status as the party's choice, Ike sent the Vice President a detailed memorandum in January about the campaign and possible running mates. Milton's reservations about Nixon dated back to 1952, yet when it became apparent that the Vice President would be the party's presidential candidate Milton offered his counsel and support. On July 13, Nixon wrote Milton, "The major problem I will take into the campaign is the almost frightening weakening of the Republican Party throughout the country. Present indications are that I will have to run 7 to 8 percentage points ahead of the party in most states in order to win. The President, of course, was able to do this, but it will take an extraordinary effort if I can pull it off this time."

Once again Milton was mentioned as a possible vice-presidential candidate and Ike discouraged the speculation. "That might look like an attempt at establishing a bit of a dynasty," he said. "I would have none of that. And I tell you much more emphatically, he wouldn't have it." Rockefeller, whom Ike would have supported for the vice presidency, flatly rejected Nixon's offer. Two Eisenhower favorites, Secretary Anderson and Lodge, were the finalists for the vice-presidential nomination and Anderson was not interested. Under the circumstances Lodge's selection was acceptable to the White House and seemed to offer popular appeal.

Ike's coolness toward Nixon was still evident: At the convention he did not remain for Nixon's nomination after his own speech. He neatly deflated Nixon's campaign slogan "Experience Counts" when he was asked to name some Nixon contribution to Administration policy. "If you give me a week, I might think of one," said Ike. "I don't remember." In Ike's judgment, Nixon committed a tactical error by agreeing to the television debates with Kennedy, a lesser-known quantity. Following the first debate, on September 26, Kennedy surged ahead in the polls.

During the early and middle phases of the fall campaign Ike did not take an active role. Whatever his feelings about Nixon he was the defender of the Eisenhower record and his election would be interpreted as a vote of confidence in Ike's eight years. Kennedy's criticism of the Administration with alarmist charges of a "missile gap" behind the Soviet Union had been an irritant. So had his charges that the Eisenhower administration had been aware that Cuban revolutionary Fidel Castro was a Communist, yet stood by complacently while he seized power. Kennedy called for Castro's overthrow and exploited the issue as if Cuba had really been America's to lose. On defense matters he talked as if he knew more than Ike. The Gallup poll indicated that Kennedy had extended his lead during October, and a letter to the White House from Rockefeller said that only Ike could save New York for Nixon.

Strangely enough, Nixon and his campaign strategists did not ask Ike to become involved until the last days of the campaign.

Had he been asked, Ike would have started campaigning much earlier, but Nixon's staff was so anxious to run their own campaign that it was even suggested that they did not need presidential help. Eisenhower's intervention in the last eight days of the campaign was a rejuvenating tonic for Nixon's campaign. Theodore H. White, covering the campaign, wrote, "Eisenhower has, and retains, a magic in American politics that is peculiarly his: he makes people happy . . . he conducts politics in his own way, personally and effectively." In joint appearances with his candidate, Ike received the greater cheers and applause and there were numerous posters that said "WE LIKE IKE, BUT WE BACK JACK." Still, Ike's presence and his hard-hitting remarks about Kennedy's inexperience were dramatic and effective. On election eve Ike talked of his responsibilities in World War II and the White House, reviewed with pride the accomplishments of his administration, and warmly endorsed Nixon and Lodge. "And now, after the last campaign speech that as your President I shall ever make to you," said Ike, "I say good night—may God bless you all and our beloved country."

By the narrowest of margins, Kennedy squeezed ahead of Nixon to win the November 8 election. There had been a strong Nixon surge in the final week of the campaign to which Ike had contributed, and the Vice President fell short by only 113,000 votes out of nearly 69 million. The morning after the election Ike sourly remarked to a member of his cabinet that Nixon's campaign managers blew the election by not making more extensive use of him. Shortly afterward Ike wrote a friend that the outcome was like getting hit with a baseball bat. "His disappointment was very deep, very genuine," said Milton years later. To John, Ike ruefully said that the Democratic victory was a repudiation of his presidency and added that he might as well have "been having fun" for the last eight years.

The Eisenhower era was approaching an end when America's oldest President would be succeeded by the youngest man ever elected. Ike was still revered by two thirds of his countrymen and if there were no trumpets to salute his accomplishments they had been considerable nonetheless. Building the federal highway system had been an event of great importance, no less so than the transcontinental railroad more than a century earlier. His civil-rights law and intervention at Little Rock were significant thrusts against racial bigotry. The paranoia and viciousness of the McCarthy nightmare had long since quieted after his deft handling of the Wisconsin demagogue. In the tense atmosphere of the Cold War, he brought to an end a war that he had inherited and came down on the side of peace when hard liners sought military adventure elsewhere. His personal diplomacy and good will had provided an opening in dealing with the Communist world and he refused to be pushed into an arms race with the Soviet Union. Ike had served his nation well in war and in peacetime and finally, at the age of seventy, he was ready to play the role he had naïvely hoped for at the end of World War II: elder statesman.

Chapter Nineteen

ELDER STATESMEN

In the winter of his presidency, the nation's first warrior-statesman made an eloquent call for national unity and a warning against "permanent" alliances with foreign powers. George Washington's Farewell Address carried a special significance that has endured for nearly two centuries. With a young Democrat, who had campaigned on the theme that America needed more missile power, about to take office, Ike chose to renew the Washington tradition with a farewell speech to the nation. Milton assisted him with the organization and revision of the speech as Ike took careful aim at the same problems that his successor would address in a saber-rattling inaugural speech.

It was 8:30 P.M. on January 17, 1961, when Ike went on the air for the last time as President and delivered an address that would be long remembered. "Three days from now," he said, "after a half a century in the service of our country, I shall lay down the responsibilities of office as, in traditional and solemn ceremony, the authority of the presidency is vested in my successor. . . . We now stand ten years past the midpoint of a century that has witnessed four major wars among great nations. Three of these involved our own country. Despite these holocausts America is today the strongest, the most influential and most productive nation in the world. Understandably proud of this preeminence, we yet realize that America's leadership and prestige depend, not merely upon our unmatched material progress, riches and military strength, but on how we use our power in the interests of world peace and human betterment."

He spoke of the great rivalry with the Soviet Union: "We face a hostile ideology. . . . Unhappily the danger it poses promises to be of indefinite duration. To meet it successfully, there is called for not so much the emotional and transitory sacrifices of crisis, but rather those which enable us to carry forward steadily, surely, and without complaint the burdens of a prolonged and complex struggle."

In the last third of the speech came Ike's answer to those militant cold warriors who had pictured the nation in grave danger from without and who demanded additional billions for the defense budget to overcome a nonexistent "missile gap": "This conjunction of an immense military establishment and a large arms industry is new in the American experience. The total influence—economic, political, even spiritual—is felt in every city, every State house, every office of the federal government. We recognize the imperative need for this development. Yet we must not fail to comprehend its grave implications. Our toil, resources and livelihood are all involved; so is the very structure of our society.

"In the councils of government, we must guard against the acquisition of unwarranted influence, whether sought or unsought, by the military-industrial complex. The potential for the disastrous rise of misplaced power exists and will persist.

"We must never let the weight of this combination endanger our liberties or democratic processes. We should take nothing for granted. Only an alert and knowledgeable citizenry can compel the proper meshing of the huge industrial and military machinery of defense with our peaceful methods and goals so that security and liberty may prosper together."

There were dangers, too, he said, in permitting the military establishment to control academic research: "A government contract becomes virtually a substitute for intellectual curiosity. . . . The prospect of domination of the nation's scholars by Federal employment, project allocations, and the power of money is ever present—and is gravely to be regarded.

"Yet, in holding scientific research and discovery in respect, as we should, we must also be alert to the equal and opposite danger that public policy could itself become the captive of a scientific technological elite."

In closing, the old soldier expressed the hope that "all peoples will come to live together in a peace guaranteed by the binding force of mutual respect and love."

Walter Lippmann, who had been one of the most persistent critics of the Eisenhower administration, compared the farewell address favorably to that of Washington's: "Washington made the theme of his farewell address a warning against allowing the influence of foreign governments to invade our political life. That was then the menace to the civilian power. Now Eisenhower, speaking from his experience and looking ahead, is concerned with a contemporary threat to the supremacy of the civilian power."

The farewell speech, which would become the most quoted of all Ike's addresses, had stressed a basic tenet of American thought in language that was both straightforward and provocative. Kennedy's inaugural address struck a different tone with its ringing rhetoric and proclamation that "the torch has been passed to a new generation of Americans, born in this century." Kennedy boasted: "In the long history of the world, only a few generations have been granted the role of defending freedom in its hour of maximum danger. I do not shrink from this responsibility; I welcome it." The young President was summoning a nation to put its resources into the Cold War and his advisers were the same hard liners whose counterrevolutionary strategy Ike had scorned.

Personal relations between the new President and Ike had been cordial, and Kennedy had made a strong impression by coming alone to meet Ike to begin the transition. As a matter of principle, Ike discouraged members of his administration from accepting appointments under Kennedy. When it was reported that he was in favor of Undersecretary of State C. Douglas Dillon accepting Kennedy's invitation to become Secretary of the Treasury, a corrective was hastily sent to Dillon. In a "Dear Doug" letter, Ike wrote: "Obviously, it is no part of my responsibility to try, unduly, to influence you, but I do want to make it clear that on balance I am against the proposal.

"Even if you could have, in advance, a solid guarantee that you would be the sole authority in determining upon matters that fall within the scope of Treasury responsibility, it is inconceivable to me that any President would, in practice, retain only nominal control over these important operations. But without such unbreakable guarantee, you would become a scapegoat of the radicals."

Dillon, then fifty-one, and once mentioned by Ike as a possible presidential candidate, joined the Kennedy administration as would Henry Cabot Lodge in later months. If it rankled that former protégés sat in the court of another leader, Ike made his own counsel available to Kennedy. Following the Bay of Pigs debacle in April of 1961, Ike lunched with Kennedy at Camp David and said afterward: "I am still in favor of the United States supporting the man who has to carry the responsibility for our foreign affairs."

President Kennedy also approached Milton for help in the wake of the Bay of Pigs disaster. Kennedy had agreed to Castro's offer to trade five hundred American tractors for the twelve hundred Cuban rebels captured during the invasion, but since diplomatic relations with Cuba had been severed the funding would be raised privately. To head the committee, Kennedy called Milton, Eleanor Roosevelt, Walter Reuther, Cardinal Cushing, and George Romney and asked them to serve. Only Romney, then campaigning for the governorship of Michigan, declined. Milton accepted with the understanding that Kennedy would explain publicly that the committee's work was mandated by the President. When Kennedy failed to follow through with his commitment and disavowed any association with the "Tractors for Freedom Committee," some congressmen protested that Milton and his colleagues were violating the Logan Act, the law that prohibits private citizens from interfering with foreign policy. Feeling that Kennedy had betrayed him, Milton sent the President a stern letter that was ultimately referred to Secretary of State Dean Rusk. Sympathetic to Milton, Rusk offered to help coordinate the committee's actions. Castro suggested that Milton or Mrs. Roosevelt come to Havana and personally negotiate for the prisoners, but Milton held that the Cuban Premier was more interested in propaganda than negotiation and moreover such diplomacy should be handled through proper channels. Ultimately Castro raised his demand to $28 million and the committee dissolved. In Milton's seven-page official biography he cites the tractors' episode as "my one bad experience with a president." For Milton the break with Kennedy was somewhat wrenching. "If it hadn't been for this unhappy experience," he said, "I suspect I would have done a good deal of work for him."

"Ike must have told Milton to be more careful about answering his phone," President Kennedy told an aide, "especially when the White House is calling." In fact, Ike had been highly skeptical about the tractors' proposal yet told Milton that a personal request from the President should be accepted as a matter of duty.

The winding-down process is painful and difficult for any President and Ike had lived in the rarefied atmosphere of the Supreme Command, a university presidency, NATO, and the White House for the better part of two decades. On moving to Gettysburg in 1961, Ike did not know how to use a dial telephone nor did he have a driver's license. John Eisenhower, who lived on the farm while on a two-year leave to help Ike with his memoirs, drove his father to his office on the Gettysburg College campus. On one occasion John loaded a rifle to cover Ike's departure from the office to the car when a threat had been made on the general's life and the demented person was reportedly in the vicinity. In a 1974 interview, Mamie Eisenhower recalled with some trepidation that the observation tower near their farm was closed off because of threats against Ike.

Working on his memoirs became Ike's primary activity in 1961 and much of the next three years. Most American Presidents had not left a written record of their administrations other than their public papers and state documents, but in the 1950s the memoirs of Herbert Hoover and Harry Truman were published and received wide recognition. At the White House John urged his father to undertake such a project in retirement and finally convinced him. Taking a two-year leave from the Army, John became Ike's collaborator and by March of 1961 had produced outlines for both volumes of *The White House Years*. Doubleday, which had published *Crusade in Europe,* was again the publisher, but Congress had closed the capital gains loophole from which Ike had benefited so greatly and his payment would be straight royalties. As always, Milton was an editorial consultant and critic and frequently conferred with Ike about the memoirs. During his last year in the White House, John organized his father's presidential papers and arranged for their transfer to Gettysburg so that primary-source material would be readily available. In their discussions Ike and his son usually worked smoothly but there were sometimes differences. "He could act a little contemptuous of my opinions at times," said John. When John suggested that CIA director Allen Dulles should be criticized strongly for the U-2 fiasco, Ike banged the table with his hand and said: "Damn it, John, I'm writing this book." John retorted, "You sure are. Do it your way."

Ike's refusal to disclose his unvarnished opinions of contemporaries was in keeping with the bland tone he set in the two volumes. "The style is flat, sometimes banal," a friendly reviewer wrote of *Waging Peace* in the *Wall Street Journal*, "most of the comments are predictable and conventional. And the author's aversion to hurting anyone's feelings, a most amiable trait in itself and part of the popular 'Ike' image, takes some of the spice and sense of drama out of the historical picture." The first volume, *Mandate for Change*, was published in late 1963, and Columbia University historian Allan Nevins wrote: "Eisenhower does more than tell the story of his crowded White House years, with many revelations of fact—he paints a portrait of himself which in genial honesty and completeness is unmatched in presidential literature." Less charitable reviewers said that the book was downright boring. *Waging Peace*, the second volume, was published in 1965 and covered Ike's second term. John resigned from the Army in 1963 to help complete the project and in so doing passed up an assignment to the Army War College and the prospect of future high command. "Dad had done so well in the military," explains John, "I thought it best to try another profession."

Following the completion of the massive presidential memoirs Ike wrote an informal autobiography of his early life and of the period between World War II and the White House. Titled *At Ease: Stories I Tell to Friends*, the book was written without the assistance of a team of researchers and was his own book. John said it was his father's best work and most literary critics seemed to share that viewpoint. Written in a warm, breezy, anecdotal style, the book provided numerous insights into the Eisenhower character and background. For ten months *At Ease* was on the best-seller lists and it was the selection of two major book clubs.

Life at Gettysburg was most agreeable with Ike and Mamie and they would often spend their evenings sitting in their glass-enclosed porch with its panoramic view of the Civil War battlefield. When Ike painted, Mamie would read or play solitaire. During his first term Ike spent $215,000 to build a new farmhouse and renovate the grounds. Thousands of dollars more in tax-free gifts were donated to the Eisenhowers for the farm. Journalist Drew Pearson reported in 1960 that the machinery, livestock, and horticultural goods given to Ike were worth more than $300,000. Ike's acceptance of the gifts generated little criticism in that pre-Watergate age, but he was sensitive enough to comment on a ceremonial sword presented to George Washington: "Do you suppose they investigated him for getting that?" At a press conference he said, "I never accept gifts that I believe have any [selfish] motive whatever behind them."

If some scrambling newspaper reporters attempted to investigate Ike's farm, most of the press corps was complacent and the Women's National Press Club even gave him "Blue Bonnet," a prize Black Angus calf. Among the other notable gifts were a $4,000 tractor with a radio and cigarette lighter; two flower gardens; an orchid greenhouse; twelve Chippendale chairs; a $3,000 putting green with a $1,000 yearly maintenance contract; a fireplace that had once been used in the White House; a power-tool shop; a $2,300 Grandma Moses painting; and fifty white pine trees for his driveway, one from each state Republican Party. The Eisenhowers later donated the farm to the National Park Service with the provision that they would have lifetime use of its facilities, tax free.

Ike and Mamie often vacationed on the grounds of the Augusta National Golf Club, where a two-story brick country home had been built just for them near the tenth tee. The house, known as "Mamie's Cabin," was the inspiration of their close friend Clifford Roberts, founder of the club and driving force behind the Master's Golf Tournament. In the winter, the Eisenhowers took their private railroad car to Palm Desert, California, where they stayed at the El Dorado Country Club.

As the nation's most prominent Republican, Ike was still expected to play a political role and on several occasions he hosted Republican picnics at Gettysburg. In 1962, he campaigned for Richard Nixon in the latter's unsuccessful race for governor of California and vigorously supported William W. Scranton for governor of Pennsylvania. When Pennsylvania's Republican power brokers settled on mountebank Judge Robert E. Woodside as their candidate for the governorship, Ike told Senator Hugh Scott that the judge would be a "miserable" choice. With Scott, Ike had attempted to persuade former Defense Secretary Thomas Gates and Scranton to become candidates. When both declined, Ike urged Scott to consider making the race himself. Through deft maneuvering Scott forced the Republican leadership to shift their support to the young, progressive Scranton. Ike then called Scranton to Gettysburg and said, "What it all comes down to, Bill, is a four-letter word—duty." Scranton consented and went on to win so impressive a victory that overnight he emerged as a ranking contender for the 1964 Republican presidential nomination.

Both Rockefeller and Arizona Senator Barry Goldwater had been critics of the Eisenhower administration and Ike had little enthusiasm for either of the Republican presidential hopefuls. His first choice—as it had been for years—was the elusive Robert B. Anderson, but the former Treasury Secretary rebuffed all efforts to make him a presidential candidate and would not be persuaded. Ike also was prepared to work for General Alfred Gruenther or General Lucius Clay, should one of them stand for the nomination and yet neither of the old soldiers had the public following that would have justified a candidacy. Out of office, Ike had no shyness about publicly suggesting that Milton Eisenhower would make a great President and he encouraged friends to explore the possibility of a national campaign for his younger brother. In September of 1963, with Ike's blessing, Milton became chairman of the Critical Issues Council of the Republican Citizens Committee. A month later, Ike arranged for Milton to be the only speaker besides himself at his own seventy-third birthday party. Ike said Milton was "the best qualified man to be President of the United

States" and urged Republicans to pick a candidate of sincerity and integrity. In an interview at Palm Desert in early 1964, Ike was more reflective about Milton's chances: "He is sixty-five, and that's something of a drawback. And the presidency is something I wouldn't wish on him."

As the president of Johns Hopkins University, Milton was a pillar of the Eastern Establishment and one of the nation's foremost educators. Milton went to Hopkins in 1956 not only because it was among the most prestigious of American universities but also because Baltimore was only a forty-five-minute train ride from Washington. "Hopkins was a very different kind of institution for Milton," said a longtime associate. "It gave a new thrust to his career." There was some concern that Milton's lack of a Ph.D. degree might cause some uneasiness at an institution renowned for its advanced graduate programs. For Milton, it did not seem to be a handicap, for he had no scholarly pretensions and yet became thoroughly absorbed in all aspects of the university. "The presidents of Yale and Harvard didn't have Ph.D.s," said Milton. "I do think if you don't come out of the scholarly ranks, that you have to have something as a good substitute. In my case, it was the work I did in government—foreign affairs, economics, and agriculture gave me an acceptability for the positions I occupied. Running a university is a terribly difficult job. You have to provide educational leadership. If you don't, it won't exist. You may not be a scholar in the academic sense but you have to have a great responsibility and understanding for scholarship."

One reason for Milton's appointment was his reputation as a fund raiser. Money had made Hopkins one of the nation's preeminent universities in the late 1800s, and a fiscal crunch had brought a period of stagnation. Hopkins was founded in 1874 with the largest private grant made for educational purposes during America's first century—seven million dollars. Its medical school became one of the world's most prestigious and other graduate departments were celebrated for their mature scholarship and innovative seminar methods. Unhappily, the value of the university's principal investments declined sharply not long after 1900 and, for most of the years between 1910 and Milton's appointment, Hopkins operated at a deficit. There had been no major building programs since the great Depression and many of the academic buildings were overcrowded and obsolete. Once the nation's highest, faculty salaries were no longer competitive with other great universities. Hopkins needed nothing less than a miracle worker and Milton eagerly accepted the challenge. In his first year the university finished with a modest reserve and there would be no deficits for the rest of his presidency. Working with trustees, department heads, and faculty members, Milton was determined to restore Hopkins to eminence among universities. To a remarkable degree he succeeded and through his efforts Hopkins experienced its greatest period of growth since the Gilded Age. More than seventy-five million dollars was spent to expand the physical plant, and the university endowment was doubled. Twelve endowed faculty chairs were created with private gifts and faculty salaries became the fourth highest in the country. "Milton was a superb fund raiser," said a former Hopkins associate. "People trust him instantly and he's persuasive without being a salesman. His well-known name was also an advantage and he was an excellent representative for the university."

Indeed, Milton Eisenhower brought Hopkins a special prominence as only a public figure can bring. Through his offices Hopkins obtained such visiting lecturers as British Prime Minister Harold Macmillan and Lyndon Johnson. Faculty members cherished an invitation to Milton's home and the opportunity to talk informally with such friends as Dean Rusk, Charles Bohlen, and other grey eminences. Milton's quiet and natural manner impressed Hopkins' administrators, faculty, and students. "He asks keen and perceptive questions," said a dean, "and you end up doing most of the talking." Milton won over undergraduates by showing up at football games and making a standard practice of inviting all interested students for rap sessions in the presidential residence when his study light was on.

Although Maryland was a Democratic stronghold, it was generally conceded that Milton could probably win the governorship or a Senate seat if he wanted to enter Republican politics. Malcolm Moos, a political science professor at Hopkins who was chairman of the Republican Central Committee for Baltimore City, approached Milton as early as 1957 to suggest that he run for the

Senate in 1958. Always concerned about the "dynasty" issue, Milton was hesitant to consider making any active campaign while Ike remained in the White House. In addition, he was just beginning his rebuilding program at Hopkins and was committed to following through. Milton also would not have challenged incumbent Republican Senator J. Glenn Beall, with whom he had a warm relationship. When Maryland's other Republican senator, John Marshall Butler, announced his retirement in December of 1961, Milton was immediately boomed as the logical successor. Senator Beall declared that Milton "would make the best possible candidate Maryland could find" and added: "I believe I can say right now the party wants him." Beall and former Governor Theodore R. McKeldin privately urged Milton to run for Butler's seat. As a senator, Milton would have the opportunity to confront the global and national issues that he was so passionately interested in. If he entertained presidential or vice-presidential ambitions the Senate election could demonstrate what most political leaders suspected—that Milton had vote-getting potential not unlike his brother's. In Kansas and again in Pennsylvania, Milton declined the overtures made by political leaders partly because he had no zest for political battle and the inevitable personal attacks. The situation in Maryland was much different than it had been elsewhere. His role at Johns Hopkins gave him the aura of a scholar-statesman and Milton was, like Ike, considered "above partisanship." Milton's friends and associates were enthusiastic about what seemed to be a most glittering opportunity for another Eisenhower to emerge. On December 13, 1961, Milton disappointed his avid supporters by saying that he would not leave Hopkins. "I have given no thought whatever to running for elective office in Maryland," he said, "and I cannot really conceive of a set of circumstances that would induce me to think seriously about it. I came here to do what I can to help Hopkins reach ever higher levels of excellence in teaching and research and I find great satisfaction in my university assignment. My obligations to the university are unfinished. I have no thought of leaving."

Years later Milton admitted that he had given serious thought to accepting the 1962 nomination: "The only political position I ever thought about and I think I would have liked to have achieved would have been the Senate. The Republicans offered me the nomination without opposition and I think I could have easily been elected. But my conscience wouldn't let me do it. Everyone thought I was crazy. But I was only halfway through a rather comprehensive program and I just couldn't leave Hopkins until the job was finished." Without Milton, Maryland's Republicans lost the Senate seat to Democrat Daniel Brewster, and the noncandidate stayed on the job at Hopkins.

Milton's refusal to seek office in 1962 showed that he was not interested in running for the presidency two years later, and Ike's public endorsement would not be enough to make the younger brother a serious contender. He shrank from such suggestions yet at the same time was interested in advancing the candidacy of other Republican moderates.

Ike was scheduled to meet with some of his oldest political associates on the weekend of November 23, 1963, to discuss possible Republican presidential candidates. Earlier in the month Ike had called on Henry Cabot Lodge, then serving as ambassador to South Vietnam, to return and campaign as the "common sense" candidate for President. Milton thought Lodge had been a lazy campaigner as the vice-presidential candidate in 1960 and disapproved of him as presidential material. Milton's first choice was Scranton of Pennsylvania. The planned November meeting never took place, for President Kennedy was assassinated on Friday afternoon and Ike drove from Gettysburg to Washington the next day to mourn the slain President. Lyndon B. Johnson invited Ike to meet with him in the grandly Victorian Executive Office Building and they talked for more than an hour. After their meeting Ike wrote a confidential memorandum for Johnson which urged him to make a brief speech before a joint congressional session. "You hope," Ike concluded, "that people of government and the entire nation may now mobilize their hearts, their hands and their resources for one purpose—to increase the spiritual and material resources of the nation and to advance her prestige and her capacity for leadership in the world for peace." Johnson said later that he was deeply touched by Ike's thoughtfulness and publicly acknowledged the former President's contribution.

A moratorium on campaigning followed the Kennedy assassination and the Eisenhowers carefully observed it, as did the Republican presidential hopefuls. By the beginning of 1964, the campaign had formally begun and Goldwater and Rockefeller seemed to be the only Republican candidates. At Scranton's invitation Milton came to the governor's mansion at Indiantown Gap in the early winter. "We spent twenty-four hours together," Milton recalls, "and I urged him to come out as an active candidate. But in a way Bill Scranton never really wanted to be in politics. He had to be persuaded to run for Congress and for governor. He never really wanted to be President. He loved his family life—his wife was in Switzerland when I visited him—and he didn't like having her away." Milton returned to Baltimore without a candidate.

On March 10, Henry Cabot Lodge won the New Hampshire primary in an avalanche of write-in votes and suddenly was the front runner in national polls. An old film clip of Ike praising Lodge had been the centerpiece of a highly effective television commercial. Lodge's victory was reminiscent of Ike's own early triumphs in 1952, for like Ike, Lodge was serving abroad in a sensitive position and disavowing any interest in the nomination. Oregon was the next major primary state and Lodge's name was on the ballot. When Goldwater's campaign manager there sent Ike a telegram asking him to repudiate his appearance in the Lodge television commercial Ike responded that the film was a "definite misrepresentation" if it suggested that he was endorsing Lodge. The commercials were withdrawn and Ike's action undermined Lodge's chances. Although two major polls showed Lodge ahead in Oregon and *Time* and *The Saturday Evening Post* published glowing Lodge cover stories on the eve of the primary, the momentum was shifting to Rockefeller, whose strenuous campaign and slogan "He Cared Enough to Come" were scoring points. Rockefeller quipped, "It looks like I'm the Lone Ranger, the only one left in this campaign." Challenging Lodge to return from Saigon and debate the issues and questioning the legality of Lodge running for office while serving as a diplomat, Rockefeller made a strong finish. On May 15, Rockefeller eliminated Lodge with a stunning upset in the Oregon vote. Two weeks later came the all-important California primary and the Oregon victory had made Rockefeller a favorite over Goldwater. That Goldwater might win the nomination in spite of his weak showing in the contested primaries was a most unpleasant realization for Ike.

On May 25, Ike published a statement on the front page of the New York *Herald Tribune* that described the kind of candidate he hoped his party would nominate with such adjectives as "responsible," "forward-looking," and "positive." Rockefeller's forces were elated by the apparent endorsement and Goldwater, appearing at a campus rally, displayed a long arrow sticking out his back. Former Treasury Secretary Humphrey, a Goldwaterite, and still a close friend of Ike's, called Gettysburg and warned his former boss that unless he disavowed newspaper interpretations of the article he would be smack in the middle of a bitter intraparty struggle. One day before the California voting, Ike snapped at a news conference: "You people tried to read Goldwater out of the party. I didn't." Whatever help Ike's May 25 statement had been to Rockefeller was neutralized. Ike would not condemn Goldwater as a right-wing extremist as Rockefeller had done.

In the meantime, Goldwater shrewdly arranged a breakfast meeting with Milton in Washington just two days before the California primary. Goldwater asked for the meeting to discuss Milton's work as chairman of the Critical Issues Council of the Republican Citizens Committee. Edgar Eisenhower, Goldwater's chairman in Washington State, had been the intermediary. Because Goldwater had been a critic of the Critical Issues Council and of the Eisenhower administration ("a dime-store New Deal"), Milton saw little reason for the meeting, but as a courtesy to a leading presidential candidate of his party he accepted the invitation. Goldwater told Milton he had read all of the council's position papers and with the exception of their liberal civil-rights paper he supported them all. A dozen photographers were gathered in the hall when Goldwater escorted a taciturn Milton out of his Senate office and the senator said that they were in agreement that Republicans should stop attacking each other and concentrate their fire on President Johnson. The widely published photographs of Barry and Milton suggested that the Eisenhowers were acknowledging Goldwater as the soon-to-be-crowned leader of the Republican Party.

On June 2, Goldwater received 51.4 percent of the vote in California's winner-take-all primary, a plurality of 68,000 votes out of more than 2 million. Rockefeller was finished as a contender and Goldwater had moved into a commanding lead. Unless Ike himself led the effort to "Stop Goldwater," the Arizona senator probably could not be denied the nomination.

Oddly enough Ike had cited Goldwater as a possible future presidential candidate in the early 1950s when he told Hazlett that the Republicans had many bright young stars. By 1957, Goldwater had broken with Ike and called the Administration's fiscal policies "a betrayal of the people's trust." In defense policy Goldwater advocated the use of atomic weapons and said that NATO field commanders should be able to use them at their discretion. He called for "total victory" against international communism. Goldwater's call for a return to the values and traditions of an earlier and less complex era had enormous appeal for conservatives and his rugged individualism was genuine. Goldwater condemned the social welfare legacy of the New Deal and he voted against the 1964 Civil Rights Act, which placed him in the company of southern segregationists.

Ike was far from pleased with Goldwater as a presidential candidate and in an off-the-record conversation with reporter Merriman Smith said that the senator's foreign policies were "dangerous." To former aide Arthur Larson Ike confided that he was deeply troubled by the Goldwater threat and went on to conclude that the senator was "nuts." Milton's judgment was equally critical: "My attitude toward Goldwater didn't have much to do with his conservatism," Milton recalled in a 1977 interview. "I just felt that he did not have the background and the knowledge that a President of the United States needed. I also felt that neither an extreme rightist nor leftist could be elected." On the Saturday that followed the California primary Ike proposed coming to Harrisburg to meet with Governor Scranton, but the governor instead offered to meet Ike at Gettysburg. It had been Ike's persuasion that convinced Scranton to make himself available for the governorship in 1962, and now the old soldier similarly urged Scranton to run for the presidency. Scranton left the meeting with the clear impression that Ike was going to endorse him. The National Governors Conference was to begin the next day in Cleveland and Scranton was expected to announce his candidacy on a nationally televised interview program. Soon after the Ike-Scranton conference there were reports that the former President would join Scranton in Cleveland as the leader of still another American crusade.

George Humphrey called Ike at Gettysburg and bluntly told him that endorsing Scranton would be a mistake that would divide the party and would also prove embarrassing to Humphrey because Ike was to be a house guest at the former Cabinet Secretary's suburban Cleveland mansion during the Governors Conference. Another Eisenhower administration stalwart, former Postmaster General Arthur Summerfield, had called Gettysburg to recommend against Ike's participation in a Scranton campaign. Humphrey's opinion carried more weight and Ike agreed that he would do nothing to embarrass his host during the conference. When Scranton reached Cleveland he received a message that Ike wanted him to call Gettysburg. Scranton's aides assumed that the former President wanted to give the governor some friendly encouragement before Scranton appeared on "Face the Nation." What happened instead was that Ike expressed dismay about the reports of his own anti-Goldwater activity and told Scranton: "I don't want to be part of a 'stop anybody' cabal, and I don't think you should be." Visibly shaken, Scranton appeared inept and stumbling in the television interview and would not commit himself to a campaign for the nomination.

Scranton's humiliation was complete, for Ike had ruined what should have been a forceful debut in presidential politics. Richard Nixon came to Cleveland and tried to organize a campaign for Michigan Governor George Romney following Scranton's dismal performance. What most observers did not know at the time was that Ike had been largely responsible for Scranton's weak and ineffective appearance and one fellow governor cruelly referred to the reluctant candidate as "Gutless Bill." Years later Goldwater said, "Ike would have probably supported him but Scranton never showed the courage to come out and fight for it."

Yet Ike also had been an unwilling warrior and his vacillation astonished members of his own family. Milton and John Eisenhower were disappointed that Ike's mercurial behavior had sabotaged Scranton. Later in the week Goldwater voted against the 1964 Civil Rights bill, and further embarrassed Ike, whose administration had initiated historic advances in civil rights. He called Scranton and lamented the Goldwater vote, urging the governor to make known his pro-civil-rights views and to reconsider running for the presidency. Ike stated publicly that he hoped the Republicans would choose a candidate who favored equality for blacks. On Friday, June 12, at the Maryland Republican Convention, Scranton announced his candidacy. "I knew that I never had a chance to be nominated," Scranton told me in 1974. "I ran primarily out of concern for the future of the party. Republicans were being portrayed as a white supremacy party and that really threw me off—it was so contrary to the party's record. I was disturbed about what was happening to the party. I wasn't personally ambitious for power."

From Gettysburg came Ike's statement that competition for the nomination would be healthy for the party: "I welcome the entry of Governor Scranton, whom I have long admired, into the contest." Henry Cabot Lodge resigned as ambassador to South Vietnam to return and assist the Scranton campaign and Lodge privately urged Ike to become a full-fledged Scranton ally. Rockefeller turned over his vast political resources to Scranton and the New York governor asked Ike to publicly join the battle. There would be no preconvention endorsement from the former President, but his family and most of his longtime political associates were now committed to Scranton.

On June 18, Scranton released a letter of endorsement from Milton, whom he had been consulting on a daily basis. The letter set forth Milton's philosophy of moderate Republicanism: "Your courageous decision to seek the Republican nomination for the presidency is tremendously heartening to all who are deeply concerned about the direction our nation has been taking since January 1961, and who wish now to work hard for a Republican of sound philosophy who will change that direction," wrote Milton.

"In the 14 years I have known you, I have admired the thorough study you give each critical issue facing the nation, the calm and wise judgments you express and the courageous way you stand for what you deem to be right.

"I know that you stand for complete integrity in government, for fiscal responsibility, for having government promote, not deaden, the creative abilities of all citizens within our competitive free system; for having government promote the general welfare in all those evolving situations which cannot be handled by the people themselves, and having essential public responsibility carried out by local and state governments when possible, by the federal government when necessary, for assuring absolute equality for all citziens regardless of race, color, or national origin; for a sound foreign policy within which each critical development may be wisely judged and consistent action fearlessly taken."

Scranton had called Milton on the eve of his announcement and asked him to do a "great favor," namely, place Scranton's name in nomination at the Republican Convention at San Francisco. Flattered that Scranton had chosen him over such prominent supporters as Rockefeller and Lodge, Milton explained that he was not a member of the Maryland delegation. Scranton replied that arrangements would be made for Milton to be seated as a delegate. Announcement of Milton's selection as the nominator was one of the high points of the Scranton campaign, and the governor said that Ike was "delighted" and had commented further that "it was the best news he had heard yet."

As promised, Scranton secured Milton a place in the Maryland delegation. Goldwater's Maryland chairman, Fife Symington, challenged the legality of substituting Milton for another delegate and was going to ask the Maryland caucus to reject Milton's credentials. Though Milton did not ordinarily welcome such controversy he sensed that such tactics by Goldwater forces might work to Scranton's benefit at San Francisco in the same way that Eisenhower's "Fair Play" amendment had at the 1952 convention. Goldwater, however, recognized that defeating Milton Eisenhower would be widely interpreted as a disservice to a distinguished Republican. A telegram from Goldwater to Milton said that "any objections to your being seated do not stem from any efforts on my part. I have asked my people in Maryland to desist from activities in this regard." Milton's ratification as a delegate proceeded swiftly and without further obstacles.

There was even some speculation that Goldwater might choose

Milton as his vice-presidential candidate. It was said that Milton, as a progressive, would add philosophical balance to a ticket headed by the conservative Goldwater and would strengthen Republican chances in the industrial states of the Northeast. Goldwater's criticism of the Eisenhower administration, however, would have made it difficult for Milton to have accepted, and Goldwater made it clear that he had strong reservations about Milton. "One Eisenhower in a generation is enough," said the salty Goldwater. Goldwater elaborated in a 1977 interview that while Milton was highly respected as an educator he lacked political aptitude.

In San Francisco the Scranton partisans clung to the hope that Ike might change his mind and deliver a ringing endorsement. Two Scranton advisers, a then little-known Harvard political scientist named Henry Kissinger and James Reichley, anxiously met with Milton to see if Ike might endorse the Scranton platform proposal that only the President and not NATO field commanders should have authority to detonate nuclear weapons. While Ike approved of the Scranton resolution and seemed ready to endorse it, he soon retreated on the basis that an ex-President should not indulge in such controversies. Nor would Ike help Rockefeller and Romney in their call for a liberal civil-rights platform.

To Norman Mailer it all came down to Ike's advancing age and his wish not to hurt anyone's feelings. "Something had been dying in him for years," wrote Mailer, "the proportions and magnitude of his own death no doubt, and he was going down into the cruelest of fates for an old man, he was hooked on love like an addict, not large love, but the kind of mild tolerant love which shields an old man from hatred. It was obvious that Eisenhower had a deep fear of the forces which were for Goldwater. He did not mind with full pride any longer if people felt contempt for him, but he did not want to be hated hard by anyone."

During the convention's Tuesday session, Ike delivered one of the most hard-hitting speeches of the convention and its tone was closer to Goldwater than Scranton. "Let us not be guilty," said Ike, "of maudlin sympathy for the criminal, who, roaming the streets with the switchblade knife and illegal firearm, seeking a helpless prey, suddenly becomes upon apprehension, a poor underprivileged person who counts upon the compassion of our society and the laxness or weaknesses of too many courts to forgive his offense." It was Ike's most vocal attack on the liberal policies of the Warren Court, but what brought the most rousing ovation at the Cow Palace was his criticism of the press: "Let us particularly scorn the divisive efforts of those outside our family, including sensation-seeking columnists and commentators, who couldn't care less about the good of our party." Then he urged the party to "renew our strength from the fountain of unity."

Milton's speech was impressive and demonstrated why Ike had so often talked of him in presidential terms. The convention anchorman from NBC, Chet Huntley, observed that Milton had been the only rational voice at the convention and one columnist suggested that President Johnson would do well to consider Milton as his Democratic vice-presidential running mate. At the end of the first ballot, Goldwater had 883 delegates to Scranton's 214 and Rockefeller's 114. For Vice President, nominee Goldwater selected an obscure New York congressman, William E. Miller, whose conservatism was as doctrinaire as Goldwater's.

There had been many ugly moments at the convention, with the booing and jeering of Rockefeller perhaps the most savage. Ike was particularly disturbed by reports of a "hoodlum harassing" the wife of a speaker and someone molesting his niece, then serving as a convention page, who tearfully reported the incident to him. As a result of these and other emotional incidents, Ike would urge the party's national committee to reform its convention procedures by curbing noisy demonstrations and reducing the number of delegates.

In a very real sense the Goldwater nomination meant the end of the Eisenhower era of the Republican Party. Goldwater's criticism of Ike's presidency had brought him notoriety and set him apart from Republican moderates; his critical references to "me-too-ism" was a repudiation of Ike's essential nonpartisanship and the idealistic promise of modern Republicanism. His acceptance speech defiantly challenged the Eisenhower style: "I would remind you that extremism in the defense of liberty is no vice. And let me remind you that moderation in the pursuit of justice is no virtue."

Goldwater attempted to soothe Ike by explaining that during the Normandy invasion Eisenhower himself had been an extremist in defense of liberty. Though Ike was unpersuaded by the ridiculous historical analogy, he did appreciate Goldwater's continuing conciliatory efforts toward him and agreed to participate in a party-unity gathering in Hershey, Pennsylvania. The defeated Republican hopefuls—Scranton, Rockefeller, Nixon, and Romney—joined Ike and Goldwater to discuss the campaign against President Johnson. Ike rated the GOP summit as less than a success because of Goldwater's emphatic denial that his Hershey speech was conciliatory. In a letter to Milton on August 14, Ike wrote: "You will recall some of the disparaging comments he made about the Republican Administration of 1953–1961; others he directed toward me personally. Now, however, he has without explanation or apology gone out of his way to pay compliments both to me and to my administration. Obviously he *means* to conciliate but not to admit it."

Goldwater made another mistake, said Ike, when he "allowed himself to get tangled into questions involving tactics in Vietnam (concerning which even a lifelong military man would not want to comment without a knowledge of all the facts). . . . This defensive trait, bordering upon belligerency, seemed to be frequently evident for the simple reason that he has made so many statements in quick reaction to questions of the past that he seems to be in a bit of hot water all the time when he is questioned about them. Possibly we have here an unsuspected 'inferiority complex.'

"On the other hand, there is no question of his sincerity, honesty and innate decency. I am sure that in any Administration of his there would be no tendency to gloss over such things as the Bobby Baker case. . . .

"My prediction is that because of his fear of ever appearing to say 'I was wrong,' he will not be quite as successful in uniting the leadership as I had hoped and, at the same time, will find his press conferences taking on the nature of a 'cross examination.' The young man he has made Chairman of the National Committee [N. Dean Burch] looks to me to be a rather able individual, but I am not sure that any adviser can help Barry overcome the one defect I mention—indeed some of them may encourage him in it.

"In any event, he is *our* candidate. While I get tired at times when hearing the 'two party system' given credit for every American advance since 1800 A.D., I still firmly believe in it, and deplore the tactics of those temperamental 'switch arounders' who take themselves so seriously."

A month later, Ike appeared with Goldwater on a half-hour television program that had the lowest audience ratings of the time period and a forgettable dialogue between the normally salty characters. Unable to overcome his extremist image, Goldwater was trounced in the November election. Johnson won forty-four states and the District of Columbia and a plurality of almost sixteen million votes. "It is all too obvious," wrote Ike, "that the Republican Party suffered further distortion of its image in the 1964 campaign." Ike concluded that many Republicans held the "mistaken impression that their party's national ticket had abandoned many traditional Republican principles and leaned toward reactionary, extremist, and racist fringes."

A month after the election Ike met with Nixon and Goldwater in New York and called for the replacement of Dean Burch as Republican national chairman. As a result of this meeting it was agreed that Ohio's shrewd and nonideological Ray Bliss should become national chairman. The subsequent election of Bliss was an important beginning in the Republican recovery. In the summer of 1965, Ike hosted four hundred Republican leaders for a picnic at Gettysburg, and it was clear that the former President did not want the party to experience another debacle. What Ike had been stressing since the Goldwater defeat was the necessity for Republicans to remind the nation that they were indeed the party of Lincoln and were committed to social justice. "There is a very real danger," Ike wrote in a 1965 magazine article, "not just to the major parties but to our whole political system itself in attempts to cram voters into narrow ideological compartments."

In the meantime, Ike was often consulted by President Johnson. Although Johnson's aggressive war policies in Vietnam were radically different than Ike's had been, the former President expressed public support for the military build-up. Johnson cited the SEATO treaty of the Eisenhower administration as a binding commitment to intervene in Vietnam and by implication blamed Ike for the unpopular war. When Ike could no longer tolerate Johnson's revisionist history, he issued a statement that emphasized it was economic and technical aid that the Eisenhower administration had promised and delivered. "Ike was bitterly opposed to getting into Vietnam," recalled Milton in 1976. "But after we got in, it was a different matter. While he might have discussed it in his private papers, he didn't speak out publicly. To have done so, he felt, would have given strength and confidence to the enemy."

During the Johnson years, Milton was also a presidential confidant and on occasion Johnson would send a helicopter to Johns Hopkins that would bring the university president directly to the White House. On April 7, 1965, Johnson made a major Vietnam speech at Hopkins, announcing that he was prepared to participate in "unconditional discussions" to end the war, but the fighting continued. John Eisenhower says that it is impossible to determine how Ike would have handled Vietnam had he remained President. "I'm inclined to think," he says, "that he would not have sent ground troops in, but I don't know."

Ike's popularity remained towering and in the last two years of the Johnson presidency, Eisenhower led the Gallup poll's list of most admired Americans. As the nation's patriarch he suggested some political reforms that were innovative and somewhat unorthodox: limiting senators and representatives to twelve years of service and restoring the tradition of citizen representation; making congressional terms four years instead of two, and having the elections held in presidential years; limiting federal judges to twenty-year terms with mandatory retirement at age seventy-two, explaining that "when a man is removed from the mainstream of life, his opinions and actions are likely to become inflexible." There had been few substantive changes in the Constitution since the document was written by its revolutionary-era framers and Ike made the argument that his proposals would "make the government work better." To amend the Constitution was not a task for an old man, for it is a long and extremely difficult process, but his proposals were to be cited for more than a decade by advocates of constitutional reform.

All of the contenders for the Republican presidential nomination flew to Ike's side and sought advice and, most of all, endorsement. Ike's first choice was former Pennsylvania Governor William Scranton, whom he had failed to support when it counted most in 1964. Because of an anachronistic state constitution, Scranton was ineligible to run for a second term as governor and, though still a young man, announced his retirement from politics in 1967. Milton still looked upon Scranton as the most ideal presidential candidate and was prepared to openly back him once again. So the brothers Eisenhower were in agreement. Ike urged Scranton to reconsider his withdrawal from politics with the promise of active support for the second Scranton presidential campaign. This time Scranton would not be persuaded, and in later years he would reject appointments as Secretary of State and Republican vice-presidential candidate. Another Eisenhower favorite was Illinois Senator Charles Percy, who had first been brought to Ike's attention by Milton in the 1950s. In 1961, Ike had written Percy, then president of Bell & Howell, about a possible political career: "I look forward at some future date to supporting you for political office—and should it be the highest office in the land my satisfaction will be all the greater." Defeated for the Illinois governorship in the 1964 Johnson landslide, Percy proved resilient enough to come back two years later and score a landslide himself against the much-respected Democratic senator, Paul H. Douglas. With that spectacular triumph Percy was instantly touted as the golden boy of moderate Republicanism and a presidential contender. Years later Percy described Ike as the "controlling influence that caused me to come into public life . . . the only man who could have caused me to seek elective office."

Percy eliminated himself as a presidential candidate during a November 2, 1967, meeting with Nixon at Milton's home in Baltimore. Milton had arranged for the meeting between his longtime friend, Percy, and the durable Nixon, hoping that it would enhance Percy's chances for the vice presidency. For nearly five hours the three men talked about issues and personalities, with Nixon conceding that Percy was himself a threat to win the nomination and Percy responding that with only two years in the Senate he was not yet qualified for the presidency. Though Percy had conducted an exploratory campaign in strategic primary states and showed modest but steady gains in public-opinion polls, his decision was firm—1968 would not be his year.

At a 1967 news conference, Ike listed Percy, Rockefeller, Romney, and Reagan as men whom he could support for the presidency in 1968. Sitting beside her husband, Mamie loudly whispered that there had been an omission: "You forgot Dick!" "Oh yes," said Ike, "Dick Nixon—a fine American." Ike's enthusiasm for his Vice President had always been well under control, although by 1967 he observed to former aide Arthur Larson that Nixon had "really matured." Michigan Governor George Romney was the early front runner on the basis of his high standing in public-opinion polls among Republicans and in trial heats with President Johnson. Romney's verbal blunders were reminiscent of Goldwater's faux pas, and Ike commented that Romney had "lost much ground in the public mind" following a statement about being "brainwashed" during a visit to Vietnam. With friends Ike was more blunt, saying that Romney sounded "like a man in panic" and lacked the heft to be President. Romney's criticism of Johnson's Vietnam policy as morally wrong and unjustified would be ultimately vindicated, but it did not set well with Ike who continued to defend Johnson's war. Ike's assessment of Romney's decline was realistic and in March, before the New Hampshire primary, the governor surprised the nation by terminating his candidacy. The Republican field had narrowed to Nixon and the still undeclared Rockefeller and Reagan.

On April 29, 1968, at Palm Desert, Ike suffered his fourth heart attack and was under intensive care for several weeks at March Air Force Hospital. In May, he was flown to Washington where he would receive further treatment and convalesce at Walter Reed Hospital. His condition was frail but there were signs of improvement. On June 15, there was another though milder heart attack. Among his visitors shortly afterward was Nixon, the undisputed front runner for the nomination, following a series of primary-election victories. Mamie had not been at all shy about wearing a large Nixon button in public and John appeared on the platform with Nixon at Portland's elegant Benson Hotel to celebrate Nixon's Oregon primary triumph. Since late 1967, David Eisenhower, Ike's only grandson, had been campaigning for Nixon. During a television interview in Oregon Nixon had proudly disclosed that David was going to become his son-in-law, announcing the engagement of Ike's namesake to his own attractive daughter Julie. "You can't beat a Nixon-Ike combination," said Romney about Nixon's extensive use of the young couple during the New Hampshire primary campaign. It had been at Mamie's urging that David look up Julie, when he was enrolled at Amherst College and she was attending Smith College, and Mamie was a strong Nixon partisan. "I wish," said an Eisenhower friend, "that Mamie would have done half as much for Ike as she did for Nixon." What Nixon wanted in the summer of 1968 was a preconvention endorsement from Ike. Milton did not think Ike should be pressured to make any political statement and felt that Ike had no obligation to endorse Nixon. "I always thought that undue influence was put on him [Ike] when he was approaching the end," said Milton, "that brought him to depart from his tradition of not intervening before the convention." Milton held Mamie in large part responsible for the Nixon endorsement. On July 18, Ike endorsed Nixon from his hospital bed as "a man of great reading, a man of great intelligence, a man of great decisiveness" whose "nomination and election would serve the best interest of the United States." Ike said reports that he had reservations about Nixon's capabilities were "complete misapprehension." Nixon termed the endorsement "immensely helpful" and "a real lift," while Rockefeller said anything short of an endorsement "would be very embarrassing for him [Nixon]" because of Julie's engagement to David.

Milton had very definite reservations about Nixon, and for that reason was rather crudely denied a place in the Maryland delegation to the Republican Convention. In 1966, a group of liberal Republicans had called on Milton to run for governor and were told that their candidate wanted to fulfill his obligations to Johns Hopkins. With Milton not running, Spiro T. Agnew, then chief executive of suburban Baltimore County, received the nomination and won the election because he campaigned as a civil-rights progressive while his Democratic opponent, George Mahoney, appealed to racism. When it became known that Milton planned to retire as president of Hopkins in 1968, some Republicans said hopefully that at last Milton would be free to run for the Senate. "I think he'd make a strong candidate," said Newton Steers, the state's Republican chairman. For a different reason, Milton declined to run against Democratic Senator Daniel Brewster. "I was nearly seventy," recalled Milton, "and was too old." Milton supported an exceptionally able and progressive congressman from western Maryland, Charles McC. Mathias, and served as chairman of Citizens for Mathias. Despite a Democratic registration edge of 3 to 1, Mathias defeated Senator Brewster. Like Mathias, Angew had been for Scranton in 1964 and recognized Milton as a nationally prominent Republican moderate. "When he was Baltimore County executive, we had lunch several times," said Milton. "We talked a lot about the economy. When he became governor, Agnew was the leading figure in the United States in trying to organize Rockefeller's 1968 presidential campaign." Because of Milton's old ties with Rockefeller, Agnew was deferential to the Hopkins president during this period. So unimpressed with Agnew was Rockefeller that he neglected to notify him that an expected announcement of candidacy was instead a withdrawal statement. Publicly humiliated, Agnew dropped his support when Rockefeller changed his mind two months later. Nixon had made overtures to the governor and hinted that he was being considered for Vice President. The ambitious Agnew purged Milton from the delegation as a demonstration of his eagerness to please Nixon. "Agnew had called me early in the spring and asked me to be a delegate," said Milton a decade later. "But after the Rockefeller incident he called again and said, 'I'm sorry, Dr. Eisenhower, I can't put your name up for the delegation. You'd be for Rockefeller and I'm putting together a Nixon delegation.' I slapped down the phone and never talked with him again. I got invitations to various dinners and receptions for Agnew and just threw them in the wastebasket. He was a political chameleon, who was so ambitious that he would say anything or flop anywhere to advance his career."

His exclusion from the delegation through Agnew's insensitivity was, to be sure, a disappointment. Whatever bitterness Milton felt at the time was soon eclipsed by a prestigious appointment. The nation had been jolted by the brutal assassinations of Martin Luther King, Jr., and Robert F. Kennedy, two of its most vital and vibrant young leaders. On June 7, the day after Kennedy's death, President Johnson called Milton to ask that he serve as chairman of a presidential commission that would study the causes of violence in American society. When Johnson told Milton the names of some of the commission's other members, Milton's rejoinder was that surely one of them might better serve as chairman. In a time of crisis, said Johnson, a national figure was needed and Milton's reputation for objectivity and fairness made him the best possible choice. It was the famed "Johnson treatment" and Milton could not refuse. For the next year and a half Milton would supervise hearings, conferences, and the research of some two hundred scholars. "Violence in the United States has risen to alarmingly high levels," the commission's report said. "Whether one considers assassination, group violence, or individual acts of violence, the decade of the 1960s was considerably more violent than the several decades preceding it and ranks among the most violent in our history. The United States is the clear leader among modern, stable democratic nations in its rates of homicide, assault, rape, and robbery, and it is at least among the highest in incidence of group violence and assassination. . . . The American people know the threat. They demand that violence be brought to a halt." Among the commission's recommendations was a national firearms policy that would limit the availability of handguns. When no such law was passed the era of handgun politics continued in later years with assassination attempts on Alabama Governor George Wallace and President Gerald Ford. Unless strong measures were taken, warned Milton, there would be still more violence. A ban on handguns was a partial solution, he said. "There are now some forty-three million handguns in circulation," he said in 1976, "increasing at a rate of three million a year. The handguns are being used in 54 percent of all murders—and in most assassinations. It may be politically unpopular to be for gun control today. But in a couple more years, the political disadvantage will be against those opposing gun control." Sadly, Milton also concluded that a more restricted method of campaigning should be used by presidential candidates. "In some countries," he said, "dictators have been shot for political reasons. But in the United States, assassinations have been committed by nuts, unbalanced people. You can double Secret Service protection and take other measures, yet as long as the President insists on barnstorming the country, he is still a target. I think the President must consider other methods to be in touch with the people. He cannot continue to be exposed in the traditional way."

In August of 1968, Ike addressed the Republican Convention in a speech that was taped for television and shown at the Miami convention hall. Before the broadcast Congressman Richard Schweiker described Ike as the "spirit of Republican renaissance" who "brought new life and new hope" to the nation. Schweiker presented a gold delegate's badge to John Eisenhower, for his father. For Republicans Ike's speech summoned the nostalgia of conventions past and national election triumphs, and delegates listened with attentive respect. On Vietnam Ike warned against a quick political settlement: "Once we begin to compete over how best to contrive an American retreat in such a struggle, then we are heading for trouble. It is one thing to call for a peaceful settlement of this struggle. It is quite another to call for retreat by America. The latter is the best way I know to stockpile tragedy for our children." Typically, there was no partisanship in Ike's speech and he criticized neither the Democratic Party nor the Johnson administration. "Here at home," he said, "let us first remind ourselves of the greatness of this nation and its people."

The next day, Ike had another heart attack, a serious one, and the nation sensed that the old warrior might never leave the hospital. Nixon was nominated and invoked Ike's name in his acceptance speech: "General Eisenhower, as you know, lies critically ill in the Walter Reed Hospital tonight. I have talked, however, with Mrs. Eisenhower on the telephone. She tells me . . . there is nothing that he lives more for and there is nothing that would lift him more than to win in November. And I say, let's win this one for Ike."

Two weeks later, there was another heart attack and Democratic leaders quietly discussed postponing their party's convention if Ike died. By the end of the month, however, Ike rallied and was no longer on the critical list. On October 14, he celebrated his seventy-eighth birthday and President Johnson declared a national "Salute to Eisenhower" week. Nixon made periodic visits during the campaign "to get some good advice." John Eisenhower was directing Nixon's campaign in Pennsylvania, David was busily campaigning, and Mamie, too, made appearances for Nixon. Although Nixon held a wide lead in the early polls it was diminishing in the final days of the campaign. Vice President Hubert Humphrey, the Democratic candidate, had finally united his party and his campaign gained dramatic momentum when President Johnson announced a halt to the bombing of North Vietnam.

On election eve a statement was released by the Nixon staff that was purported to have been written by Ike from his hospital room, yet Walter Reed officials reported that it had been written by an aide at Gettysburg. The statement noted that polls indicated that "the American people may have been swayed by President Johnson's recent order to stop our attacks on North Vietnam." It praised Nixon's "statesmanship" in refusing to make a political issue of the war and concluded: "It would be supreme irony if these statesmanlike positions of Richard Nixon, maintained despite the greatest provocation, should now be turned into instruments of political injury to him." For good measure, it was arranged to have David Eisenhower read excerpts from Ike's statement during Nixon's election eve telethon.

Nixon narrowly won and Ike seemed pleased with the result. After the election Nixon often visited at Walter Reed and each newly appointed Cabinet Secretary came to Ward Eight at Ike's invitation. That Ike was too frail to attend the weddings of his grandchildren, Barbara Anne in November, and David in December, was a disappointment, but his condition had improved enough by the end of the year that John and other family members discussed Ike's possible return to Gettysburg. On Christmas, Ike presented Mamie a handwritten letter that expressed his gratitude to the hospital staff for helping him to enjoy "one more merry Christmas." Ike knew that it would be his last Christmas and Mamie wept as she read the letter, for she recognized that it was a moment to cherish.

In February, Ike underwent surgery to remove another intestinal obstruction. His condition was weakening and on March 28 his heart stopped for the last time. As he lay dying Ike spoke softly to Mamie: "I've always loved my wife. I've always loved my children. I've always loved my grandchildren. And I have always loved my country."

With Roosevelt, Churchill, and De Gaulle, Ike had truly been one of the giants of his age. "America will be a lonely land without him," said Lyndon Johnson. "But America will always be a better nation—stronger, safer, more conscious of its heritage, more certain of its destiny—because Ike was with us when America needed him."

Chapter Twenty

KEEPERS OF THE FLAME

He was always the figure slightly to the rear and somewhat out of focus in dozens of photographs—yellowing pictures taken in the bloody Europe of 1944; a snapshot of him and his father in cap and gown with the solemn pillars of Columbia University in the background; a grainy wire-service photo of the President and his son, also his assistant and adviser, striding out of the White House; a picture of father and son working on the White House memoirs during the early '60s at Gettysburg. Such would be the visible record of John Eisenhower, Dwight David Eisenhower's only son. More than a son, though, he was for many years his father's alter ego, his trusted confidant, his discreet emissary to world leaders and men of power. Since the early days of World War II, the massive shadow of Dwight Eisenhower had enveloped John, and yet the son wanted nothing more than to establish his own identity. It followed then that John would resign from the Army. "Dad had done so well in the military," he said, "that I thought it best to try another profession." Years before, at West Point, John had predicted that he would one day leave the military to become a writer. On resigning his commission, he became a senior editor for Doubleday and in that position would help Ike complete the memoirs.

Though John did not have political ambitions his name was

often mentioned as a candidate for the Pennsylvania governorship, the Senate, and Congress. In 1960, a poll taken by a Democratic senator demonstrated that John Eisenhower would command surprising strength as a presidential candidate. It was, of course, the famous name that made John different. From colonial days, Americans have shown a willingness to elect members of dynastic families to public office. In the nineteenth century, a presidential son, John Quincy Adams, and a presidential grandson, Benjamin Harrison, were themselves elected to the presidency. In more recent times, another presidential son, Robert Taft, was a national political leader for more than a generation and three times a serious contender for the presidency. Two of Franklin Roosevelt's sons went into politics, but neither attained national prominence in his own right and their ambitions were unfulfilled: James losing the governorship of California, and Franklin, Jr., losing the Democratic nomination for governor of New York and election as state attorney general.

In 1966, John Eisenhower was considered a strong possibility for the Pennsylvania governorship. It was well known that Scranton, the outgoing governor, was somewhat restrained in his enthusiasm for Lieutenant Governor Raymond Shafer and by contrast held John in high regard. Scranton and others talked with John about his possible candidacy, but the younger Eisenhower took himself out of consideration and endorsed Shafer, who was subsequently elected. "The reason that various people have tried to get me involved in politics is because of Dad and the famous name," says John.

If the Eisenhower legend brought John recognition, it also brought the inevitable comparisons between father and son. "If you want to dwell on it," said John, "you can drive yourself crazy."

Winston Churchill's only son, Randolph, was similarly overshadowed by his father and would attribute his often crude behavior to a desire for a separate identity. "I wanted a show of my own," said Randolph, "so struggling to establish my own individuality and personality, I often said and wrote reckless things, which I suppose if I hadn't felt this frustration I would have tempered down."

A Washington lawyer and diplomat who knew both Randolph and John made this comparison: "As sons of great men, they had an awfully heavy burden to carry. John is not a showman. He shies away from adulation—it's not his thing. Randolph liked attention and was a showboat. Randolph was a better speaker than his father but he had no discipline and did not work at it like Winston, who would spend hours working on a sentence. John is not a speaker at all. But I've got great respect for him because he has picked a different career and, unlike Randolph Churchill, he has done something. John is a fine military historian."

In 1964, John resigned as an editor with Doubleday as the second volume of Ike's memoirs was completed, and he accepted a $16,600-a-year job as executive vice president of Freedoms Foundation at Valley Forge. John and Barbara purchased a two-story, five-bedroom colonial house near Phoenixville and they quickly became fond of the historic area where Washington's troops had spent the Revolutionary War winter of 1777–78. Unhappily enough, John found himself cast as the foundation's star fund raiser. Established in 1949 to "build an understanding of The American Way of Life," Freedoms Foundation is best known as the patriotic organization which annually gives out medals and cash prizes on Washington's Birthday. Ike himself presented the first awards, in 1950, and later would serve as chairman of the foundation's trustees and honorary chairman. By letting the organization use his name, Ike helped them attract some $15 million in contributions during their first two decades. Over the years the foundation's golden hustler had been Kenneth Wells. When John became executive vice president, however, Wells seemed more interested in spending the funds that Eisenhower solicited, and John was given the responsibilities of paying for the awards and administrative expenses. After thirteen months John was thoroughly disenchanted with his job and decided to at last begin a writing career of his own.

In 1965, John agreed to serve as a technical adviser on a motion picture about the Battle of the Bulge, and that project evolved into his first book, *The Bitter Woods,* an authoritative history of the Ardennes campaign. To research the book John spent months studying primary-source material at the World War II archives in Alexandria and official army histories; and he traveled abroad for interviews with Field Marshal Montgomery and General Hasso von Manteuffel. Other family members assisted John: Barbara Eisenhower went to business school for secretarial training and typed John's final manuscript, and Ike offered his thoughts and reactions to the manuscript and confided to Mamie that the book was "good." Published in January of 1969, *The Bitter Woods* was both a critical success and a best seller. "John S. D. Eisenhower writes with power," wrote military historian S. L. A. Marshall. "His imagination flames and his prose flows. His first work leaves no doubt that he is a military historian born." *Saturday Review's* assessment was also favorable: "A powerful narrative that is authoritative, accurate, and instructive, frequently fascinating, sometimes dramatic or humorous, and only occasionally difficult to follow."

During the period between delivery of the final manuscript and publication of his book, John became involved in the 1968 presidential campaign. His candidate was Richard Nixon, soon to become an in-law with the marriage of David to Julie Nixon. Although John had misgivings about Nixon, Mamie and Barbara were longtime Nixon supporters, and by late spring John had endorsed Nixon as well. Following the Miami convention John became Pennsylvania chairman of Citizens for Nixon and Agnew. "I worked pretty hard in the campaign," he said, "but I didn't want any payoff. I told Mr. Nixon that I was willing to do what I could, but I emphasized that I was one guy who wasn't worried about a job because I had already negotiated a new book contract."

His next book was scheduled to be a history of the Grand Alliance of World War II, but it would not be written for another decade. Early in 1969, General Andrew Goodpaster, John's onetime White House colleague, called John with the news that Nixon wanted to appoint him as ambassador to Belgium. "Do they really want me or is this a political payoff for the use of the name?" asked John. Assured by Goodpaster that he was indeed wanted on the basis of his experience and background, John accepted. "John did not want to be an ambassador," recalls a friend who served in the Nixon administration. "It was his wife's idea.

She's very outgoing and social. John isn't. An ambassador doesn't have a policy role in today's diplomacy. He's judged on his social performance and John doesn't like that kind of thing."

For John, an essentially shy man who values his privacy, the endless round of diplomatic parties at the Common Market, NATO, and the embassies was disenchanting. "It was pretty grim," he says. "I didn't like the damned cocktail circuit." Some State Department veterans complained about John's attitude. *Time* characterized him as a "diplomat by appointment and a historian by choice."

In the meantime there was renewed interest in John as a candidate for governor of Pennsylvania. "There has been a quiet, but effective word-of-mouth campaign for young Eisenhower," said a Republican leader. "This has been going on in various sections of the state." John's service in Belgium made him all the more attractive to Pennsylvania Republicans because the Harrisburg administration of Governor Raymond Shafer had been the most unpopular in recent memory and the party's best hope of victory in 1970 appeared to be with a candidate not closely tied to Shafer. Above all else, John struck Republicans as a winner. "His name carries magic," said Saul Kohler, who was then Washington correspondent for the Philadelphia *Inquirer*. "There's no doubt that he could have had the nomination if he had wanted it and probably won the election, too."

Urging John to return from Brussels and seek the governorship was Dick Butera, who had served as Eisenhower's executive director in the 1968 Nixon campaign. During 1968 Butera said that John demonstrated extraordinary popular appeal. "In Scranton we went into a diner and everybody in the place stood up and applauded John," recalled Butera years later. Wherever John went in Pennsylvania, he received a warm response. At one point John asked Butera if they could "stand the biddy circuit" for another year.

John's appointment as ambassador did not diminish Butera's enthusiasm. By phone and through correspondence he pressed John to become a candidate. According to a plan devised by Butera and other Montgomery County Republican moderates, an elaborate "Welcome Home" ceremony would be held for John.

Shortly afterward, John would be "drafted" by the Republican state committee as its gubernatorial candidate.

The scenario of another Eisenhower returning from Europe to enter Republican politics was not to be. John turned down those who sought his gubernatorial candidacy and was later embarrassed when a group of insurgent Republicans formed a "Draft Eisenhower" committee, urging that he seek the Republican nomination for the Senate against Minority Leader Hugh Scott.

In a letter to Scott, John wrote: "Naturally my position remains the same as it always has, that I should stay in this post long enough to learn to do a good job. I suppose that from now on I will have to answer any similar communications—if any more come in—with rather 'Shermanistic' terms."

So John continued as ambassador rather than seek elective office in Pennsylvania. There were, to be sure, some pleasant aspects of the ambassadorship and his relations with King Baudouin were friendly. "The King was kind of naïve at first," says John. "He thought I had a red-hot line to the President and could get them whatever they wanted."

By August of 1971, however, there were severe financial strains. After two years of running the embassy he "could not make ends meet financially." Several years later he said, "Only a millionaire can afford to serve at Paris or London, but Brussels was supposed to be an embassy where someone of more modest means could serve. I lost around thirty thousand dollars. It didn't help matters having six thieves on the embassy staff. Food kept disappearing."

The White House announced that John resigned for "personal reasons." President Nixon said John served "with exceptional competence and in doing so has contributed significantly in strengthening longtime ties of friendship between our country and Belgium." In an editorial, the Philadelphia *Inquirer* said: "As a professional army officer, as a writer and sometime historian of impressive seriousness and respect for scholarship, and as ambassador, he has ably given of himself a humility as rare as it is impressive. With his resignation, as before, there will be inevitable speculations about political possibilities. Doubtless, among them will be suggestions of the Pennsylvania governorship. . . ."

A year later, Nixon designated John as his representative at the funeral of King Frederick IX of Denmark and at the fifth inauguration of Chiang Kai-shek as President of the Republic of China. In May of 1972, John became chairman of the Interagency Classification Review Committee, charged with preventing the overzealous use of secrecy stamps. Some progress was made in reducing by half the number of bureaucrats allowed to classify material as top secret. John's commission overruled the National Security Council in making public the controversial "top secret" Gaither Report which had warned Ike that some $44 billion in defense programs were needed to protect Americans against Soviet nuclear attack. The Central Intelligence Agency did not cooperate with the committee and John concluded somewhat ruefully that the Nixon administration "really wasn't interested in helping."

Indeed, John determined that his committee was nothing more than a public relations front. When he tried to meet with Nixon's closest aides, John had difficulty penetrating the palace guard. "My dad was much more accessible than Ehrlichman," John said. On one occasion John phoned Nixon at Camp David and was referred to H. R. Haldeman who told him curtly: "The President sends you his best wishes." Only after John drafted a resignation statement did Nixon see him. The President thanked John for his contributions and Eisenhower felt obligated to remain on the job for a few more months.

On his return from Belgium, John resumed his writing career with *Strictly Personal*, an autobiography. "There's not a lot of heavy stuff to excite historians," he said. "I just wrote it for the fun of it. I had some things to say that I didn't want to die with me." As would be expected, Ike dominates the pages of the memoir with John's boyhood recollections of "a terrifying figure" and firsthand reports of working for "the Boss" at the White House. Veteran critic John Barkham wrote, "In its candor, zest, and ability to hold the reader's attention, it promises well for the writing career of John Eisenhower." Reviewing the book in *Philadelphia* magazine, Charles MacNamera said, "Unfortunately, *Strictly Personal* is a step backward as a writer. For the most part it is as bland as its title."

John almost abandoned his writing career to enter politics in the winter of 1974. An aging congressman, John Ware, announced his retirement from Pennsylvania's Fifth District. For the first time John "thought seriously" about becoming a candidate. He discussed his plans with Drew Lewis, a friend and business associate who was the Republican gubernatorial candidate that year. "John came to see me and was all enthused about running," Lewis recalls. "I told him, 'There's a lot of good you could do and I'd certainly like to have you as a candidate. But you should also realize that there are some sacrifices you'll have to make such as picnics and the chicken circuit.' Right there John decided that he would have no part of it."

"We felt that I could probably get elected," says John. "Then Drew said he'd see me the next weekend at a Republican picnic at West Grove. I didn't even know where West Grove was. I realized, too, that campaigning would become almost a full-time occupation even in nonelection years, and I'm just not built for that degree of public exposure.

"I can carry off public appearances and speaking engagements, but they take a lot out of me. Everybody seems to presume you want the biggest job you can possibly get. I just don't buy that. It's heady stuff when they suggest that you run for governor or for Congress, but I don't know enough about Pennsylvania to run it, and I don't want to live in Washington. I want to stick with book writing." In 1973, John mused, "It doesn't seem logical or right for me to seek political office. I'd be running strictly on the old man's name."

If John had sought political office, his wife, Barbara, would have been an undeniable asset. Attractive, warm, and personable, she enjoyed the crowds that so discomfited John. William Scranton describes her as his "favorite Eisenhower" and speaks with admiration about how she moved her children from the White House to Gettysburg during the Eisenhower presidency so that they might have a more normal family life. As her children left home in the 1970s, Barbara developed a range of interests. She studied literature at Rosemont College and talked of writing a biography of Mamie. In 1978 she was approached about running for lieutenant governor of Pennsylvania. Though interested, she did not run. She may, however, seek political office in the future.

To John, writing was more stimulating and challenging than

political campaigning. "Everybody mentions the book and no one ever mentions my being ambassador," he said in 1974. "And I think that books are more enduring than politicians. After all, who remembers who was Vice President of the United States when *The Great Gatsby* was written?" John talked of future works of military history—a study of the American Revolution from the colonial defeat at Brandywine through the fateful winter at Valley Forge; a book about Civil War generals; and a history of the First World War. His next major work, though, was the Anglo-American alliance of World War II and he expressed hope that it would be "something with substance."

When called, John was still available for presidential assignments and in 1975 President Gerald Ford appointed him chairman of a commission to help relocate Vietnamese refugees. Promised a budget, White House office, and his own staff, John received minimal help from the Administration. After a nationally televised ceremony where John and Ford smiled amiably, the commission was all but ignored by the White House and John would term the experience a disappointment. "Each time I've been back to the White House my office has been further removed from the Oval Office," he noted in 1976. Like so many other well-intended initiatives of the Ford administration, the Vietnam commission was hastily conceived and quickly forgotten.

Ford's repeated tributes to Harry Truman did not set well with John nor with other members of the Eisenhower family. "My evaluation of Truman," says John, "is that he was holding thirteen spades and bid four." John also was decidedly unimpressed with such Ford appointments as Texas politician George Bush as CIA director, White House chief of staff Alexander Haig as NATO Supreme Commander, and Donald Rumsfeld as Defense Secretary.

Still, Ford was John's choice for the Republican presidential nomination. Ronald Reagan was an Eisenhower family friend but John thought that Ford, as the incumbent, was entitled to the nomination. Moreover, Reagan's fervently right-wing supporters at Kansas City were all too reminiscent of the Goldwaterites at San Francisco in 1964. John and Barbara were hopeful that Ford might choose their friend William Scranton, then serving as

United Nations ambassador, as the vice-presidential candidate, but the nominee was Kansas Senator Robert Dole. Some weeks after President Ford's defeat by Jimmy Carter, Ford was elected president of the Eisenhower Exchange Fellowships with John's approval.

As Ike's only son and as an accomplished historian, John has often been urged to write a comprehensive and formal biography of his father. Randolph Churchill's *Winston Churchill* and Margaret Truman Daniel's *Harry S. Truman* were best sellers and book-club selections and John's would surely be accorded widespread attention. John is unenthusiastic about any such project. "I wouldn't want to be known only as my dad's biographer," he says. "How could you be objective? Do you think anybody will take Margaret Truman's book seriously? I wouldn't."

It all comes back to John's effort to establish his own identity. "He really doesn't want to capitalize on the Eisenhower name," says a friend. "There's a feeling that he wants his books to be his own—without the influence of his father."

In the years since Ike's death John has spoken out when his father's reputation has come under attack. The 1975 Senate hearings on intelligence activities revealed CIA assassination plots against such foreign leaders as Cuban Premier Fidel Castro and the late African revolutionary Patrice Lumumba. Testifying before the committee, headed by Idaho Senator Frank Church, John said that Ike had confided in him about secret matters "to a very large extent" and mentioned the 1945 conversation about the atomic bomb and that as early as 1956 Ike advised him about the U-2 flights. John said that Ike would have told him about CIA assassination plans but said that Ike believed that no foreign leader was indispensable and thus assassination was not justified as a political instrument. The committee did not implicate Ike in the assassination plots and the Senate report indicated that the murder of undesirable foreign leaders was to proliferate during the Kennedy administration.

John was less than amused when the 1974 publication of Merle Miller's *Plain Speaking*, a series of interviews with Harry Truman, resurrected the old rumors about Ike's wartime relationship with his attractive driver, Kay Summersby. "I don't give a damn what

Truman thinks," John said then. "The worst thing about that book is that Mother might get hurt. I find myself wondering why anybody pays attention to Truman's foul-mouthed railings."

Miss Summersby's own memoir was published posthumously in 1977 and her version was that she and Ike had an unconsummated affair. When John learned that the American Broadcasting Company planned a dramatization of the Summersby book, he could no longer remain silent. He became indignant after reading the television script that included a crude fictional exchange between his parents: "Generals die in bed," said Ike. "So did our marriage, Ike," responded Mamie.

John had recently edited a book of his father's wartime letters to Mamie that was scheduled for 1978 publication. Originally planned to counter the Summersby book, John decided to release excerpts more than six months before his book's publication. Milton contacted Robert Donovan, associate editor of the Los Angeles *Times* and author of a favorable book about the Eisenhower presidency, and Donovan came to Valley Forge where he could examine the correspondence. Donovan wrote that the letters indicated "a poignant attachment of Eisenhower to his wife" yet failed to clarify Ike's relationship with Summersby. What the letters did do, said Donovan, was cast doubt on the Truman allegation that Ike planned to divorce Mamie.

There were wartime strains between his parents, John said, but at no time was divorce contemplated. Rumors of Ike's relationship with Summersby circulated during the war, and Mamie did make references to it in some of her letters. "I don't know if she believed the rumors," said John, "but she thought enough of them to bring it up in her letters." John said Mamie learned of the alleged affair "from husbands coming back to visit and talking to their wives. The Army was a real hotbed for that kind of thing."

John does not pretend to know the full details of the relationship between Summersby and Ike. "Nobody can bear witness that an incident did not happen," he said. "But the letters establish beyond any doubt in my mind that divorce never crossed my dad's mind.

"The relationship between my parents across the ocean was not always smooth," he said. "My reason in releasing the letters at this time was to refute the hogwash in Merle Miller's *Plain Speaking*. You can only take it lying down so long."

John did concede that had he found written evidence of an affair between his father and Summersby, the letter would have been destroyed or deposited at the Eisenhower Library with a fifty-year seal. Mamie was predictably troubled by the published reports about Ike's relationship with Summersby. "She's not terribly exposed to it," said John. "The only thing that has really disturbed her is receiving sympathy letters. Nobody likes getting sympathy letters."

Soon after Ike's death Mamie said that she could not return to Gettysburg and live alone at their farm. Some thought was given to moving back to Washington so that Mamie could be near her sister, "Mike" Moore, and numerous old friends. One factor in her ultimate decision to stay at Gettysburg was economic. She could live rent free since the farm, deeded to the government in 1967, would eventually become a National Historic Site. Her role in Gettysburg society would be limited in the years after Ike's death. "Most of my friends are all over the world," she told me in 1974. "I really don't socialize here. I don't want to be giving luncheons and dinners all the time. I'm a taxpayer. I deserve my privacy and I'm going to have it."

Her favorite topic of conversation is her husband. "Sometimes I feel like I'm fighting a one-person battle to keep his name alive," Mamie lamented to John.

In her years alone, the once plump Mamie became thin and fragile-looking. "I've lost twenty pounds since Ike died," she said, "ten pounds this year [1974]. I always wondered if I'd be a fat old lady or a thin old lady. I guess I'm finding out." During our 1974 interview, Mamie wore a long, flowing lamé gown, a pearl necklace, and a jeweled American flag. "Ike was very worried about patriotism when he was in the hospital because people weren't displaying the flag. I promised him that I'd always wear a flag. And I do—as do all of my Secret Service men."

Her second-floor sitting room, which she describes as "a sort of catch-all room," is decorated with family antiques—a marble-topped table and cut-glass rose bowl from the Doud house in Denver, a few yellowing family photographs, and her maternal grandmother's slipper stool. She seldom goes downstairs to the big, glassed-in back porch with the view of the battlefield where she spent so much time with Ike. "There's too much of him there," she said. "I don't go down there."

Ike's choice grade cattle were his hobby and in retirement he entered some of the Black Angus in the Pennsylvania Farm Show. "I couldn't have told you how many cattle we had," said Mamie. "I always said the outside was Ike's and the inside was mine. The Park Service's resident farmer now raises feeders where Ike used to have his cattle."

Although she is a woman of strong opinions and not afraid to voice them, Mamie says that she never debated political issues with Ike. "When Ike came home, he came home," she said. "He left all his work at the office. I never went to his headquarters when he was an army officer. I only went to his White House office four times—and I was invited each time."

As First Lady, she did not give speeches, never held press conferences, but did seem to enjoy her public appearances with her husband. "I was Ike's wife, John's mother, the children's grandmother," she said. "That was all I ever wanted to be. My husband was the star in the heavens. It wasn't that I didn't have my own ideas, but in my own era, the man was the head of the household. Ike was strong enough to make his own speeches. Ike and I never did the same things. For example, I knitted and he painted. There was never any competition between us."

For the most part, her public appearances were restricted to special ceremonies honoring Ike. In October of 1977, she went to Norfolk for the dedication of the Navy supercarrier *Dwight D. Eisenhower*. In 1974, she traveled to West Point for the dedication of Eisenhower Hall, a student center. There are annual trips to the Eisenhower Library at Abilene, where Ike is buried, and to Eisenhower College at Seneca Falls, New York.

The college, a small liberal-arts school founded in 1965, has had severe financial difficulties like numerous other private schools. Mamie has made the college's cause her own. "I wouldn't give a sou to any school but Eisenhower," she said. "I sold my Chrysler to raise money for the college. And I wrote an article for *Reader's*

Digest for the same reason. I'd do just about anything to help them. I think the students up there are terrific. They've really helped put heart back into me. There were four students at graduation so badly crippled they couldn't walk to the podium and pick up their diplomas. Just think of all the hardship and sacrifices they went through to get an education. It's like a family at the college. The students go up there to learn. The girls wait on tables and the boys also work their way through. There have been no confrontations and nobody has painted a moustache on any of Ike's portraits. They don't even have to put glass over the picture. Most of our young people are great. It seems that the press only emphasizes the bad ones."

"Noblesse oblige" was the motto of Mamie's Denver finishing school and she has for years supported many charitable causes. In Gettysburg, she donated funds to her Presbyterian church for an Eisenhower memorial room, and to the local hospital for a new room. "I used to send a boy and a girl to summer camp every year," she said. "Now I can just afford to send one child. I'm like a retired person. I can't get raises since I'm living on a fixed income." (Her government pension as a President's widow is $20,000 and her annual income is estimated at $60,000.)

Mamie's afternoons are, most often, reserved for reading and watching television. "I watch soap operas," she said without apology. "That's an awful name for these programs. I find them touching, very true to life. I won't look at shows about hospitals. It brings back memories of the months I spent in hospitals during Ike's illnesses." Much of this time is spent in bed. Mamie once said, "Every woman over fifty should spend a day a week in bed."

"If doctors told me I had to go to bed, I probably wouldn't enjoy it," she said. "But it does rest you. Your mind, of course, never stops, but the body is resting. That's why I don't have any wrinkles."

Mamie still wears the trademark bangs which, during the 1950s, influenced American hair styles. "Whenever I get a little bored, I go in and cut them," she said. "I've always worn them since I have a high forehead—it runs in the Carlson family."

Seldom, if ever, does she discard old clothes. Her closets on the third floor are full of dresses, gowns, hats, and almost everything else she ever wore. "I'm wearing many of my White House clothes now," she said two decades later. "They're all silk—you can't get much of that any more. It's beautiful material. And the full skirts and pleated skirts are right in style now."

Whispered and sometimes published rumors that Mamie was an alcoholic never bothered her, she insisted. "I lived with myself," she said. "I knew it wasn't so. And so did my friends. I don't think there's anybody that drinks less than I."

Because of an inner-ear affliction, Mamie sometimes walks in an unsteady manner and bumps into objects. The ailment led to rumors of a drinking problem. "I have what they call a cartoid sinus," she said, "and they can't operate on it. Your vein presses on your inner ear. I've lived with it for twenty-five years or more. I never know when it's going to hit me. Doctors tell me there's no assurance that an operation would do any good. I'll probably walk down this hall and hit the wall. I'm black and blue from walking around the house."

In addition to her equilibrium problem, Mamie suffers from claustrophobia. "I don't like being closed in," she said. When she travels to Abilene it is by car rather than airplane. "It gives me a good feeling that Ike's at peace there in Abilene," she said. "He's in his old neighborhood, surrounded by old friends. There's a place for me, too, there. But I don't like to look at it or think about it much."

Her favorite monument in Gettysburg is the statue of Ike outside his old office on the Gettysburg College campus. "I always speak to him when I pass it," she said. "During the winter I don't like to see the snow covering his head."

Mamie was a frequent guest at the Nixon White House and Nixon visited her at Gettysburg. "She was very loyal to Richard Nixon and he was very loyal to her," recalls a former Nixon aide. Asked about Nixon's resignation and the Watergate scandal, Mamie talks sadly about the hurtful pain suffered by the Nixon family. "It's been so sad," she said.

Within the family Milton had been Richard Nixon's earliest critic. As early as 1952 Milton questioned Nixon's aptitude for the presidency. "I mentioned my feelings to my own family and to my brother," said Milton. "Ike appreciated Dick Nixon's absolutely loyal and effective service. My reservations were not based upon his ability to do the job. I was concerned by the lack of a deep fundamental philosophy that would guide him in making decisions. I did not suspect that he would lie to the American people or be amoral."

Milton's 1974 book, *The President Is Calling,* a memoir of his five decades of public service, described Watergate as a "sordid period," saying that even if Nixon survived the cover-up investigation, the Administration would be tarnished by Nixon's income-tax problems, the use of federal funds to improve his Florida and California residences, the Agnew resignation and disgrace, and Nixon's "unjustified" firing of Attorney General Elliot Richardson, Deputy Attorney General Donald Ruckelshaus, and Watergate special prosecutor Archibald Cox. "I went as far as I dared go," said Milton more than two years later.

During Watergate Milton's concern was such that he openly condemned the Nixon administration in a November 15, 1973, letter in which he endorsed Illinois Senator Charles Percy for the presidency in 1976. "In my judgment," wrote Milton, "our country today is in the midst of her deepest political crisis, cursed with widespread cynicism, mistrust of government and doubt about the validity of our political processes.

"Many things need to be done but what will help above all else is the election in 1976 of a President who possesses absolute integrity, moral leadership, courage, intelligence and a middle of the road philosophy. We need a leader the people believe in. Senator Percy is that man. He is an independent man . . . whose only 'special interest' is America."

The letter helped raise $230,000 for Percy's "exploratory" campaign. In public-opinion polls, Percy trailed such familiar names as Reagan, Ford, and Rockefeller, yet Milton was hopeful that some early primary victories and national exposure would thrust Percy into serious contention for the nomination. As in the 1964 Scranton campaign, Milton gave Percy his not inconsiderable prestige. The Percy campaign was suspended early in the Ford presidency when it became evident that Ford, contrary to his own earlier statements, would run for another term. Though Milton liked Ford he was fully aware of the new President's limitations and talked privately of such alternatives as Percy, Scranton, Richardson, and Maryland Senator Mathias.

Milton fought back tears at the dedication of the Milton S. Eisenhower Library in 1967, for the occasion also marked his retirement as president of Johns Hopkins. At sixty-seven, Milton became president emeritus and cheerfully accepted the university's honors. His successor, Lincoln Gordon, was a Harvard political economist who had served as ambassador to Brazil and as Assistant Secretary of State in the Johnson administration, and was appointed university president from a field of some 150 candidates. Admittedly, Gordon had a difficult act to follow, but he was unable even to preserve the gains of the Eisenhower era.

By March of 1971, the faculty was in revolt and the university was confronted with a deficit of more than five million dollars. Gordon resigned with the recommendation that "a young and vigorous man" be appointed president. With the huge deficit and dwindling reserves the trustees felt that only one man could accomplish the miracles needed to restore Hopkins: Milton Eisenhower.

"For two weeks," Milton recalls, "the trustees, faculty, and students poured into my house and told me that nobody else could straighten things out. I had left a good record and all I could do was leave a shadow. My conscience finally took the better of my common sense and I agreed to come back."

At seventy-two, Milton was the oldest president of any American university. In his first speech Milton announced that sacrifices would have to be made at all levels. "I had to do all sorts of mean things," he recalled. "We got $700,000 in appropriations and put an austerity program into effect."

Milton called a meeting of the university community and announced that the cafeteria's annual deficit was $100,000 a year and that he was replacing its services with vending machines until the cafeteria showed a profit. At the end of the meeting, Milton received a standing ovation.

For the next ten months Milton applied his energies toward reducing the deficit, and when he announced his retirement in January, the deficit was down to two million dollars. Foundations and corporations gave nearly four million dollars and the Hopkins alumni and trustees gave more than two million dollars as tribute to Milton and the university. Milton also reduced the faculty carefully and increased student enrollment, which he called "squeezing the accordion from both ends."

"Many of the belt-tightening measures and reforms put into effect in the past ten months would probably not have been so effective or so willingly accepted if the man behind them had not possessed the humanity and ability the University needed in such crucial times," said an editorial in the *Johns Hopkins Magazine*. "Johns Hopkins is indebted to Milton Eisenhower."

Five years later Milton would recall: "Instead of a bad experience, it was one of the most glorious experiences of my life. Faculty, students, and alumni just contributed 100 percent. Everybody realized that you had to cooperate to get the job done."

Milton has no regrets about resisting efforts in three states to get him to run for political office. "I never really liked the idea of rough-and-tumble politics," he says. "I am somewhat sensitive, which might have worked against a political career but which helped give me a built-in radar system as a university president. I understood other people's feelings."

When Milton's portrait was unveiled at the Eisenhower Center in Abilene, former Kansas Senator Harry Darby said that Kansas lost "a good governor or congressman" when Milton declined to enter politics. "Who knows?" said Darby. "We might even have had another Eisenhower as President if Milton had decided to run as some of us talked to him about."

Ike hoped that one day the nation would be inspired by another President Eisenhower, and if it could not be Milton perhaps it would be David. "He spoke of it only to others, never to me," said David in 1975. As the scion of one of America's most famous families, he has been viewed for years by Republican politicians as a future star of a party that is notably lacking in young talent. With the Eisenhower name, Ike's only grandson, while still in his twenties, could talk earnestly about his scenario: practicing law in a small town and then running for Congress; moving up to the Senate; and then, finally, "a crack at the presidency."

Much of his youth was spent at the White House, and Ike

would rename Shangri-La, the presidential retreat in the Catoctin Mountains of Maryland, Camp David for him. As a youngster he would meet such historical giants as Churchill, De Gaulle, and Khrushchev; and Roy Rogers, the "King of the Cowboys," would come to David's birthday party at the White House. When the Eisenhower presidency neared a close, David sneaked through White House corridors and rooms hiding "I shall return" notes behind mirrors and pictures.

In the 1960s, David attended Exeter, one of the nation's great prep schools and graduated cum laude. Though John privately hoped that David might continue the family tradition by going to West Point, there was no parental pressure to do so. "I didn't realize until I was eighteen years old that I was disappointing anybody," said David years later, "and it turned out I disappointed everybody."

David went to Amherst and once again he would graduate cum laude, but his glittering academic record was overshadowed by his dynastic marriage to Julie Nixon. Their romance was an undeniable asset to Richard Nixon during his political comeback. When the Nixon family was discussing whether the former Vice President should make another presidential campaign, David wrote his future father-in-law a memorandum urging him to do just that. Campaigning in more than thirty states, most often with Julie, David was euphoric about the association with another presidential family. Of Nixon, the twenty-year-old David said, "He's really easygoing, a lot of fun, and has a good sense of humor—the perfect father for a teen-age serial."

There was still considerable affection nationally for Ike's namesake and grandson, and yet the Nixon bond brought controversy. Student protestors heckled David and Julie at numerous stops, and members of the radical Students for a Democratic Society shouted them down at Binghamton, New York. One of Ike's liberal admirers, Garry Wills, wrote acidly that David had become "a Nephew Tom to his generation."

After Nixon's inauguration, David found himself suddenly isolated from much of his own age group. When the brother of a close friend was killed in the Vietnam War, the friend would no longer talk to David. President Nixon contributed to the tension by disclosing that his input from American youth came from David and Julie rather than antiwar demonstrators. Because of the volatile mood of their campuses, the young Eisenhowers decided against attending their 1970 graduations where demonstrators might subject them to embarrassing taunts. David would later speak with bitterness about what he termed the excesses of the protest movement.

Although there were many privileges afforded him in the years of the Nixon presidency, David was among a handful of young men in his graduating class to go into the military. Selective service was then governed by a lottery system and David's March 31 birthday was drawn thirtieth, meaning that he was almost certain to be drafted. So David, less than eager to be a ground soldier in Vietnam, entered Naval Officer Candidates School and graduated in the top 10 percent of his class with a commission. For two years and five months, Lieutenant Junior Grade Eisenhower served in the Navy, including eleven months as an intelligence officer aboard the guided missile cruiser USS *Albany*. "I didn't mind being in the Navy," said David, "but it's just not my life."

In the summer of 1973 David worked as a sports columnist for the Philadelphia *Bulletin*. At a White House correspondents' dinner David had been offered a political column by *Bulletin* executive editor George Packard, but David expressed doubt that such an arrangement was workable and proposed instead the baseball column. Though David has a keen understanding of the game, his prose was dull and flat. A fellow *Bulletin* sportswriter said that David approached the column as if he were writing a term paper. As for his own assessment, David said, "I'm just not very aggressive. I think I've been interviewed too much. I know what people don't want to be asked and I don't ask it." Whatever his limitations, David enjoyed the experience. "I think I'd rather be a sports columnist than President," he said then.

David entered the George Washington University Law School in the fall of 1973, but his life style was hardly typical of his classmates. He lived in a luxurious $127,000 house in suburban Bethesda owned by Nixon's best friend C. G. "Bebe" Rebozo, who charged nominal rent. Once and sometimes twice a week,

President and Mrs. Nixon would drive out for dinner and cocktails.

On David's return from the Navy he discovered that concern about Watergate had done something to the family. Instinctively David rose to defend his embattled father-in-law. "Watergate will prove to be relatively inconsequential," he predicted in October of 1973. Through the winter of 1974 David asserted that his political hero had done nothing wrong, had nothing to hide, and would not be impeached. As he followed the hearings and read the Watergate transcripts David became more restrained in his public defense. By the summer he would admit that Nixon was losing "on the evidence," and the publication of the damning transcript was a severe jolt. David comforted Nixon when the disgraced President could not look other family members in the face.

Shortly before Nixon's resignation, David put another "I shall return" note behind a picture in the White House. In the days that followed, David remained among the most visible defenders of his father-in-law: coming forth to defend President Ford's unpopular pardon of Nixon and continuing to insist that Nixon was a great man with a tragic fate.

Returning from a January 1976 trip to China that included a meeting with Mao Tse-tung, David announced that the Chinese attached no significance to Watergate. It was David, with Julie, who carried the invitation from Chinese officials to Nixon for a return visit by the former President. Nixon's journey just one month later brought about a major legal and political controversy. Senator Barry Goldwater suggested that Nixon ought to remain in China and the White House maintained a discreet silence.

In the fall of 1977, when the ABC television network broadcast a fictional drama based on the Nixon White House, David responded with a vigorous Nixon defense in a *Newsweek* column. "Nixon may not be a sympathetic figure as a former president and a powerful man brought low," wrote David. "Nonetheless, he deserves protection from depersonalization, reveling in his tragedy, and bullying." Continuing to defend his father-in-law during the spring of 1978, David insisted that Nixon's unfavorable image was more a manifestation of eastern animus against California than anything else.

David's close relationship with Nixon has bound him to the most controversial political figure of the postwar generation. "If David doesn't watch it," said one friend, "he's going to be identified as a Nixon instead of an Eisenhower." Nixon had urged David to run for Congress in 1974 from a central Pennsylvania district that included Gettysburg. John Eisenhower said it was too early and somewhat presumptuous for David to run for Congress fresh out of the Navy. "John didn't want David to be in a position of capitalizing on the name and ending up with a congressional seat at twenty-five and nowhere to go ten years later," said a family friend. Concluding that he was too young, David chose to finish law school.

Much thought would be given in later years to launching a political career in Pennsylvania. "I think Pennsylvania is a place where I could establish myself in a hurry," he said. "I know people back there. It would be kind of an ideal place to start." Early in 1977, David and Julie looked at houses in suburban Bucks County where a traditionally Republican congressional seat was held by a young Democrat. Yet they moved to California, where David was writing his first book.

It was to be a biography of Ike, and David's publisher, Random House, said the book would be a major work. David had once said of Ike: "I'm really not objective about my grandfather. . . . I really don't know much about him though." After receiving a large advance, David described the project as a personal responsibility because Ike's memory was "threatened by superficiality." For David the book held the promise of linking him to his grandfather once again and truly making him an Eisenhower. It had been more than twenty years since the nation first saw him as Ike's grandson, and if David was to fulfill his grandfather's high ambitions for him it would come as an Eisenhower, not as a Nixon.

Bibliographical Essay

Any study of the Eisenhower era must begin with the Eisenhower Library in Abilene, Kansas. Ike's personal files from 1916 through 1952 have long been available to researchers and within recent months much of his personal correspondence and diaries from the White House years has also been opened. While there is little material prior to 1939, the next thirty years are richly documented. Through an arrangement made by Ike himself the Johns Hopkins University Press is publishing *The Papers of Dwight David Eisenhower*. In 1970, the five-volume *War Years* edition was published at Hopkins and another multivolume edition on the *Chief of Staff* period will soon be published. More than any other work, these volumes reveal Eisenhower's personality and character and demonstrate that he was a man of intelligence and ambition. The *Public Papers of the Presidents: Dwight D. Eisenhower, 1953–1961*, eight volumes, are important as an ongoing record of the presidential years with complete transcripts of press conferences, speeches, and some correspondence made public at the time. Robert L. Branyan and Lawrence H. Larsen, editors, *The Eisenhower Administration, 1953–1961: A Documentary History*, two volumes (Random House, 1971), is a useful and annotated compendium of material at the Eisenhower Library, although recently opened collections should be consulted to supplement this material.

The autobiographical writings of the Eisenhowers are a much

neglected resource. Ike's *At Ease: Stories I Tell to Friends* (Doubleday, 1967) is a delightful and unpretentious book of reminiscences about his early life. *Crusade in Europe* (Doubleday, 1948) is his eminently readable memoir of World War II. *Mandate for Change* (1963) and *Waging Peace* (1965) cover the White House years in massive detail. The presidential memoirs are highly significant and full of information relevant to biographers. Milton S. Eisenhower's *The President Is Calling* (Doubleday, 1974) covers the younger brother's half century in public life and was of much value in this study. Milton's earlier book, *The Wine Is Bitter* (Doubleday, 1963), is a memoir of his experiences as Ike's ambassador to Latin America. John S. D. Eisenhower's *Strictly Personal* (Doubleday, 1974) offers numerous insights into the Eisenhower family and describes Ike from a son's perspective. Ike's *Letters to Mamie* (Doubleday, 1978), which John edited and annotated, is a rich source of information about the relationship between General and Mrs. Eisenhower. Unhappily, Mamie's letters to Ike were not saved and her papers at Abilene have not been opened to researchers. Edgar Eisenhower's *Six Roads from Abilene* (Wood & Reber, 1960) is fragmented and incomplete.

There is not a definitive biography of Dwight D. Eisenhower, nor can one be written until the remaining classified material from his presidency is made available. In the meantime, Peter Lyon's *Eisenhower: Portrait of the Hero* (Little, Brown, 1974) is a competent full-scale biography. Stephen Ambrose's *The Supreme Commander* (Doubleday, 1970) is a first-rate history of Ike's wartime years by a scholar who served as an editor for the Eisenhower Papers. Based on exhaustive research, Herbert S. Parmet's *Eisenhower and the American Crusades* (Macmillan, 1972) is the most authoritative portrait of the Eisenhower presidency and a major historical work.

An important and provocative revisionist interpretation is Murray Kempton's "The Underestimation of Dwight D. Eisenhower," published in the September 1967 issue of *Esquire*. On the same theme, Garry Wills wrote about Ike in *Nixon Agonistes* (Houghton Mifflin, 1970) and challenged the unfavorable view taken of Eisenhower by Cold War liberals.

Of early Eisenhower biographies, *General Ike* by Alden Hatch (Holt, 1944) is loosely documented and must be used with caution. By contrast, *Soldier of Democracy* by Kenneth S. Davis (Doubleday, 1945) remains one of the best pieces of Eisenhower literature and is particularly useful for its material on the family's Kansas background. Kevin McCann's *Man from Abilene* (Doubleday, 1952) is an uncritical portrait by a longtime Eisenhower aide which is of some use because it does include letters and correspondence. John Gunther's *Eisenhower: The Man and the Symbol* (Harper, 1952) is a collection of magazine articles that are of limited value.

Numerous Eisenhower aides have written their accounts of service with Ike. Walter Bedell Smith's *Eisenhower's Six Great Decisions* (Longmans, 1956) and Harry Butcher's *My Three Years with Eisenhower* (Simon & Schuster, 1946) are indispensable for studying Ike's role in World War II. Kay Summersby's *Eisenhower Was My Boss* (Prentice-Hall, 1948) is an informal and readable memoir that was rewritten into *Past Forgetting: My Love Affair with Dwight D. Eisenhower* (Simon & Schuster, 1977).

Important memoirs from Eisenhower associates from the White House years include Emmet John Hughes's *The Ordeal of Power: A Political Memoir of the Eisenhower Years* (Atheneum, 1963); Arthur Larson's *Eisenhower: The President Nobody Knew* (Scribner's, 1968); Sherman Adams' *Firsthand Report: The Story of the Eisenhower Administration* (Harper, 1961); George B. Kistiakowsky's *A Scientist at the White House* (Harvard, 1976); and James R. Killian's *Sputnik, Scientists, and Eisenhower: A Memoir of the First Special Assistant to the President for Science and Technology* (MIT, 1977). Richard Nixon's *Six Crises* (Doubleday, 1962) discusses his troubled experience as Ike's Vice President while attempting to put the best possible face on his relationship with President Eisenhower.

The most important book-length treatments of President Eisenhower by contemporary journalists were Richard Rovere's *Affairs of State: The Eisenhower Years* (Farrar, Straus, 1956), an anthology of articles first published in *The New Yorker*; Robert J. Donovan's *Eisenhower: The Inside Story* (Harper, 1956), based on exclusive access to presidential papers; and Marquis Childs's *Eisenhower: Captive Hero* (Harcourt, 1958).

Of the numerous biographies of Ike's contemporaries, the most thorough and useful were Forrest Pogue's *George C. Marshall* (Viking, three volumes); John Bartlow Martin's *Adlai Stevenson of Illinois* (Doubleday, 1976) and *Adlai Stevenson and the World* (Doubleday, 1977); James MacGregor Burns's *Roosevelt: Soldier of Freedom* (Harcourt, 1971), James T. Patterson's *Mr. Republican: A Biography of Robert A. Taft* (Houghton Mifflin, 1972); Townsend Hoopes's *The Devil and John Foster Dulles* (Atlantic, Little, Brown, 1973); Robert Griffith's *The Politics of Fear: Joseph R. McCarthy and the Senate* (University of Kentucky, 1970); and Robert J. Donovan's *Conflict and Crisis: The Presidency of Harry Truman* (Norton, 1977).

Geoffrey Perrett's *Days of Sadness, Years of Triumph* (Putnam, 1973) is a vivid portrait of American life during World War II. John Morton Blum's V *Was for Victory: Politics and American Culture During World War II* (Harcourt Brace, 1976) is the best historical account of the home front. Carl Solberg's *Riding High: America in the Cold War* (Mason & Lipscomb, 1973) and William Manchester's *The Glory and the Dream* (Little, Brown, 1973) are both helpful works of popular history. Richard Kluger's *Simple Justice* (Knopf, 1975) is an extraordinary study of the *Brown* v. *Board of Education* case and of the struggle for black equality in the United States. *The Pentagon Papers: The Defense Department History of United States Decisionmaking on Vietnam* (Beacon, 1971) includes documents related to the Eisenhower administration's Indochina policy.

Index